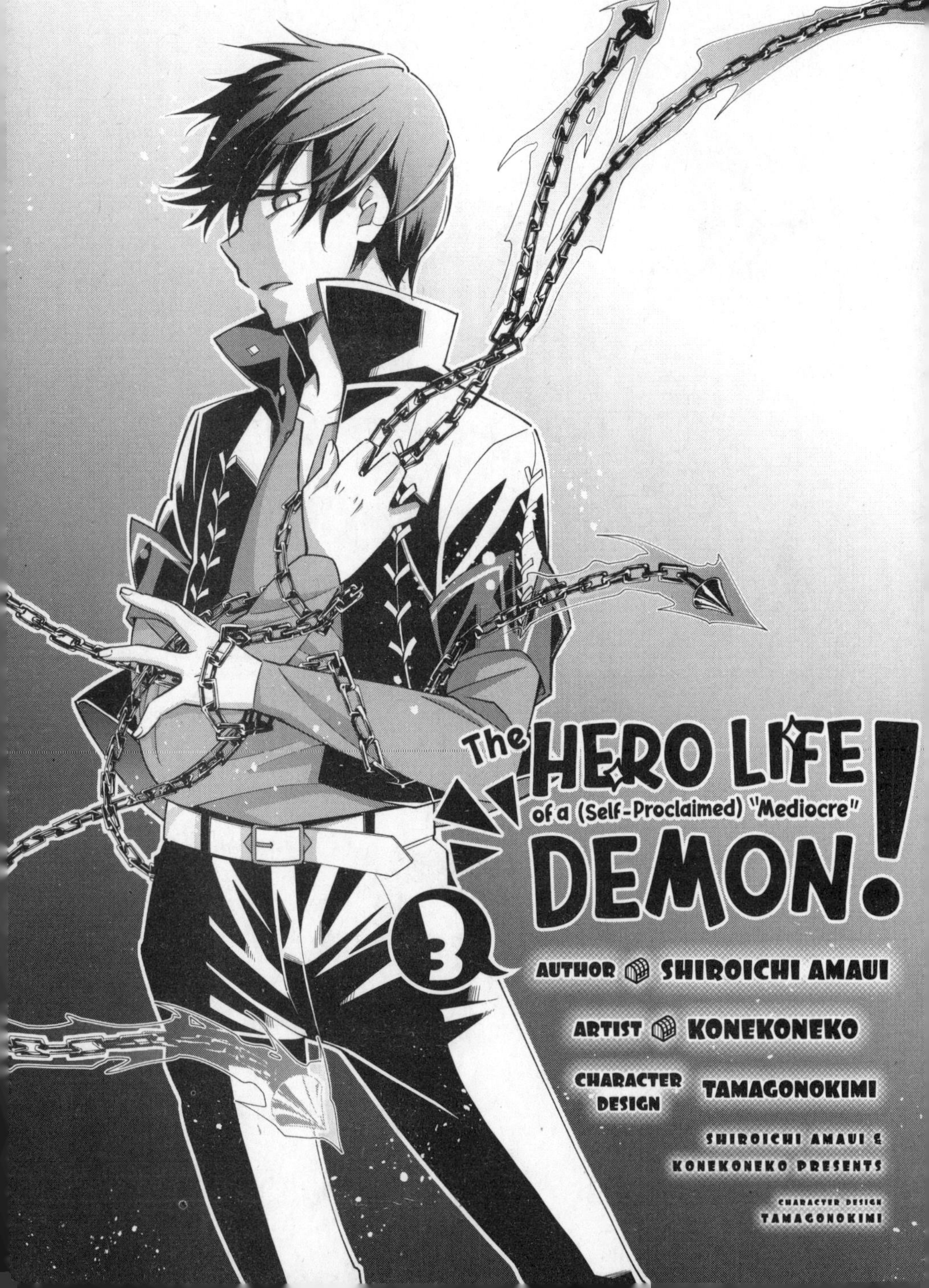

The HERO LIFE of a (Self-Proclaimed) "Mediocre" DEMON! 3

AUTHOR SHIROICHI AMAUI

ARTIST KONEKONEKO

CHARACTER DESIGN TAMAGONOKIMI

SHIROICHI AMAUI & KONEKONEKO PRESENTS

CHARACTER DESIGN TAMAGONOKIMI

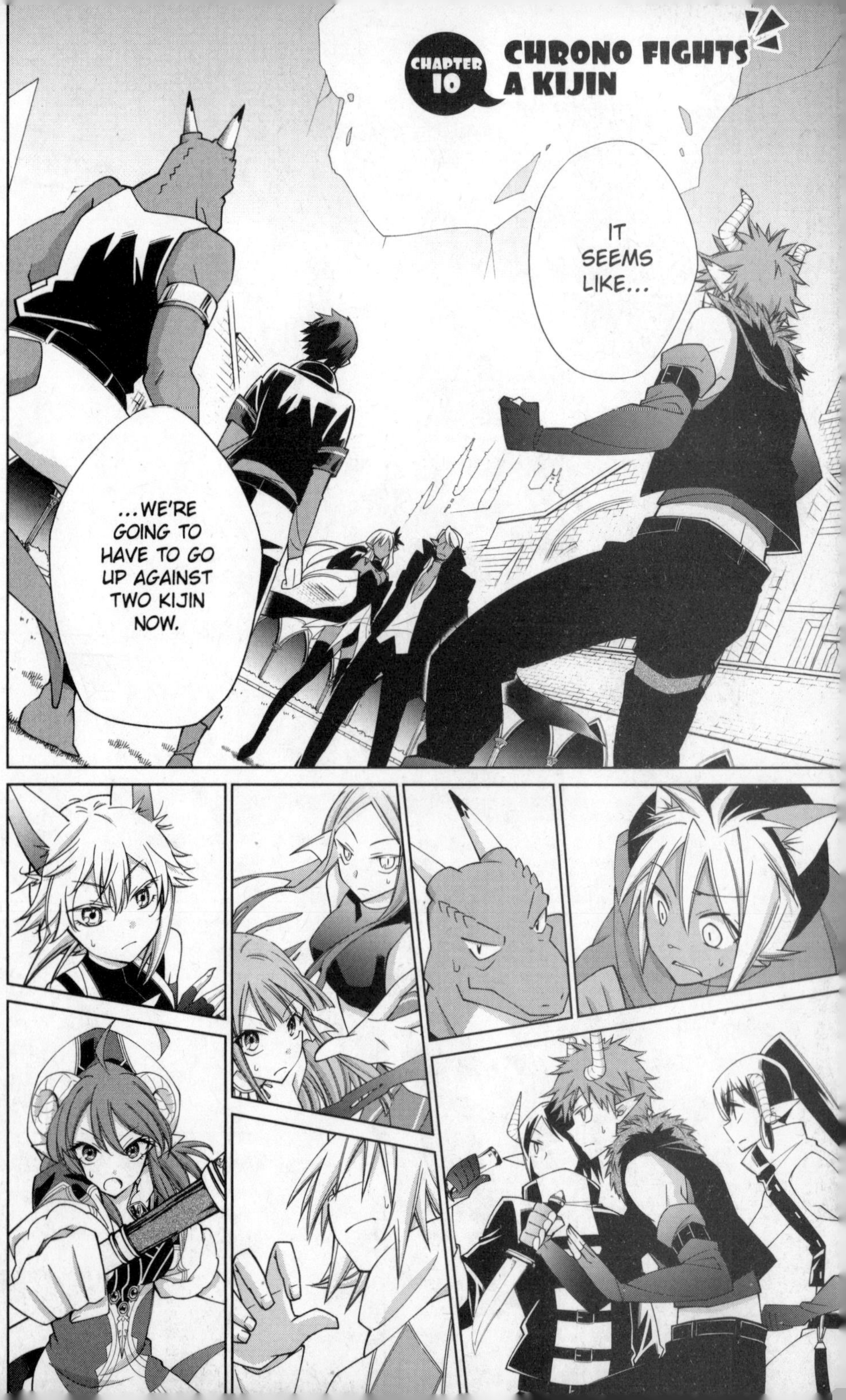
CHAPTER 10
CHRONO FIGHTS A KIJIN
IT SEEMS LIKE...
...WE'RE GOING TO HAVE TO GO UP AGAINST TWO KIJIN NOW.

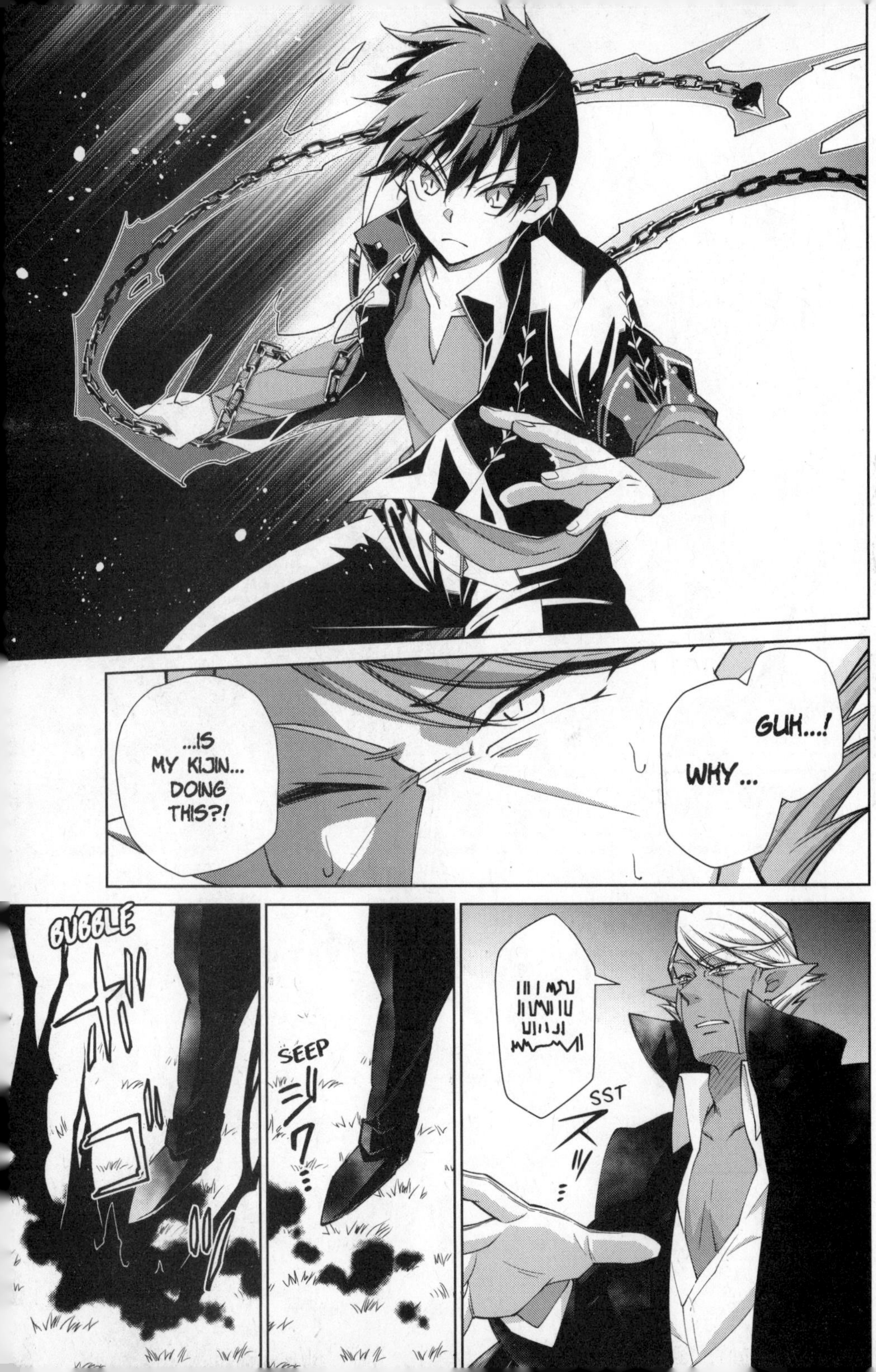
GUH...! WHY...
...IS MY KIJIN... DOING THIS?!
SST
SEEP
BUBBLE

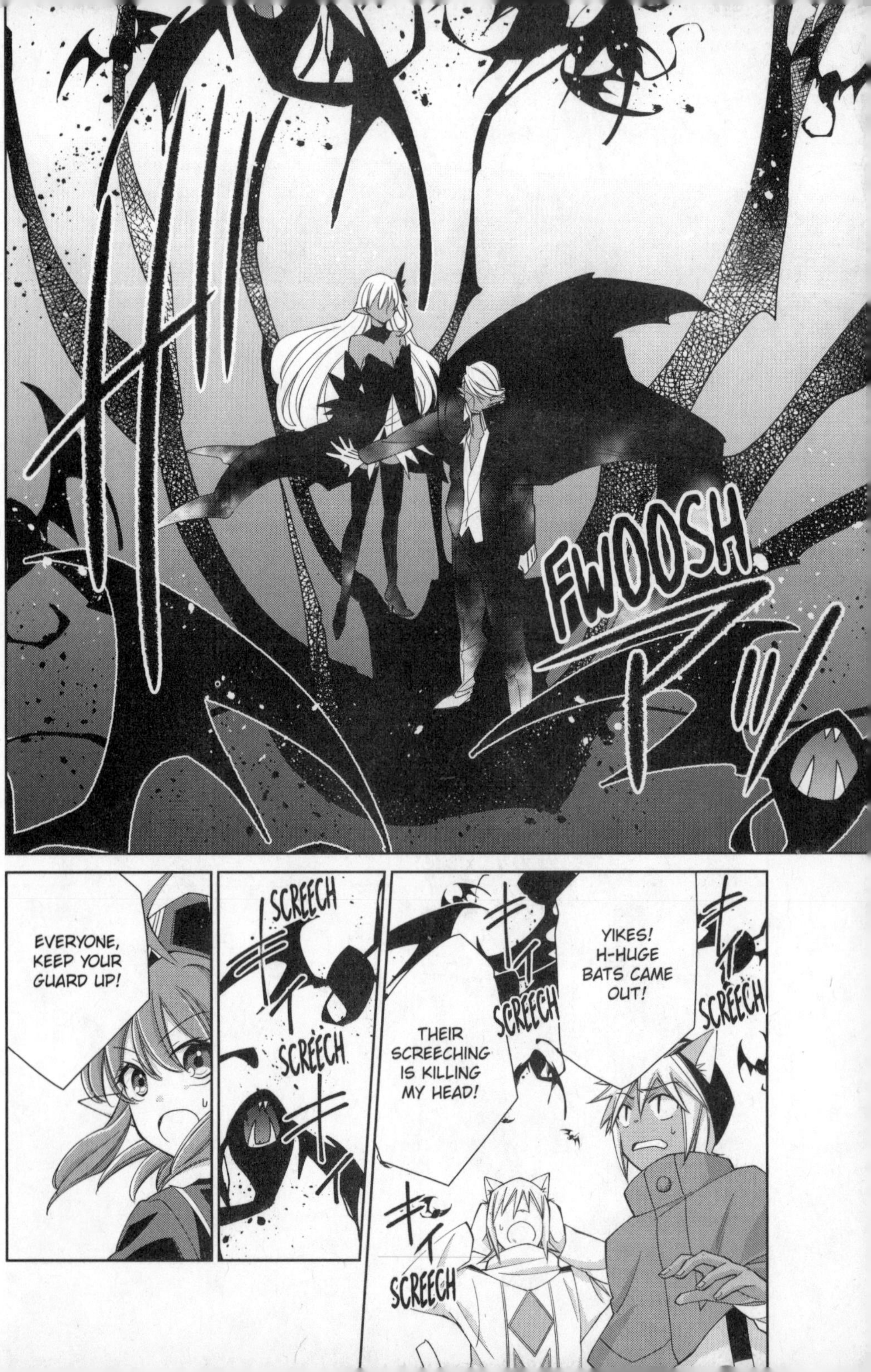
FWOOSH
SCREECH
YIKES! H-HUGE BATS CAME OUT!
SCREECH
THEIR SCREECHING IS KILLING MY HEAD!
SCREECH
SCREECH
SCREECH
EVERYONE, KEEP YOUR GUARD UP!

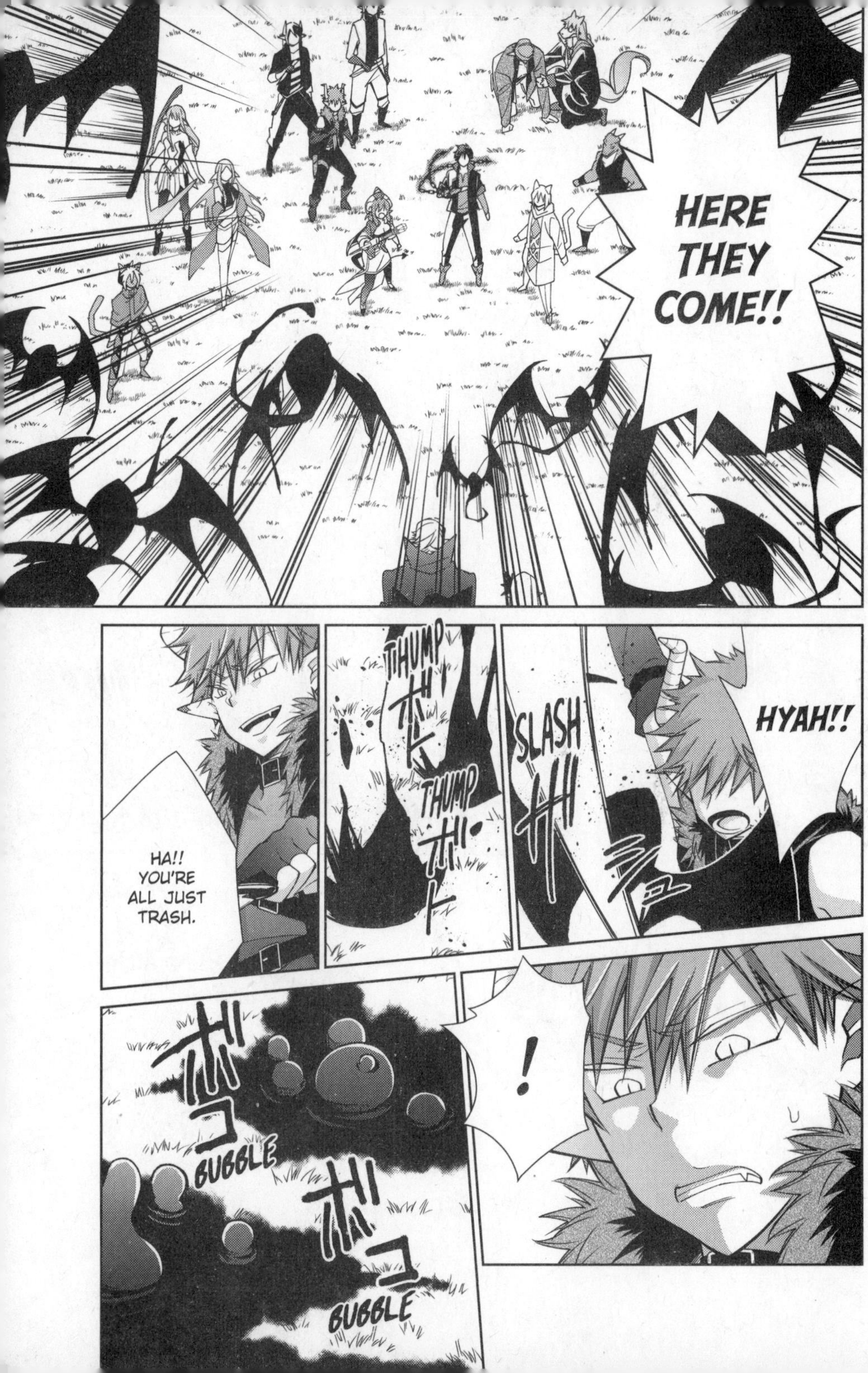
HERE THEY COME!!
HYAH!!
SLASH
THUMP
THUMP
HA!! YOU'RE ALL JUST TRASH.
!
BUBBLE
BUBBLE

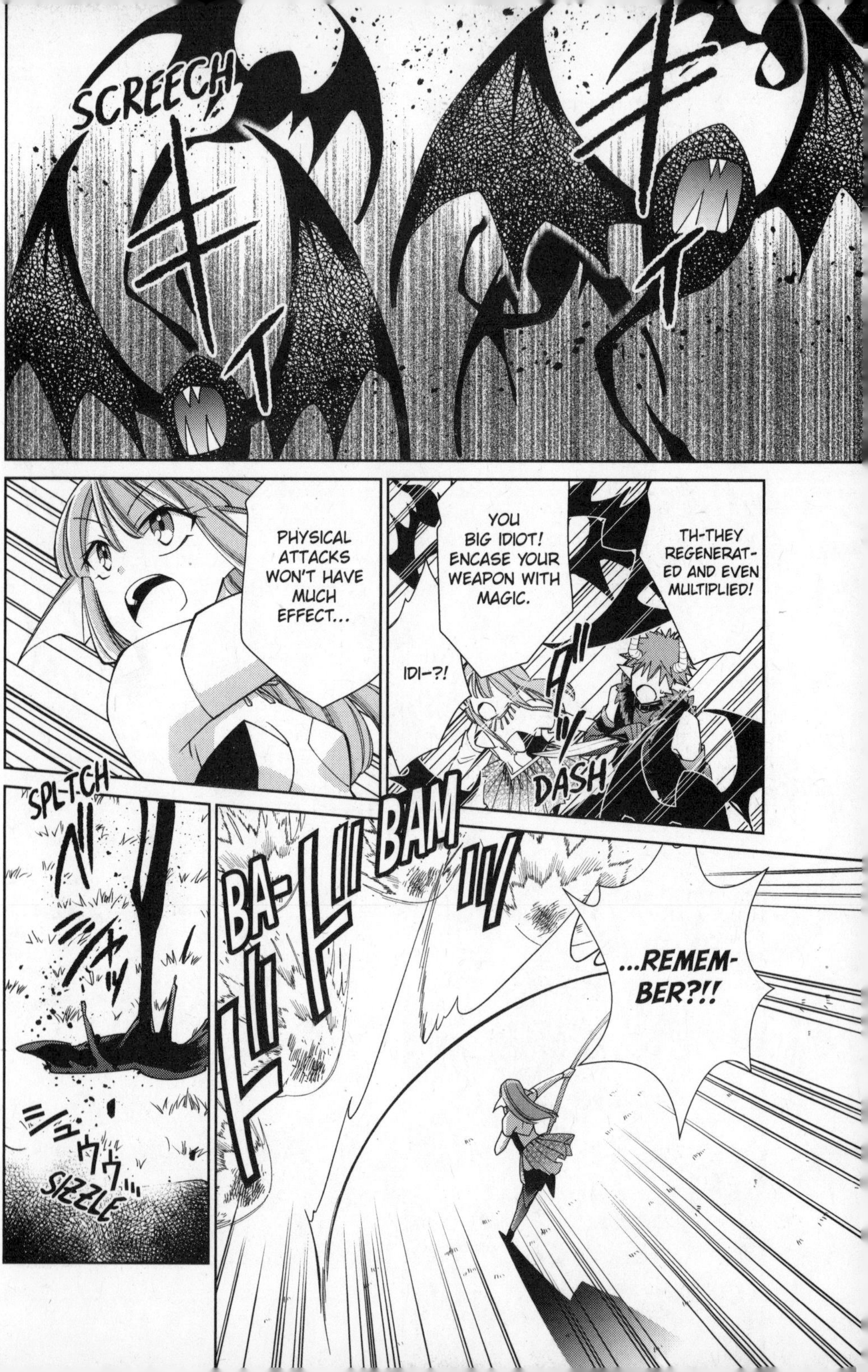
SCREECH
TH-THEY REGENERAT-ED AND EVEN MULTIPLIED!
YOU BIG IDIOT! ENCASE YOUR WEAPON WITH MAGIC.
IDI-?!
DASH
PHYSICAL ATTACKS WON'T HAVE MUCH EFFECT...
BA-LII BAM
...REMEM-BER?!!
SPL-T-CH
SIZZLE

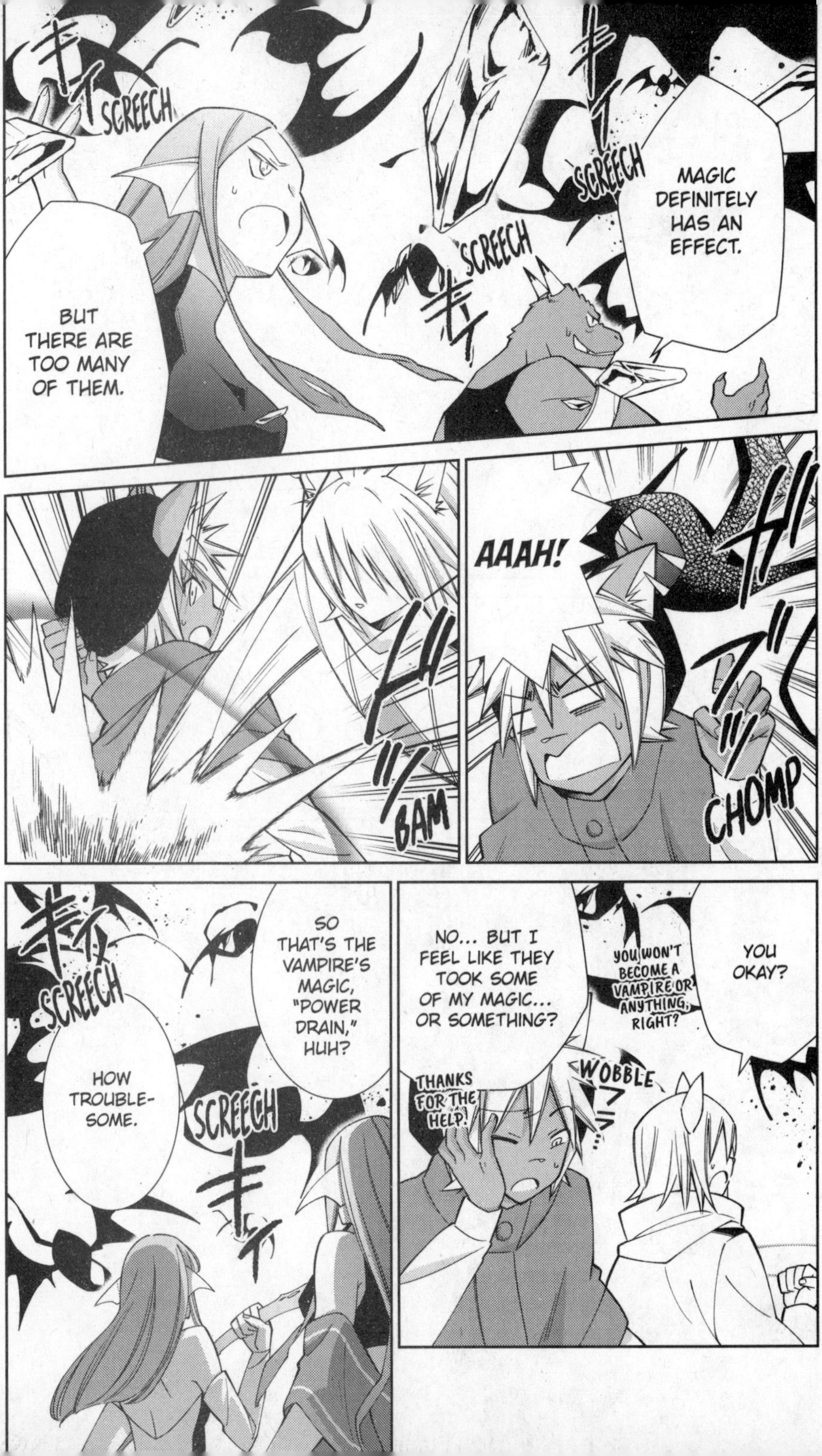
SCREECH
SCREECH
SCREECH
MAGIC DEFINITELY HAS AN EFFECT.
SCREECH
BUT THERE ARE TOO MANY OF THEM.
AAAH!
CHOMP
BAM
YOU OKAY?
YOU WON'T BECOME A VAMPIRE OR ANYTHING, RIGHT?
NO... BUT I FEEL LIKE THEY TOOK SOME OF MY MAGIC... OR SOMETHING?
WOBBLE
THANKS FOR THE HELP.
SO THAT'S THE VAMPIRE'S MAGIC, "POWER DRAIN," HUH?
SCREECH
HOW TROUBLE-SOME.
SCREECH

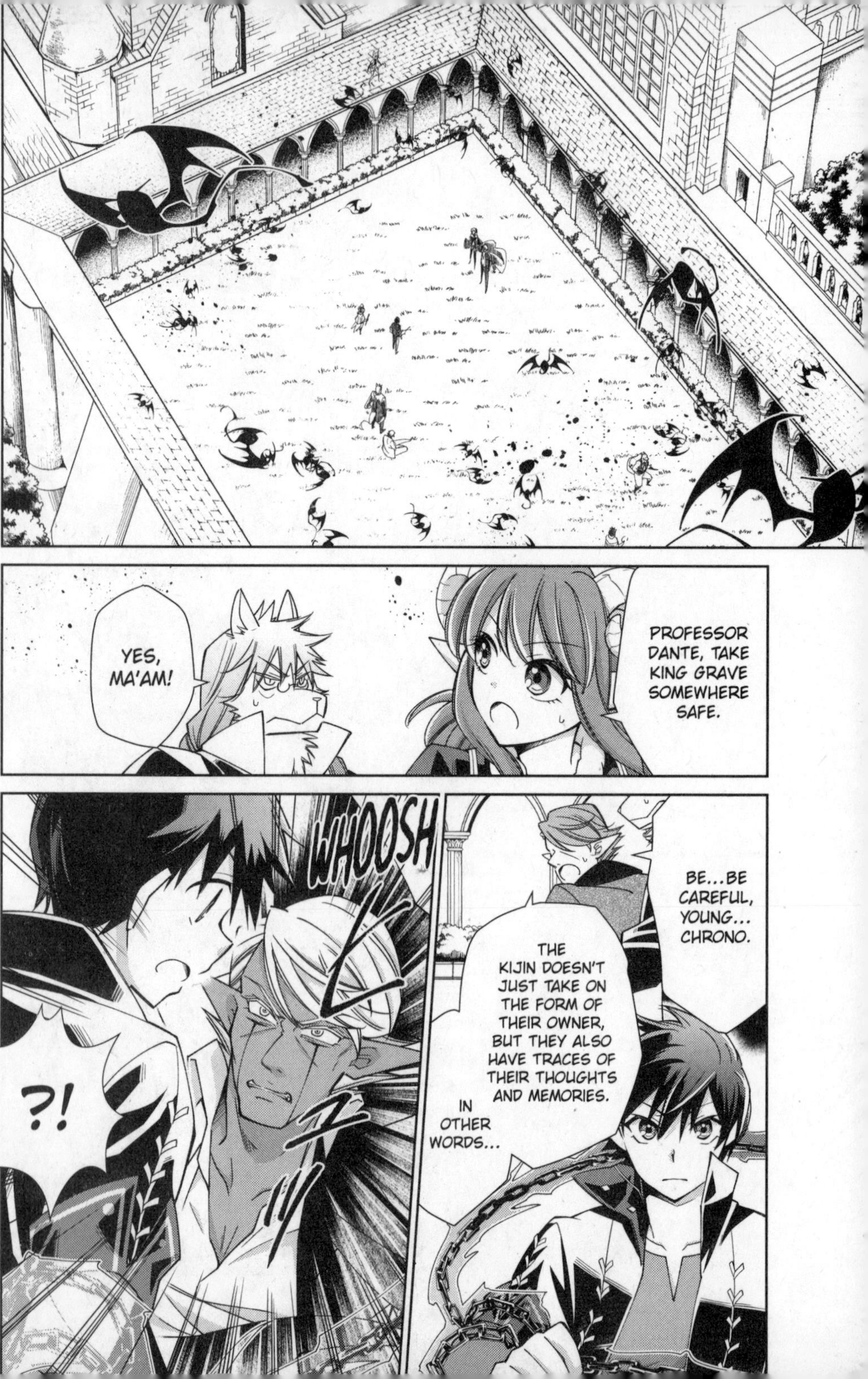
PROFESSOR DANTE, TAKE KING GRAVE SOMEWHERE SAFE.
YES, MA'AM!
BE...BE CAREFUL, YOUNG... CHRONO.
THE KIJIN DOESN'T JUST TAKE ON THE FORM OF THEIR OWNER, BUT THEY ALSO HAVE TRACES OF THEIR THOUGHTS AND MEMORIES.
IN OTHER WORDS...
WHOOSH
?!

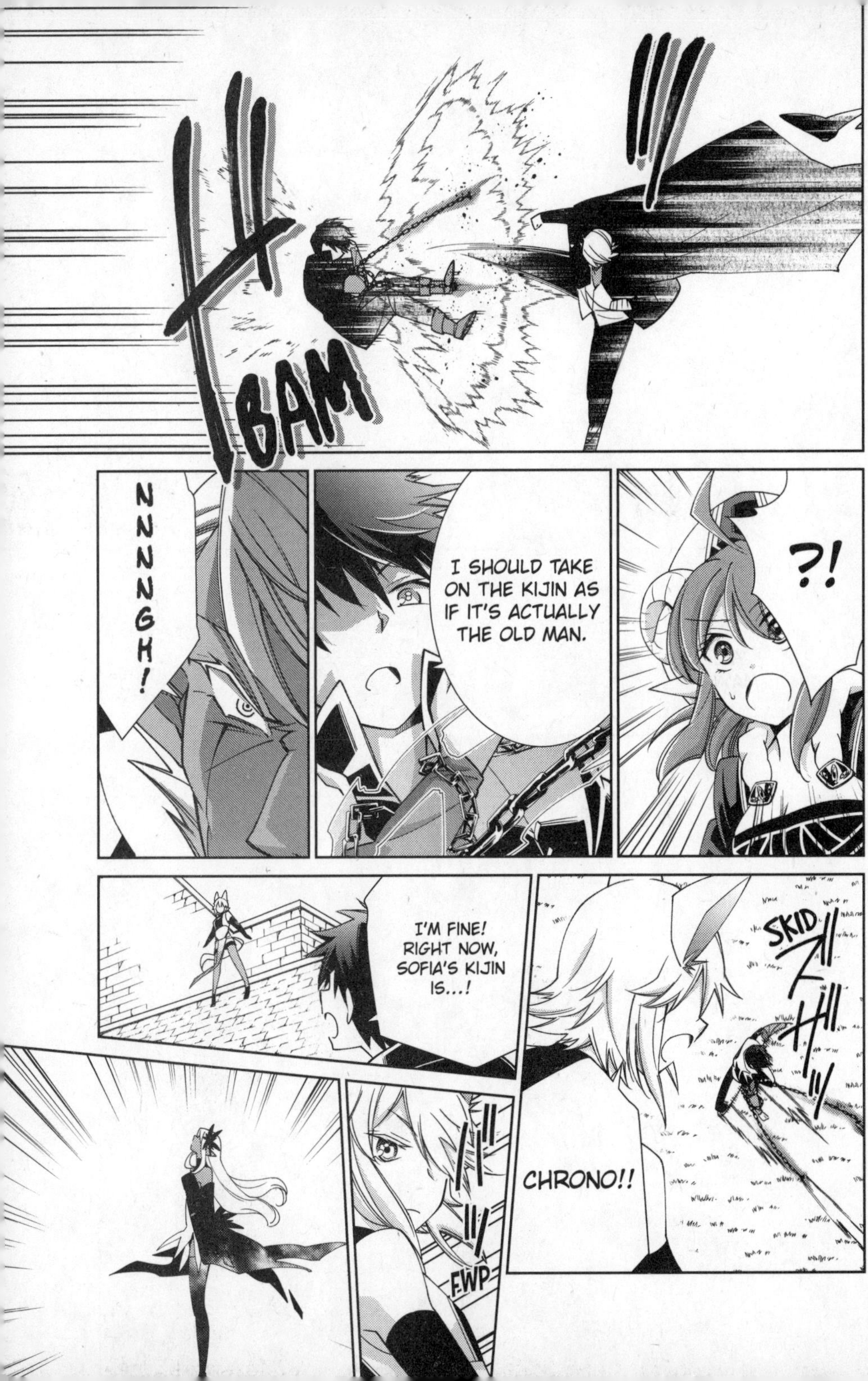
BAM
?!
I SHOULD TAKE ON THE KIJIN AS IF IT'S ACTUALLY THE OLD MAN.
NNNNNGH!
SKID
CHRONO!!
I'M FINE! RIGHT NOW, SOFIA'S KIJIN IS...!
FWP

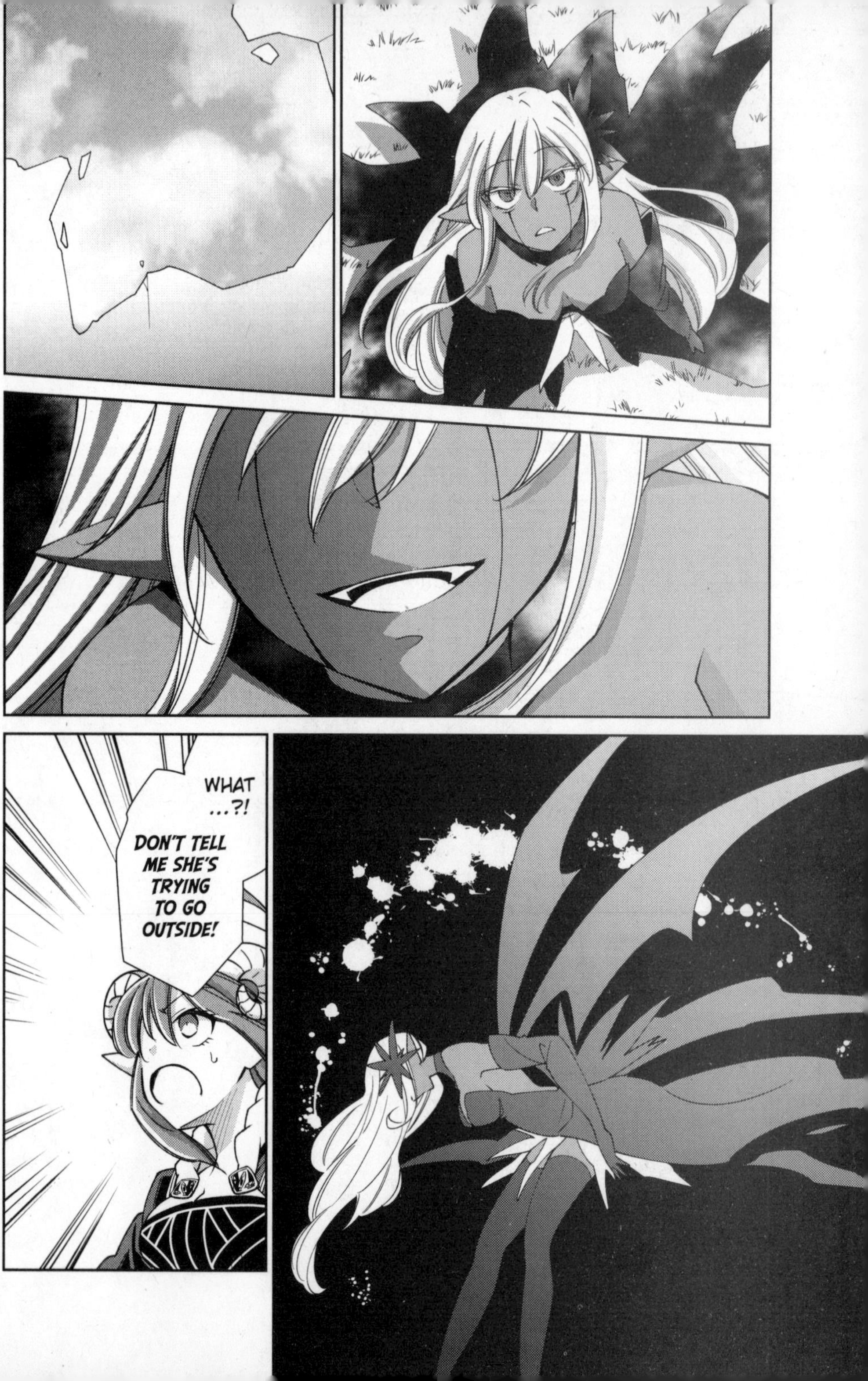
WHAT ...?!
DON'T TELL ME SHE'S TRYING TO GO OUTSIDE!

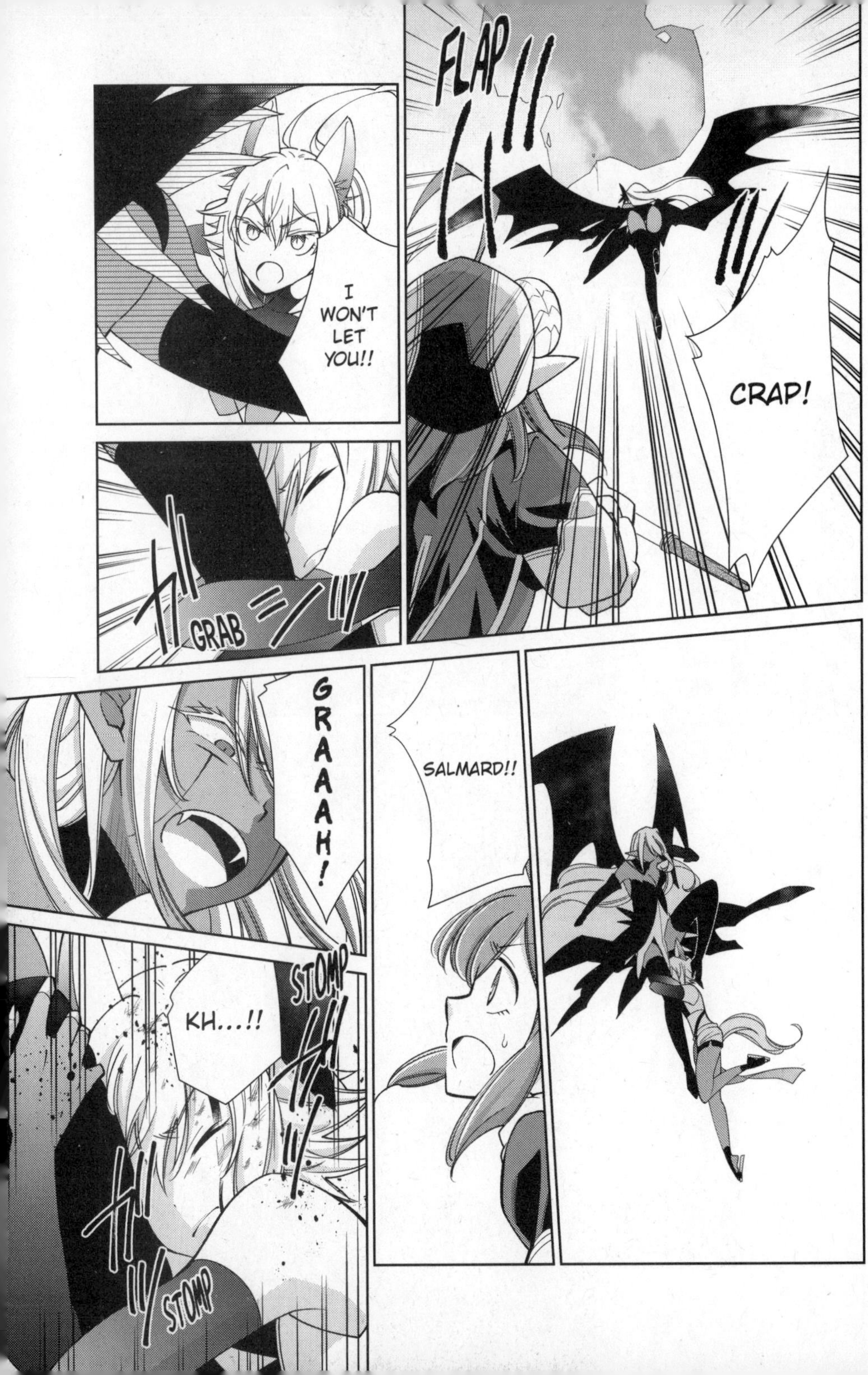
FLAP
CRAP!
I WON'T LET YOU!!
GRAB
SALMARD!!
GRAAAAH!
KH...!!
STOMP
STOMP

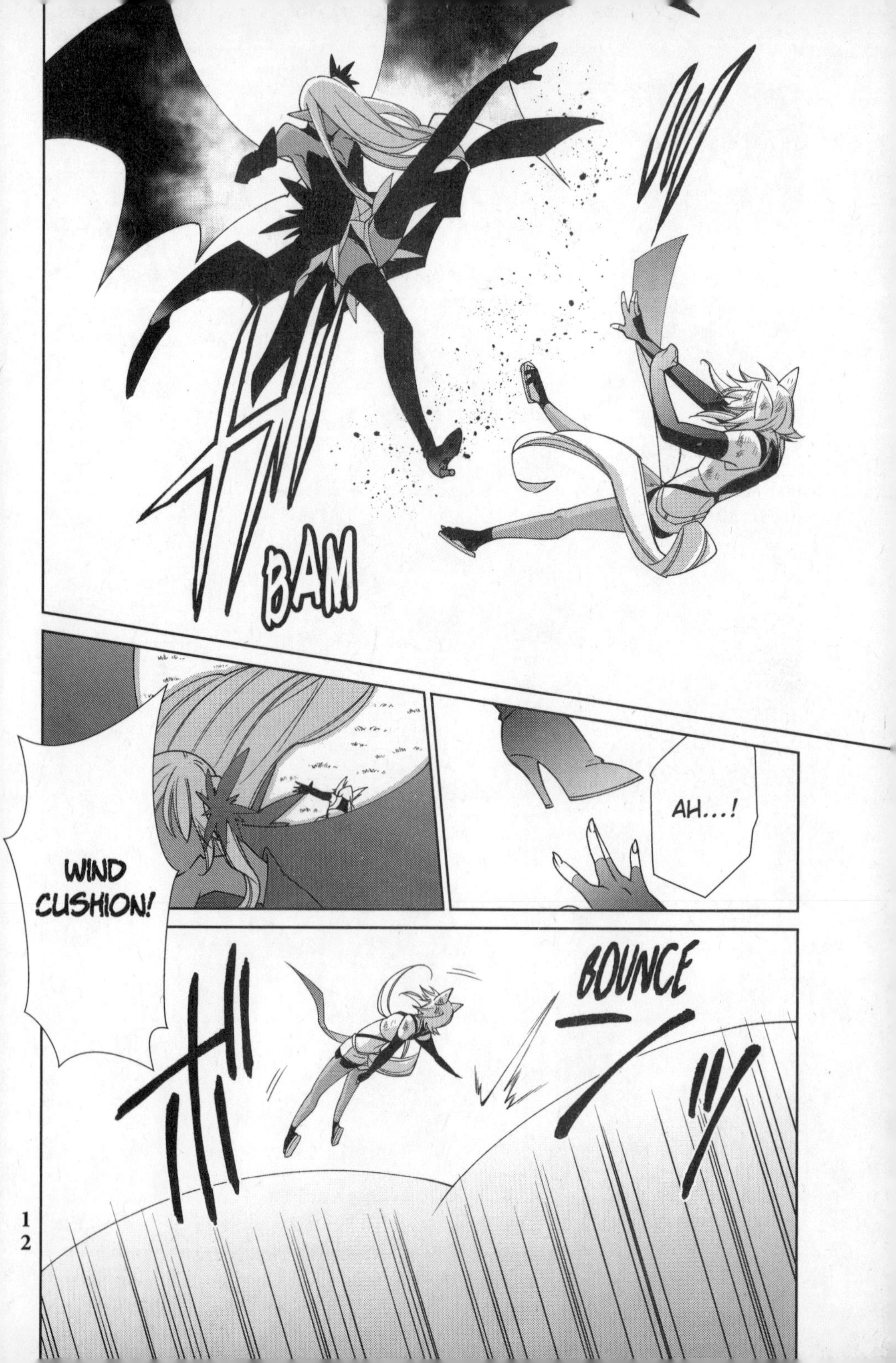
BAM
AH...!
WIND CUSHION!
BOUNCE

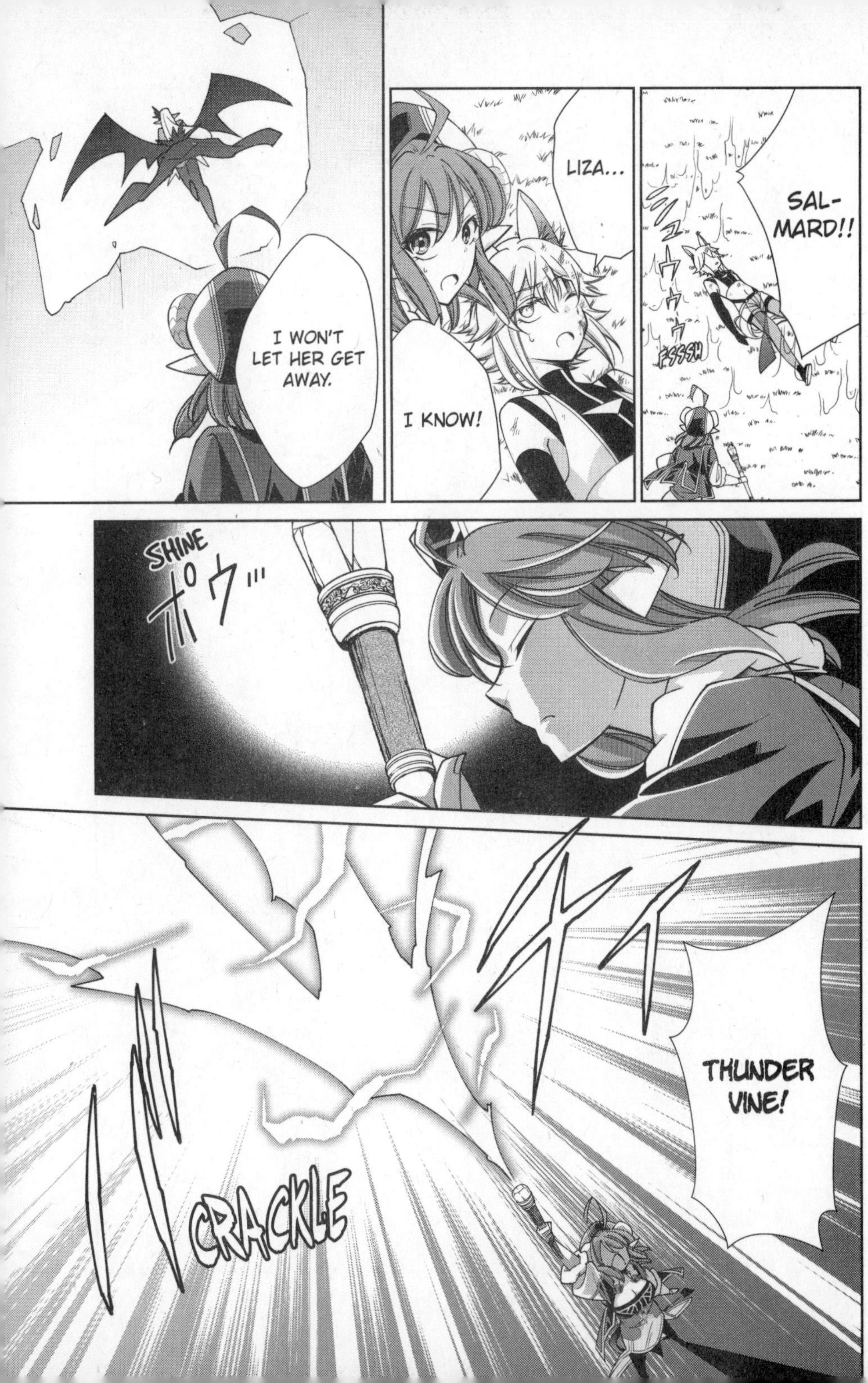
SAL-MARD!!
FSSSH
LIZA...
I KNOW!
I WON'T LET HER GET AWAY.
SHINE
THUNDER VINE!
CRACKLE

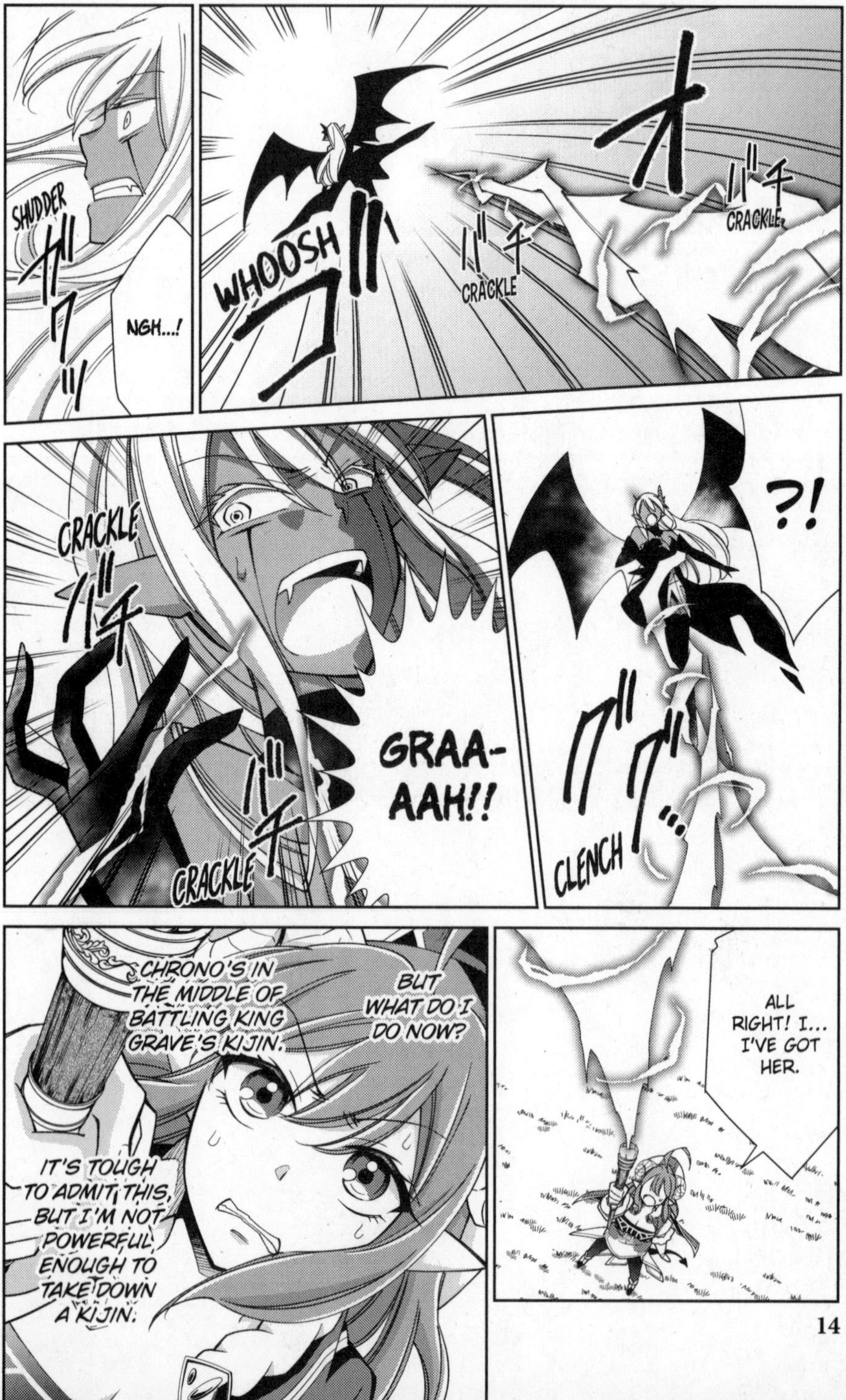
CRACKLE
CRACKLE
WHOOSH
SHUDDER
NGH...!
?!
CLENCH
CRACKLE
GRAA-AAH!!
CRACKLE
ALL RIGHT! I... I'VE GOT HER.
CHRONO'S IN THE MIDDLE OF BATTLING KING GRAVE'S KIJIN.
BUT WHAT DO I DO NOW?
IT'S TOUGH TO ADMIT THIS, BUT I'M NOT POWERFUL ENOUGH TO TAKE DOWN A KIJIN.

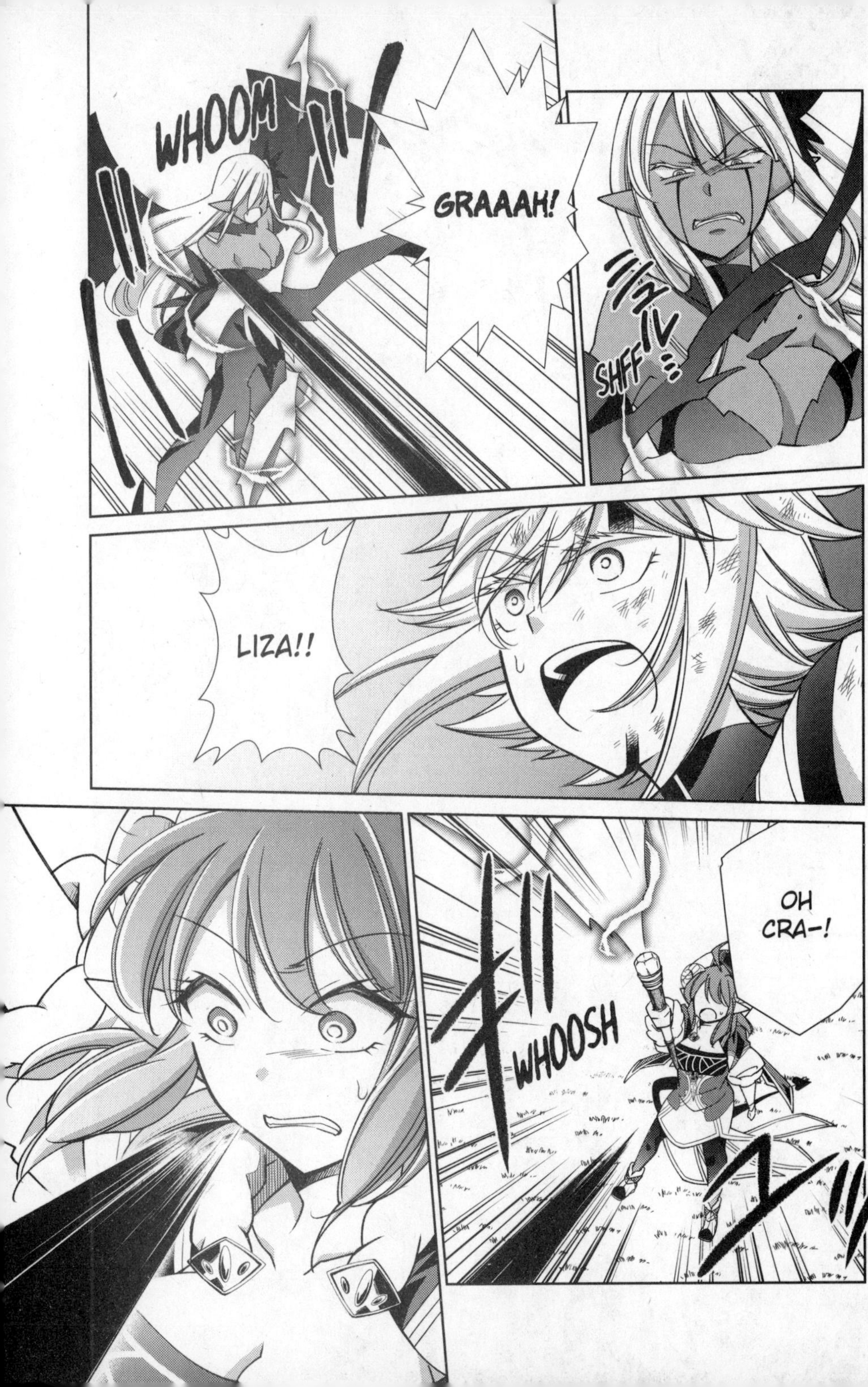
GRAAAH!
SHFF
WHOOM
LIZA!!
OH CRA-!
WHOOSH

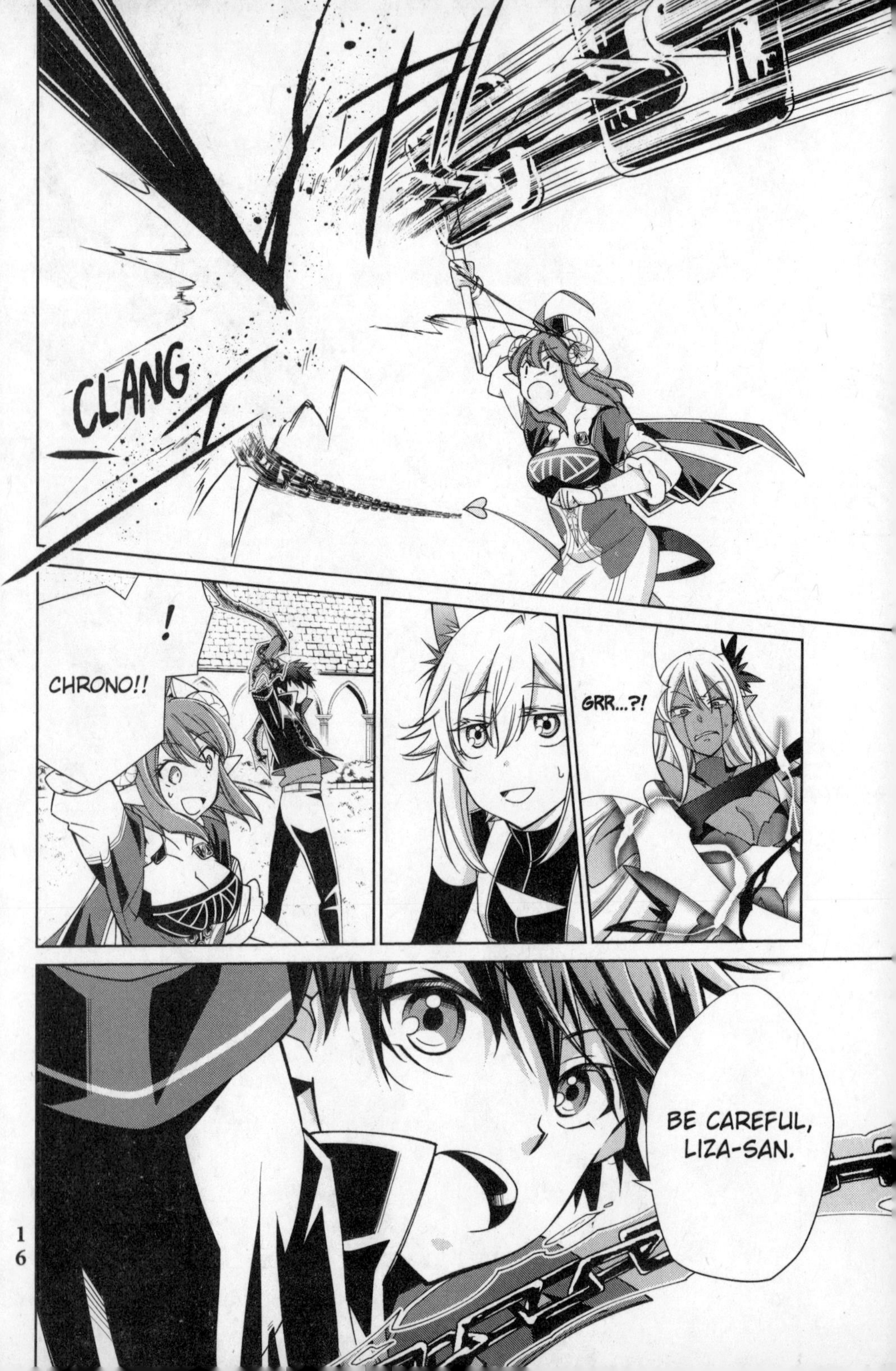
CLANG
GRR...?!
!
CHRONO!!
BE CAREFUL, LIZA-SAN.

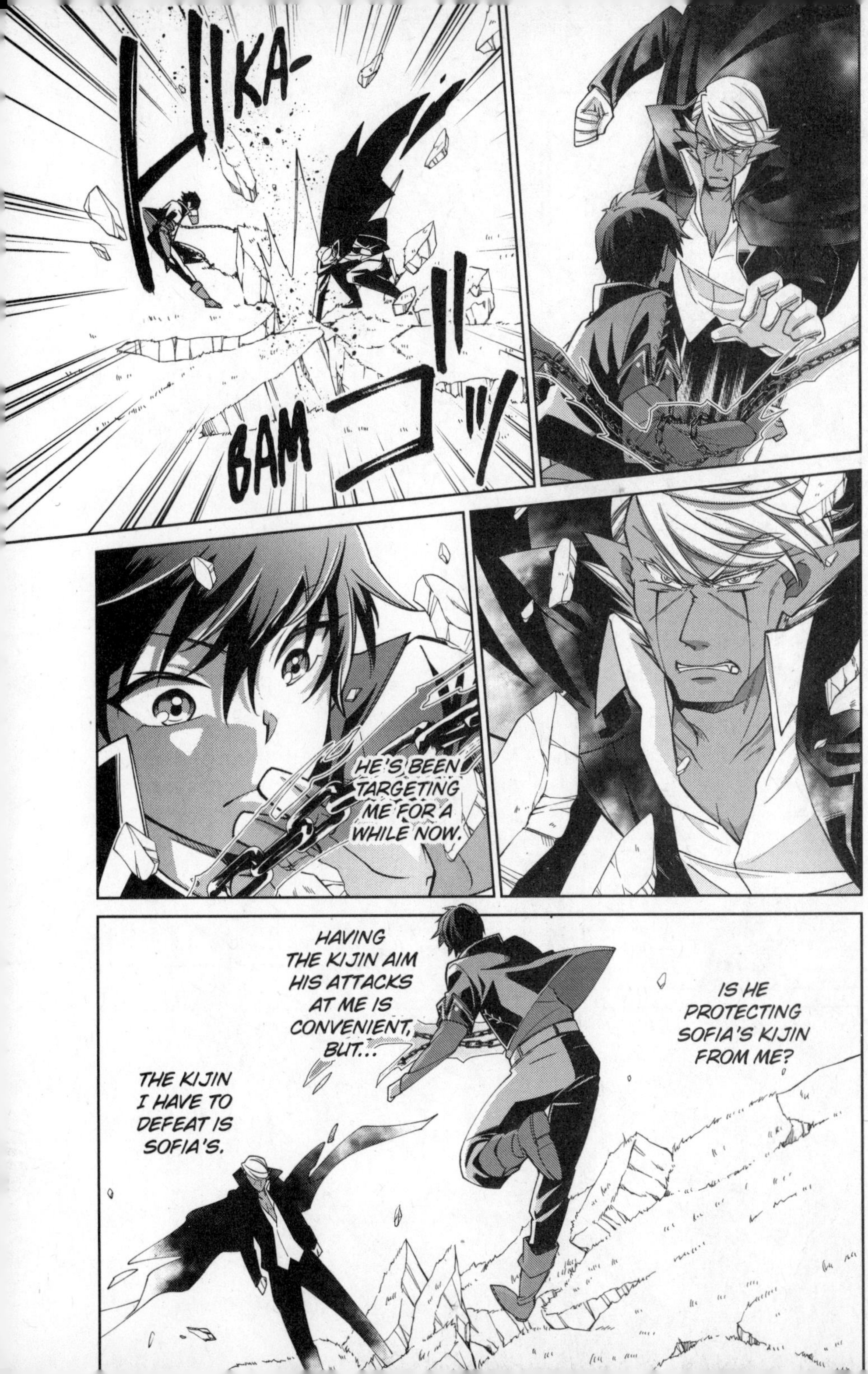
KA-
BAM
HE'S BEEN TARGETING ME FOR A WHILE NOW.
IS HE PROTECTING SOFIA'S KIJIN FROM ME?
HAVING THE KIJIN AIM HIS ATTACKS AT ME IS CONVENIENT, BUT...
THE KIJIN I HAVE TO DEFEAT IS SOFIA'S.

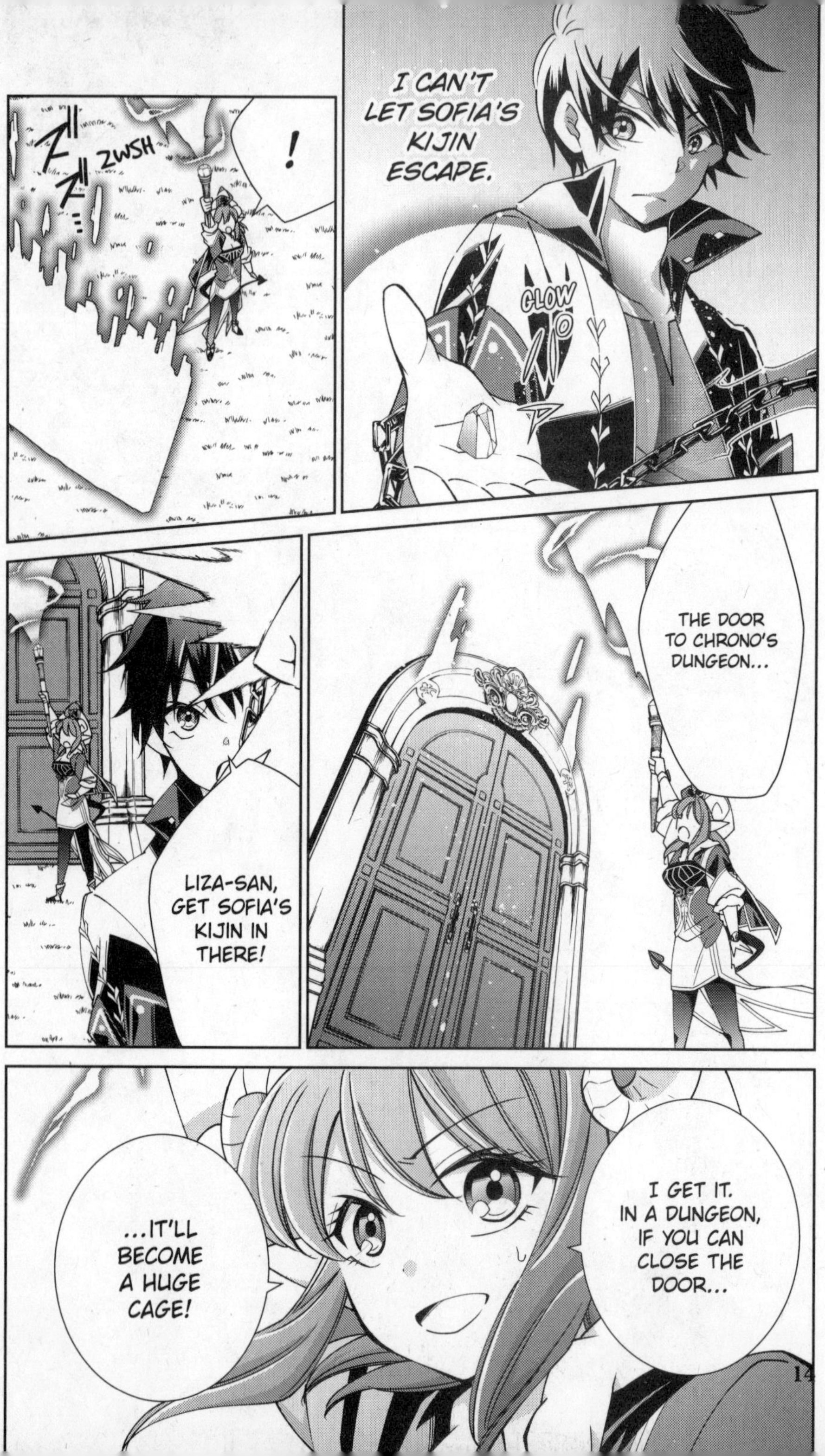
I CAN'T LET SOFIA'S KIJIN ESCAPE.
GLOW
ZWSH
!
THE DOOR TO CHRONO'S DUNGEON...
LIZA-SAN, GET SOFIA'S KIJIN IN THERE!
I GET IT. IN A DUNGEON, IF YOU CAN CLOSE THE DOOR...
...IT'LL BECOME A HUGE CAGE!

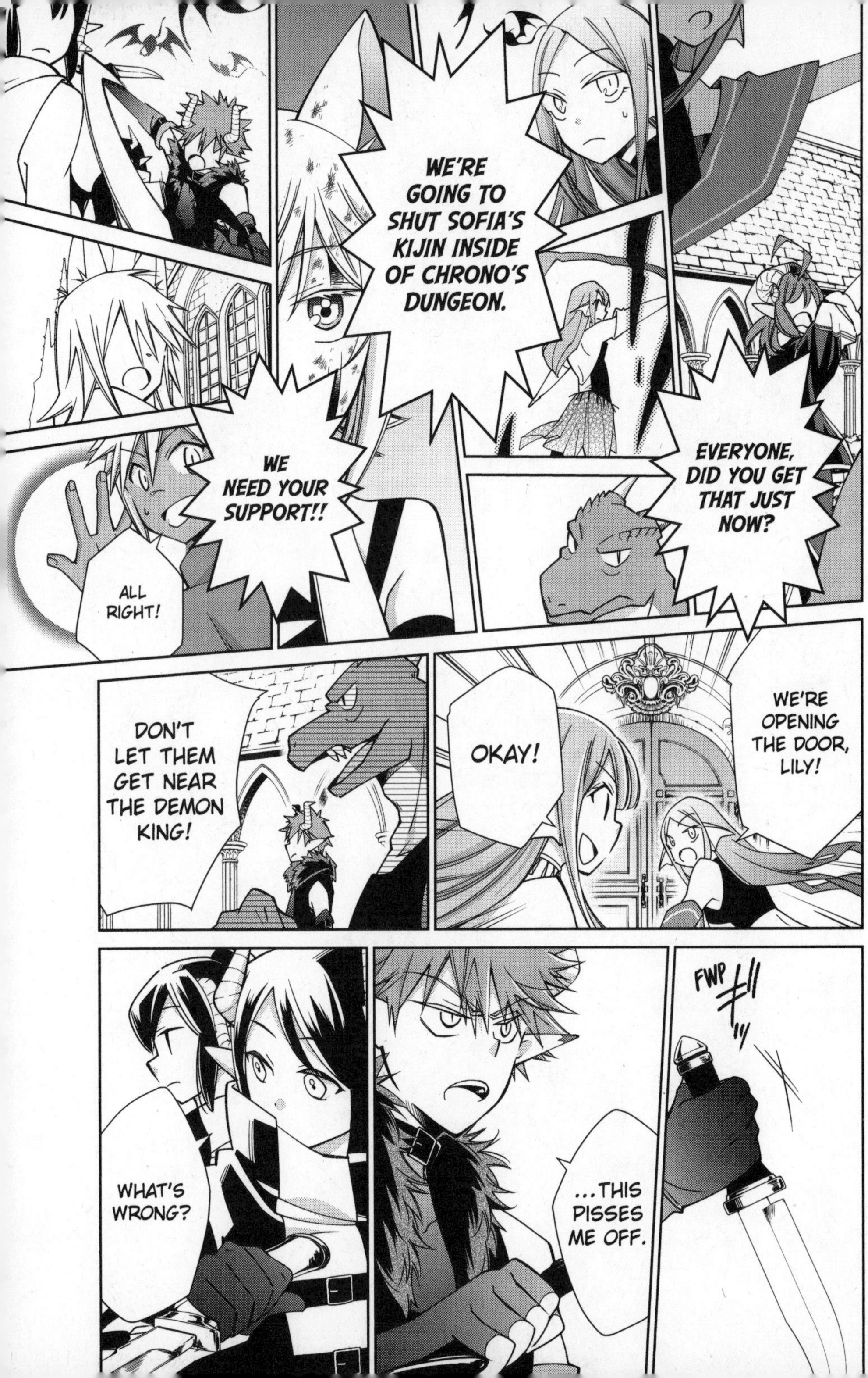
WE'RE GOING TO SHUT SOFIA'S KIJIN INSIDE OF CHRONO'S DUNGEON.
WE NEED YOUR SUPPORT!!
EVERYONE, DID YOU GET THAT JUST NOW?
ALL RIGHT!
WE'RE OPENING THE DOOR, LILY!
OKAY!
DON'T LET THEM GET NEAR THE DEMON KING!
FWP
...THIS PISSES ME OFF.
WHAT'S WRONG?

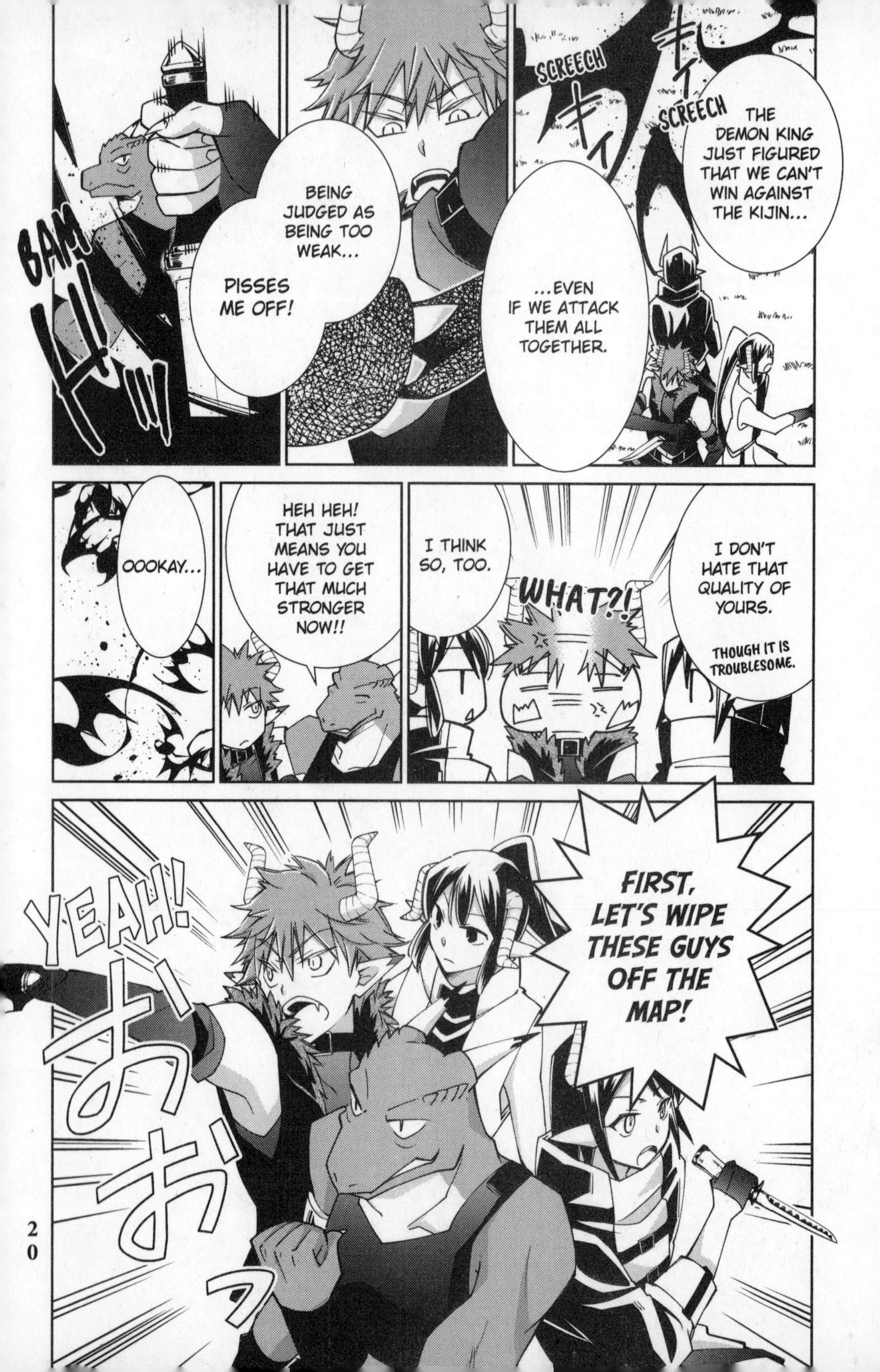
SCREECH
SCREECH
THE DEMON KING JUST FIGURED THAT WE CAN'T WIN AGAINST THE KIJIN...
...EVEN IF WE ATTACK THEM ALL TOGETHER.
BEING JUDGED AS BEING TOO WEAK...
PISSES ME OFF!
BAM
I DON'T HATE THAT QUALITY OF YOURS.
THOUGH IT IS TROUBLESOME.
I THINK SO, TOO.
WHAT?!
HEH HEH! THAT JUST MEANS YOU HAVE TO GET THAT MUCH STRONGER NOW!!
OOOKAY...
FIRST, LET'S WIPE THESE GUYS OFF THE MAP!
YEAH!

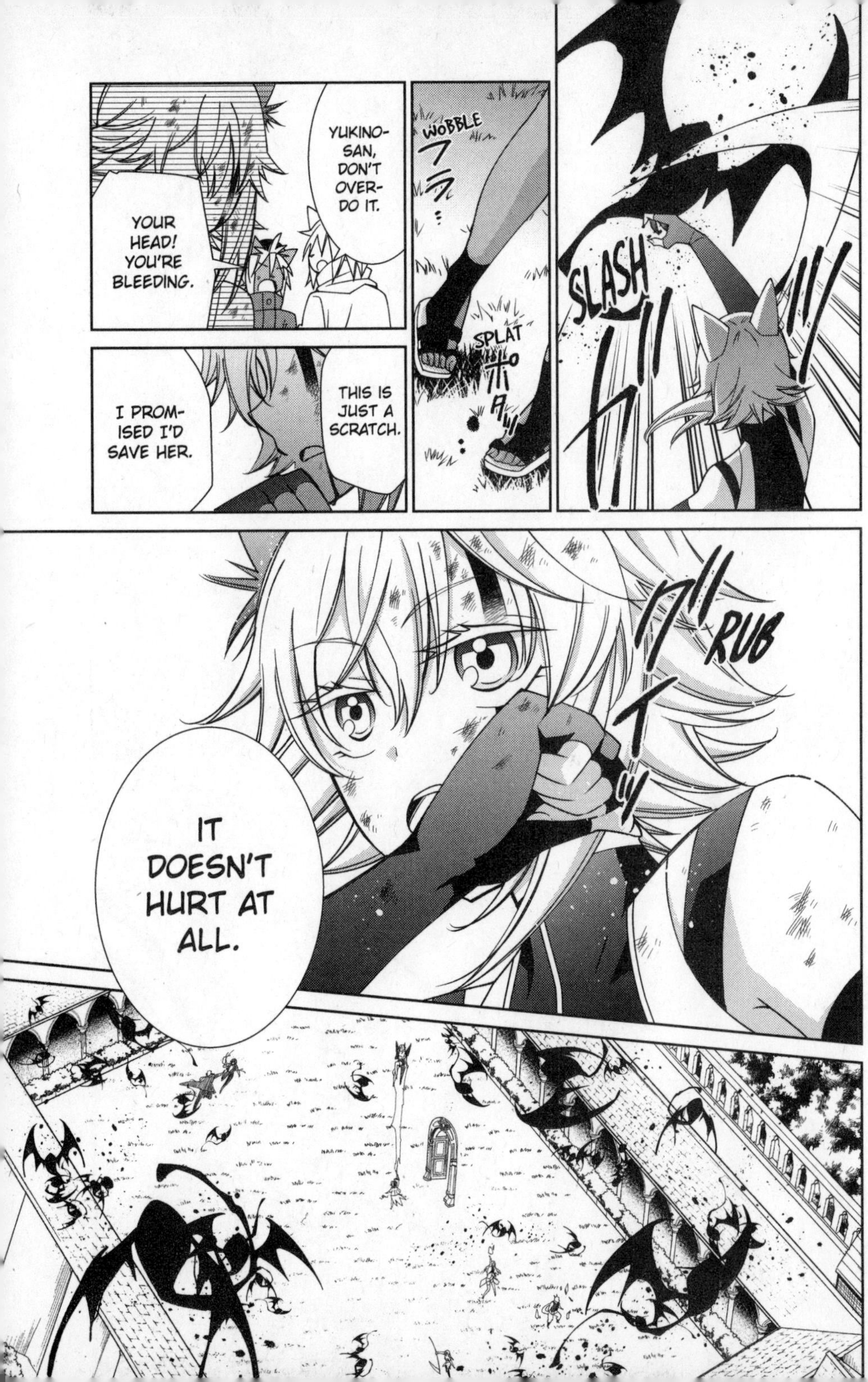
SLASH
WOBBLE
SPLAT
YUKINO-SAN, DON'T OVER-DO IT.
YOUR HEAD! YOU'RE BLEEDING.
THIS IS JUST A SCRATCH.
I PROM-ISED I'D SAVE HER.
RUB
IT DOESN'T HURT AT ALL.

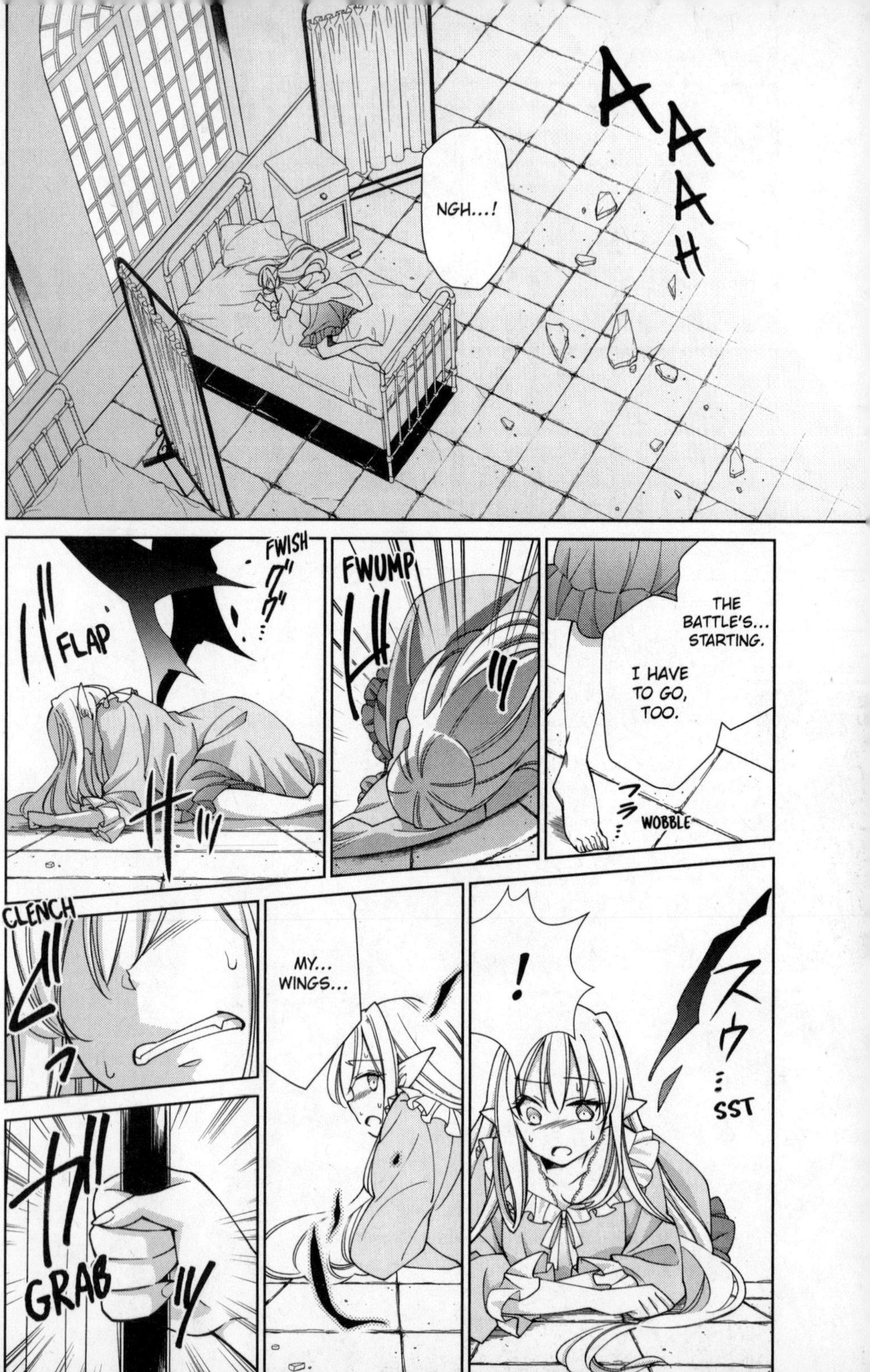
AAAH
NGH...!
THE BATTLE'S... STARTING.
I HAVE TO GO, TOO.
WOBBLE
FWUMP
FWISH
FLAP
!
SST
MY... WINGS...
CLENCH
GRAB

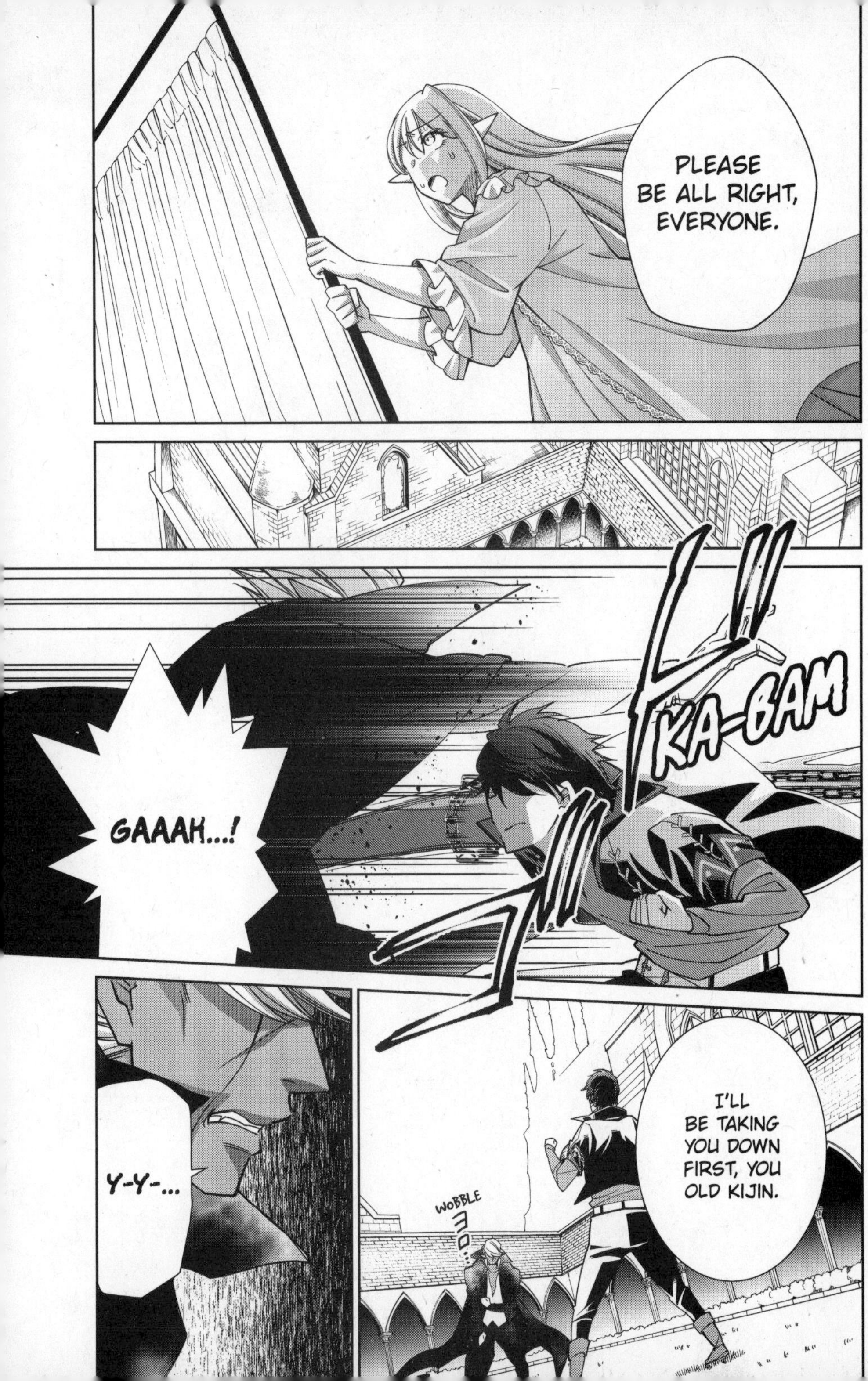
PLEASE BE ALL RIGHT, EVERYONE.
KA-BAM
GAAAH...!
I'LL BE TAKING YOU DOWN FIRST, YOU OLD KIJIN.
WOBBLE
Y-Y-...

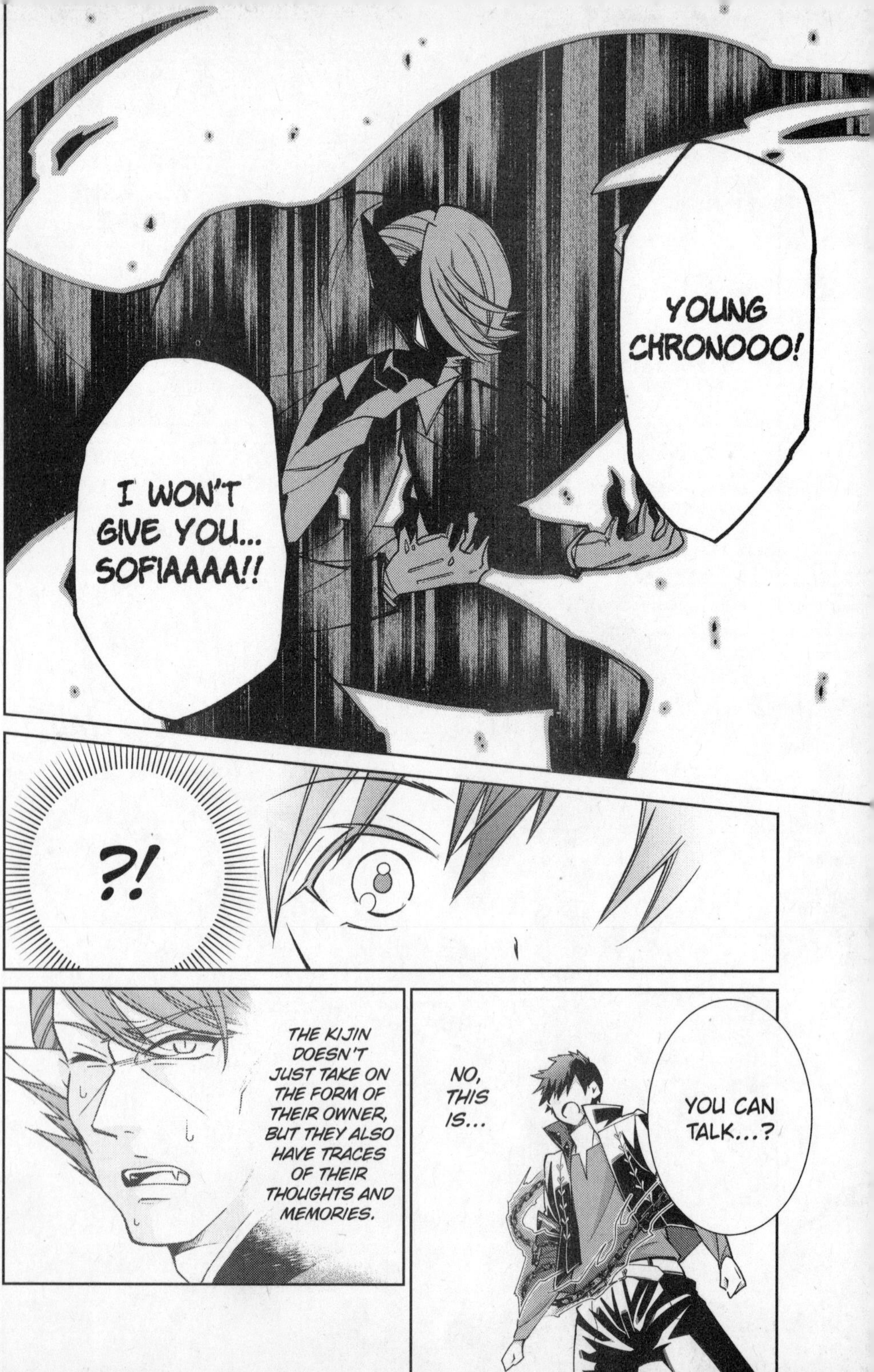
YOUNG CHRONOOO!
I WON'T GIVE YOU... SOFIAAAA!!
?!
YOU CAN TALK...?
NO, THIS IS...
THE KIJIN DOESN'T JUST TAKE ON THE FORM OF THEIR OWNER, BUT THEY ALSO HAVE TRACES OF THEIR THOUGHTS AND MEMORIES.

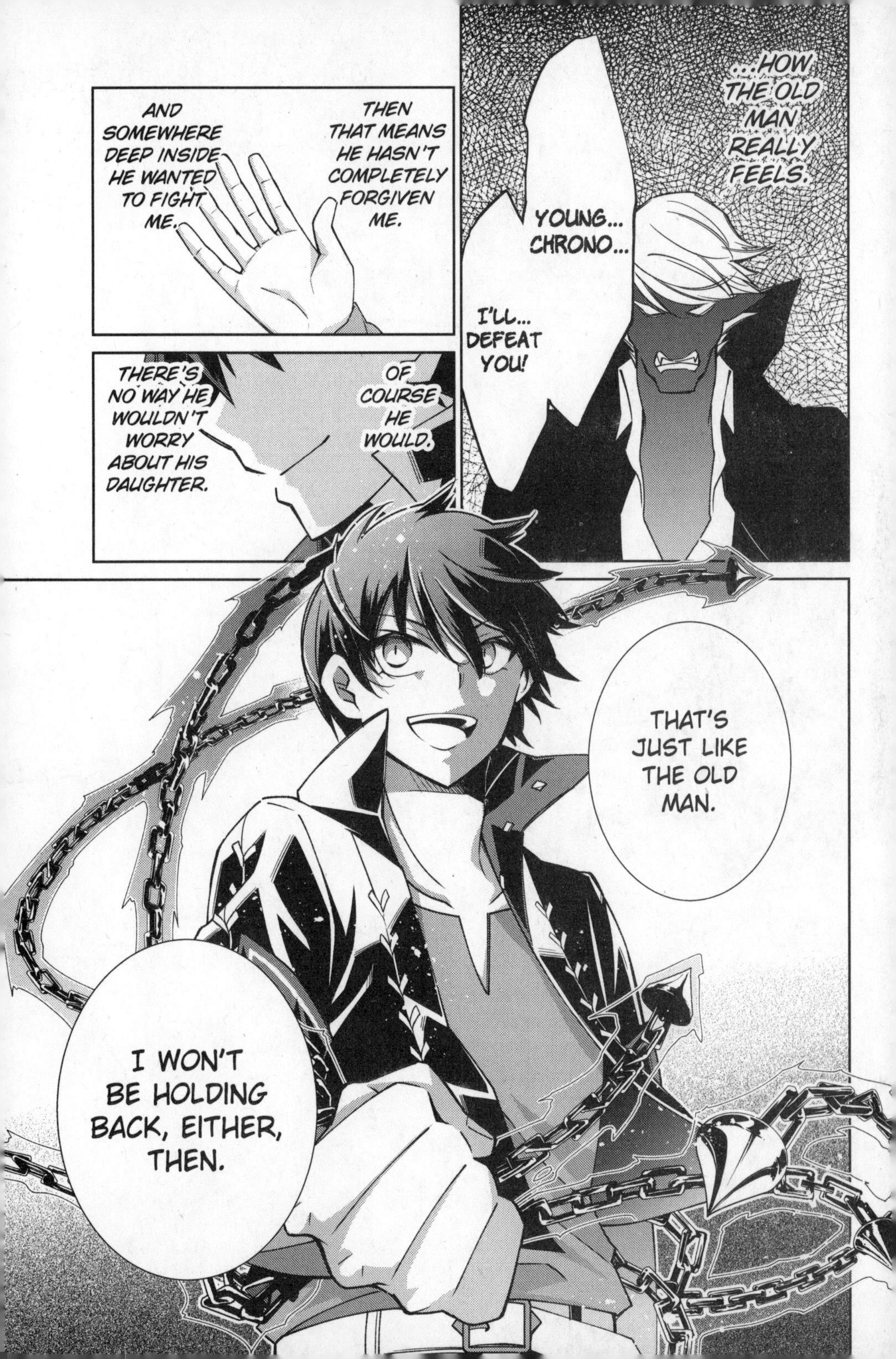
...HOW THE OLD MAN REALLY FEELS.
YOUNG... CHRONO...
I'LL... DEFEAT YOU!
THEN THAT MEANS HE HASN'T COMPLETELY FORGIVEN ME.
AND SOMEWHERE DEEP INSIDE HE WANTED TO FIGHT ME.
OF COURSE HE WOULD.
THERE'S NO WAY HE WOULDN'T WORRY ABOUT HIS DAUGHTER.
THAT'S JUST LIKE THE OLD MAN.
I WON'T BE HOLDING BACK, EITHER, THEN.

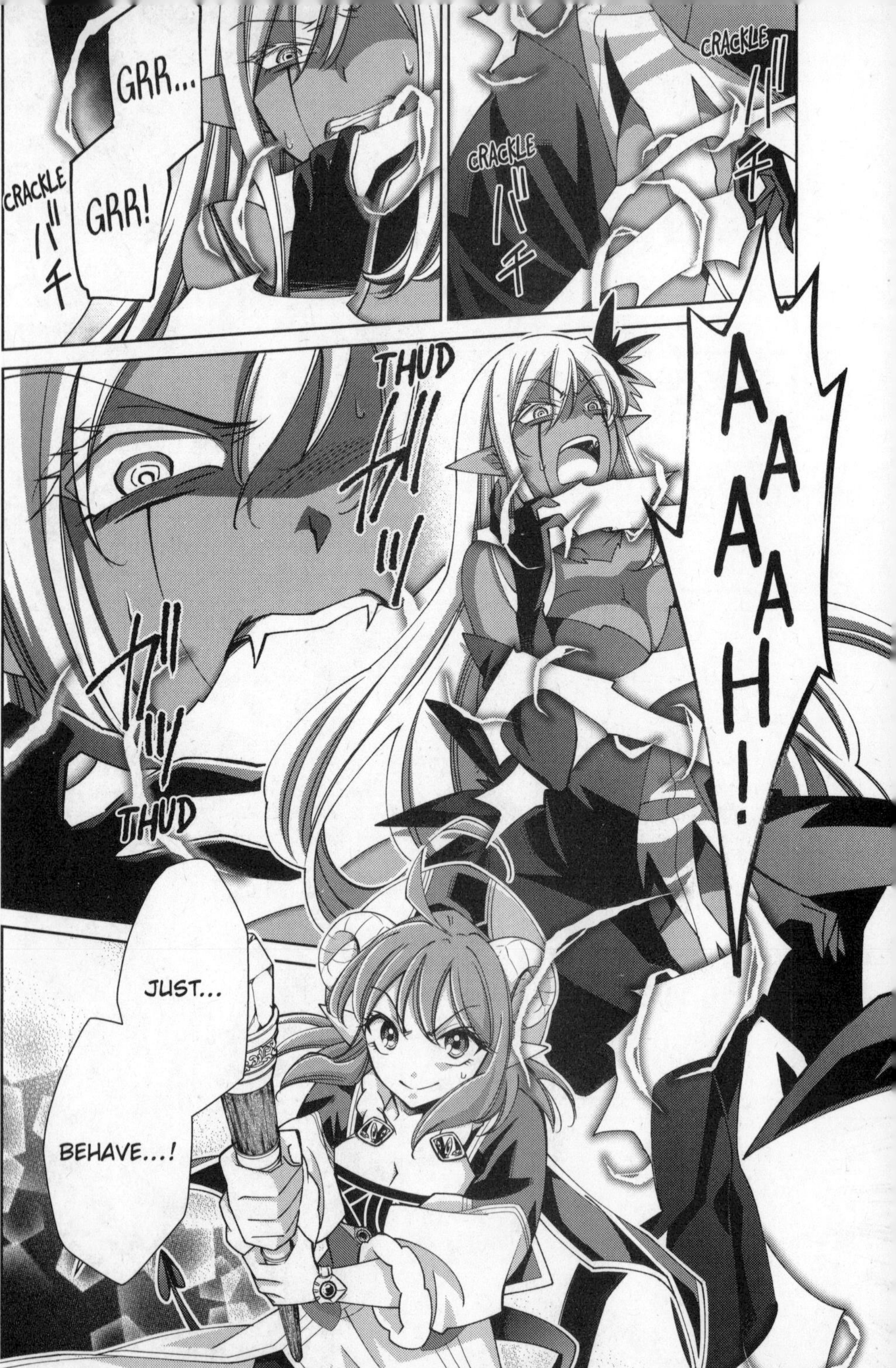
CRACKLE
バチ
CRACKLE
バチ
GRR...
CRACKLE
バチ
GRR!
AAAAH!
THUD
ガッ
ガッ
THUD
JUST...
BEHAVE...!

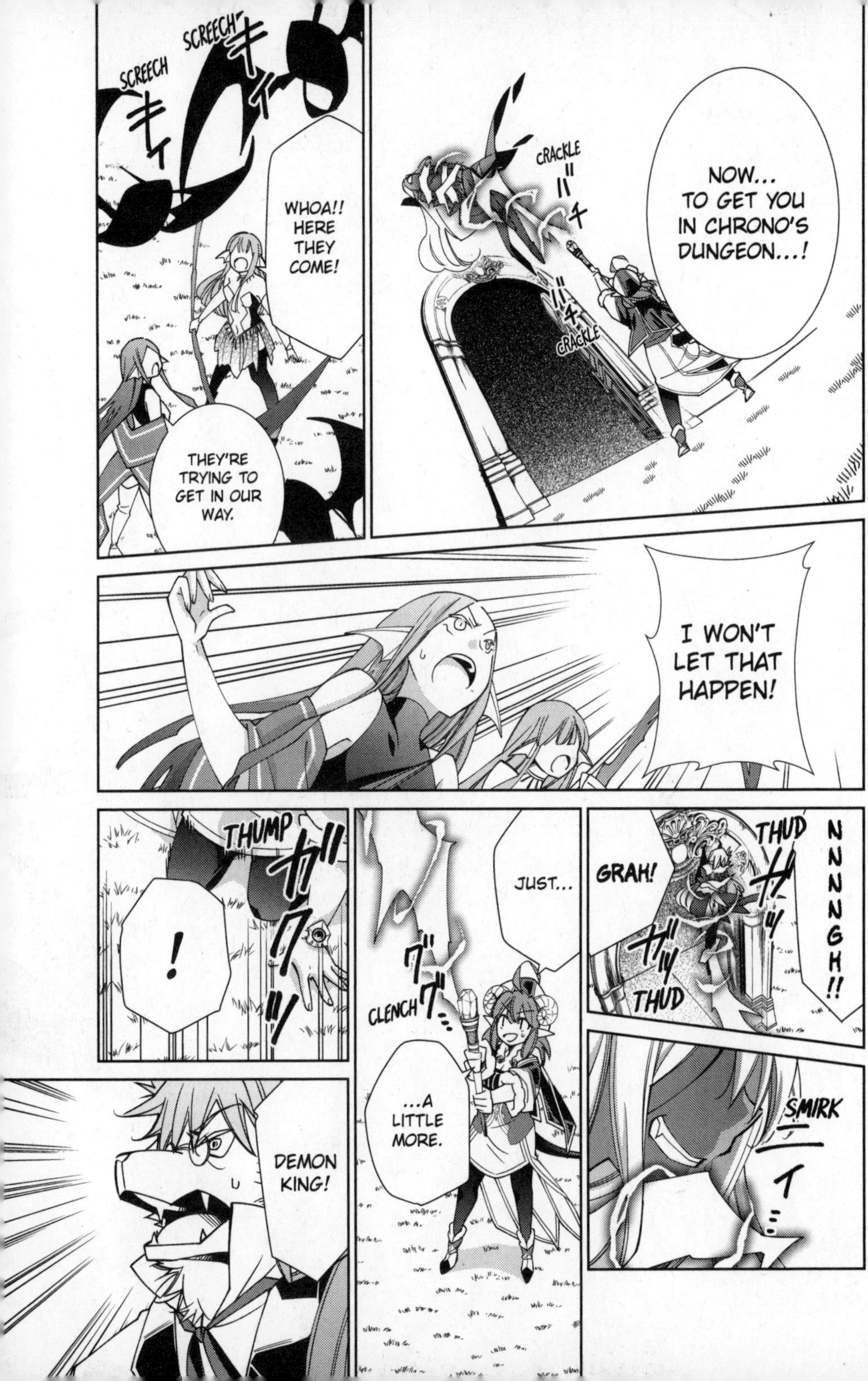
NOW... TO GET YOU IN CHRONO'S DUNGEON...!
CRACKLE
CRACKLE
SCREECH
SCREECH
WHOA!! HERE THEY COME!
THEY'RE TRYING TO GET IN OUR WAY.
I WON'T LET THAT HAPPEN!
NNNNGH!!
THUD
GRAH!
THUD
SMIRK
JUST...
CLENCH
...A LITTLE MORE.
THUMP
!
DEMON KING!

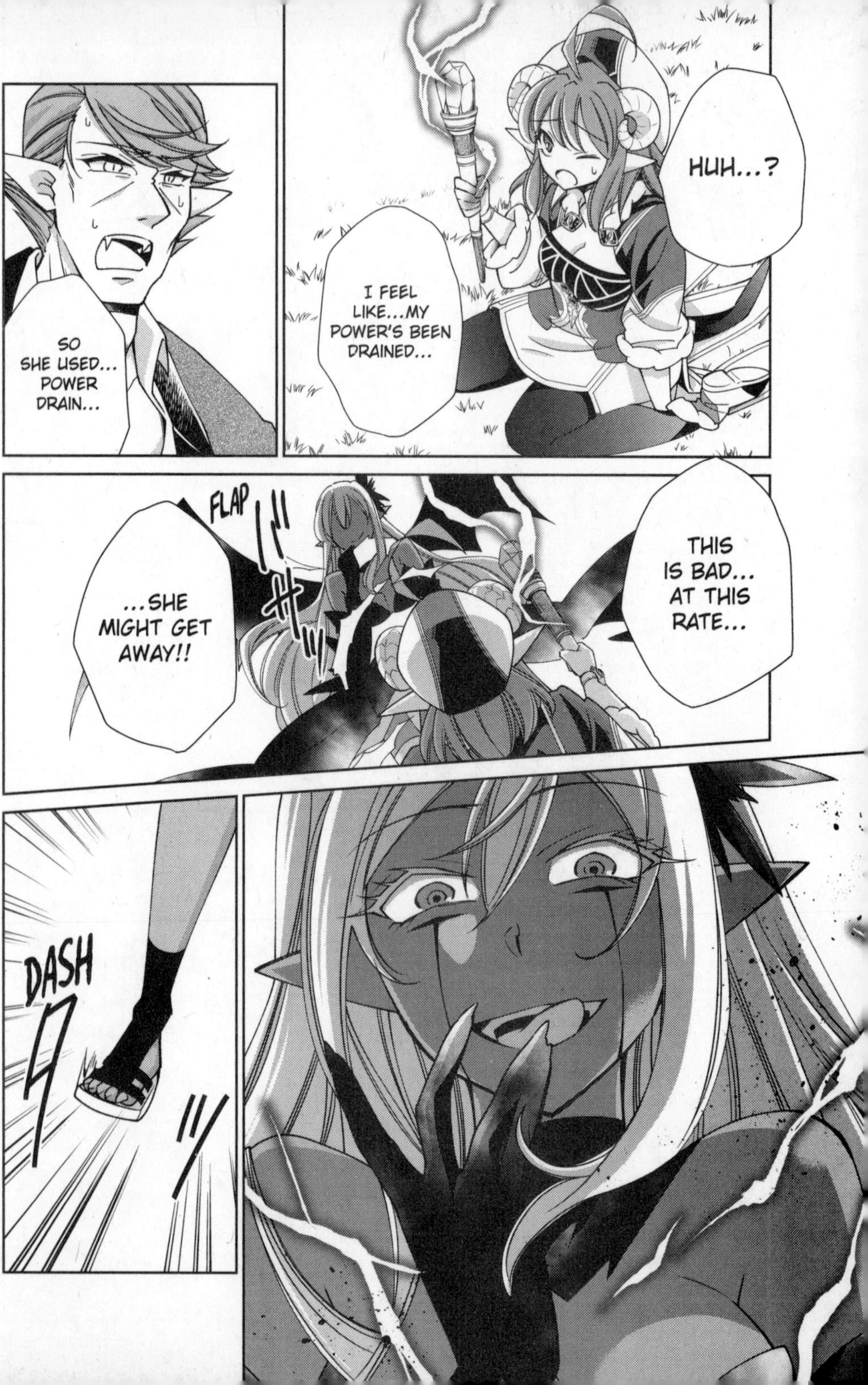
HUH...?
I FEEL LIKE...MY POWER'S BEEN DRAINED...
SO SHE USED... POWER DRAIN...
THIS IS BAD... AT THIS RATE...
FLAP
...SHE MIGHT GET AWAY!!
DASH

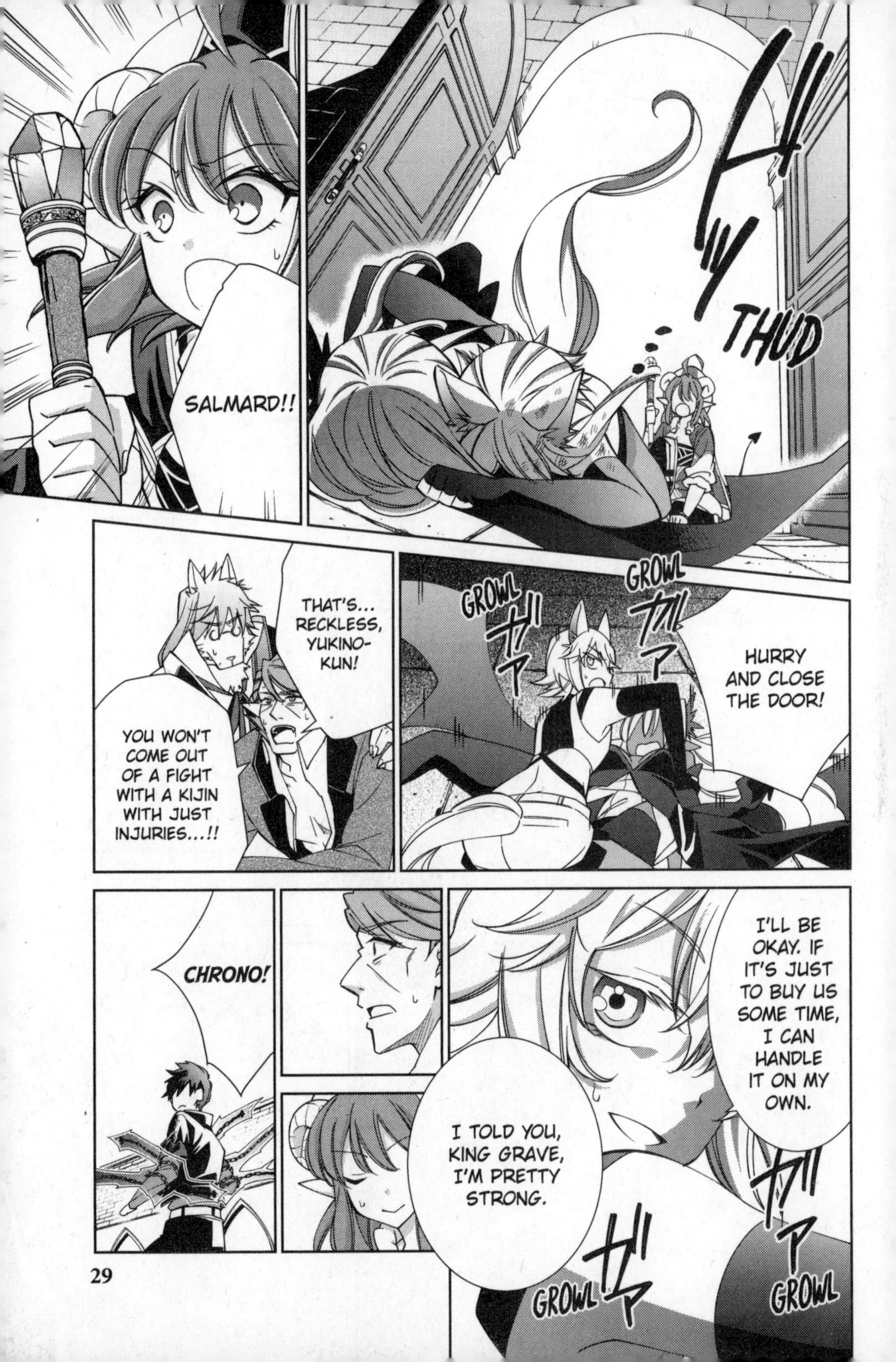
THUD
SALMARD!!
GROWL
GROWL
HURRY AND CLOSE THE DOOR!
THAT'S... RECKLESS, YUKINO-KUN!
YOU WON'T COME OUT OF A FIGHT WITH A KIJIN WITH JUST INJURIES...!!
I'LL BE OKAY. IF IT'S JUST TO BUY US SOME TIME, I CAN HANDLE IT ON MY OWN.
GROWL
GROWL
I TOLD YOU, KING GRAVE, I'M PRETTY STRONG.
CHRONO!

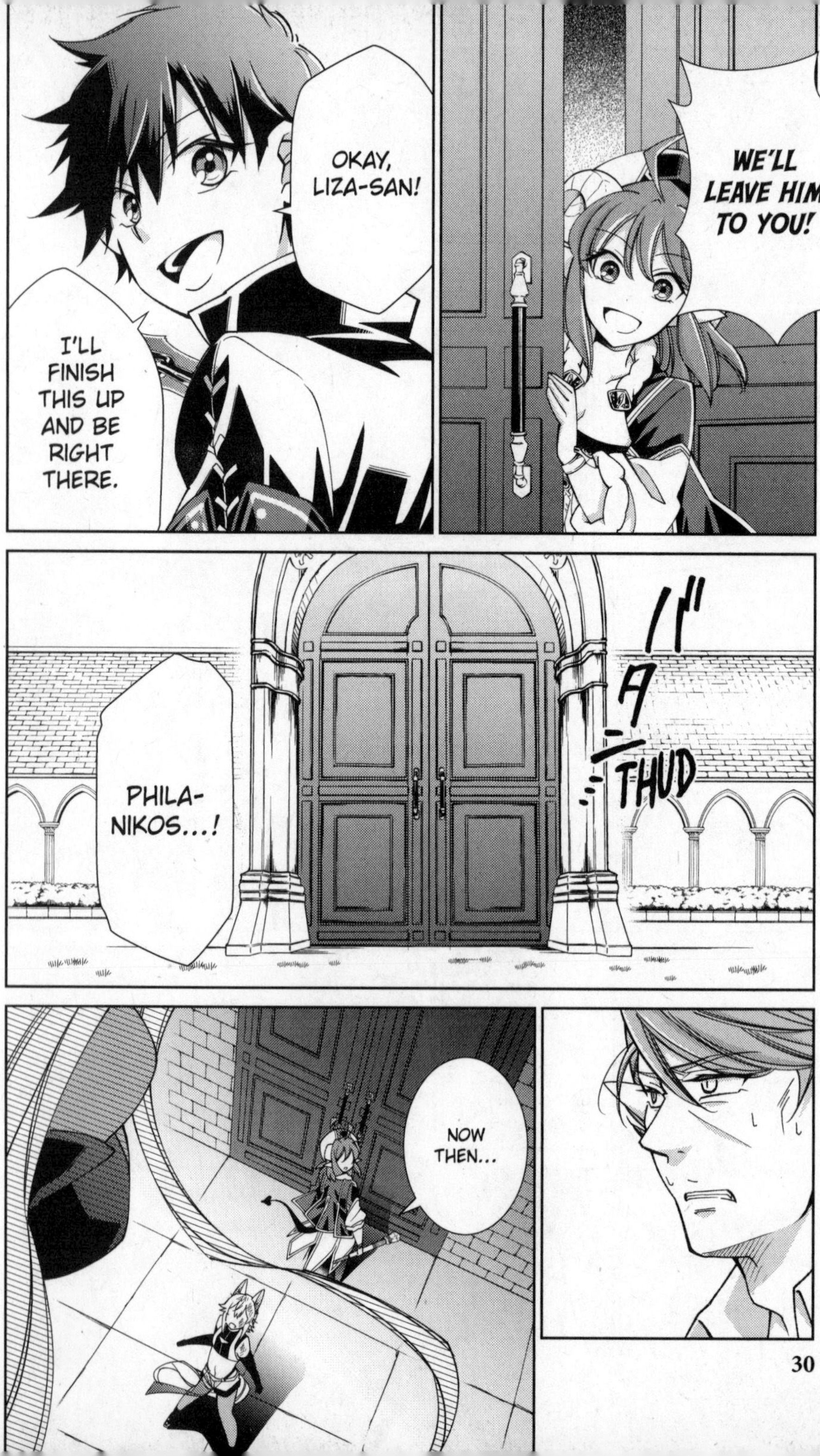
WE'LL LEAVE HIM TO YOU!
OKAY, LIZA-SAN!
I'LL FINISH THIS UP AND BE RIGHT THERE.
バタ
THUD
PHILA-NIKOS...!
NOW THEN...

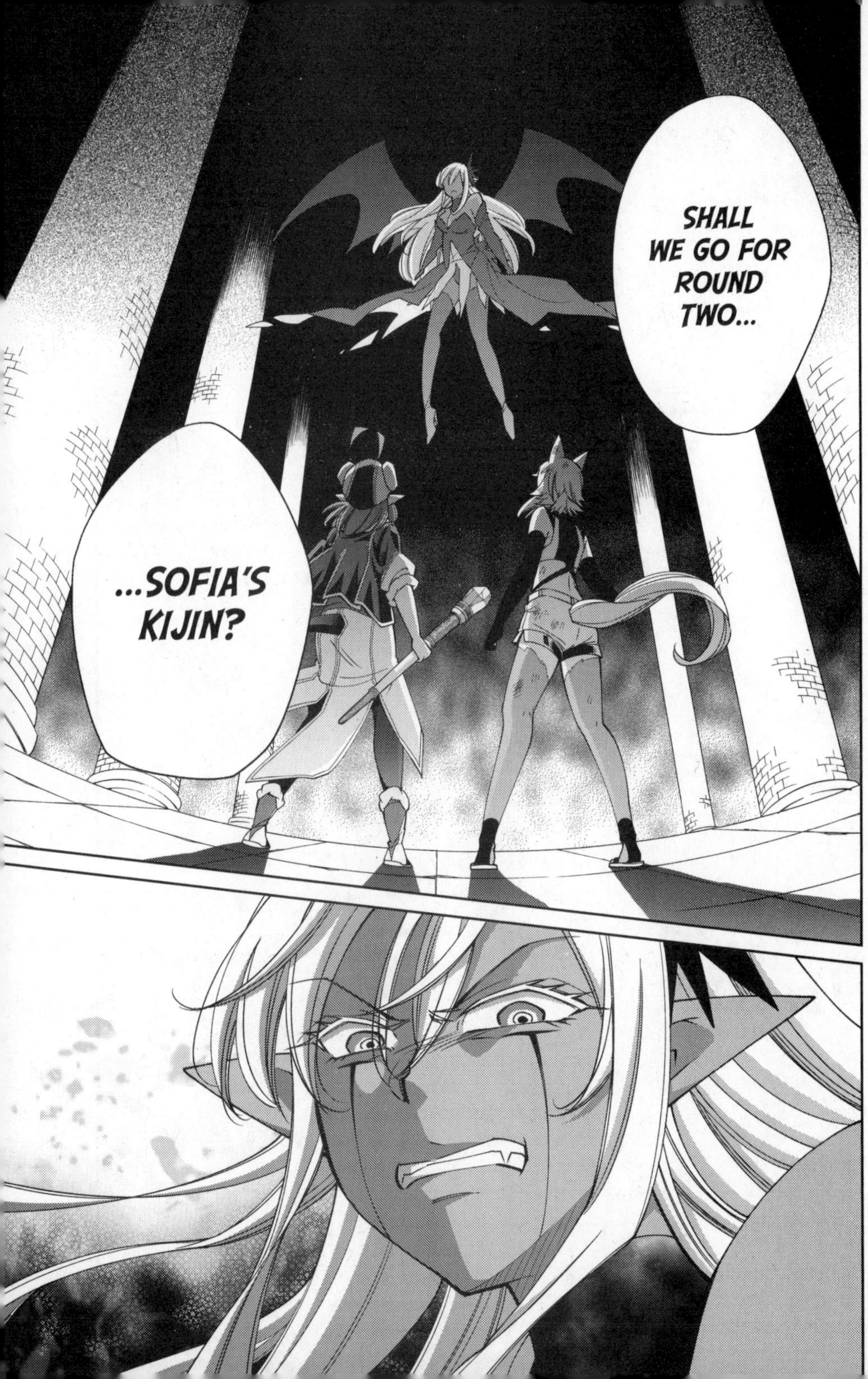
SHALL WE GO FOR ROUND TWO...
...SOFIA'S KIJIN?

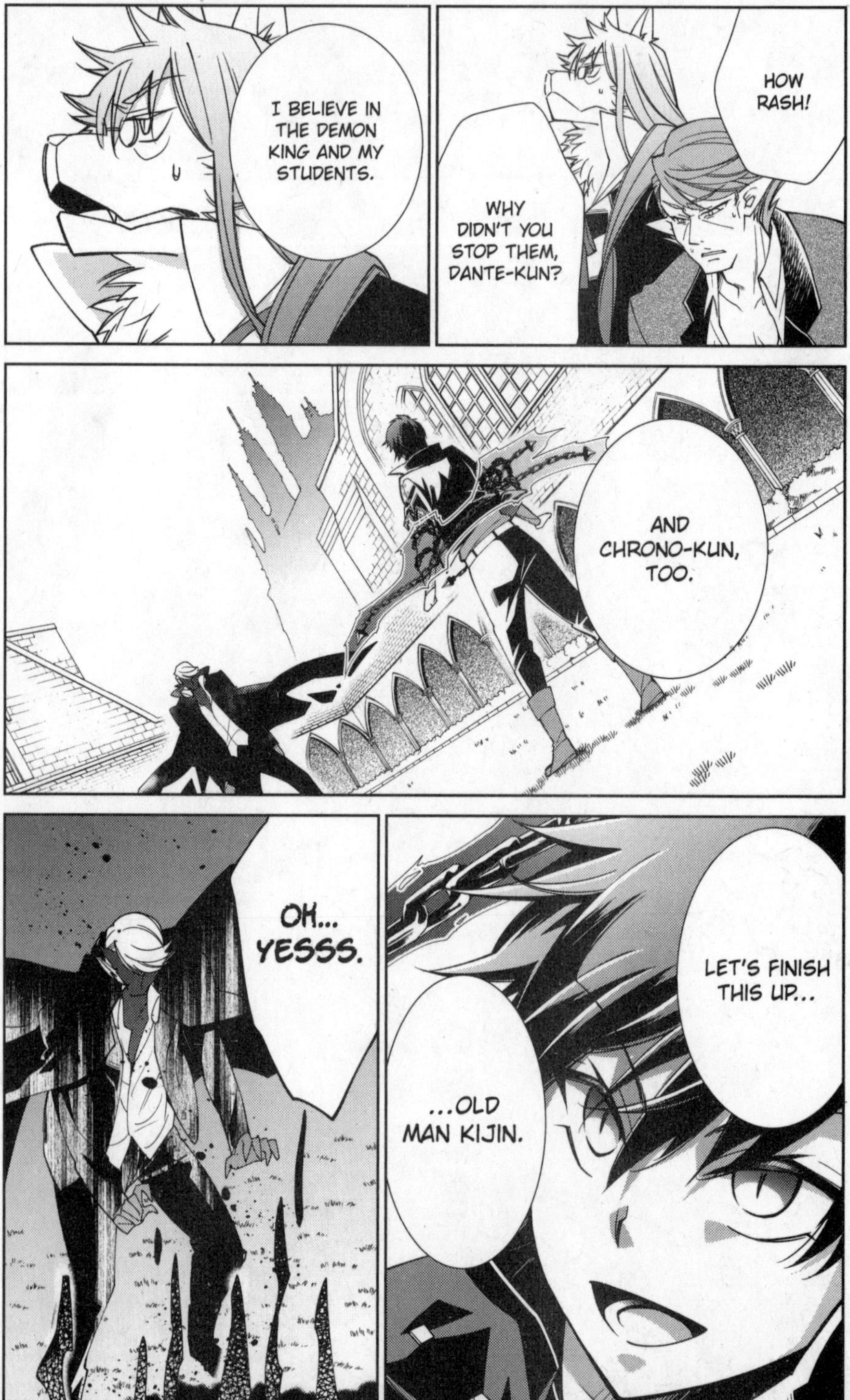
HOW RASH!
WHY DIDN'T YOU STOP THEM, DANTE-KUN?
I BELIEVE IN THE DEMON KING AND MY STUDENTS.
AND CHRONO-KUN, TOO.
LET'S FINISH THIS UP...
...OLD MAN KIJIN.
OH... YESSS.

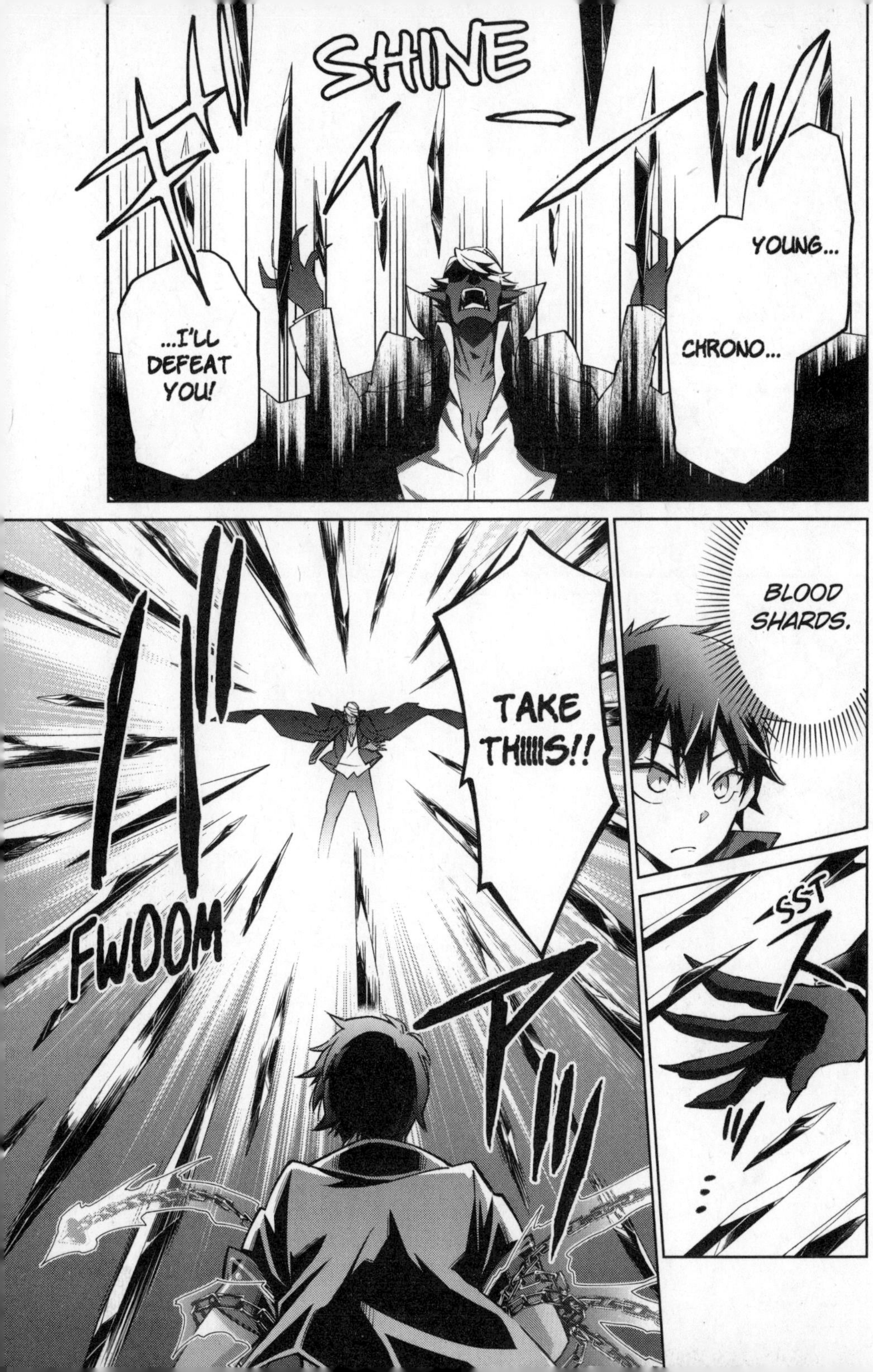
SHINE
YOUNG... CHRONO...
...I'LL DEFEAT YOU!
BLOOD SHARDS.
SST
TAKE THIIIIS!!
FWOOM

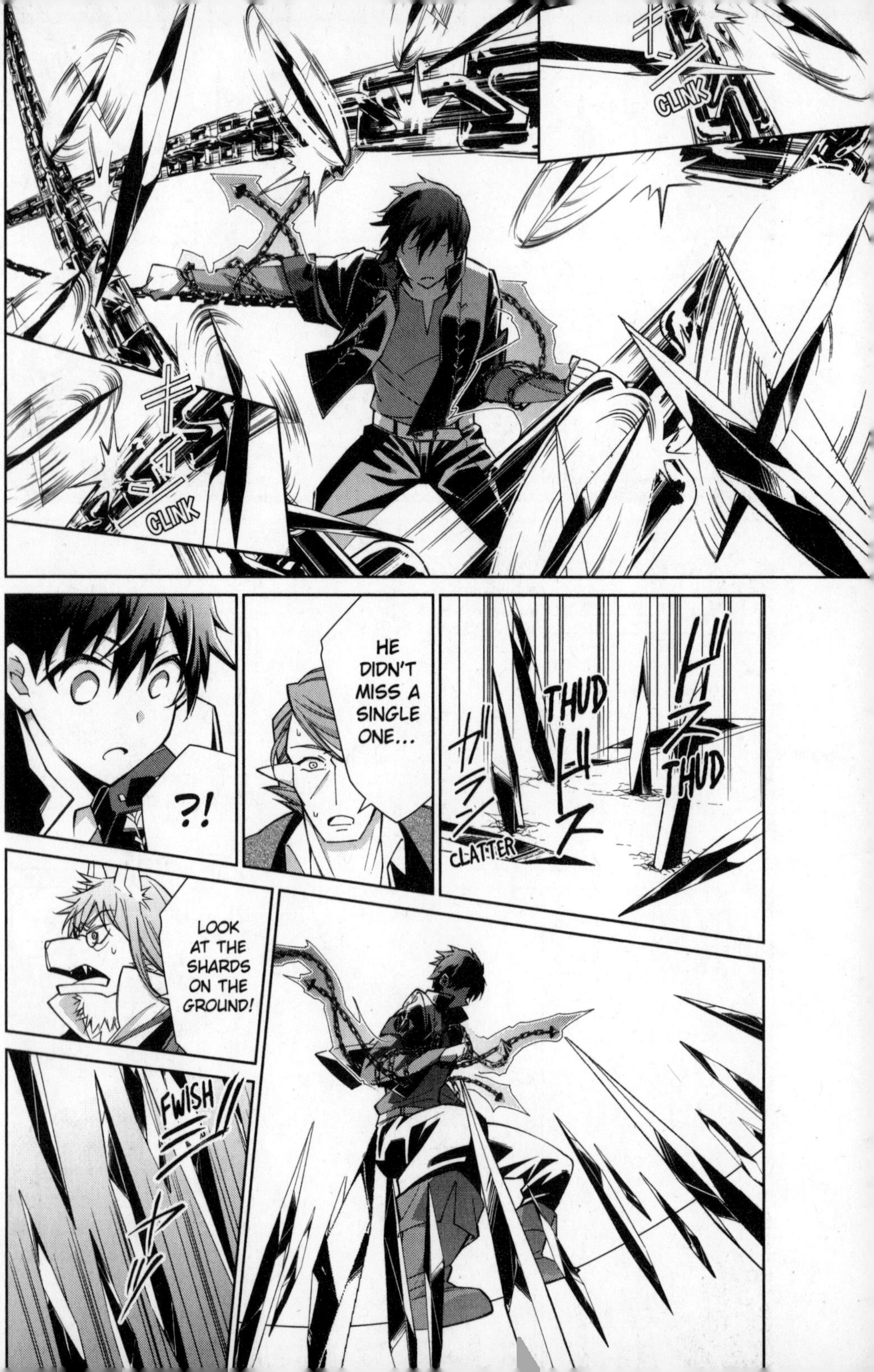
CLINK
CLINK
THUD
THUD
CLATTER
HE DIDN'T MISS A SINGLE ONE...
?!
LOOK AT THE SHARDS ON THE GROUND!
FWISH

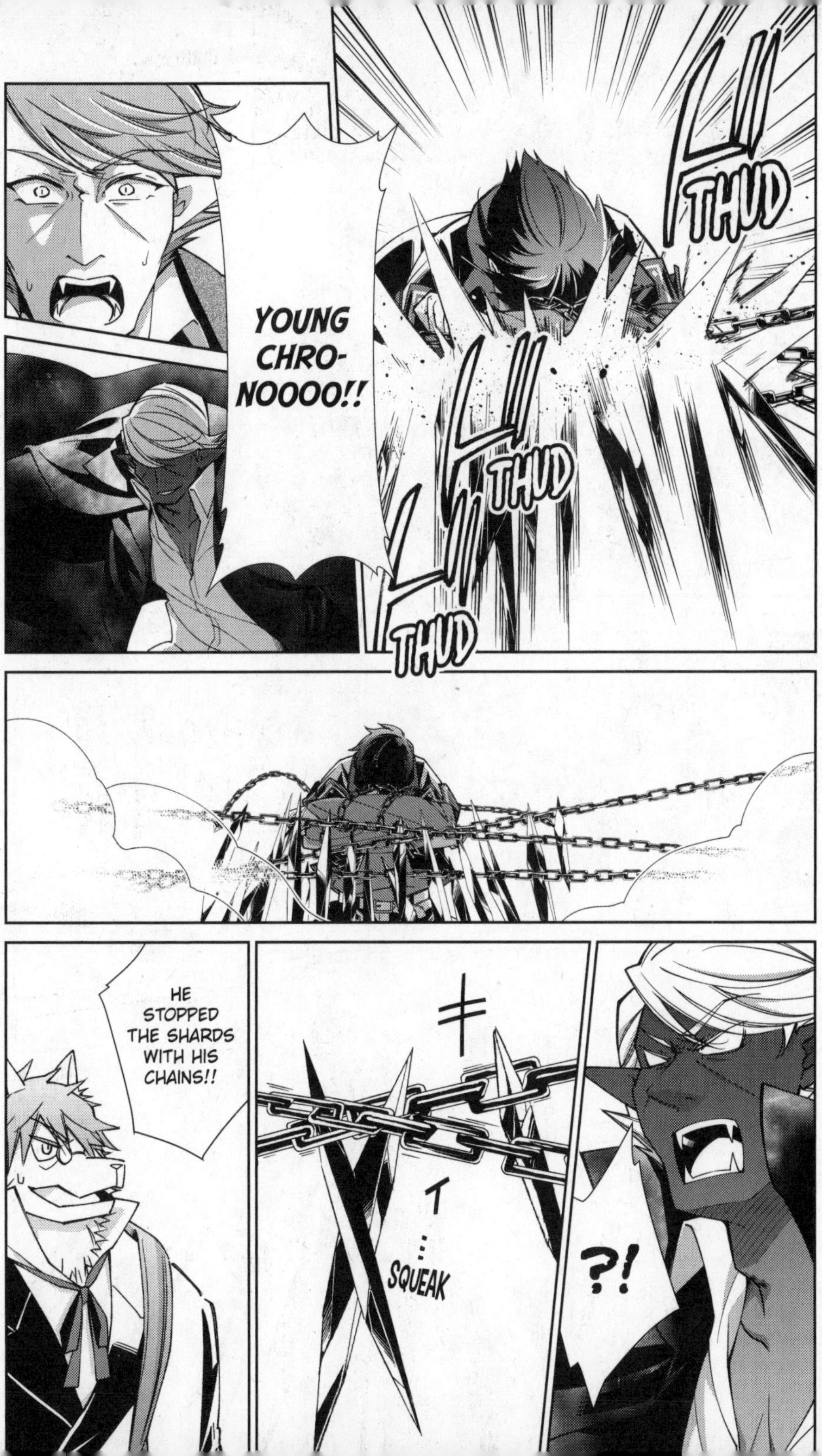
THUD
THUD
THUD
YOUNG CHRO-NOOOO!!
?!
SQUEAK
HE STOPPED THE SHARDS WITH HIS CHAINS!!

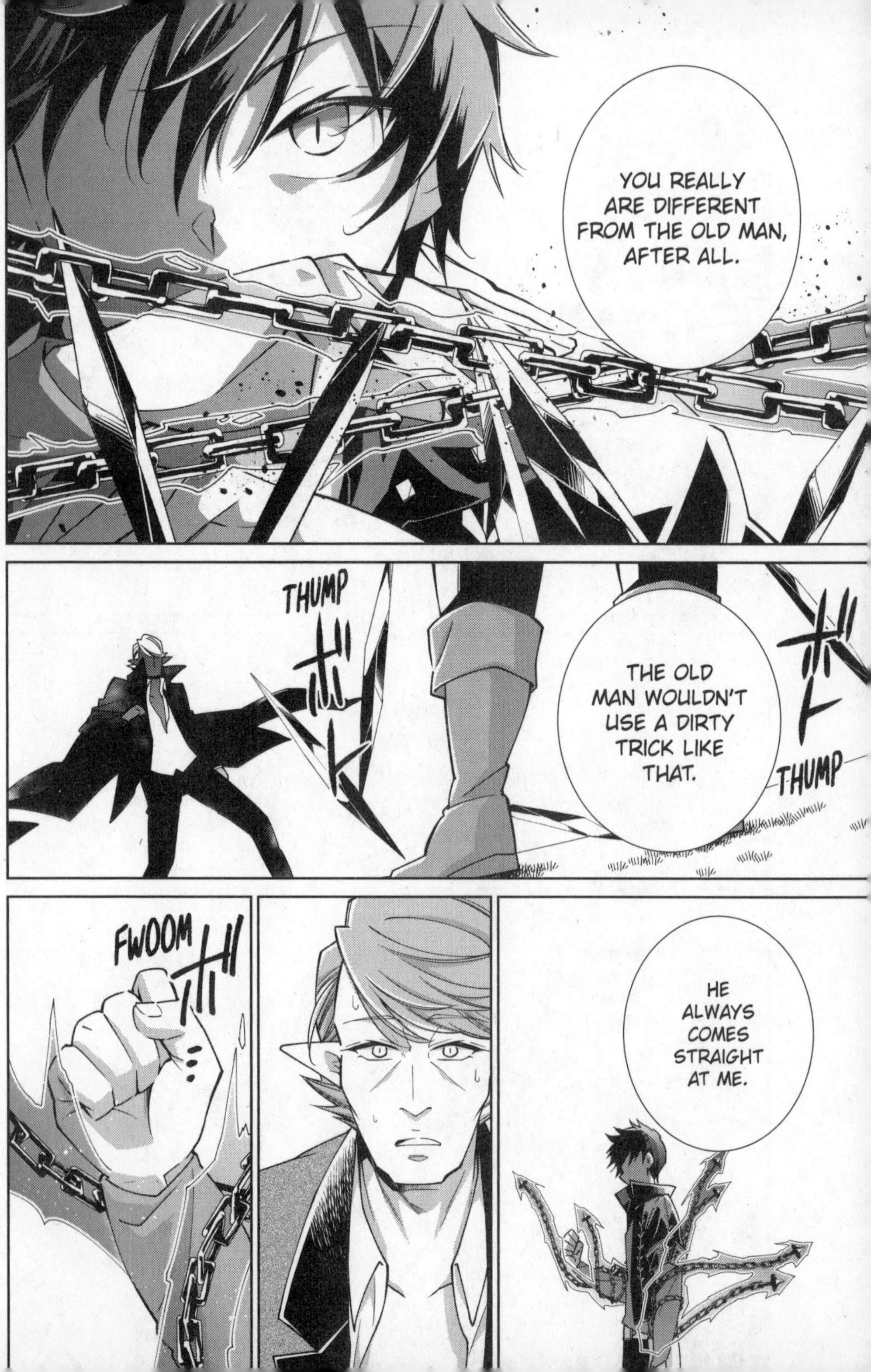
YOU REALLY ARE DIFFERENT FROM THE OLD MAN, AFTER ALL.
THUMP
THE OLD MAN WOULDN'T USE A DIRTY TRICK LIKE THAT.
THUMP
HE ALWAYS COMES STRAIGHT AT ME.
FWOOM

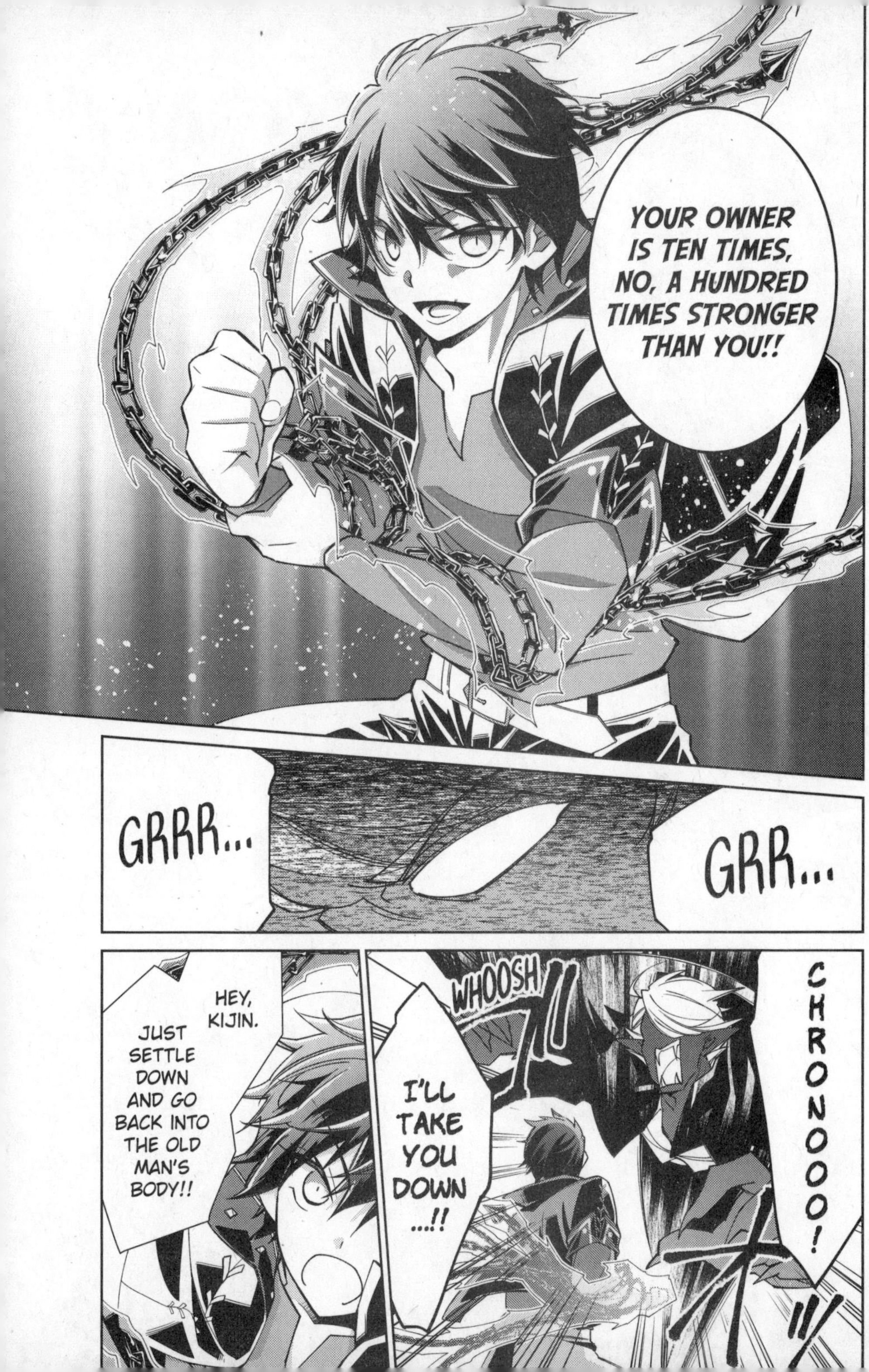
YOUR OWNER IS TEN TIMES, NO, A HUNDRED TIMES STRONGER THAN YOU!!
GRR...
GRRR...
CHRONOOOO!
WHOOSH
I'LL TAKE YOU DOWN ...!!
HEY, KIJIN.
JUST SETTLE DOWN AND GO BACK INTO THE OLD MAN'S BODY!!

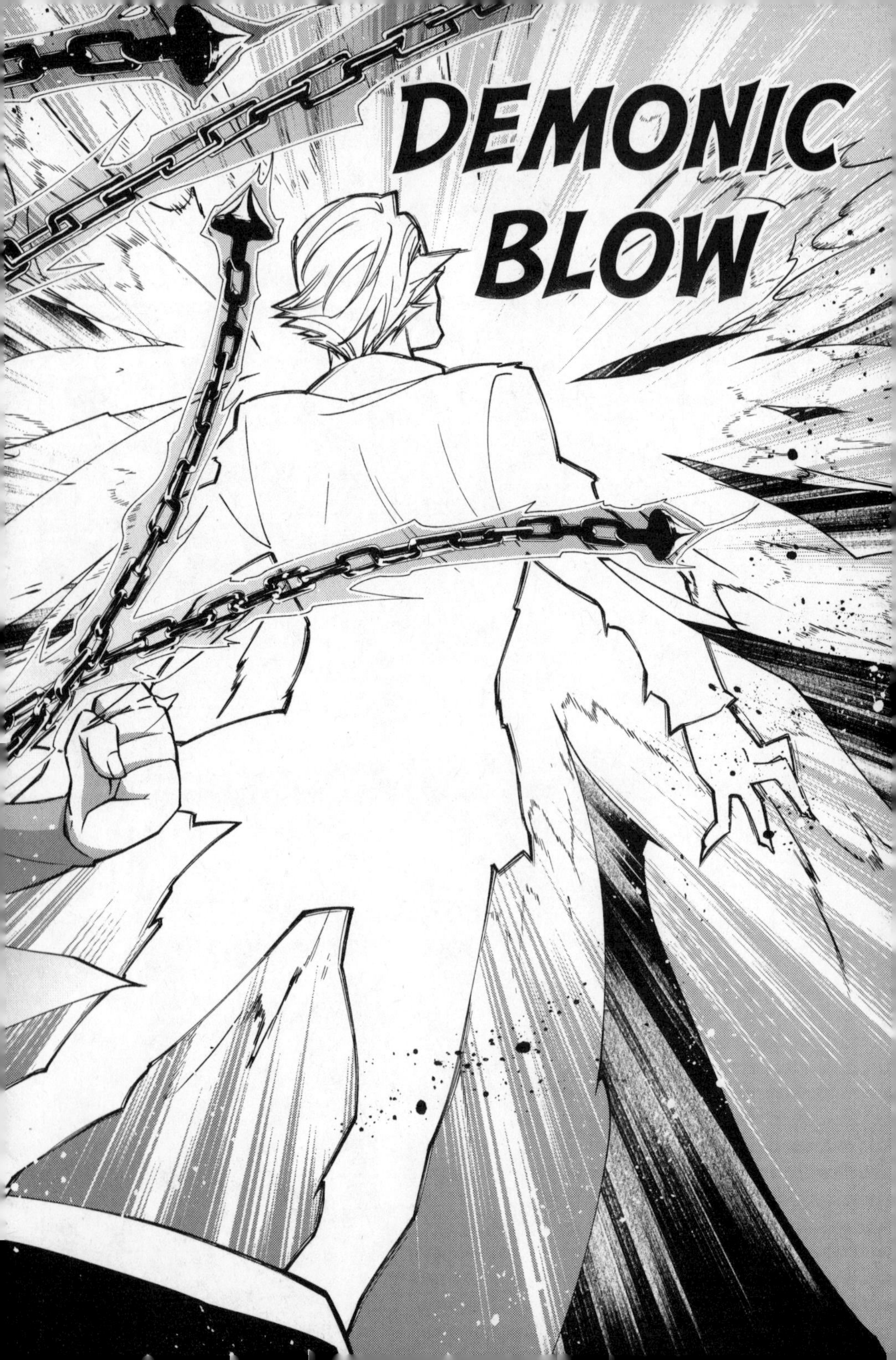
DEMONIC BLOW

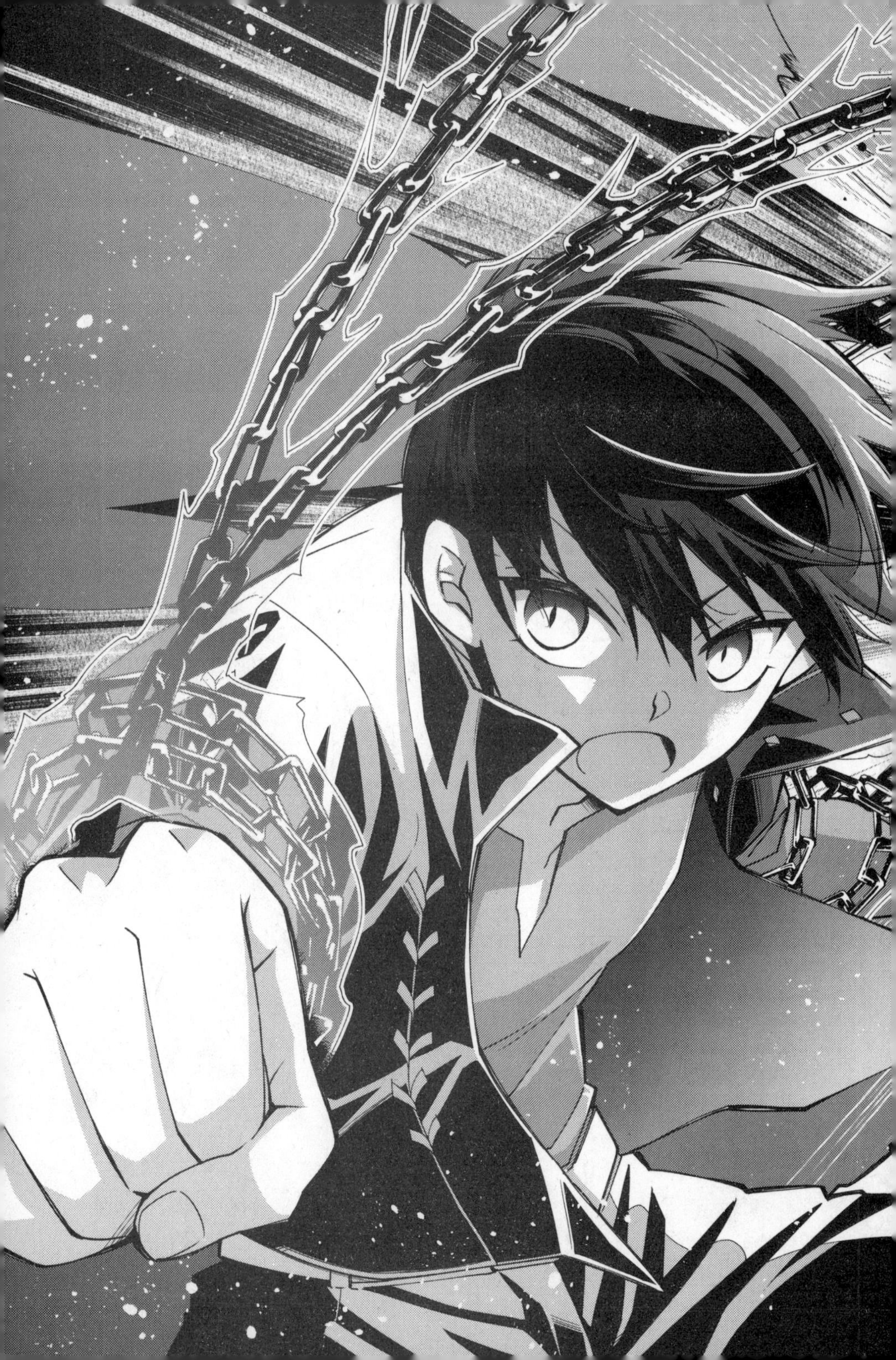

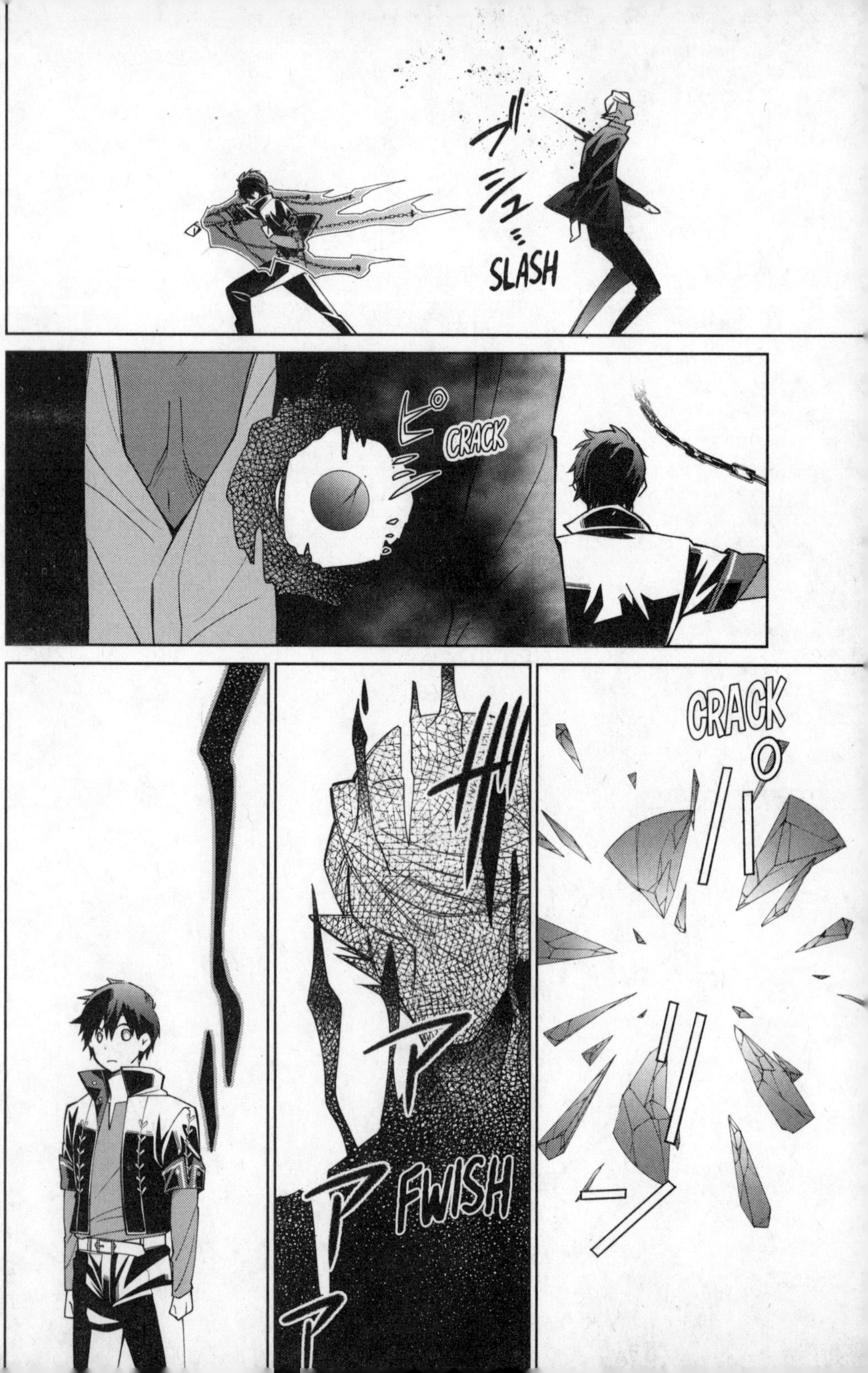
SLASH
CRACK
CRACK
FWISH

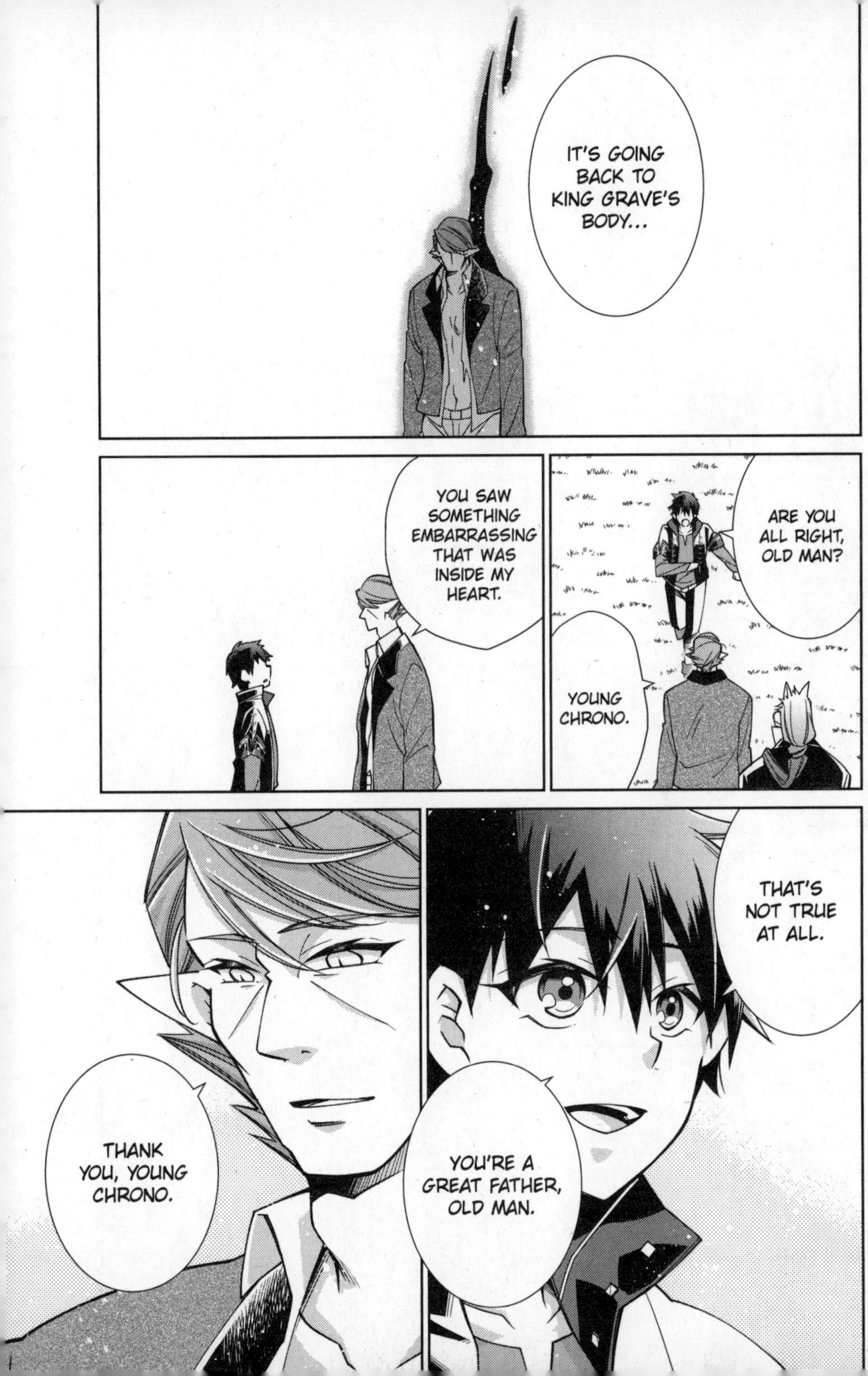
IT'S GOING BACK TO KING GRAVE'S BODY...
ARE YOU ALL RIGHT, OLD MAN?
YOUNG CHRONO.
YOU SAW SOMETHING EMBARRASSING THAT WAS INSIDE MY HEART.
THAT'S NOT TRUE AT ALL.
YOU'RE A GREAT FATHER, OLD MAN.
THANK YOU, YOUNG CHRONO.

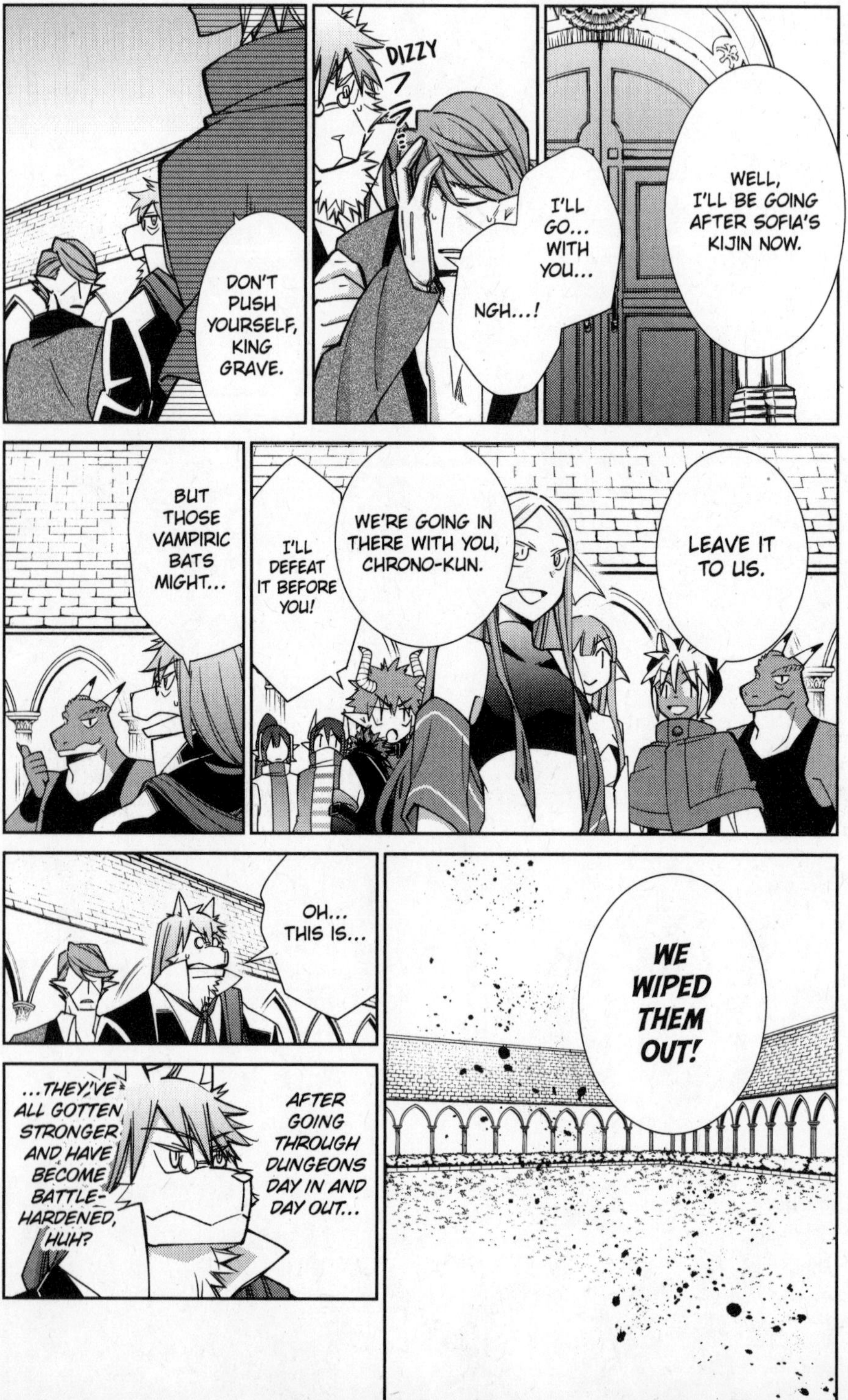
WELL, I'LL BE GOING AFTER SOFIA'S KIJIN NOW.
DIZZY
I'LL GO... WITH YOU...
NGH...!
DON'T PUSH YOURSELF, KING GRAVE.
LEAVE IT TO US.
WE'RE GOING IN THERE WITH YOU, CHRONO-KUN.
I'LL DEFEAT IT BEFORE YOU!
BUT THOSE VAMPIRIC BATS MIGHT...
WE WIPED THEM OUT!
OH... THIS IS...
AFTER GOING THROUGH DUNGEONS DAY IN AND DAY OUT...
...THEY'VE ALL GOTTEN STRONGER AND HAVE BECOME BATTLE-HARDENED, HUH?

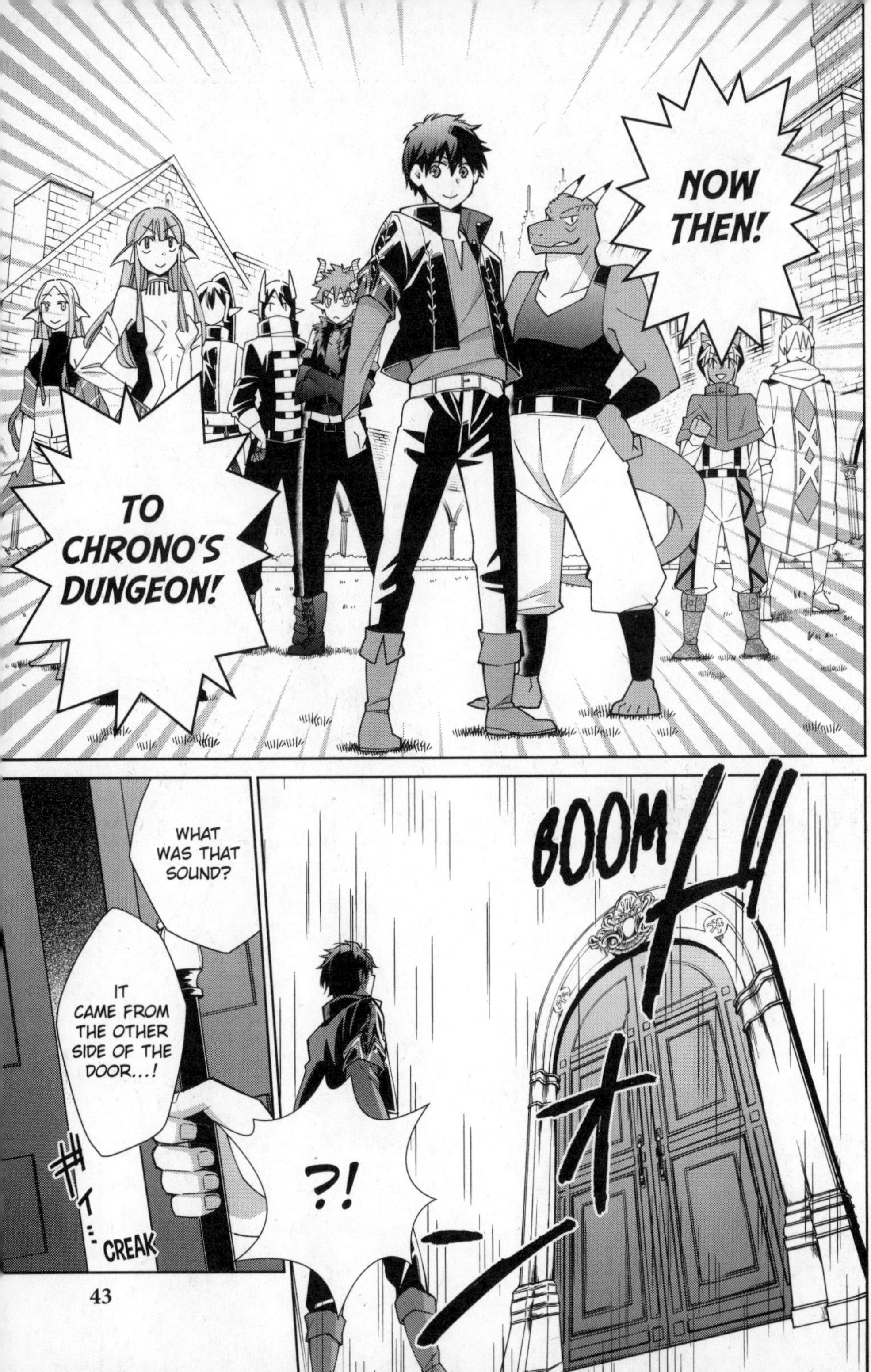
NOW THEN!
TO CHRONO'S DUNGEON!
BOOM
?!
WHAT WAS THAT SOUND?
IT CAME FROM THE OTHER SIDE OF THE DOOR...!
CREAK

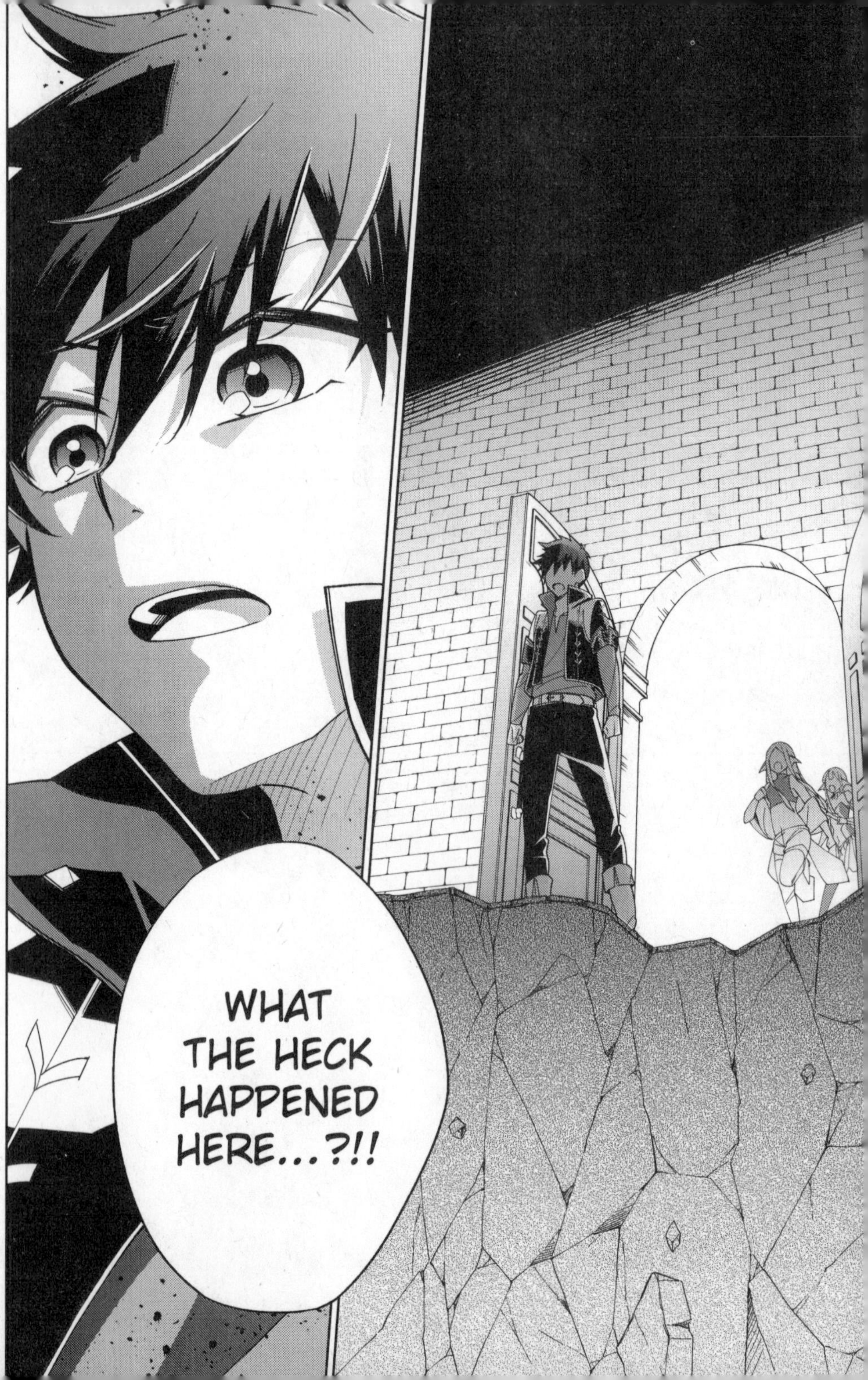
WHAT THE HECK HAPPENED HERE...?!!

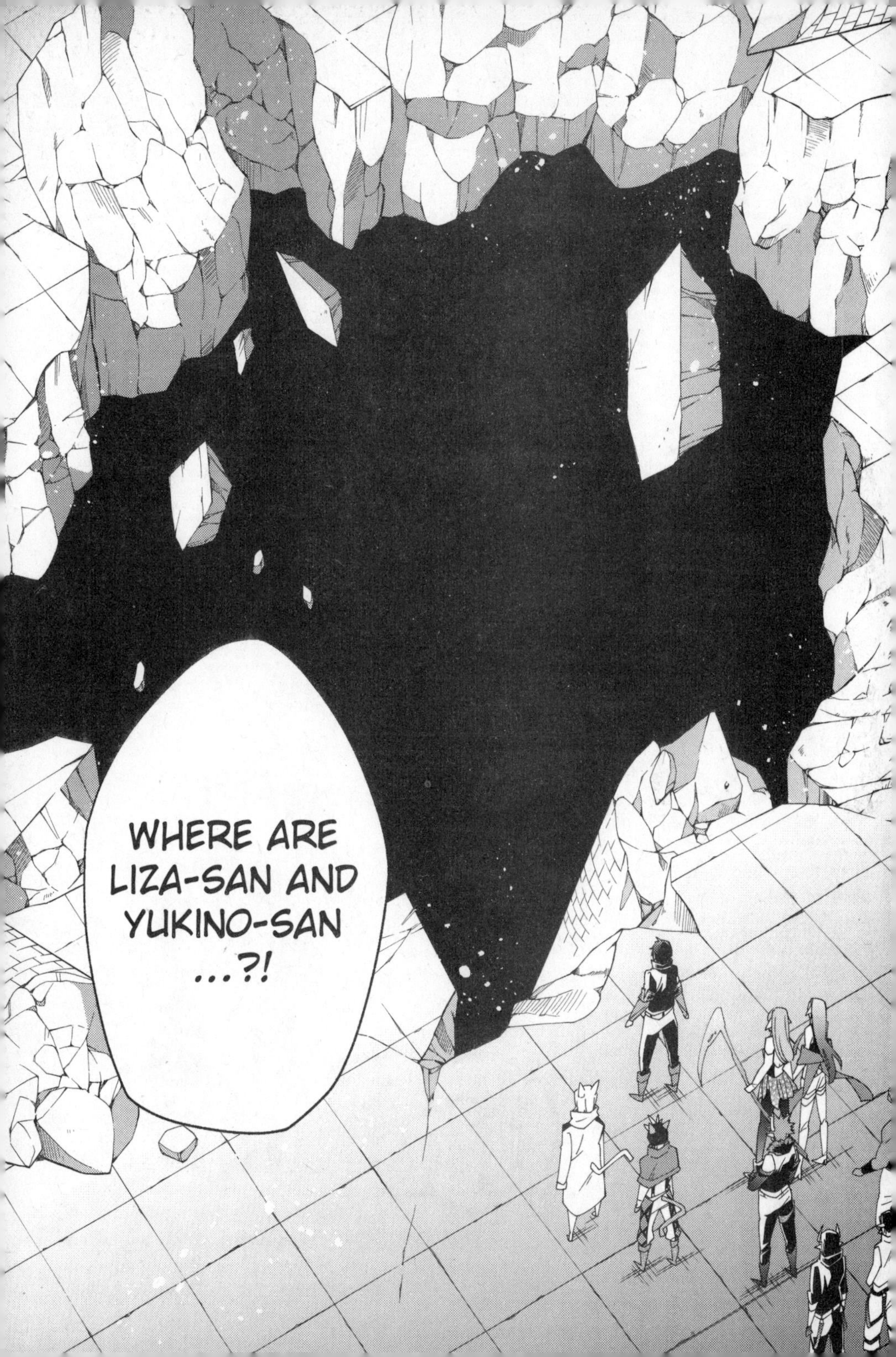
WHERE ARE LIZA-SAN AND YUKINO-SAN ...?!

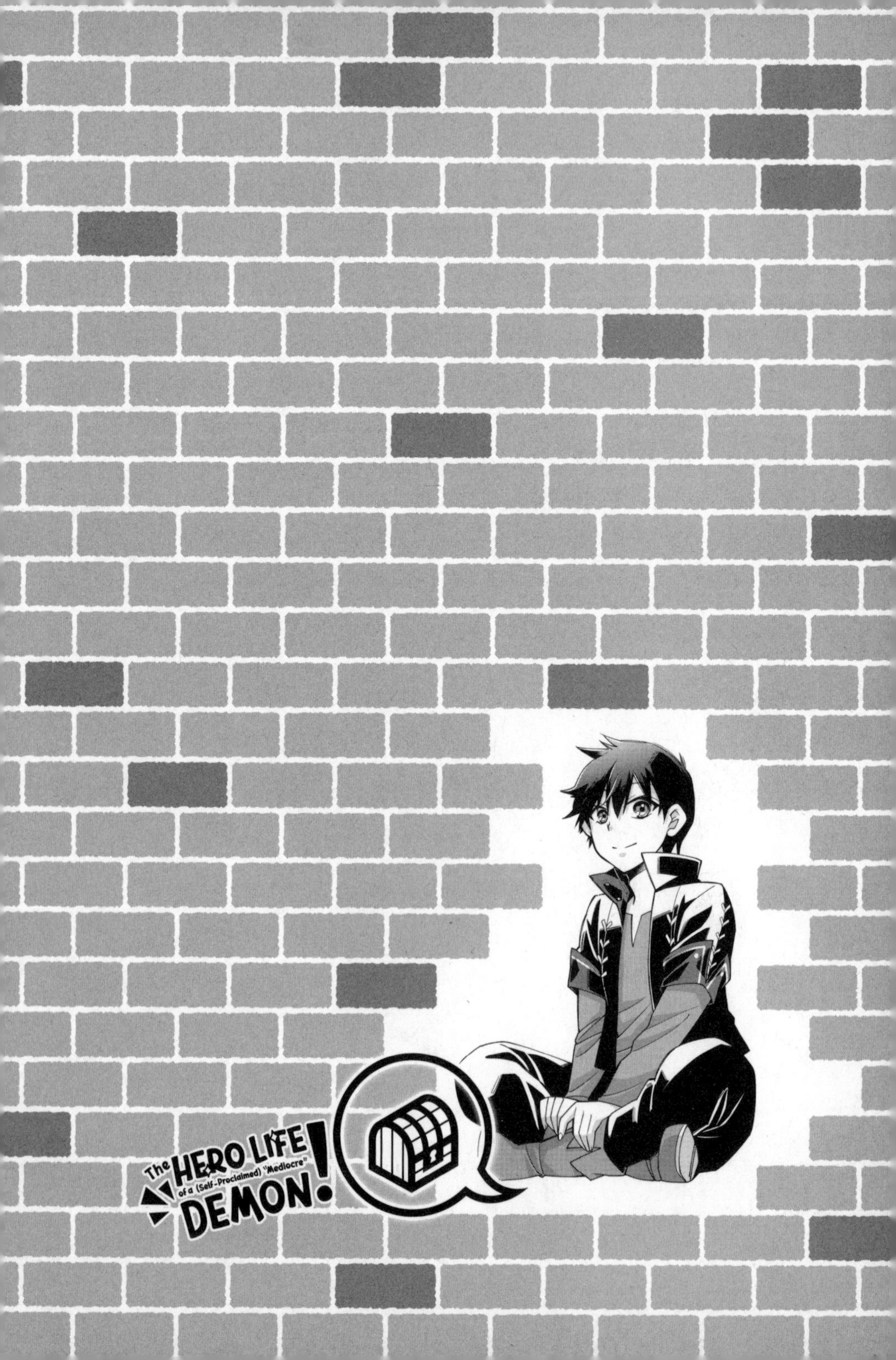
The HERO LIFE of a (Self-Proclaimed) "Mediocre" DEMON!

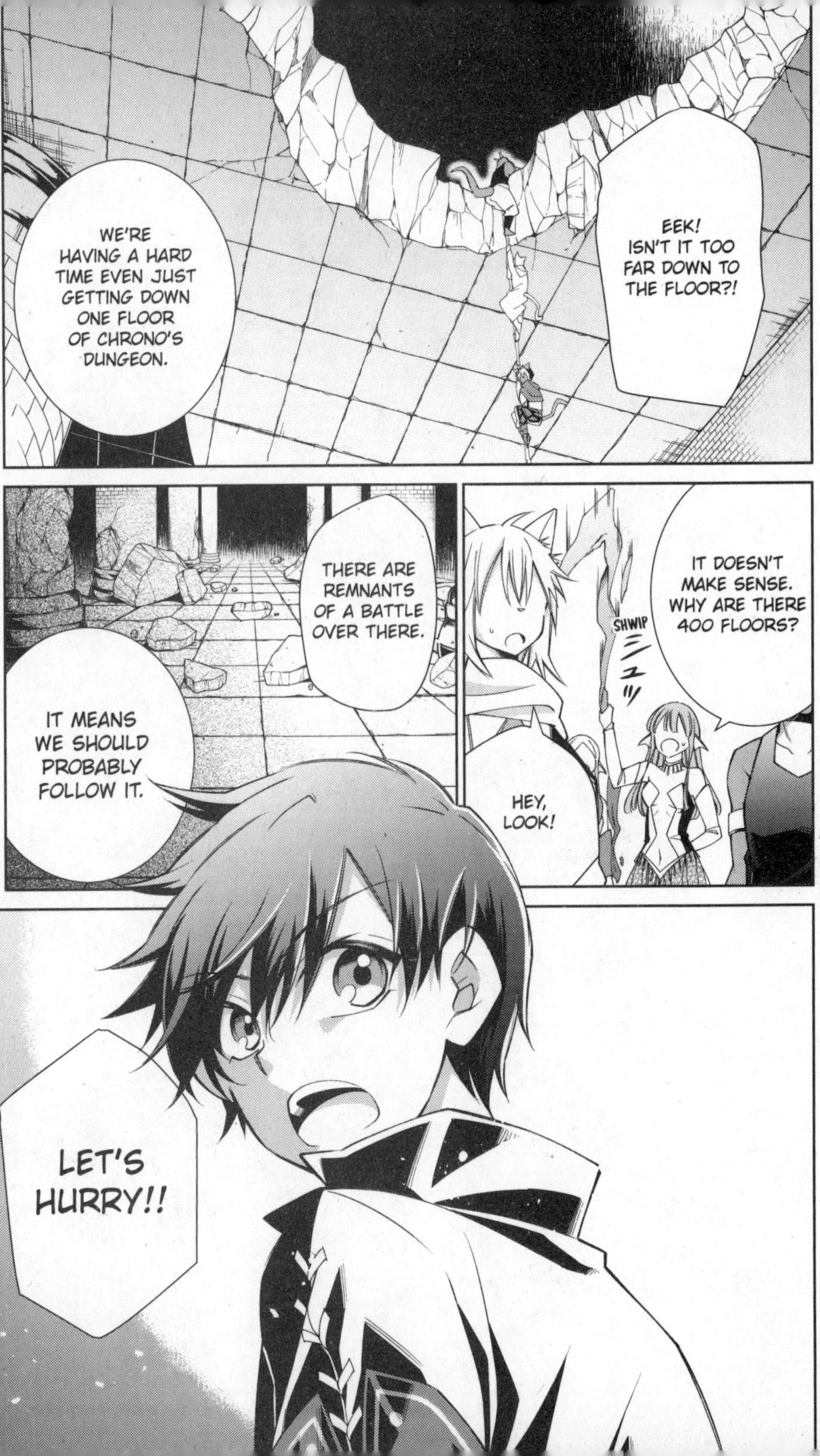
EEK! ISN'T IT TOO FAR DOWN TO THE FLOOR?!
WE'RE HAVING A HARD TIME EVEN JUST GETTING DOWN ONE FLOOR OF CHRONO'S DUNGEON.
IT DOESN'T MAKE SENSE. WHY ARE THERE 400 FLOORS?
SHWIP
HEY, LOOK!
THERE ARE REMNANTS OF A BATTLE OVER THERE.
IT MEANS WE SHOULD PROBABLY FOLLOW IT.
LET'S HURRY!!

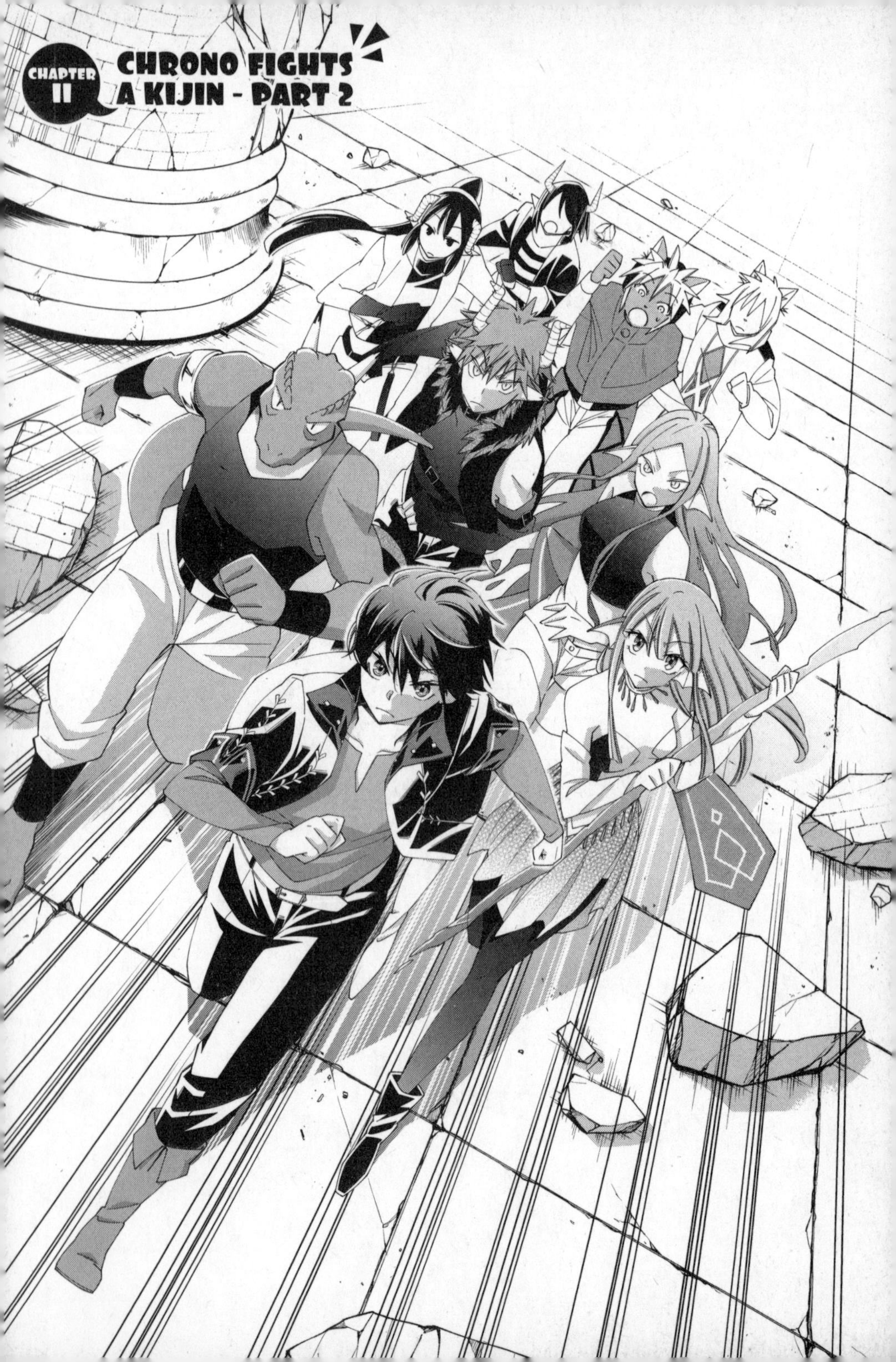
CHAPTER 11
CHRONO FIGHTS A KIJIN - PART 2

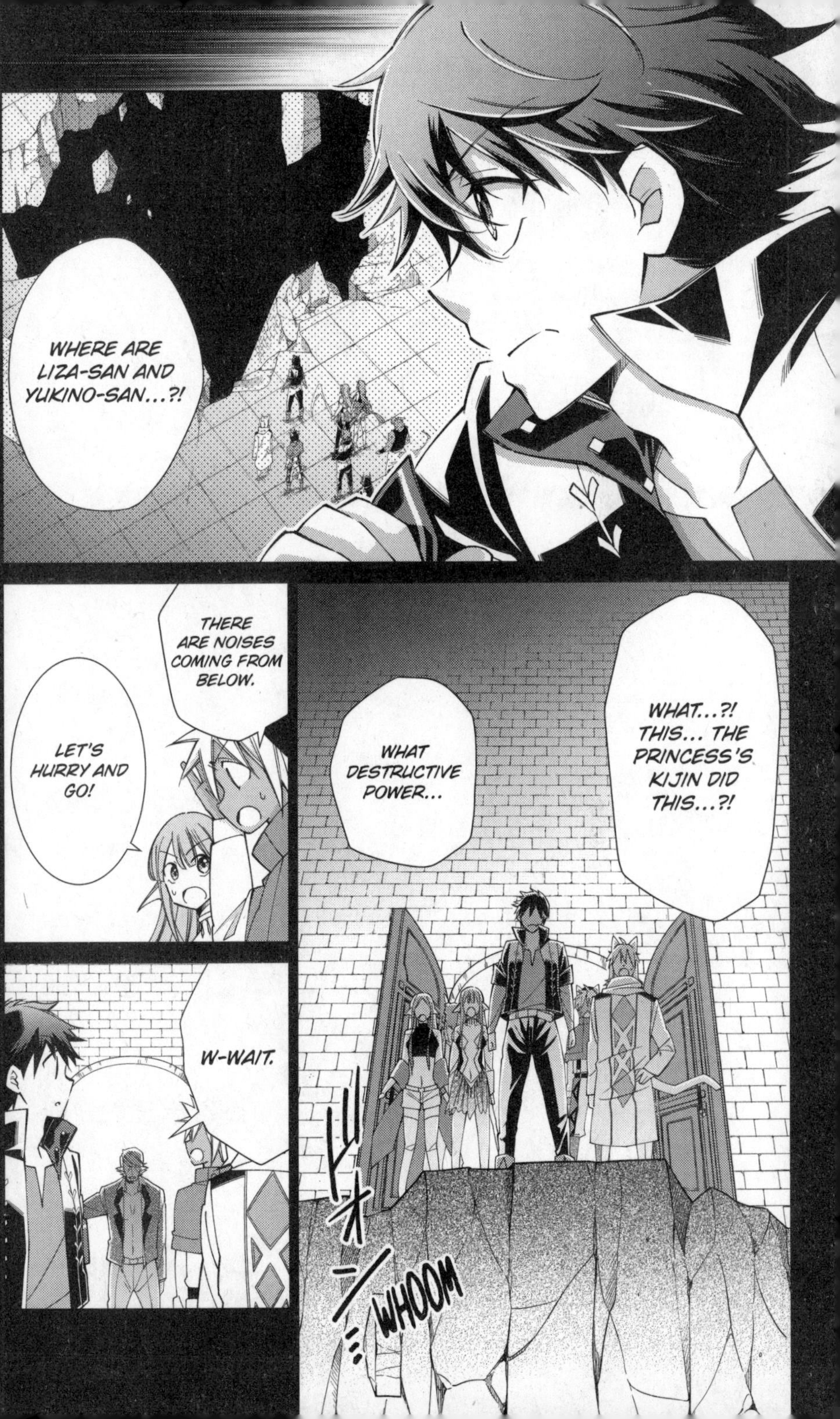
WHERE ARE LIZA-SAN AND YUKINO-SAN...?!
WHAT...?! THIS... THE PRINCESS'S KIJIN DID THIS...?!
WHAT DESTRUCTIVE POWER...
WHOOM
THERE ARE NOISES COMING FROM BELOW.
LET'S HURRY AND GO!
W-WAIT.

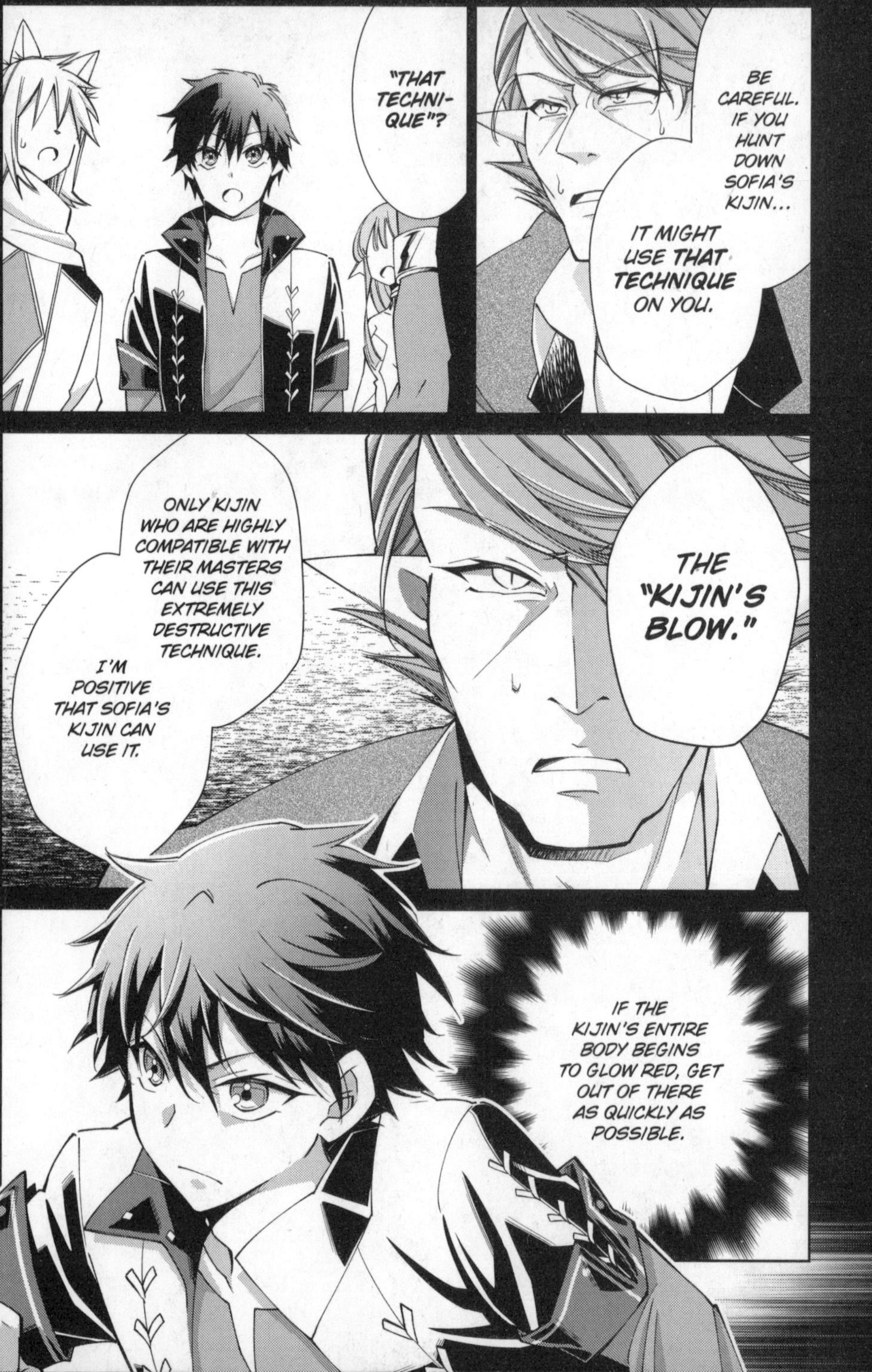
BE CAREFUL. IF YOU HUNT DOWN SOFIA'S KIJIN...
IT MIGHT USE THAT TECHNIQUE ON YOU.
"THAT TECHNI-QUE"?
THE "KIJIN'S BLOW."
ONLY KIJIN WHO ARE HIGHLY COMPATIBLE WITH THEIR MASTERS CAN USE THIS EXTREMELY DESTRUCTIVE TECHNIQUE.
I'M POSITIVE THAT SOFIA'S KIJIN CAN USE IT.
IF THE KIJIN'S ENTIRE BODY BEGINS TO GLOW RED, GET OUT OF THERE AS QUICKLY AS POSSIBLE.

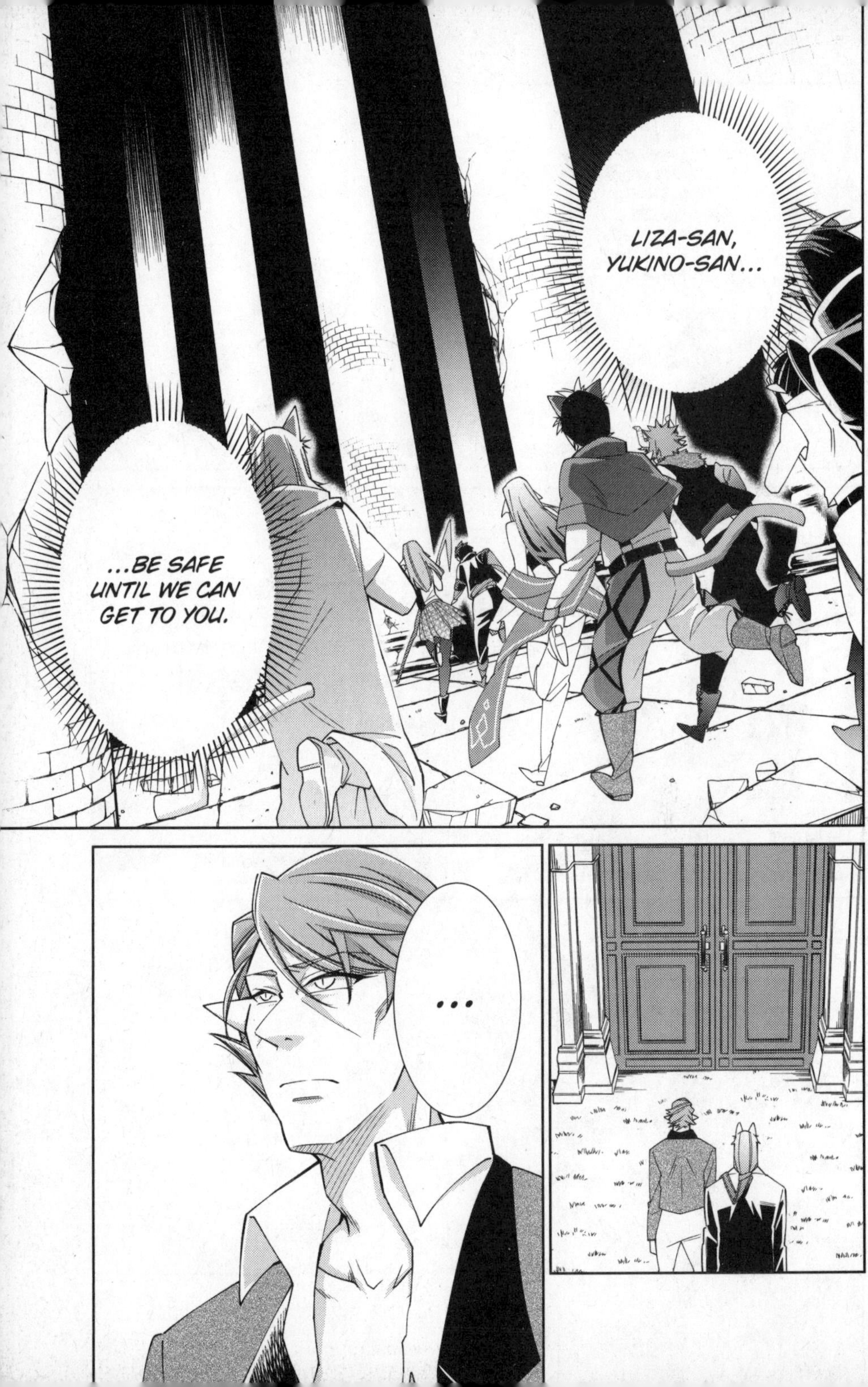
LIZA-SAN, YUKINO-SAN...
...BE SAFE UNTIL WE CAN GET TO YOU.
...

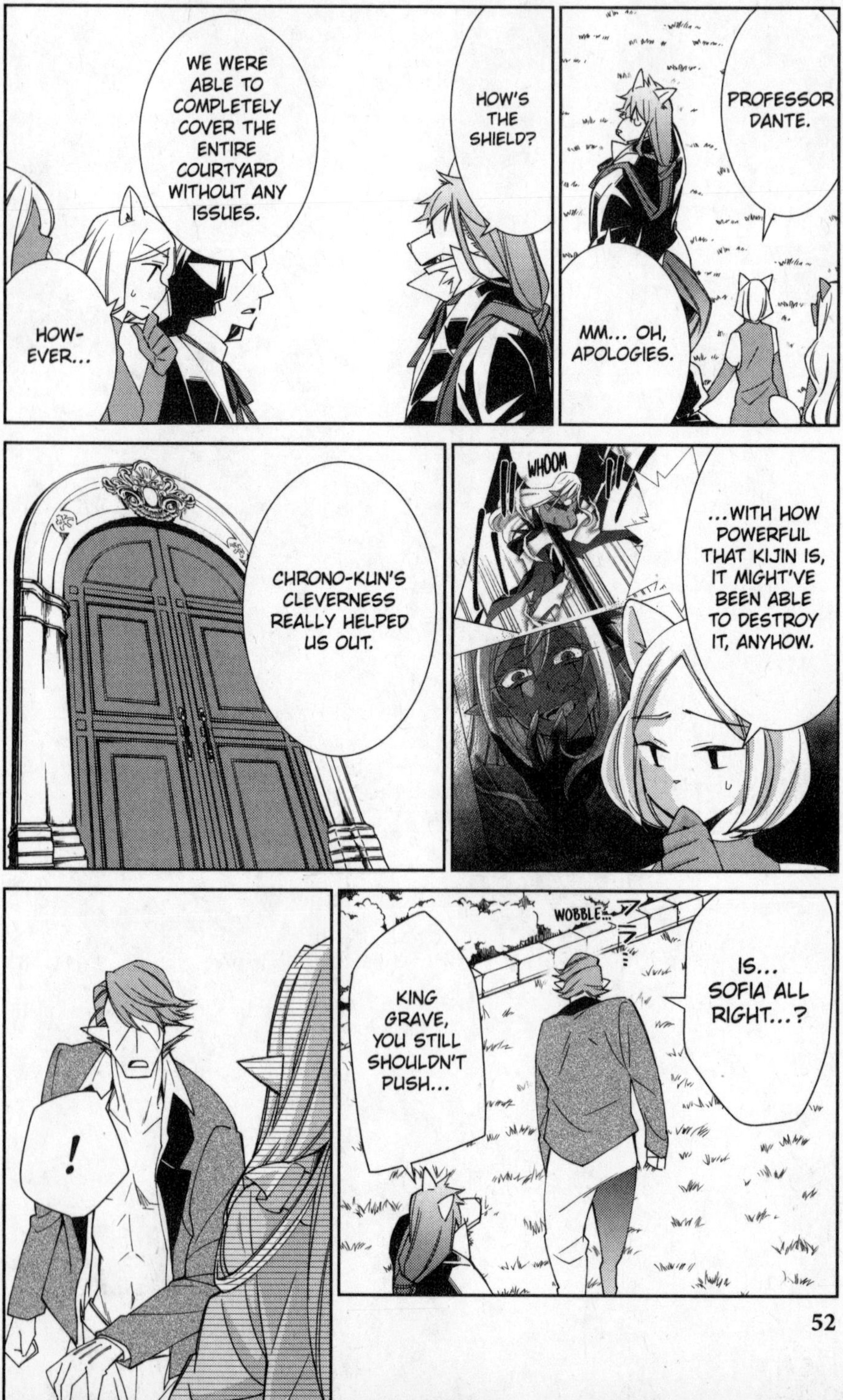
PROFESSOR DANTE.
MM... OH, APOLOGIES.
HOW'S THE SHIELD?
WE WERE ABLE TO COMPLETELY COVER THE ENTIRE COURTYARD WITHOUT ANY ISSUES.
HOW-EVER...
WHOOM
...WITH HOW POWERFUL THAT KIJIN IS, IT MIGHT'VE BEEN ABLE TO DESTROY IT, ANYHOW.
CHRONO-KUN'S CLEVERNESS REALLY HELPED US OUT.
WOBBLE...
IS... SOFIA ALL RIGHT...?
KING GRAVE, YOU STILL SHOULDN'T PUSH...
!

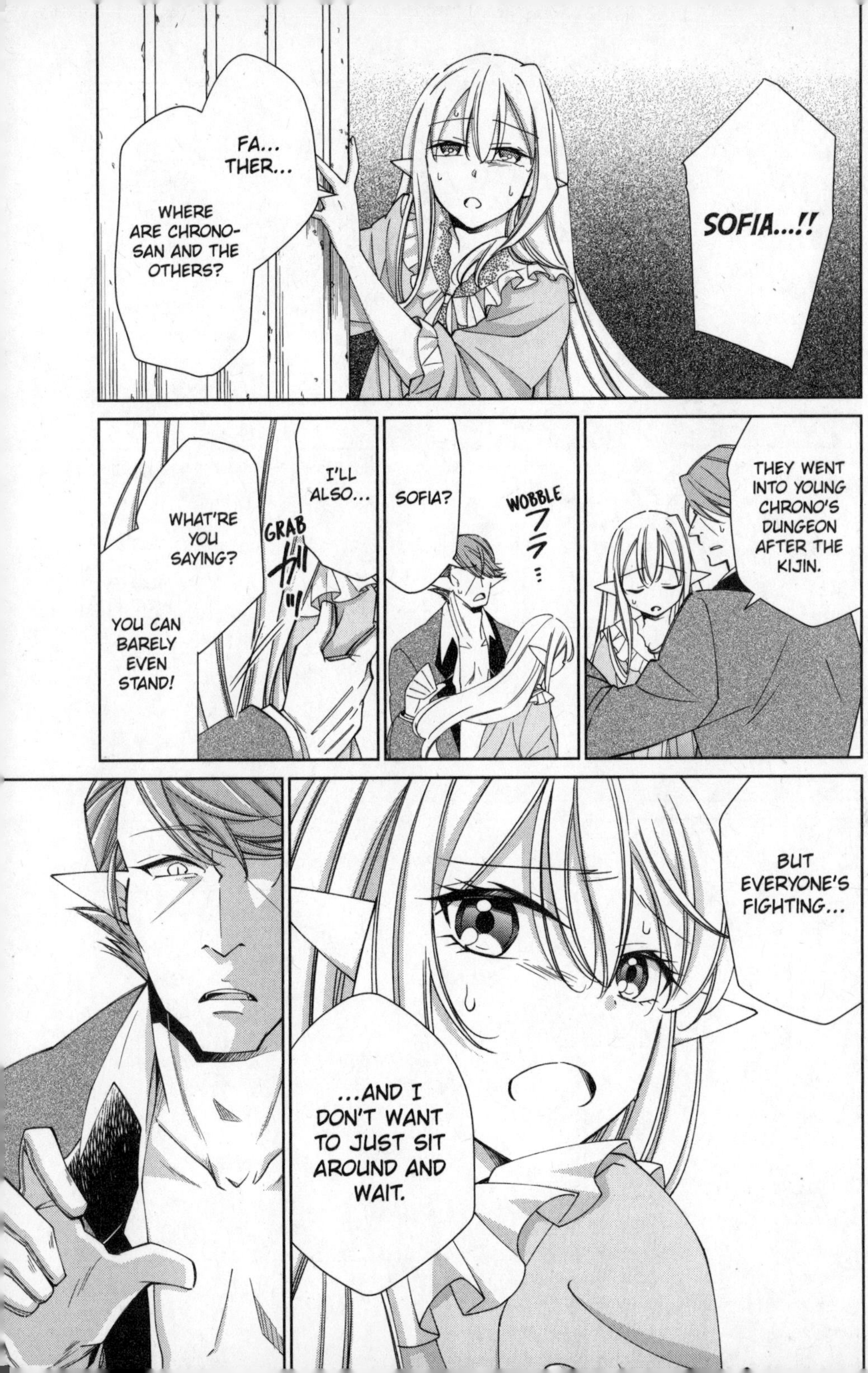
SOFIA...!!
FA... THER...
WHERE ARE CHRONO-SAN AND THE OTHERS?
THEY WENT INTO YOUNG CHRONO'S DUNGEON AFTER THE KIJIN.
WOBBLE
SOFIA?
I'LL ALSO...
GRAB
WHAT'RE YOU SAYING?
YOU CAN BARELY EVEN STAND!
BUT EVERYONE'S FIGHTING...
...AND I DON'T WANT TO JUST SIT AROUND AND WAIT.

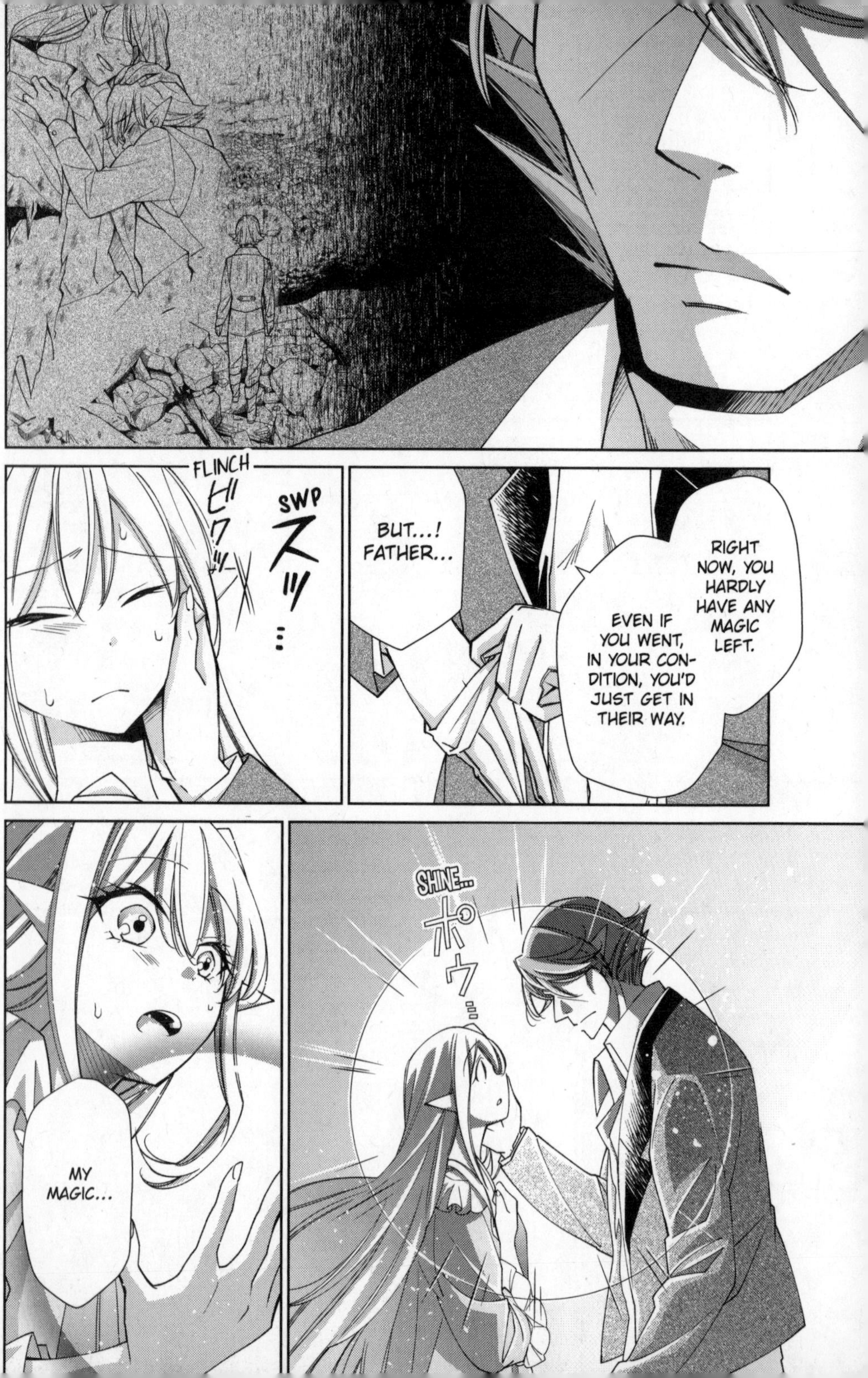
RIGHT NOW, YOU HARDLY HAVE ANY MAGIC LEFT.
EVEN IF YOU WENT, IN YOUR CON-DITION, YOU'D JUST GET IN THEIR WAY.
BUT...! FATHER...
SWP
スッ…
FLINCH
ビクッ
SHINE...
ポウ…
MY MAGIC...

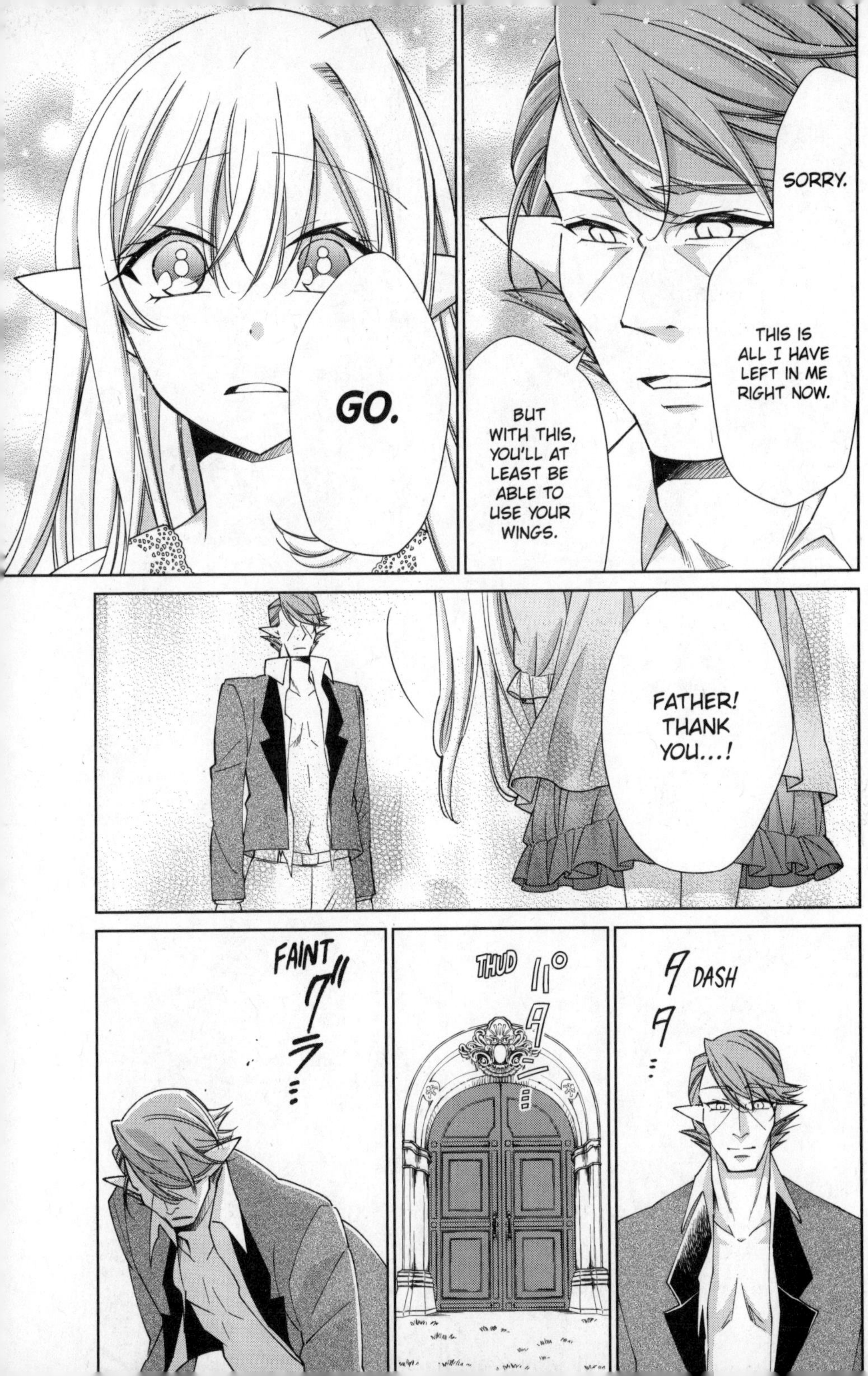
SORRY.
THIS IS ALL I HAVE LEFT IN ME RIGHT NOW.
BUT WITH THIS, YOU'LL AT LEAST BE ABLE TO USE YOUR WINGS.
GO.
FATHER! THANK YOU...!
DASH
THUD
FAINT

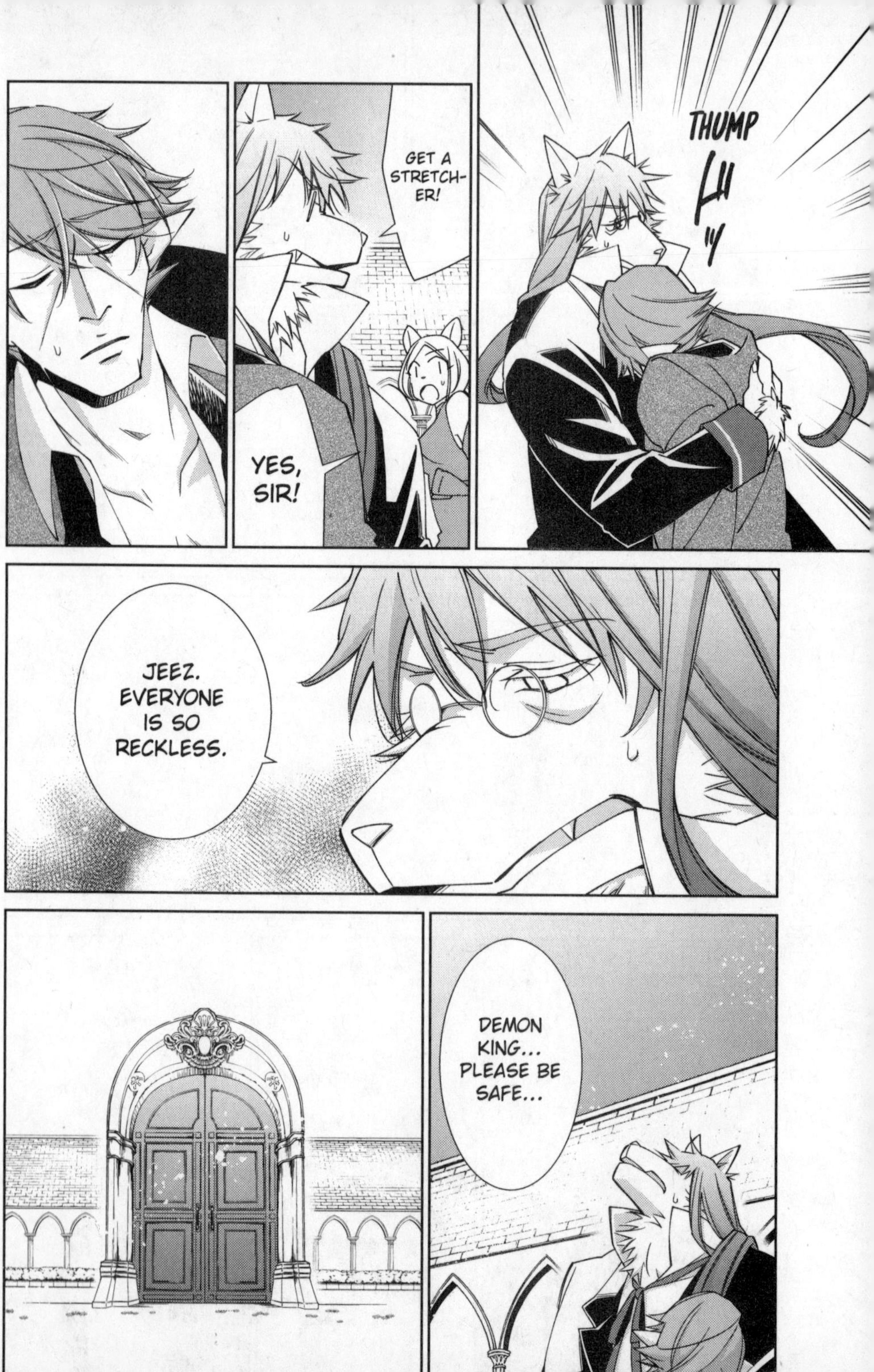
THUMP
GET A STRETCHER!
YES, SIR!
JEEZ. EVERYONE IS SO RECKLESS.
DEMON KING... PLEASE BE SAFE...

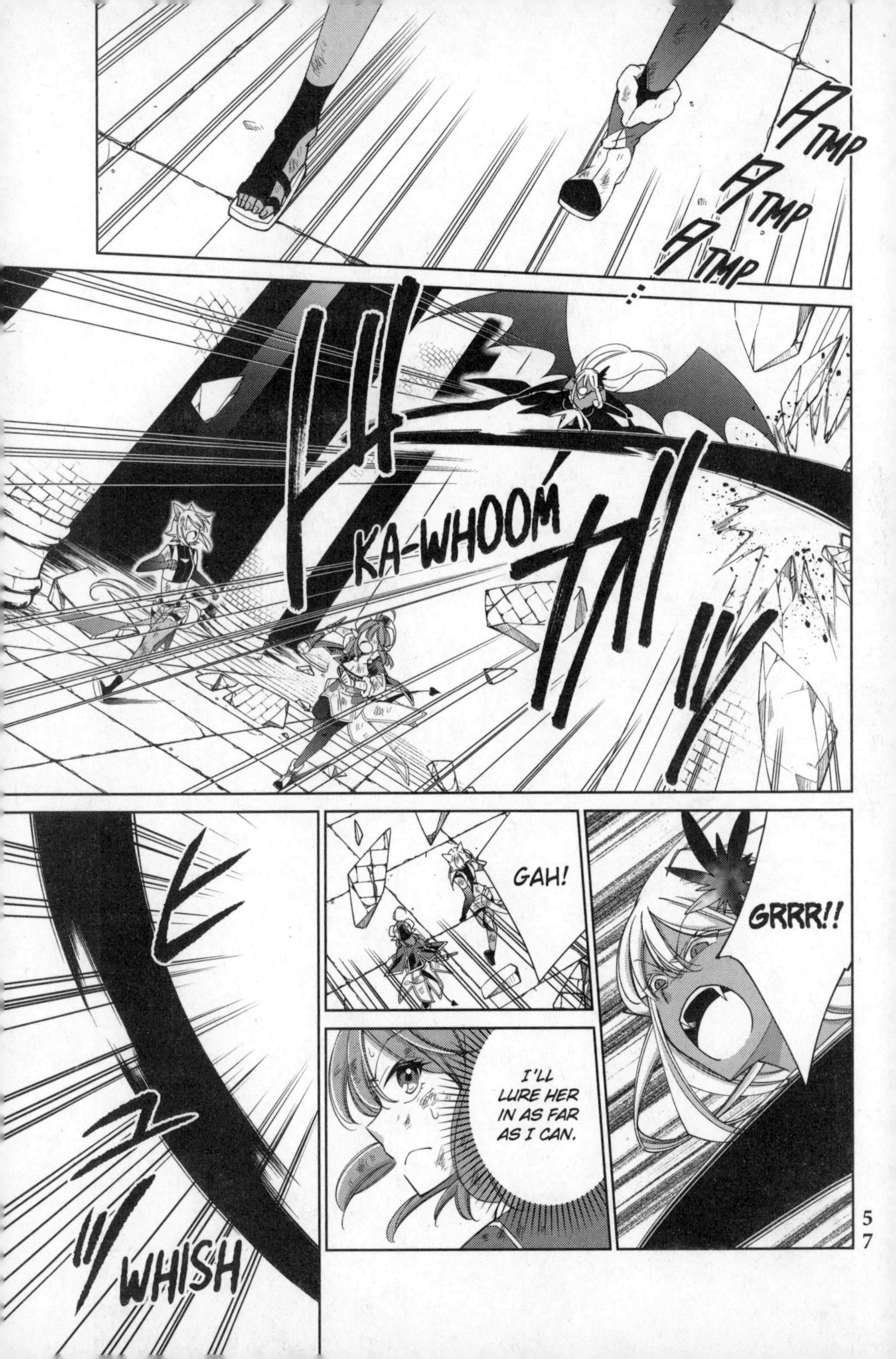
TMP
TMP
TMP
KA-WHOOM
GRRR!!
GAH!
I'LL LURE HER IN AS FAR AS I CAN.
WHISH

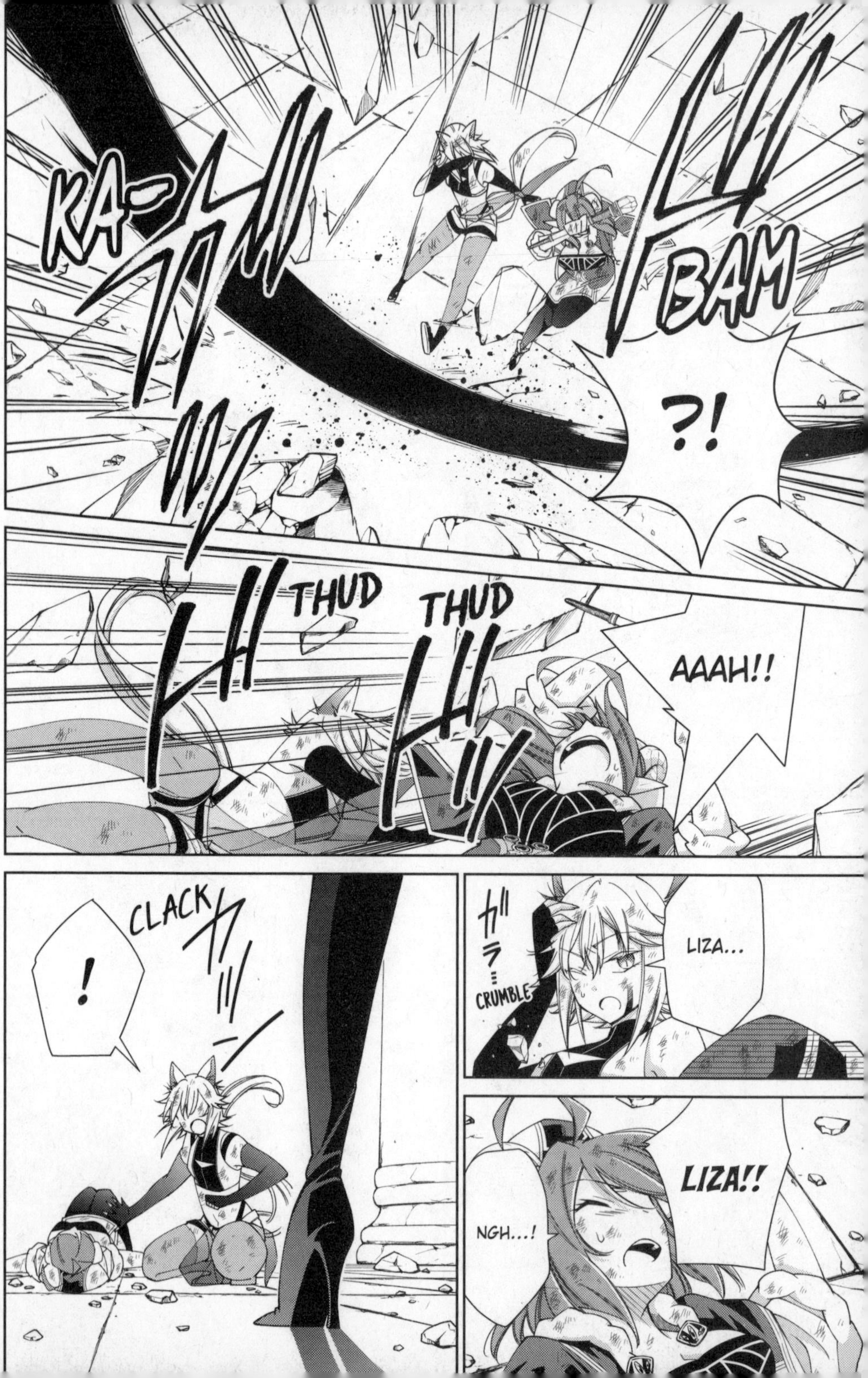
KA-
BAM
?!
AAAH!!
THUD
THUD
LIZA...
ガラ
CRUMBLE
LIZA!!
NGH...!
CLACK
!

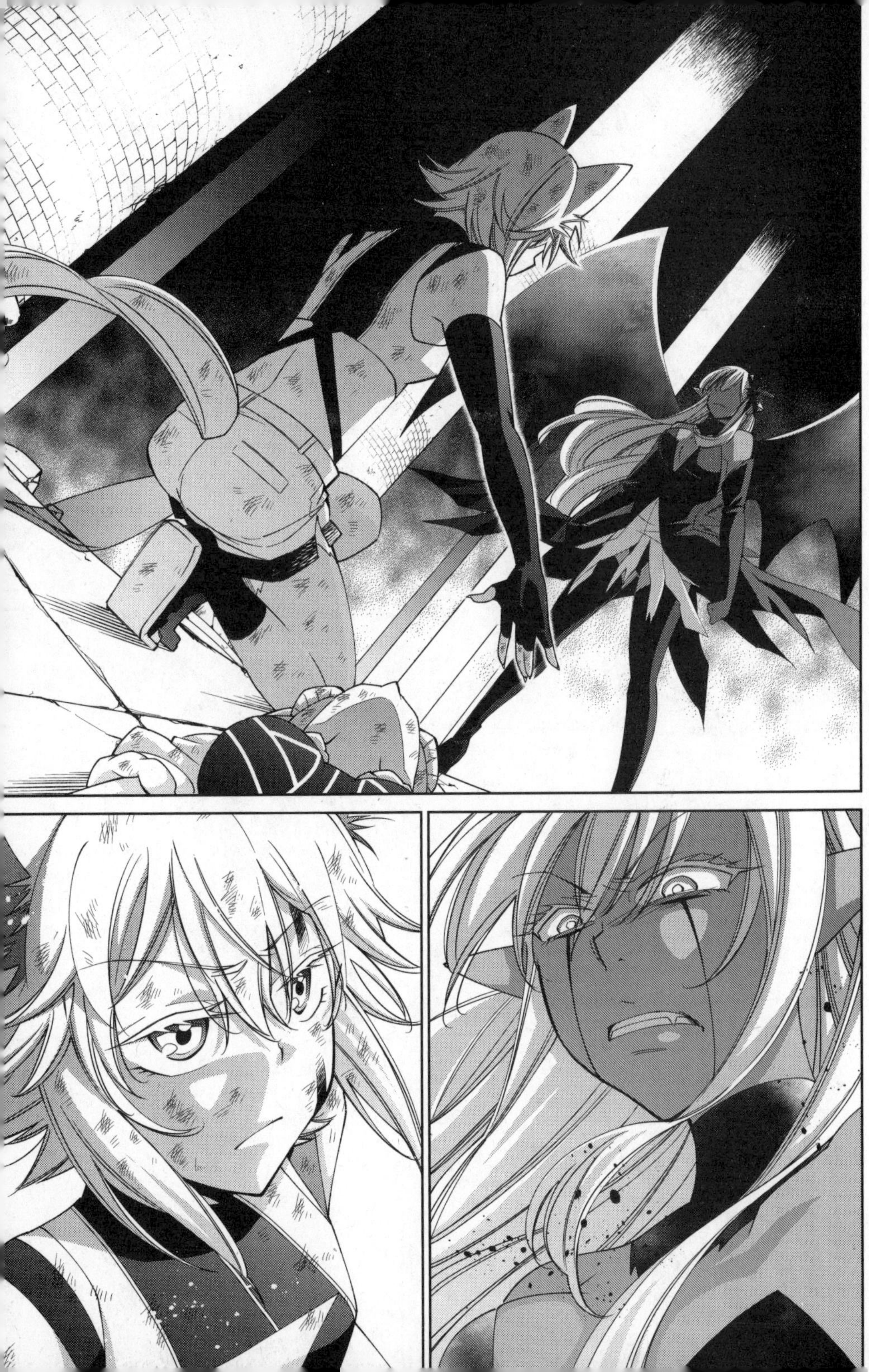

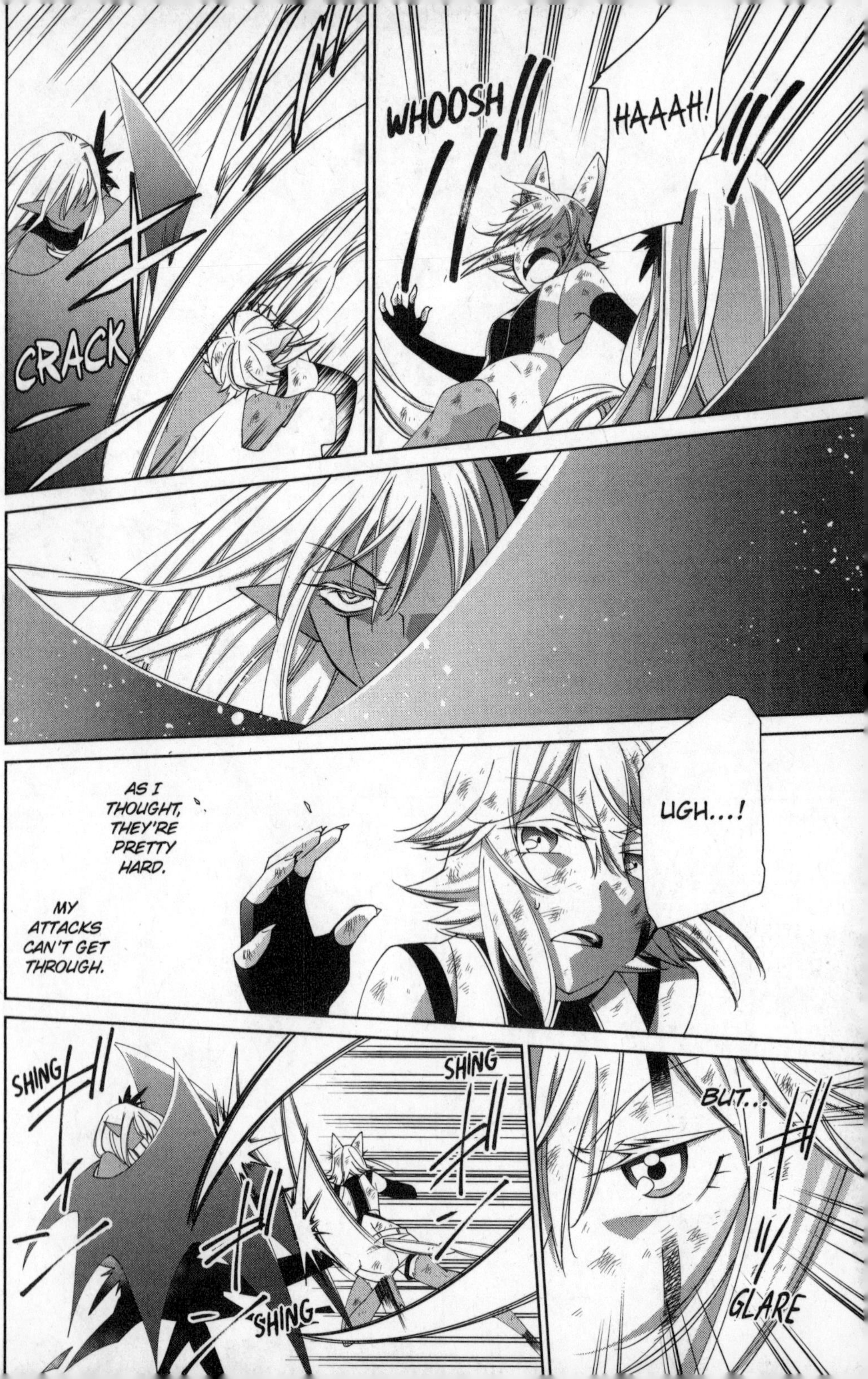
HAAAH!
WHOOSH
CRACK
UGH...!
AS I THOUGHT, THEY'RE PRETTY HARD.
MY ATTACKS CAN'T GET THROUGH.
BUT...
GLARE
SHING
SHING
SHING

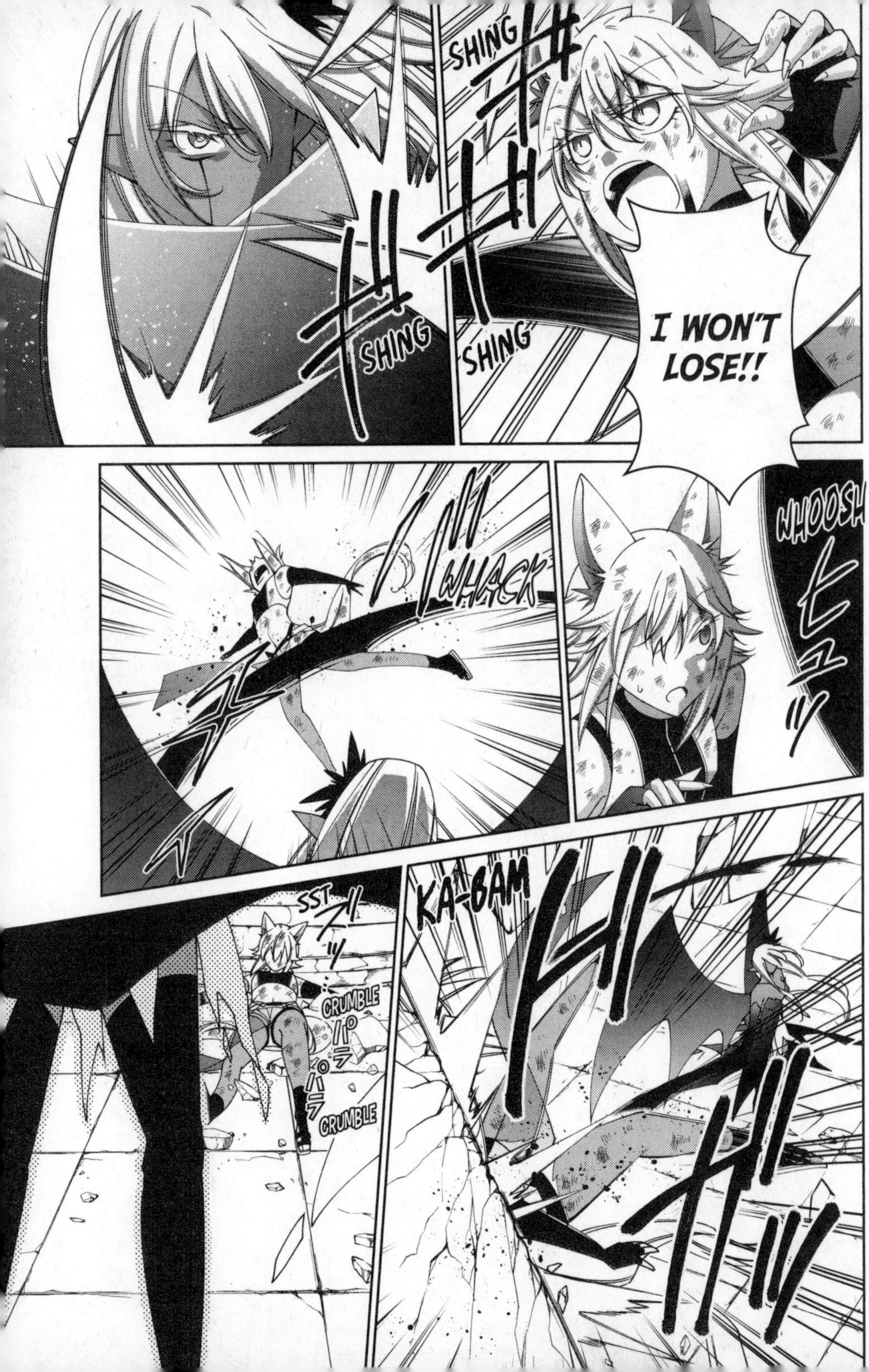
SHING
SHING
I WON'T LOSE!!
SHING
WHOOSH
ヒュッ
WHACK
KA-BAM
SST
CRUMBLE
パラ
パラ
CRUMBLE

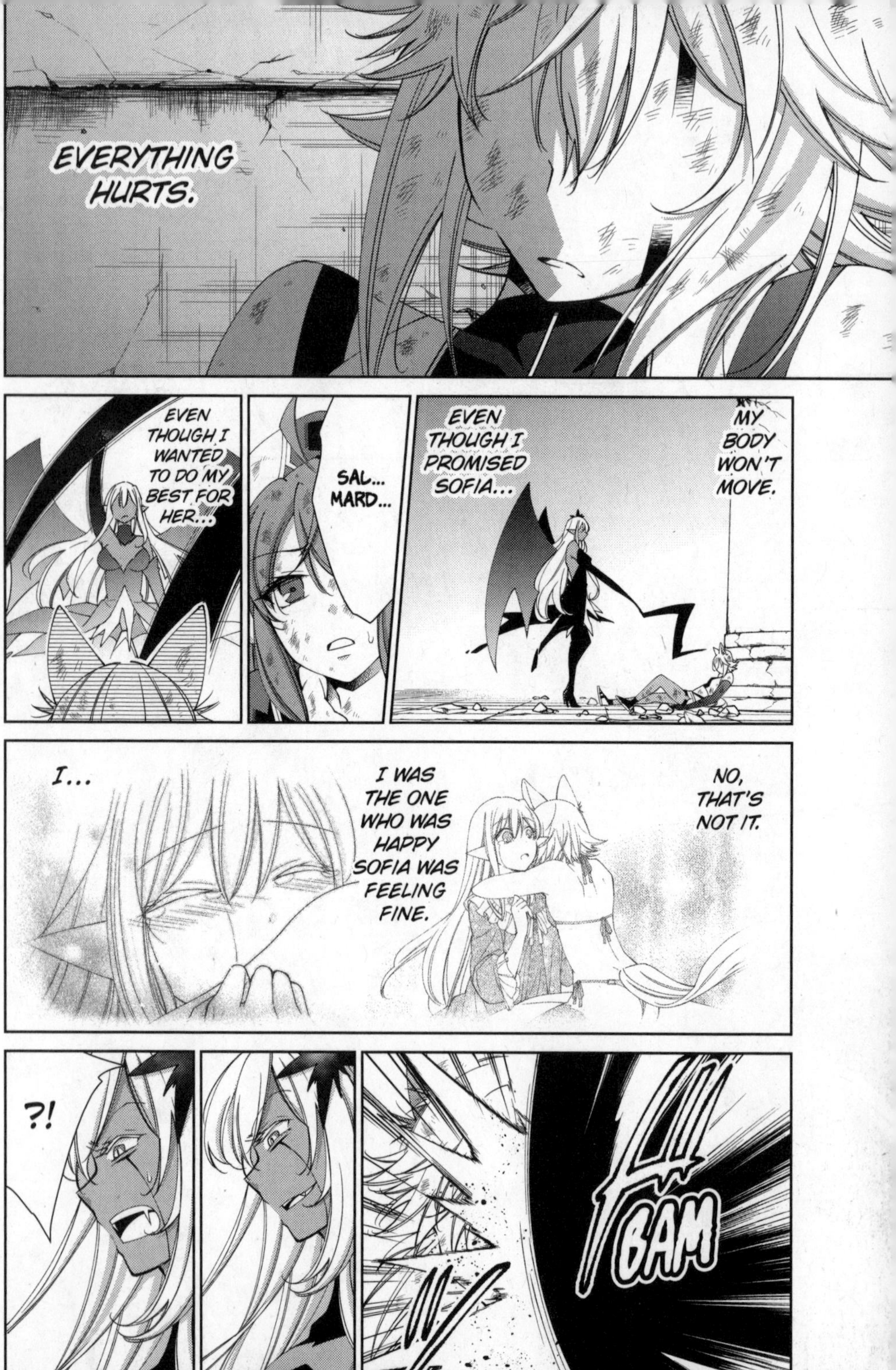
EVERYTHING HURTS.
MY BODY WON'T MOVE.
EVEN THOUGH I PROMISED SOFIA...
SAL... MARD...
EVEN THOUGH I WANTED TO DO MY BEST FOR HER...
NO, THAT'S NOT IT.
I WAS THE ONE WHO WAS HAPPY SOFIA WAS FEELING FINE.
I...
GAM
?!

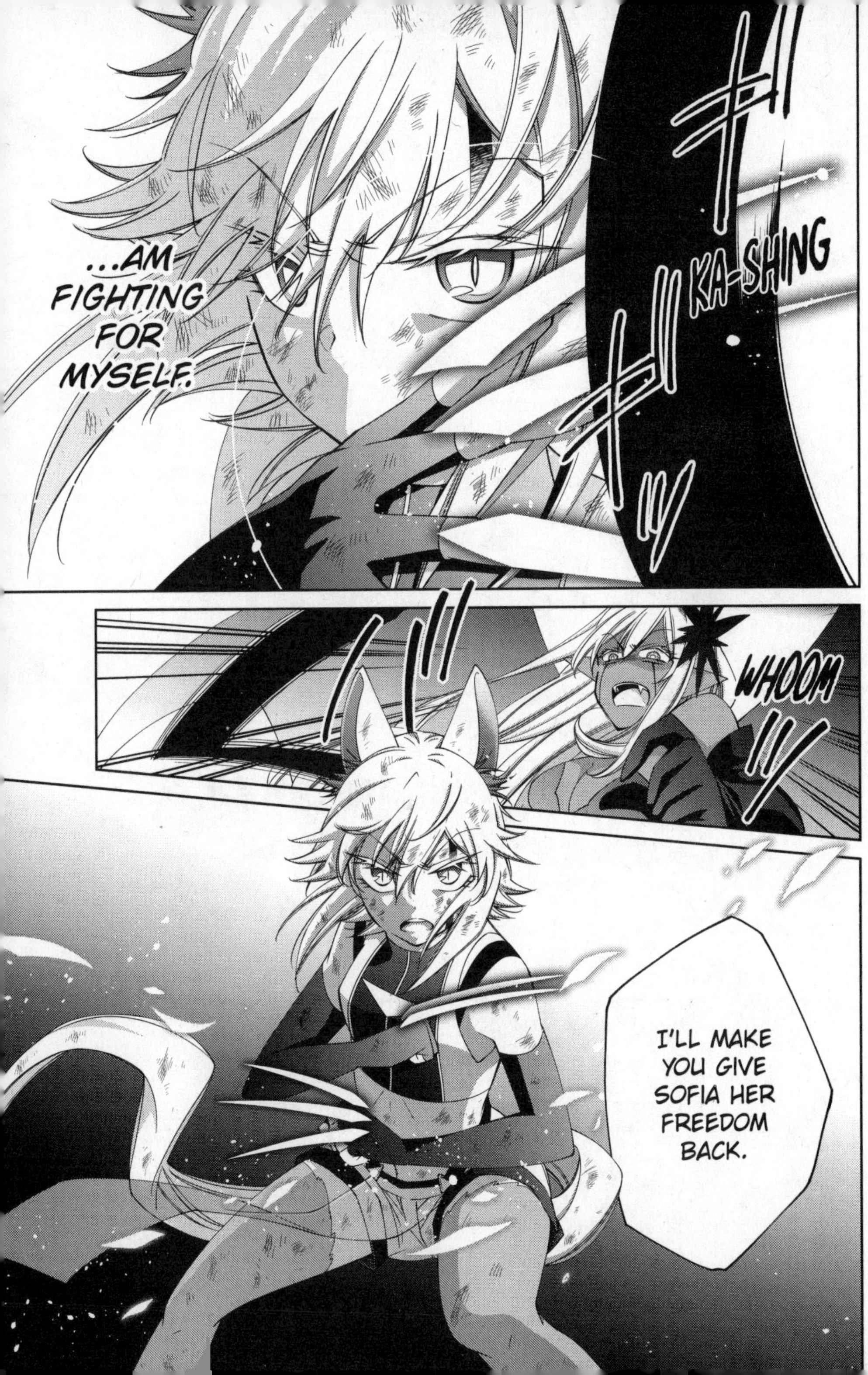
KA-SHING
...AM FIGHTING FOR MYSELF.
WHOOM
I'LL MAKE YOU GIVE SOFIA HER FREEDOM BACK.

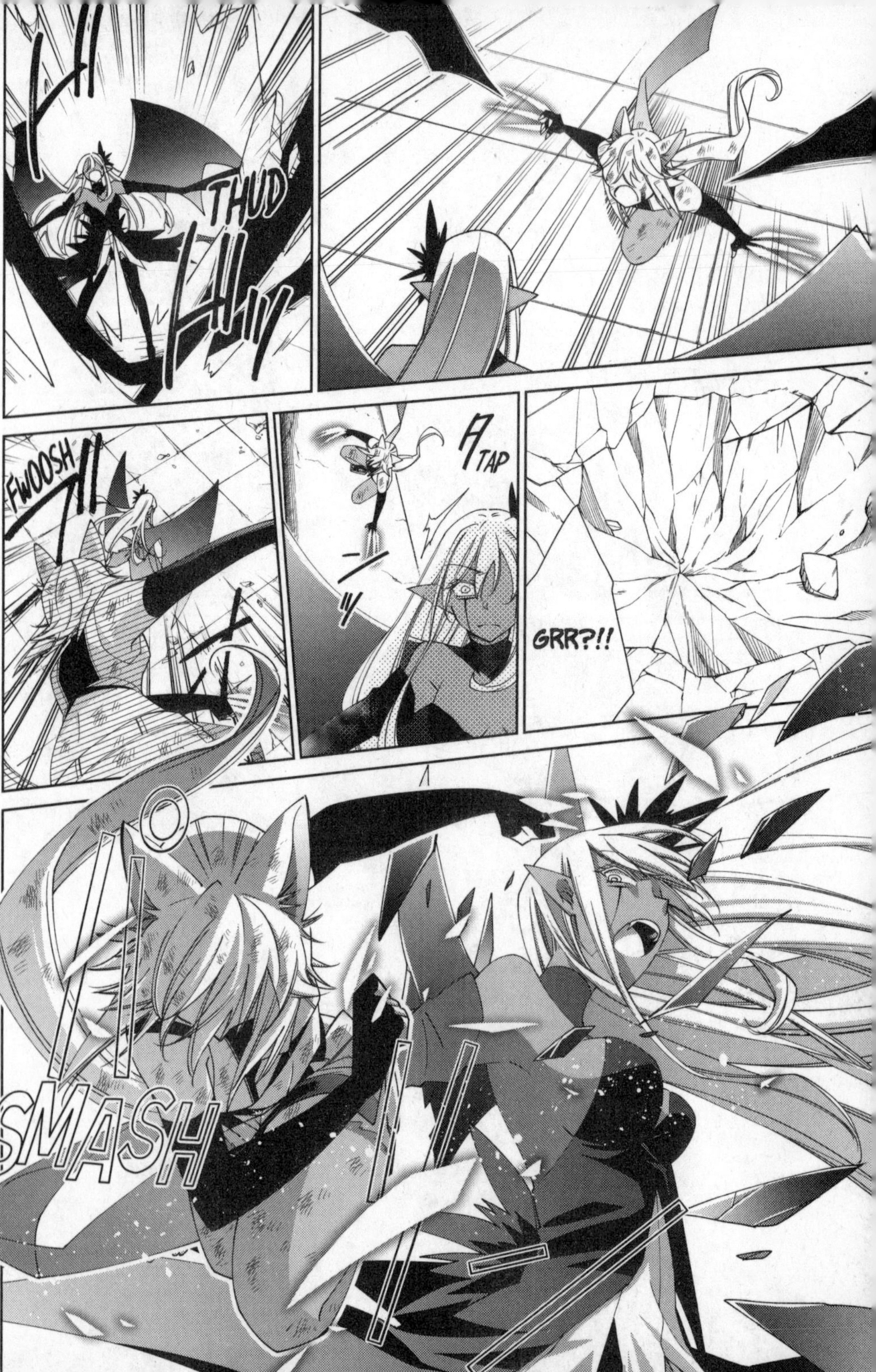

THUD
TAP
GRR?!!
FWOOSH
SMASH

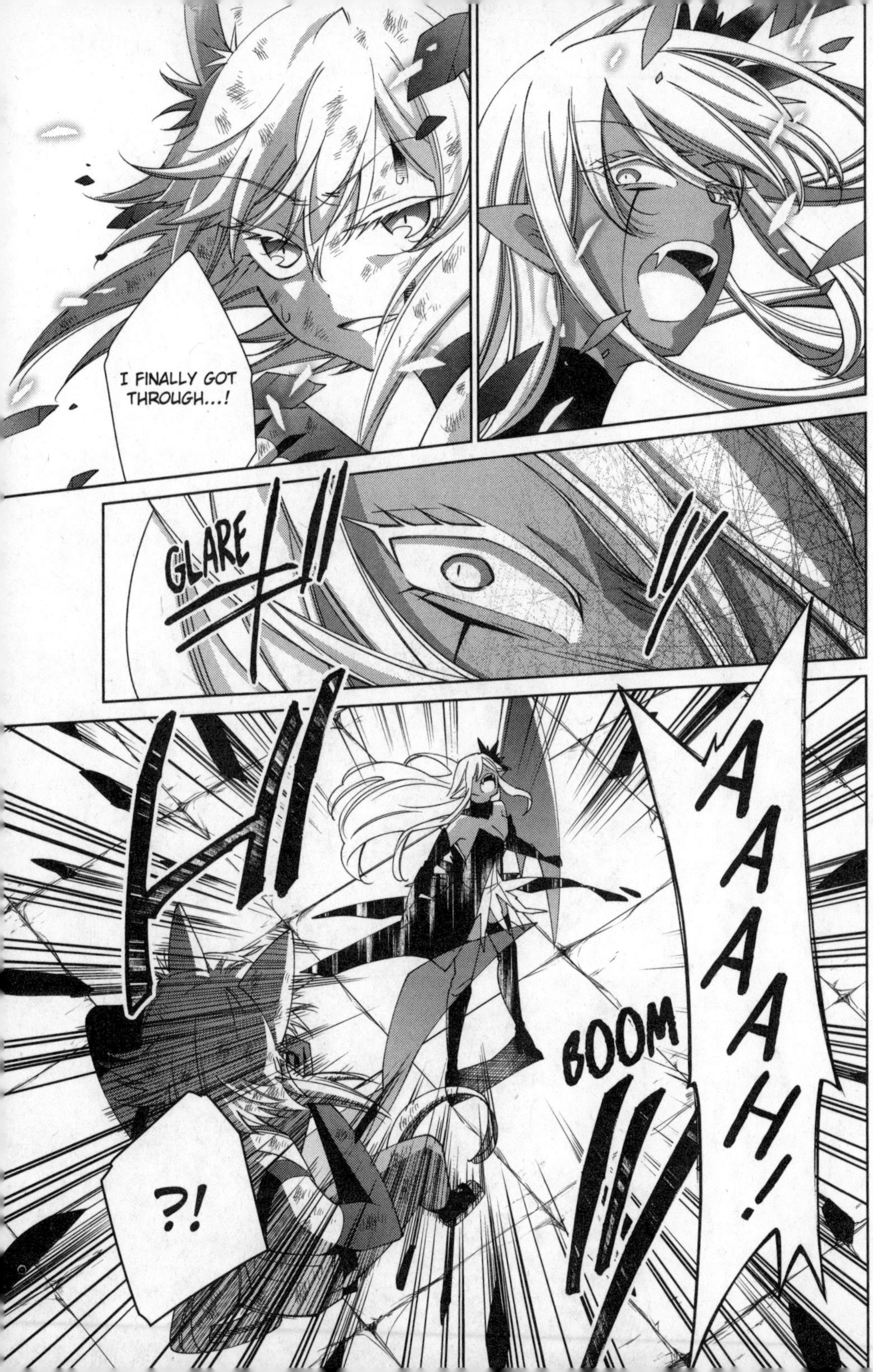
I FINALLY GOT THROUGH...!
GLARE!!
AAAAAH!!
BOOM
?!

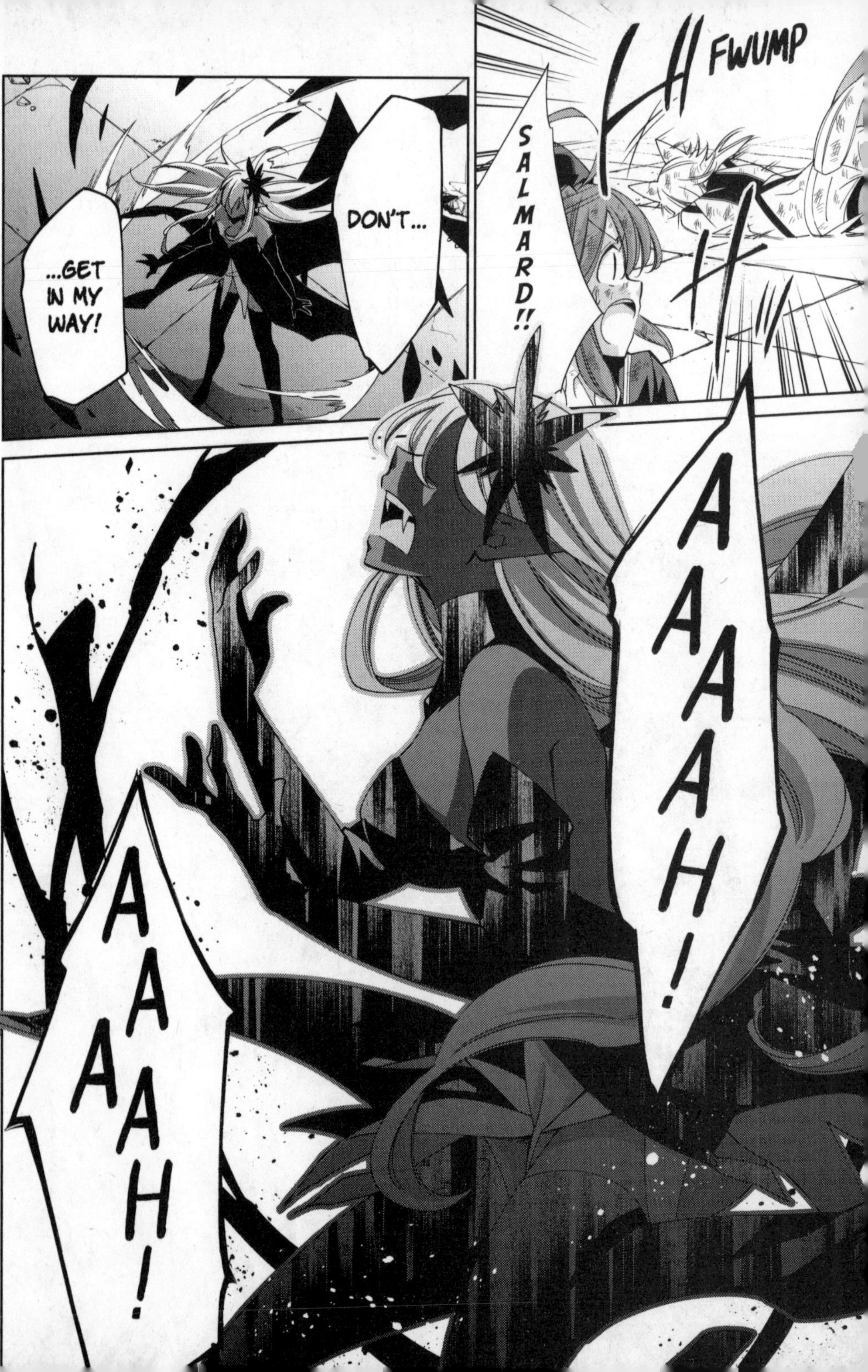
FWUMP
SALMARD!!
DON'T...
...GET IN MY WAY!
AAAAAH!
AAAAAH!

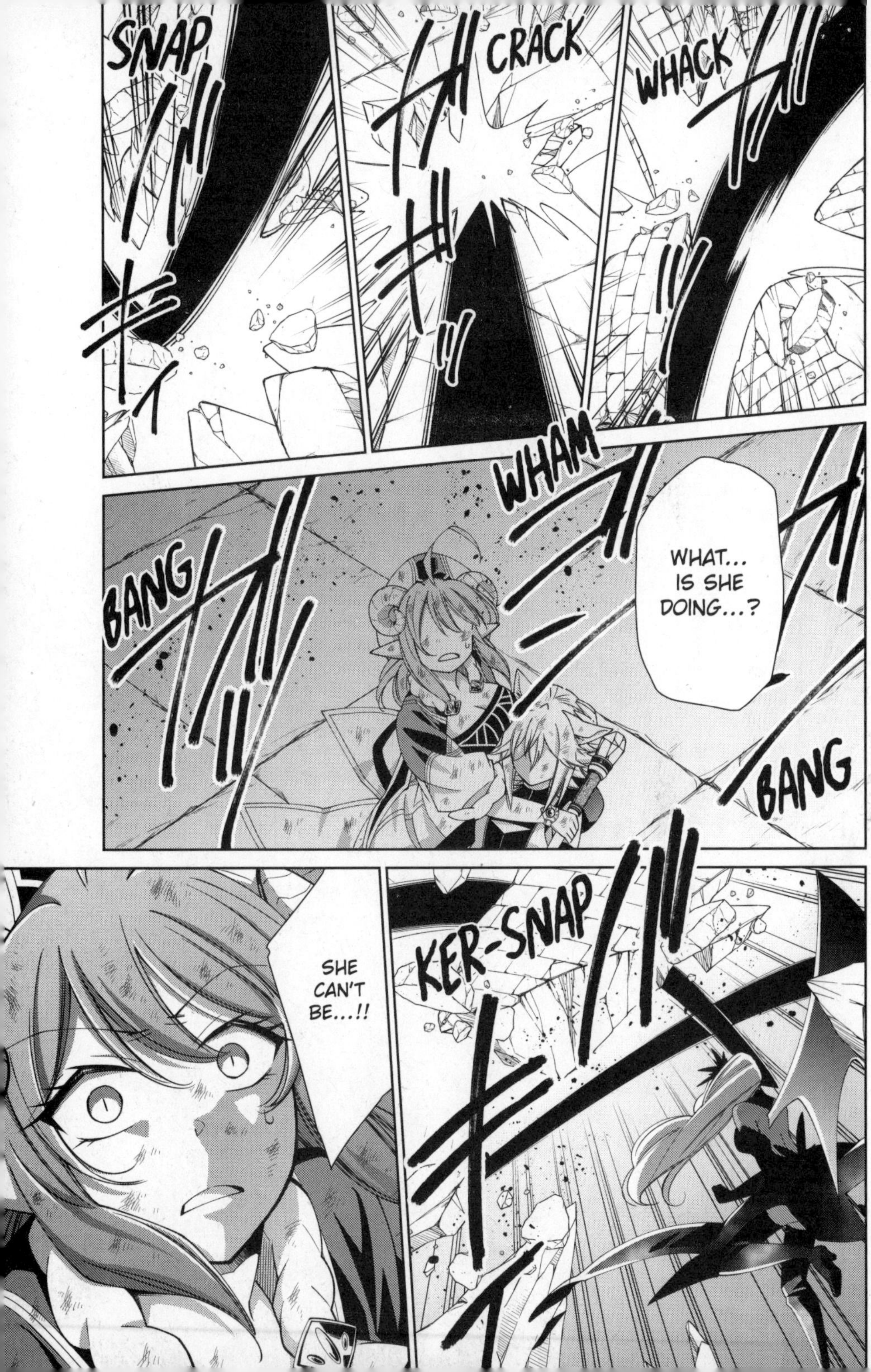
WHACK
CRACK
SNAP
WHAM
WHAT... IS SHE DOING...?
BANG
BANG
KER-SNAP
SHE CAN'T BE...!!

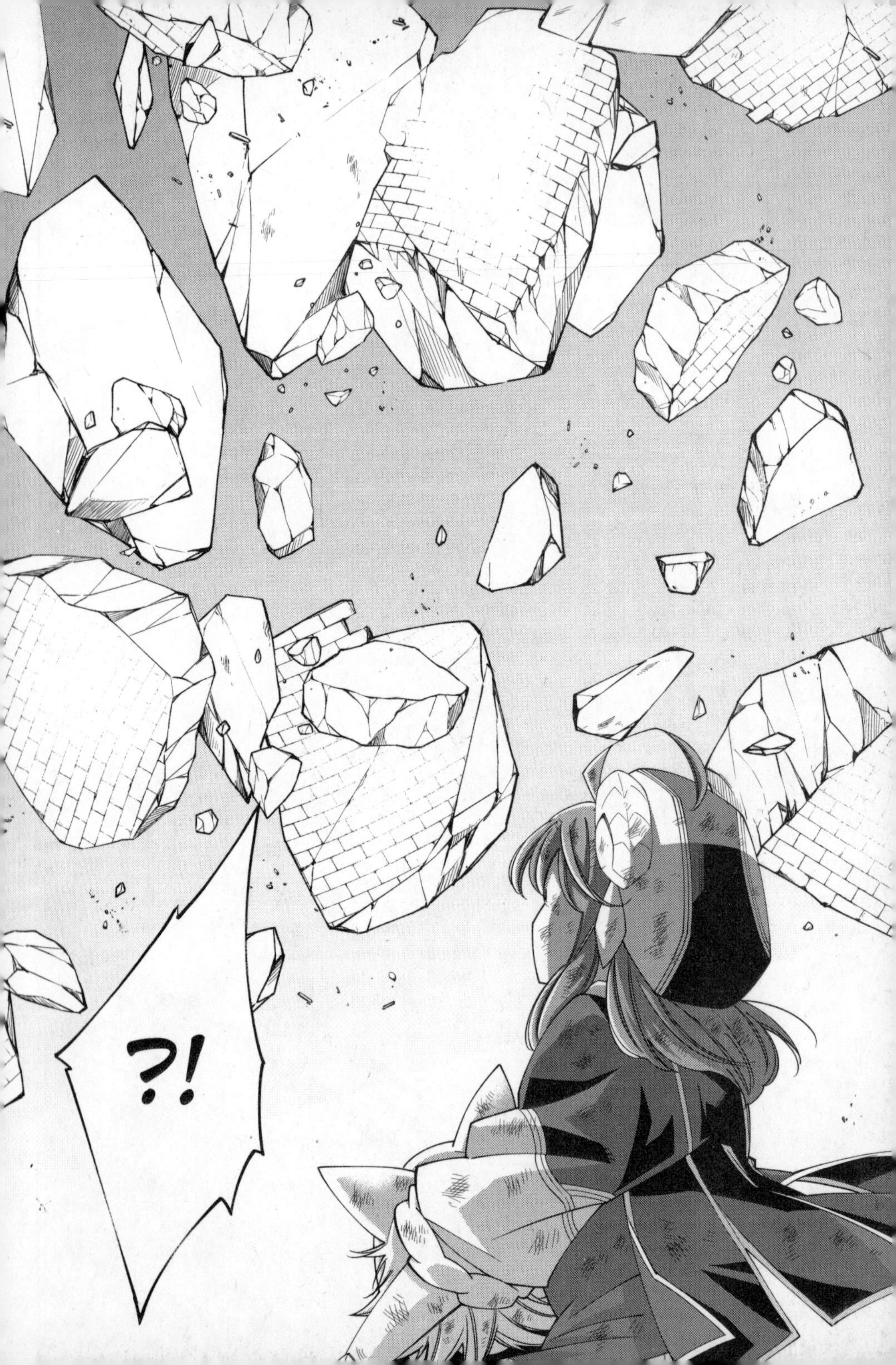
?!

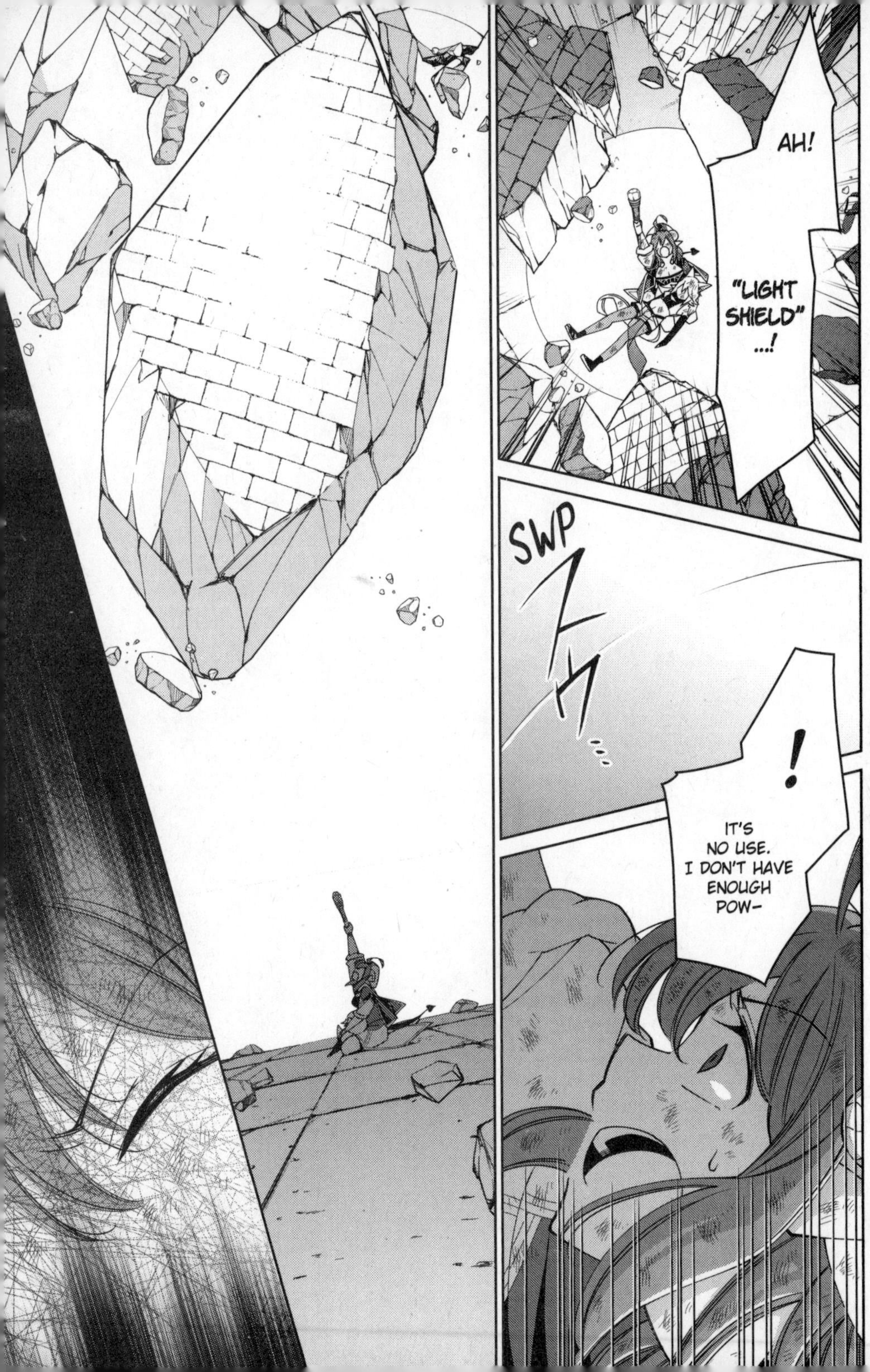
AH!
"LIGHT SHIELD" ...!
SWP
!
IT'S NO USE. I DON'T HAVE ENOUGH POW-

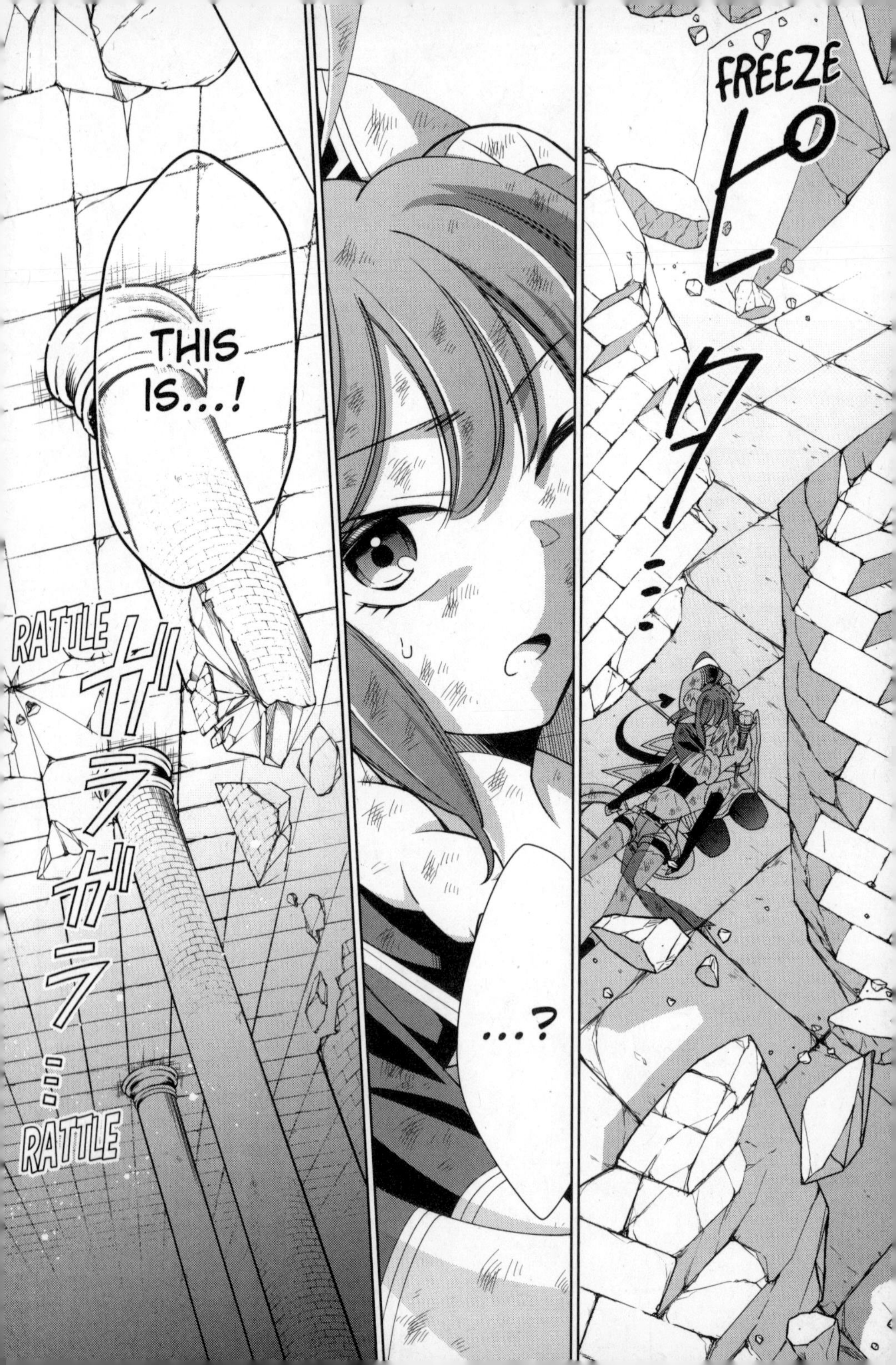
FREEZE
ピク…
...?
THIS IS...!
RATTLE
ガラガラ…
RATTLE

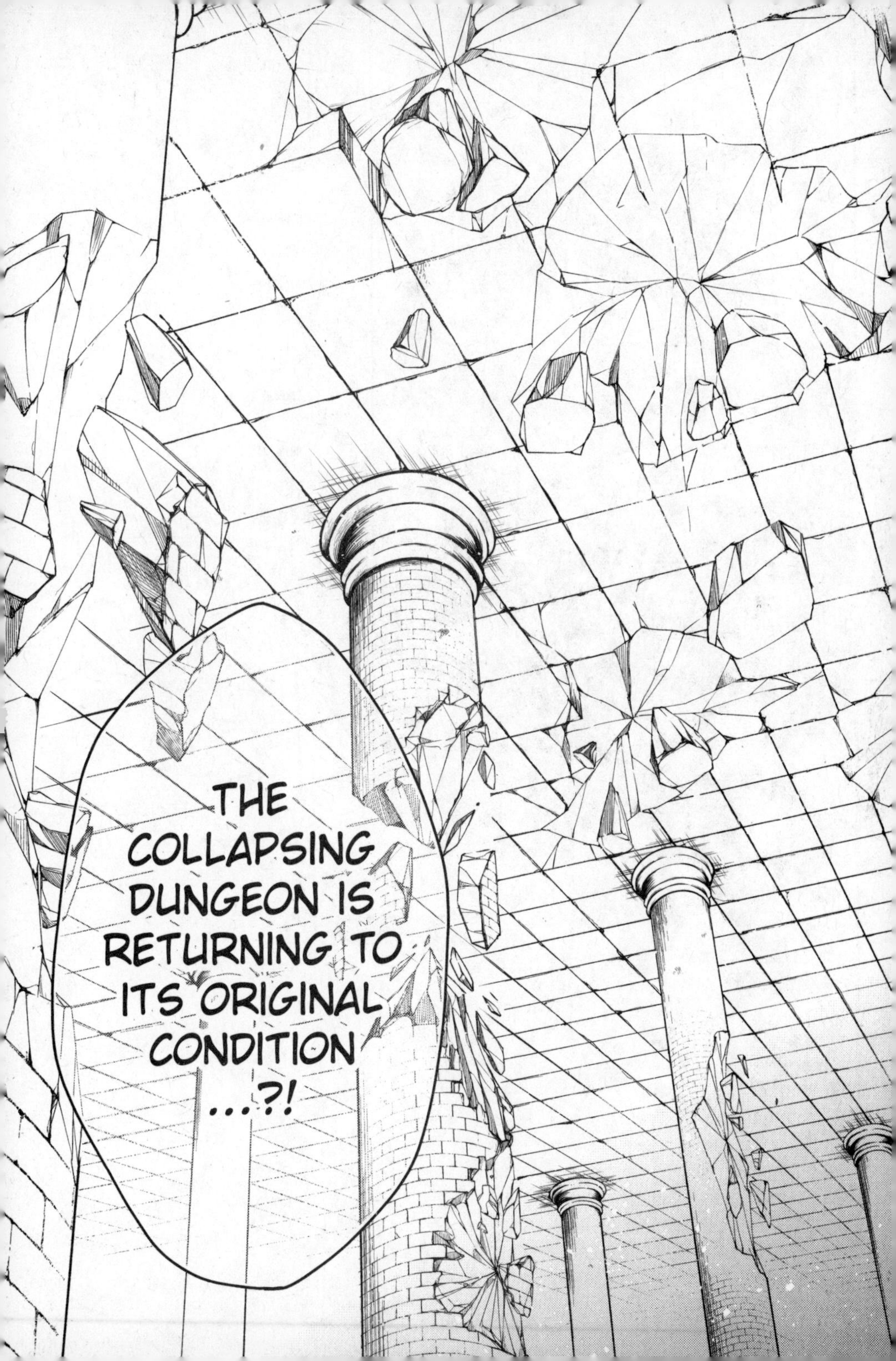
THE COLLAPSING DUNGEON IS RETURNING TO ITS ORIGINAL CONDITION ...?!

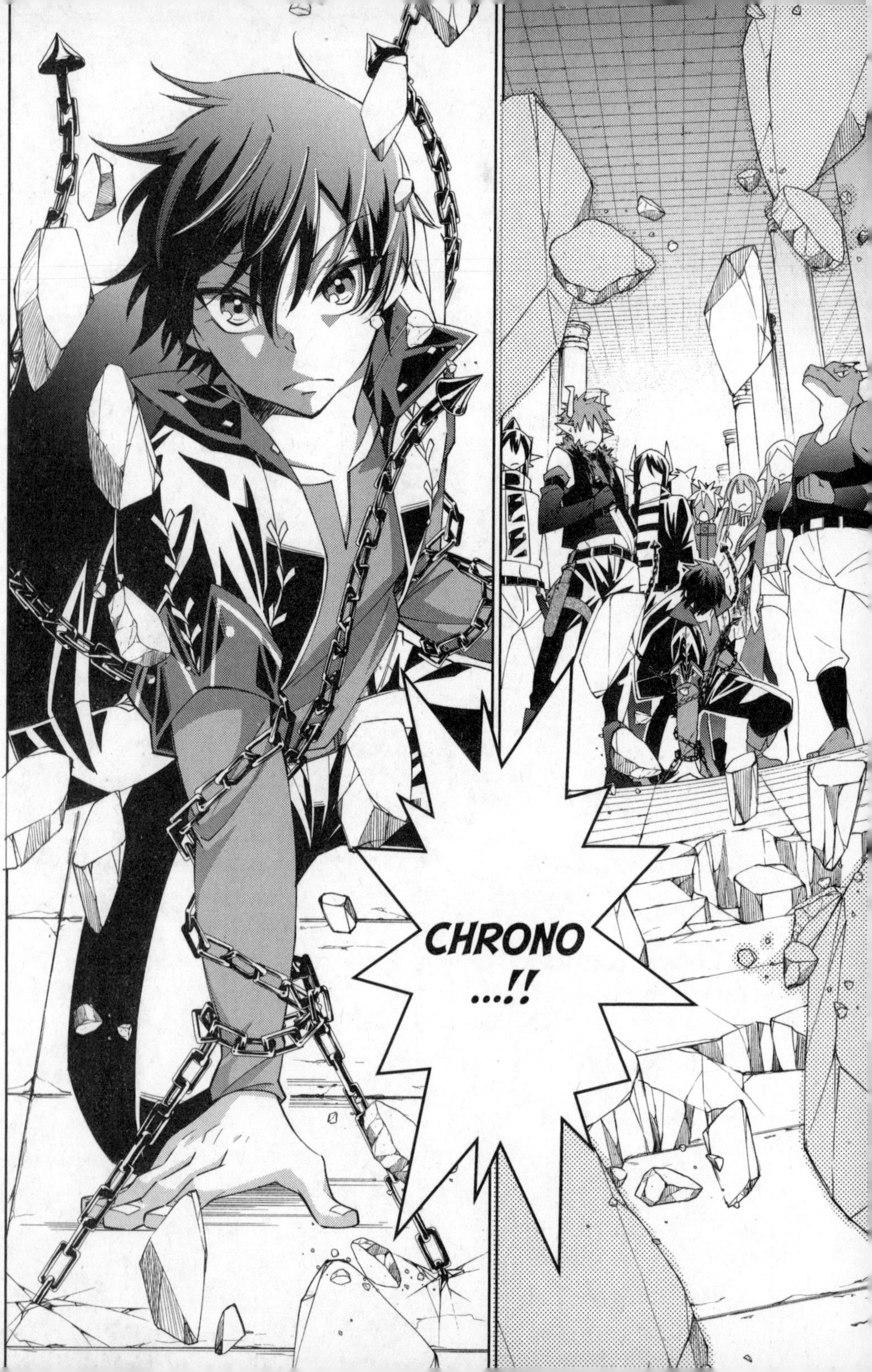
CHRONO ...!!

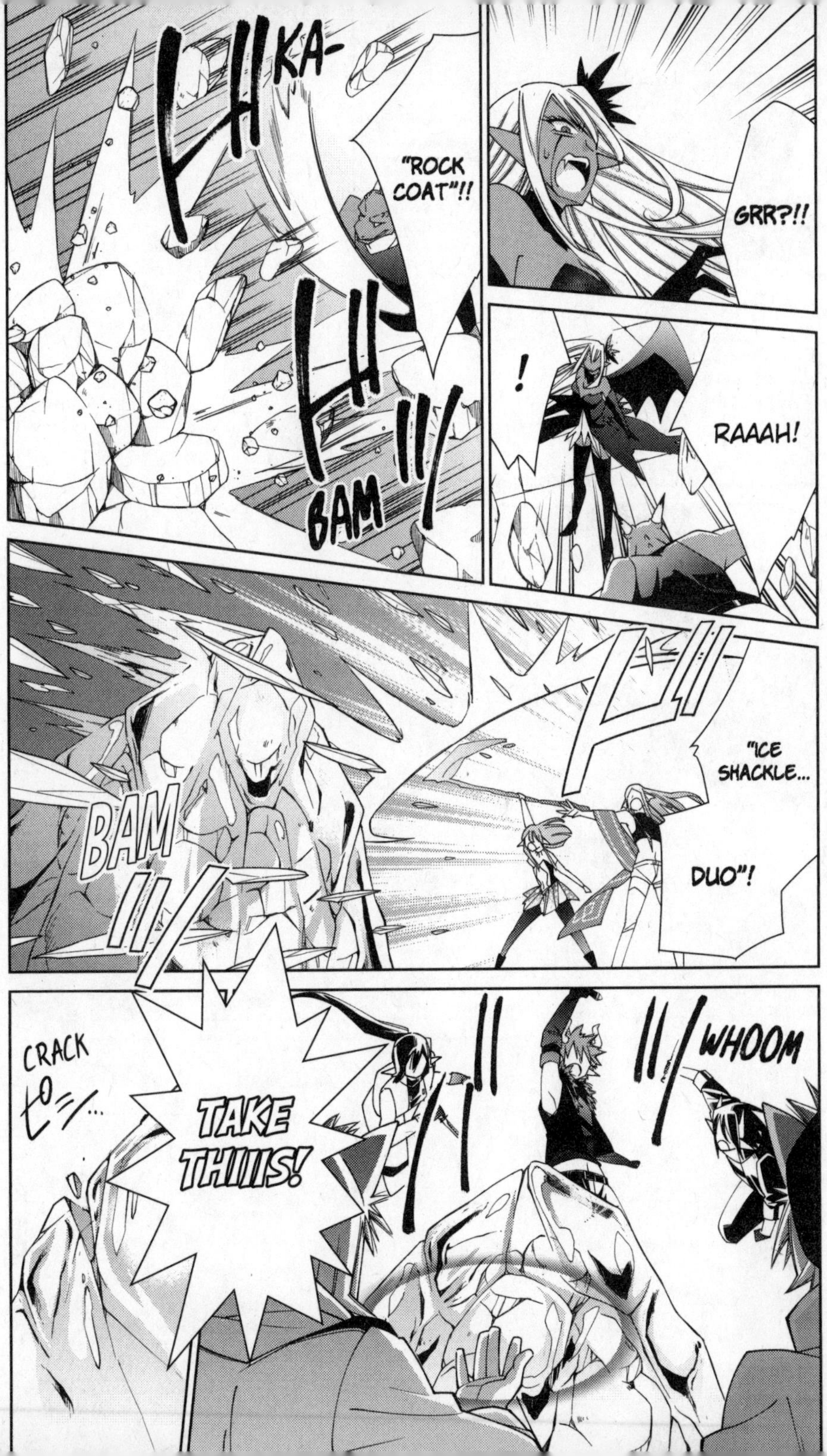
GRR?!!
!
RAAAH!
KA-
"ROCK COAT"!!
BAM
"ICE SHACKLE...
DUO"!
BAM
WHOOM
TAKE THIIIS!
CRACK

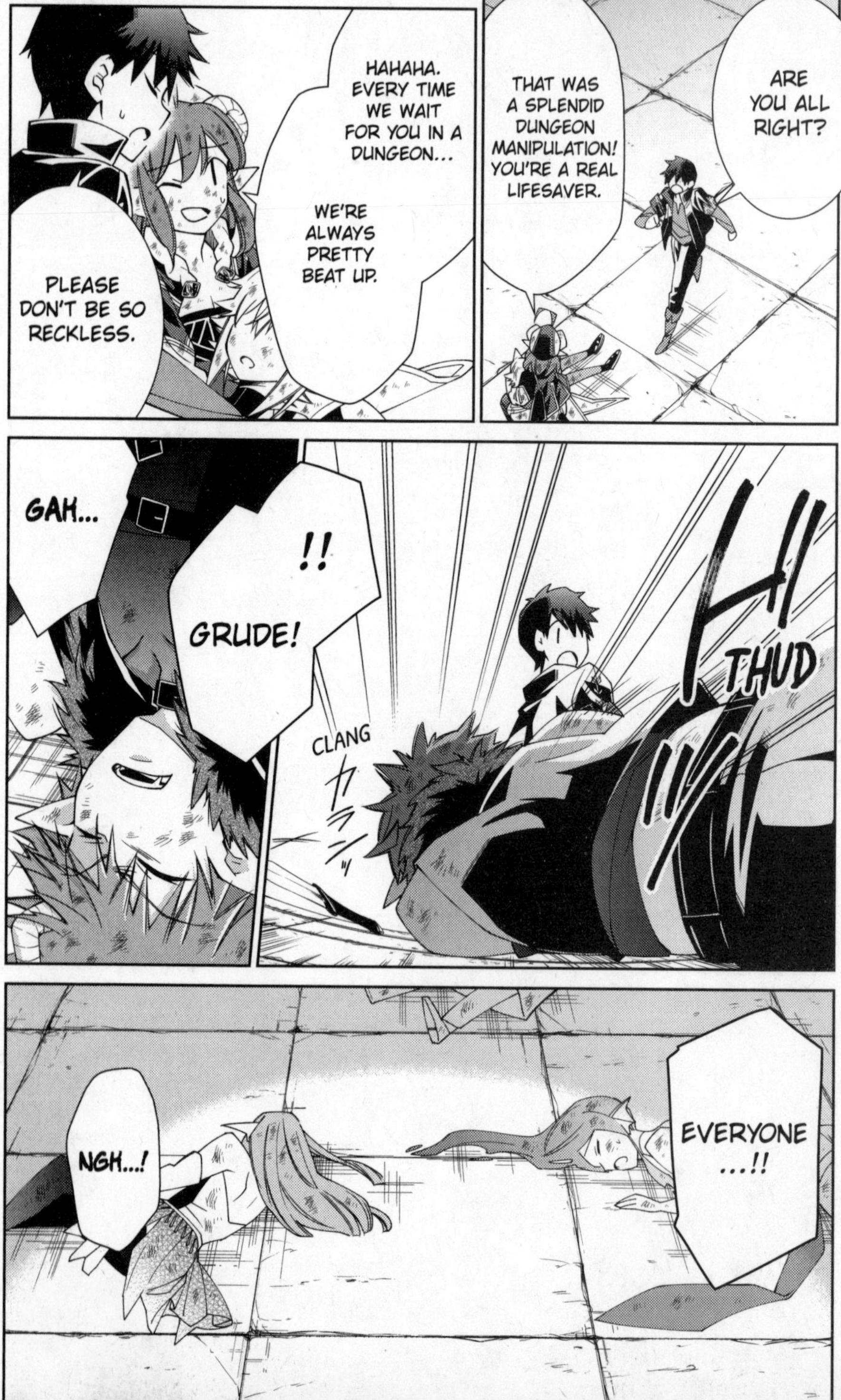
ARE YOU ALL RIGHT?
THAT WAS A SPLENDID DUNGEON MANIPULATION! YOU'RE A REAL LIFESAVER.
HAHAHA. EVERY TIME WE WAIT FOR YOU IN A DUNGEON...
WE'RE ALWAYS PRETTY BEAT UP.
PLEASE DON'T BE SO RECKLESS.
THUD
CLANG
!!
GRUDE!
GAH...
EVERYONE ...!!
NGH...!

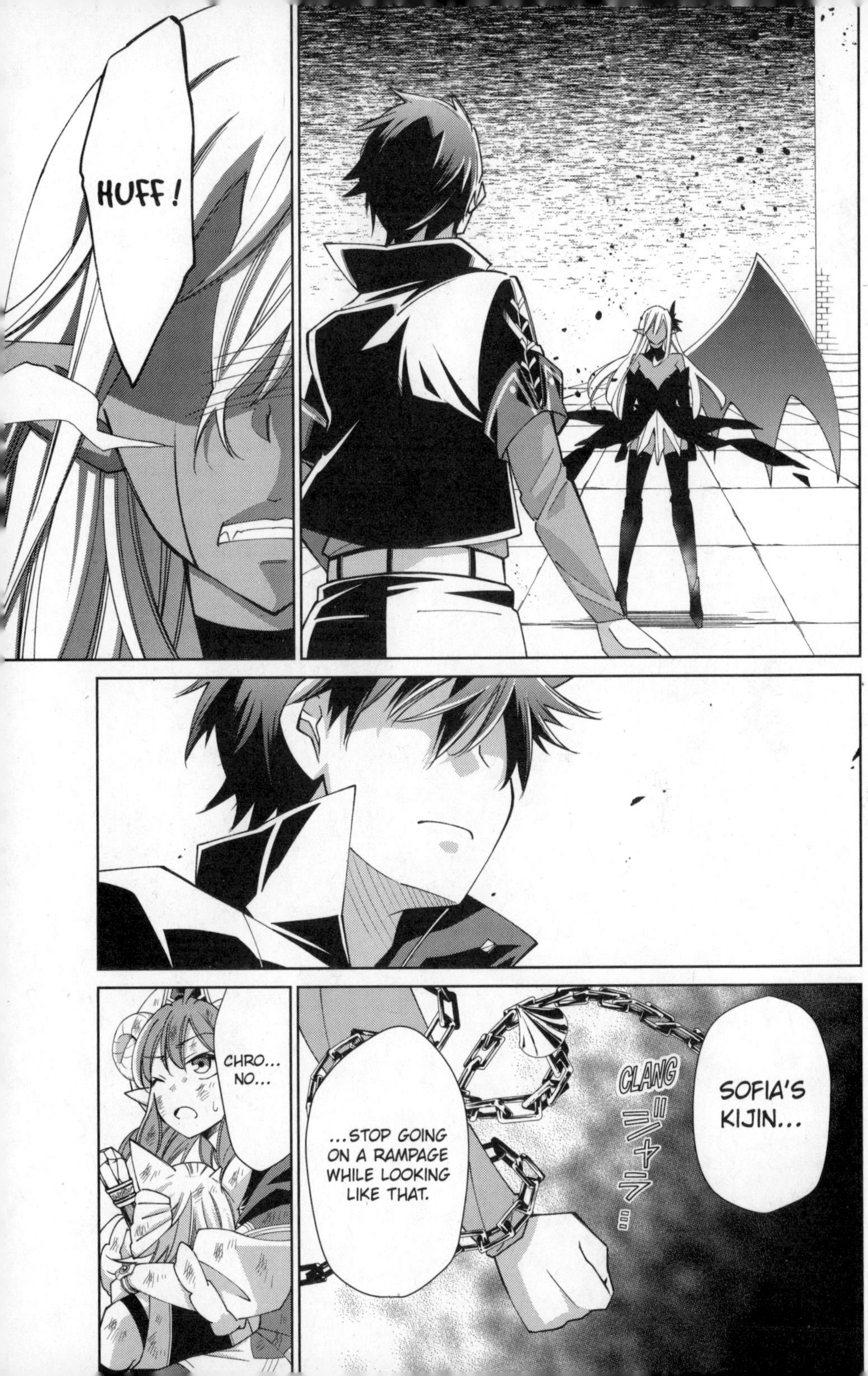
HUFF!
SOFIA'S KIJIN...
CLANG
ジャラ...
...STOP GOING ON A RAMPAGE WHILE LOOKING LIKE THAT.
CHRO... NO...

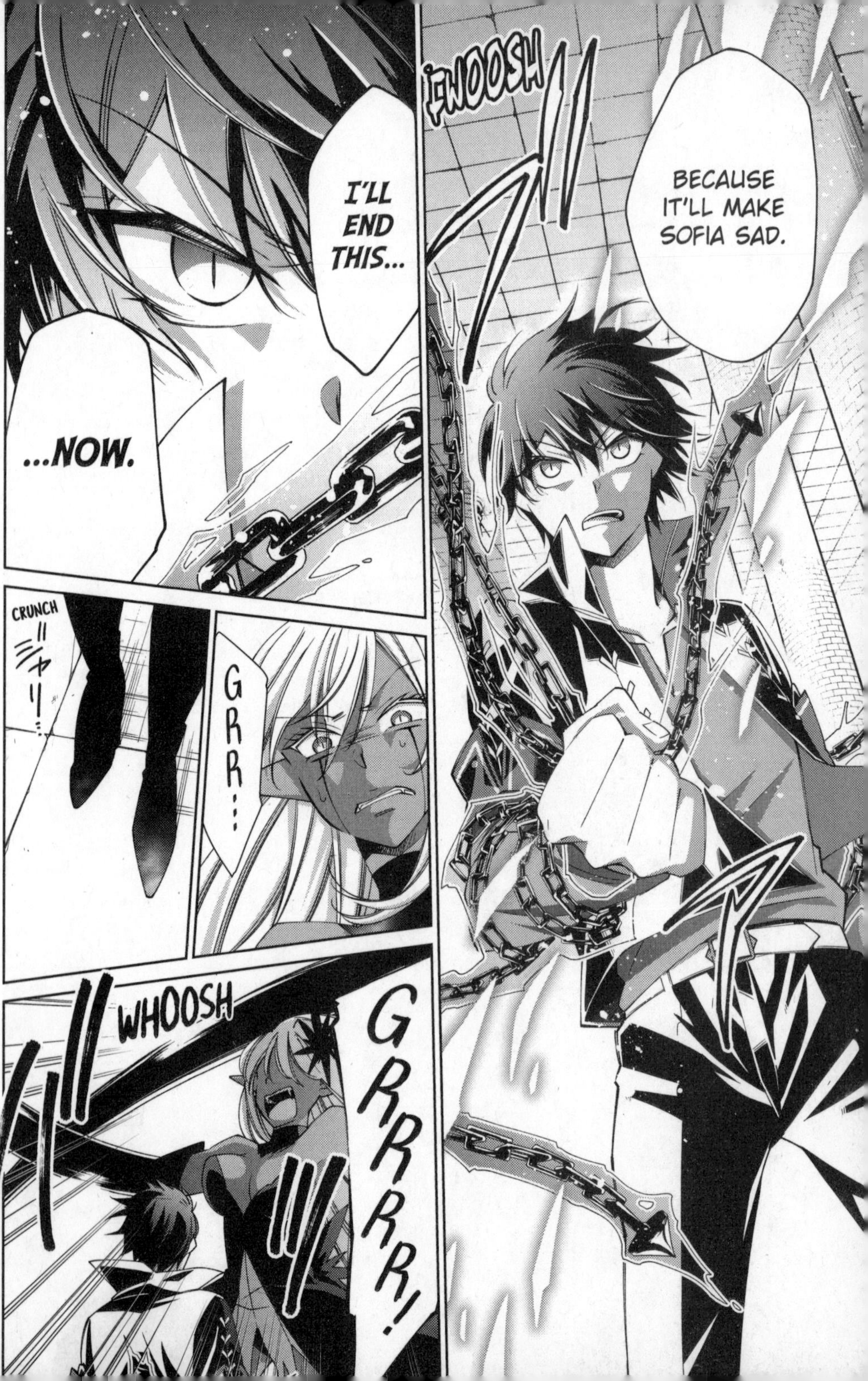
WHOOSH
BECAUSE IT'LL MAKE SOFIA SAD.
I'LL END THIS...
...NOW.
CRUNCH
GRR...
WHOOSH
GRRRR!

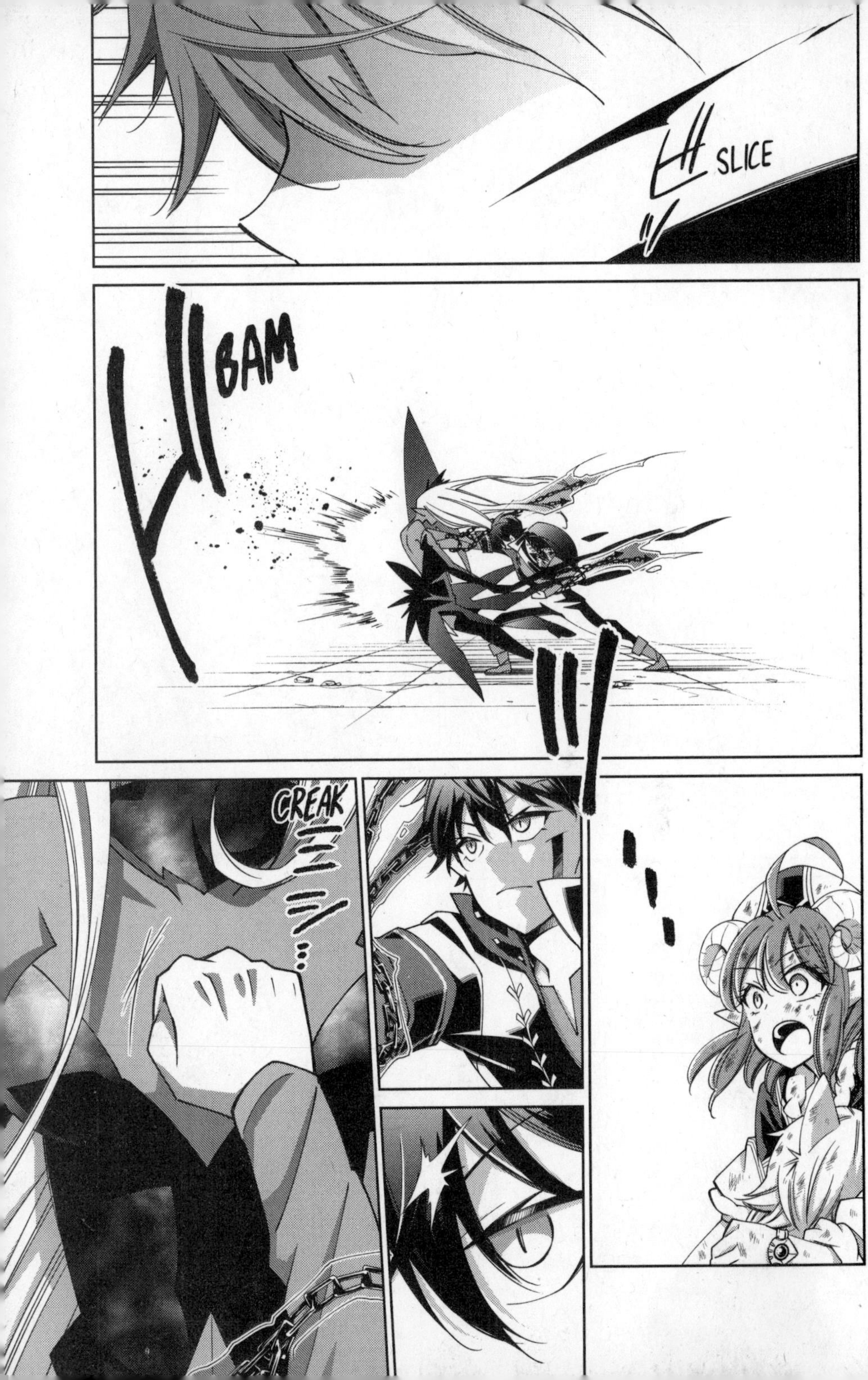
SLICE
BAM
CREAK

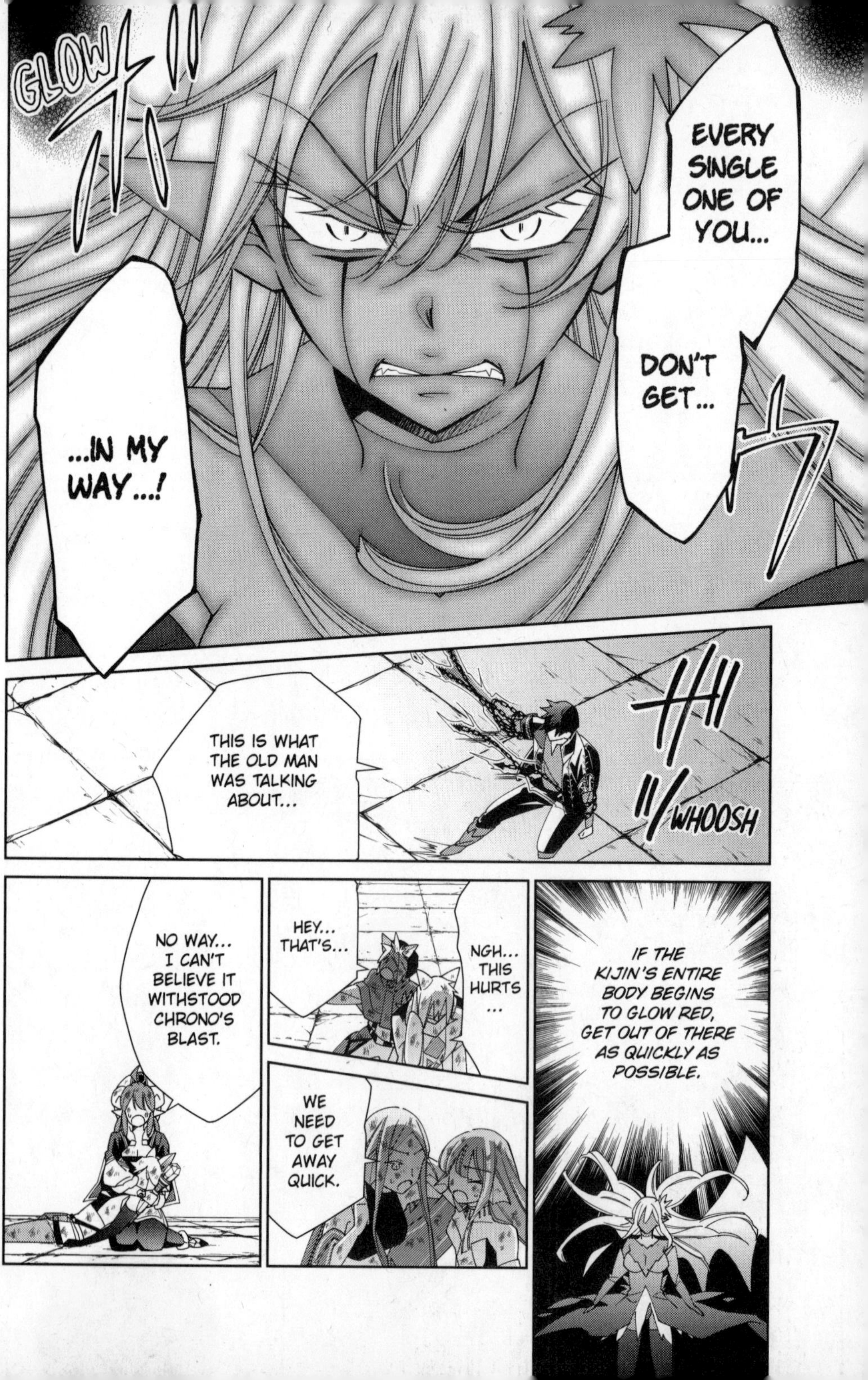
GLOW
EVERY SINGLE ONE OF YOU...
DON'T GET...
...IN MY WAY...!
WHOOSH
THIS IS WHAT THE OLD MAN WAS TALKING ABOUT...
IF THE KIJIN'S ENTIRE BODY BEGINS TO GLOW RED, GET OUT OF THERE AS QUICKLY AS POSSIBLE.
NGH... THIS HURTS...
HEY... THAT'S...
WE NEED TO GET AWAY QUICK.
NO WAY... I CAN'T BELIEVE IT WITHSTOOD CHRONO'S BLAST.

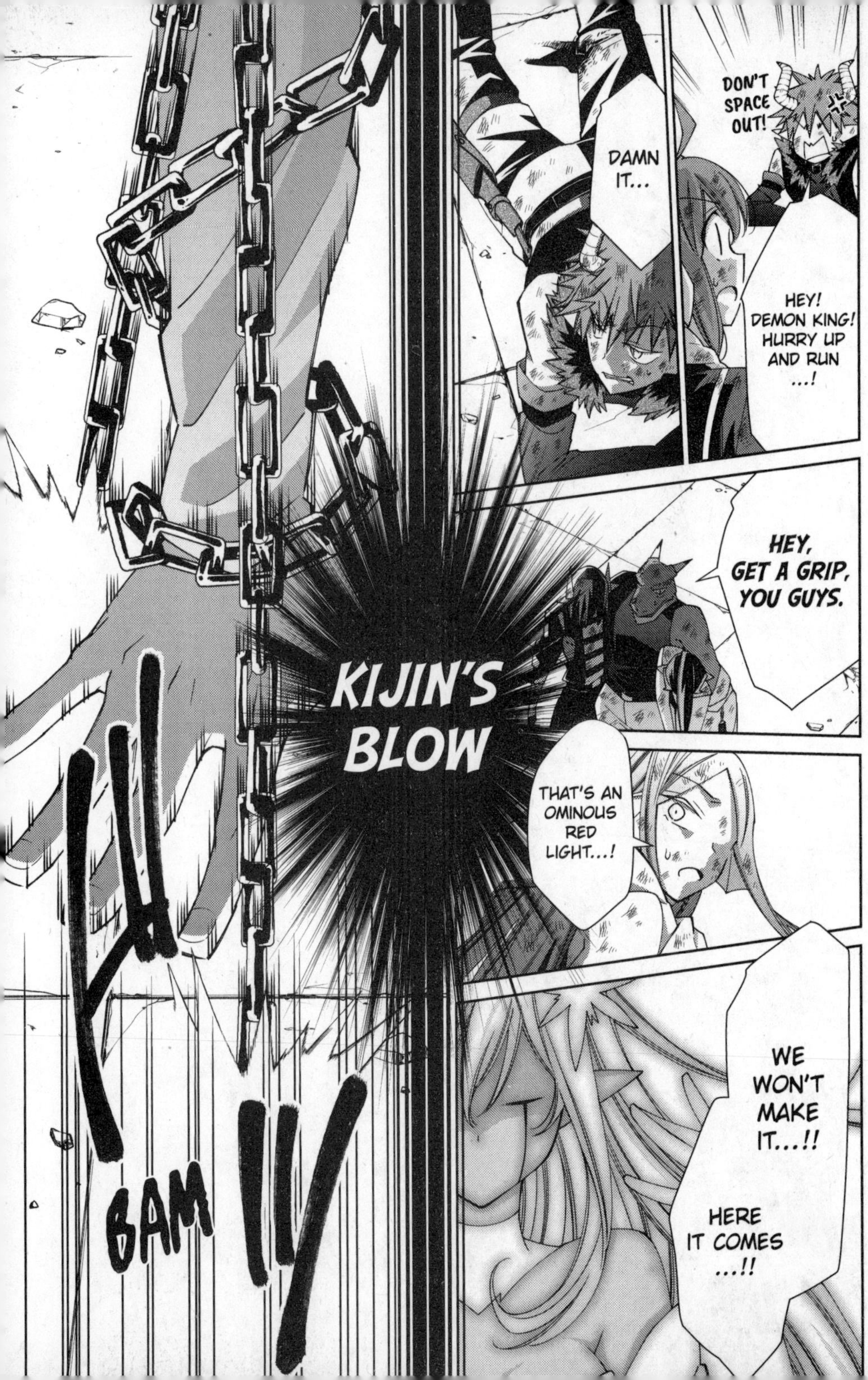
DON'T SPACE OUT!
HEY! DEMON KING! HURRY UP AND RUN ...!
DAMN IT...
HEY, GET A GRIP, YOU GUYS.
THAT'S AN OMINOUS RED LIGHT...!
WE WON'T MAKE IT...!!
HERE IT COMES ...!!
KIJIN'S BLOW
BAM!!

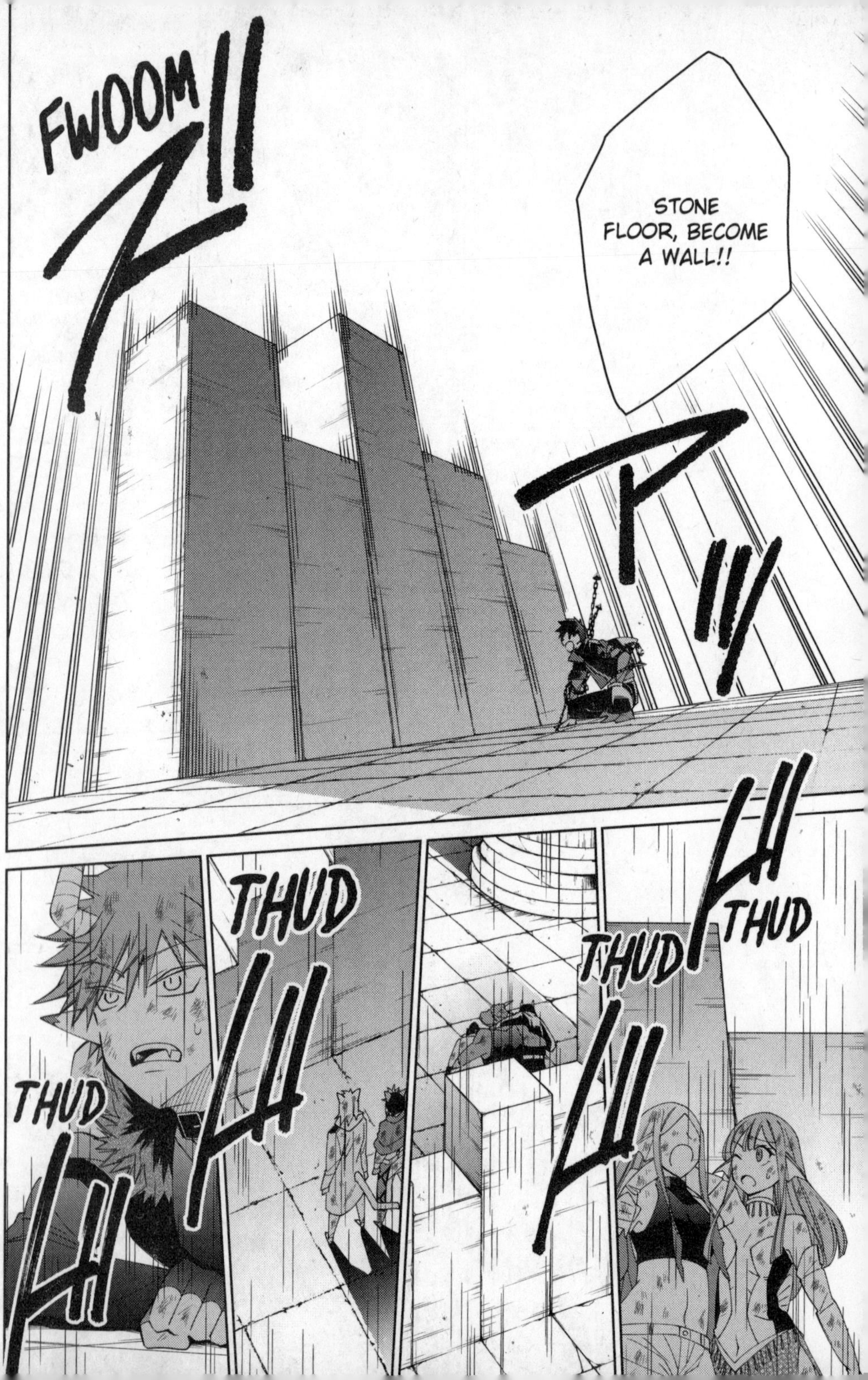
STONE FLOOR, BECOME A WALL!!
FWOOM
THUD
THUD
THUD
THUD

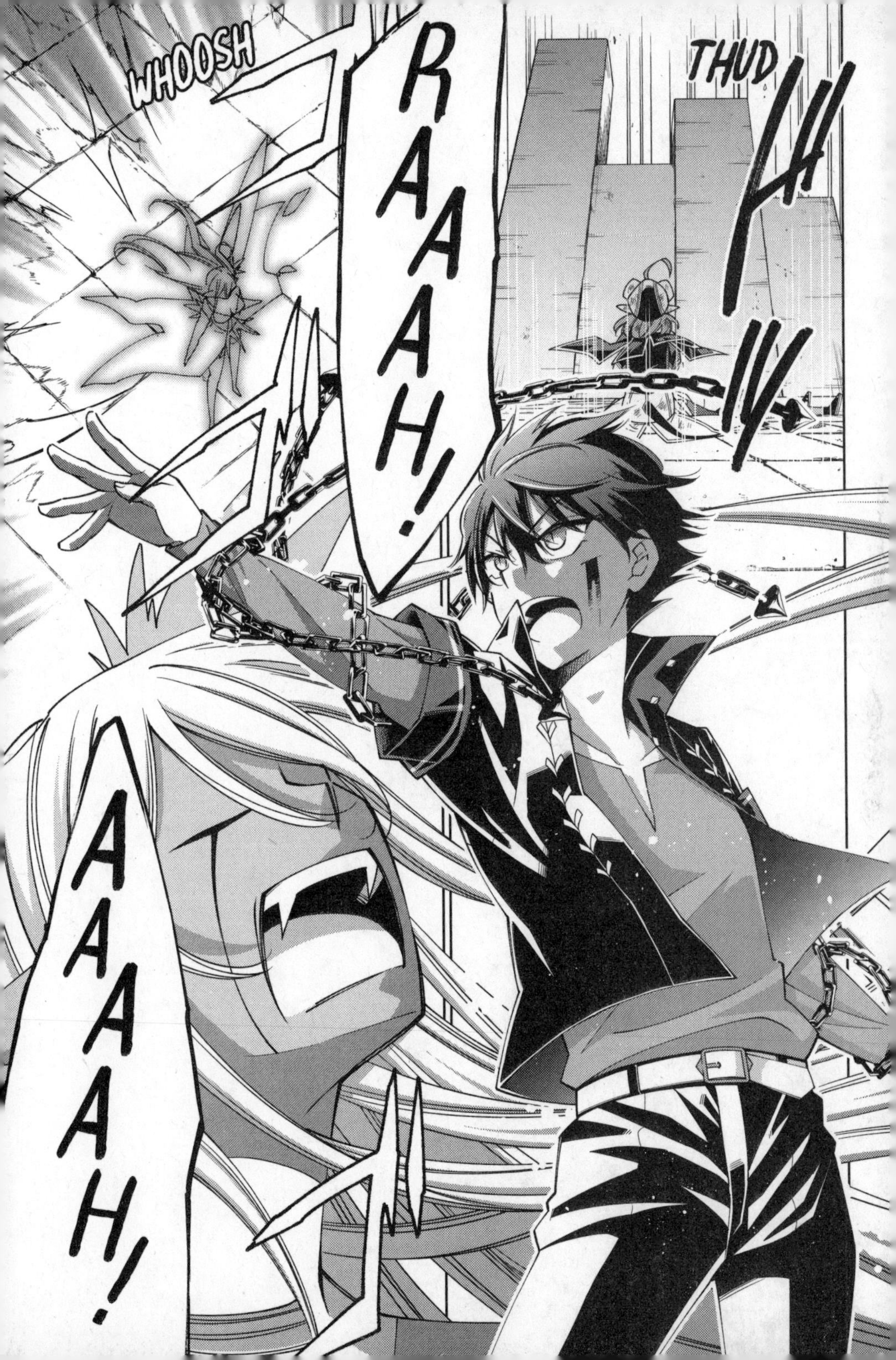
THUD
RAAAAH!!
WHOOSH
AAAAAH!!

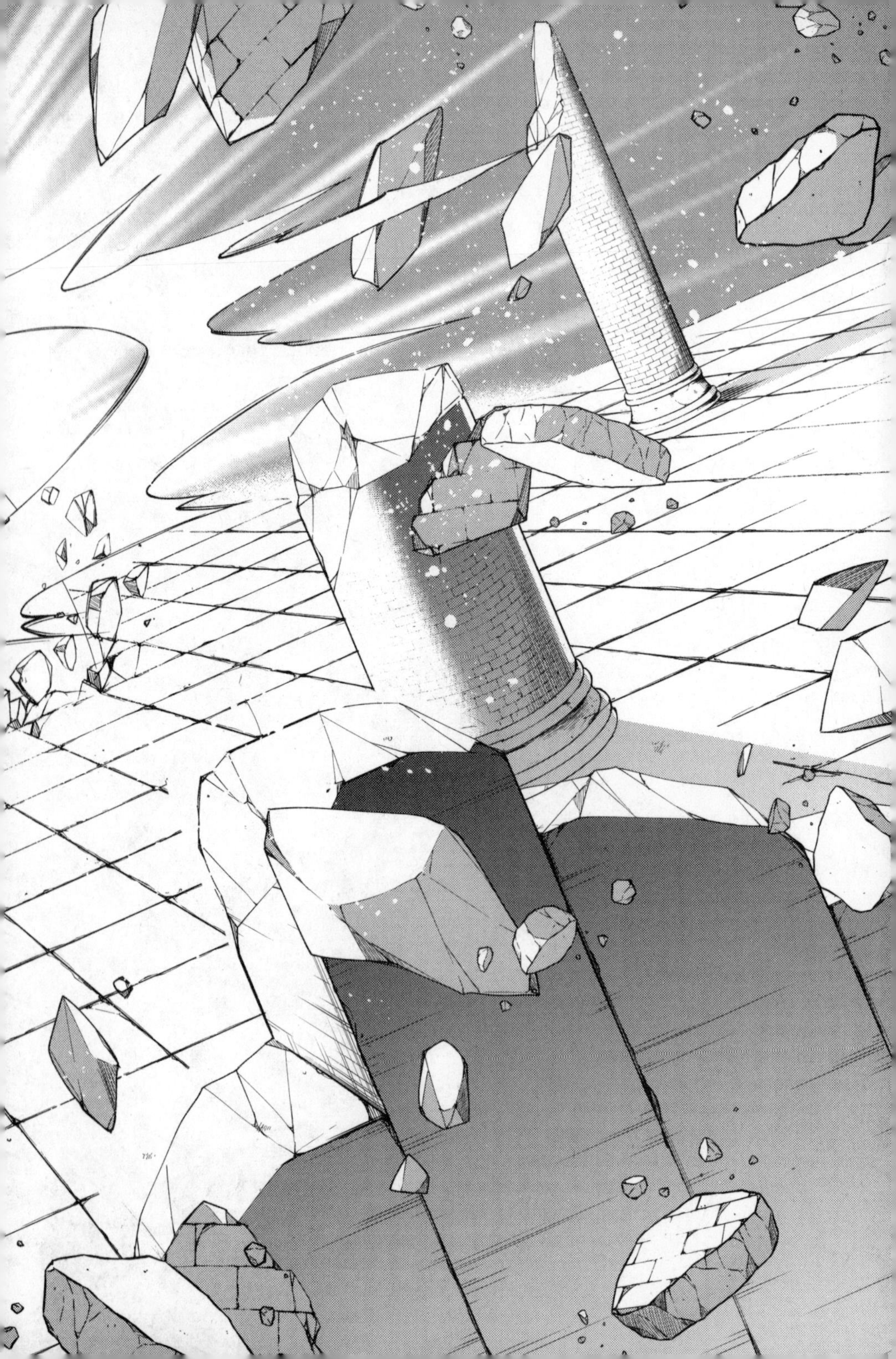

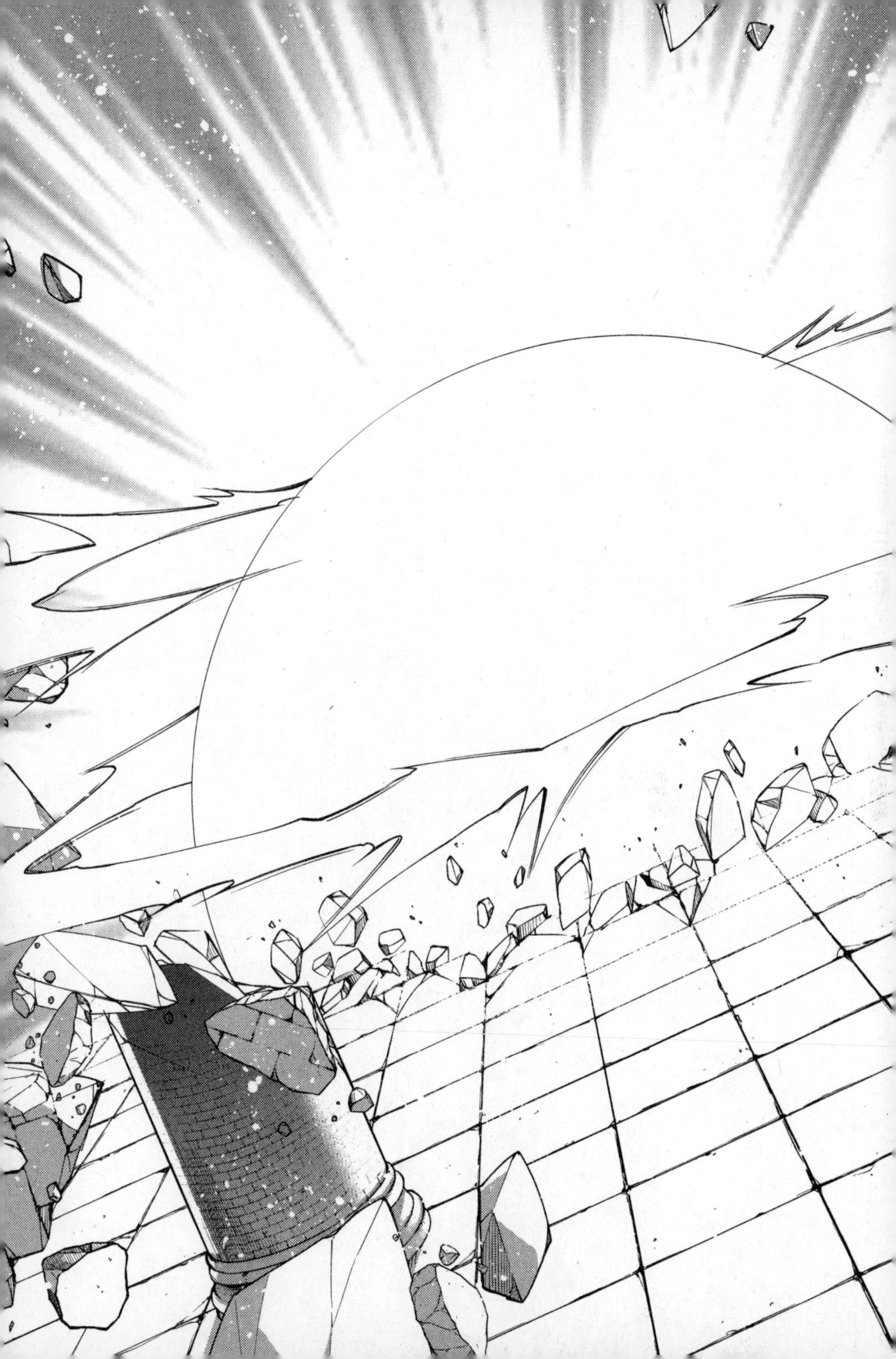

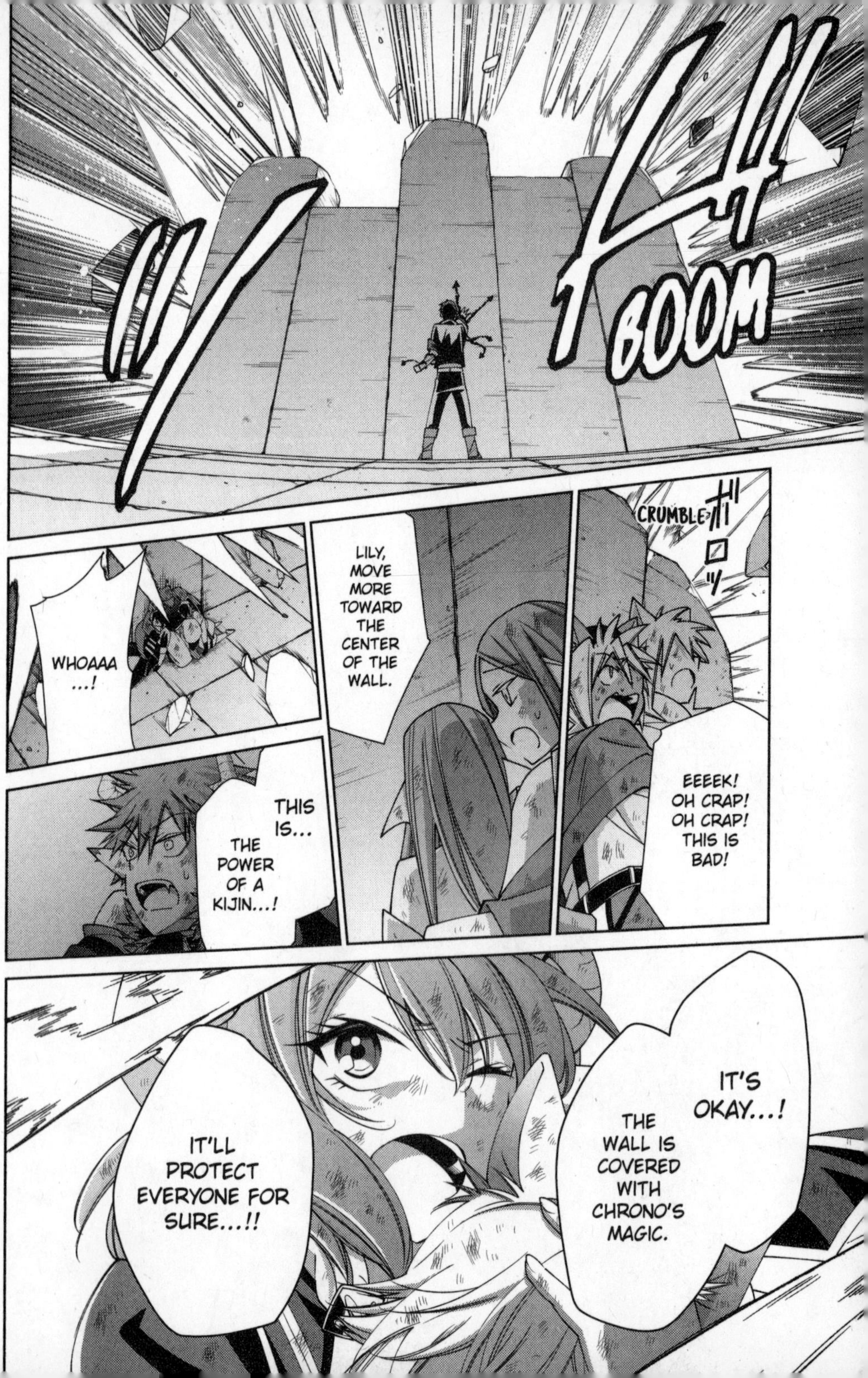
BOOM
CRUMBLE
EEEEK! OH CRAP! OH CRAP! THIS IS BAD!
LILY, MOVE MORE TOWARD THE CENTER OF THE WALL.
WHOAAA...!
THIS IS... THE POWER OF A KIJIN...!
IT'S OKAY...!
THE WALL IS COVERED WITH CHRONO'S MAGIC.
IT'LL PROTECT EVERYONE FOR SURE...!!

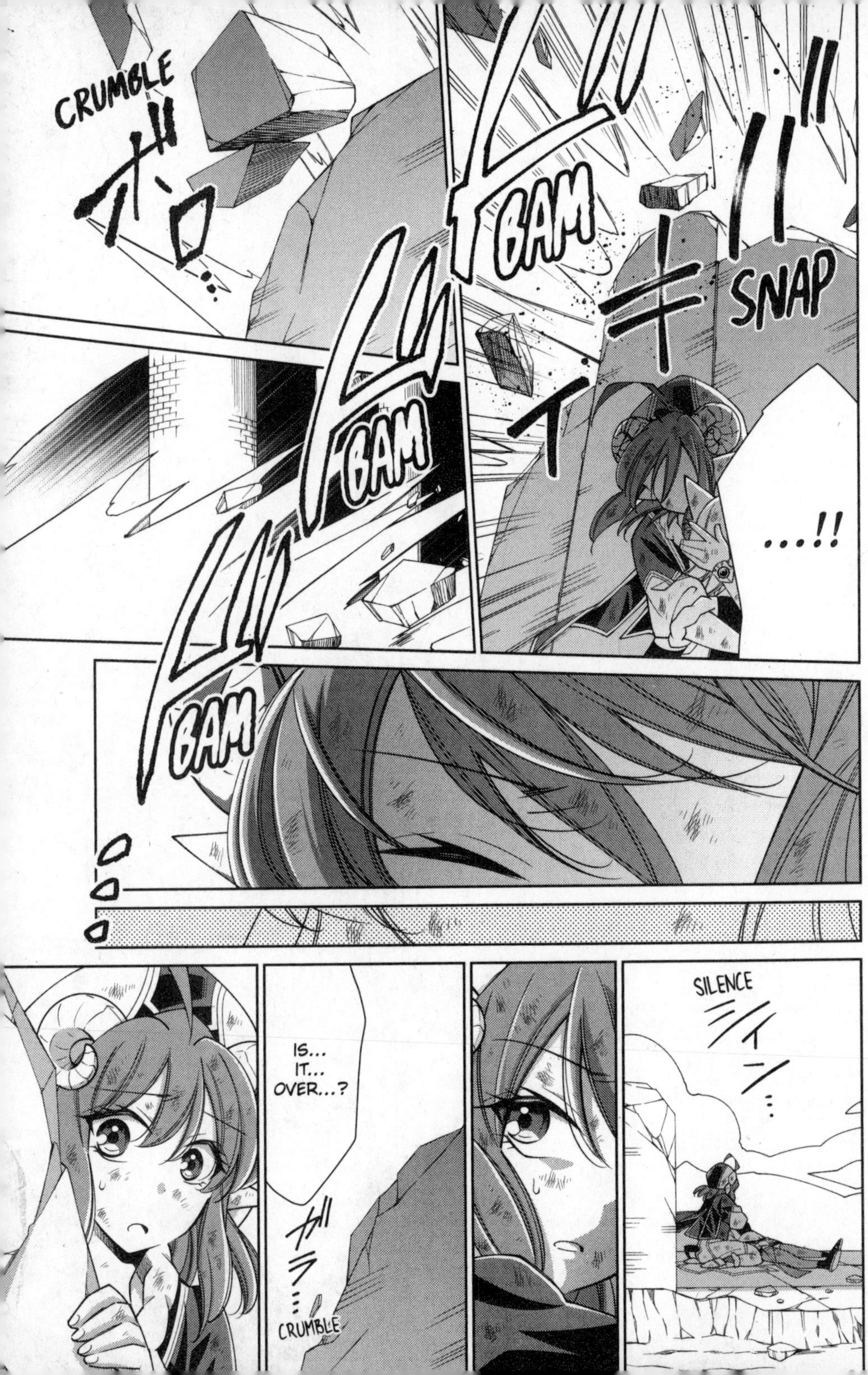
SNAP
BAM
CRUMBLE
...!!
BAM
BAM
SILENCE
IS... IT... OVER...?
CRUMBLE

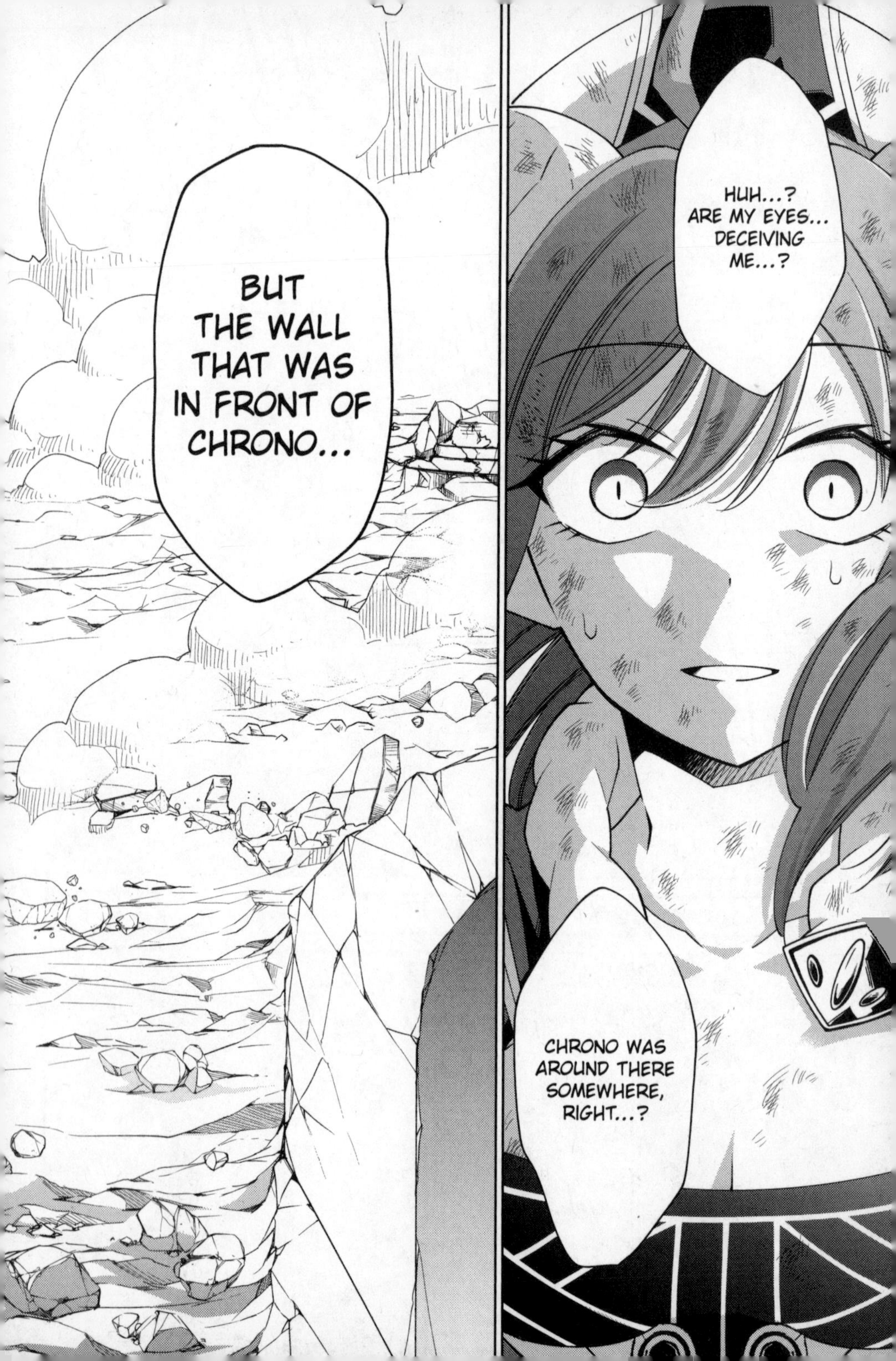
HUH...? ARE MY EYES... DECEIVING ME...?
CHRONO WAS AROUND THERE SOMEWHERE, RIGHT...?
BUT THE WALL THAT WAS IN FRONT OF CHRONO...

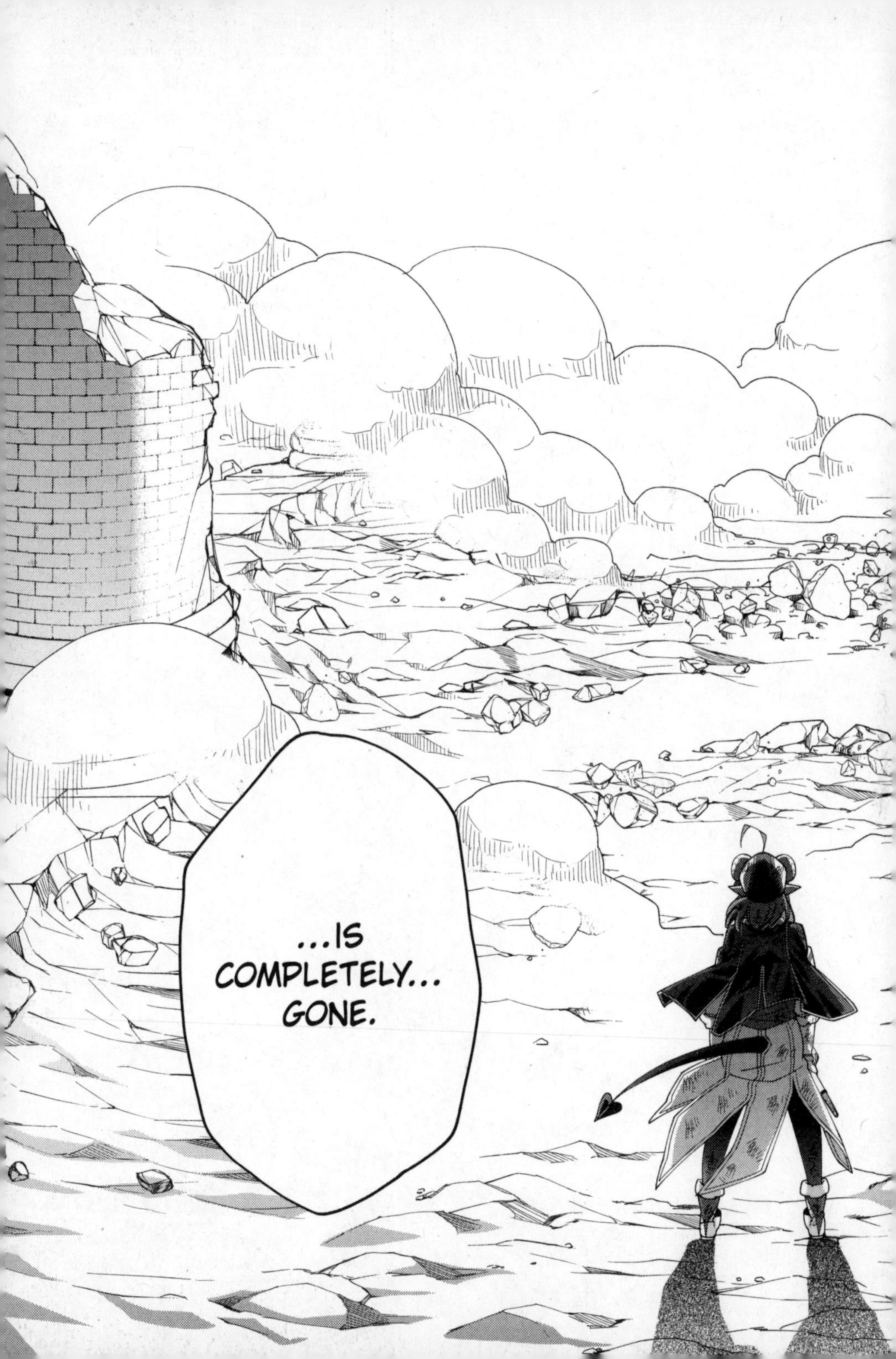
...IS COMPLETELY... GONE.

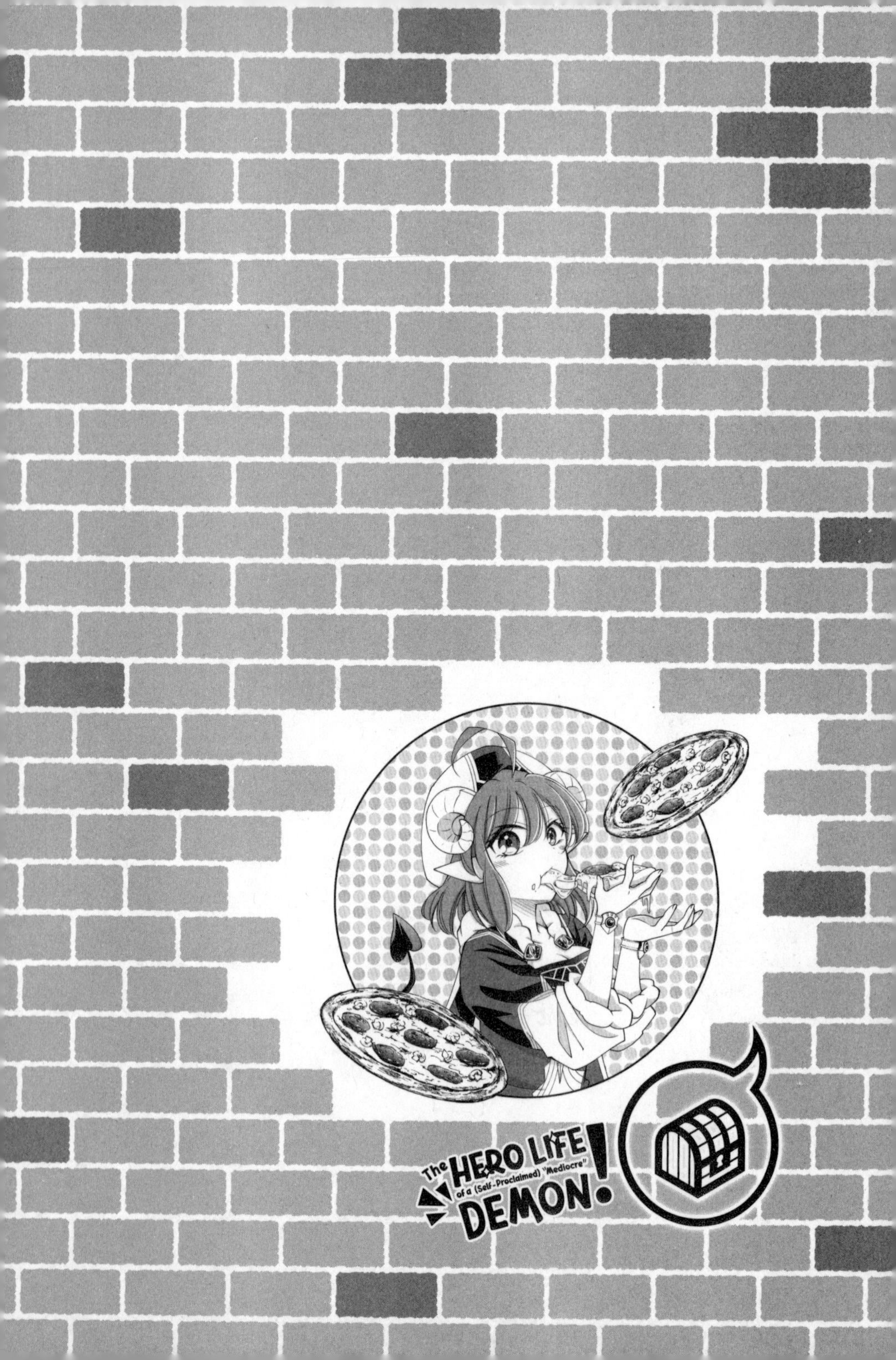
The HERO LIFE of a (Self-Proclaimed) "Mediocre" DEMON!

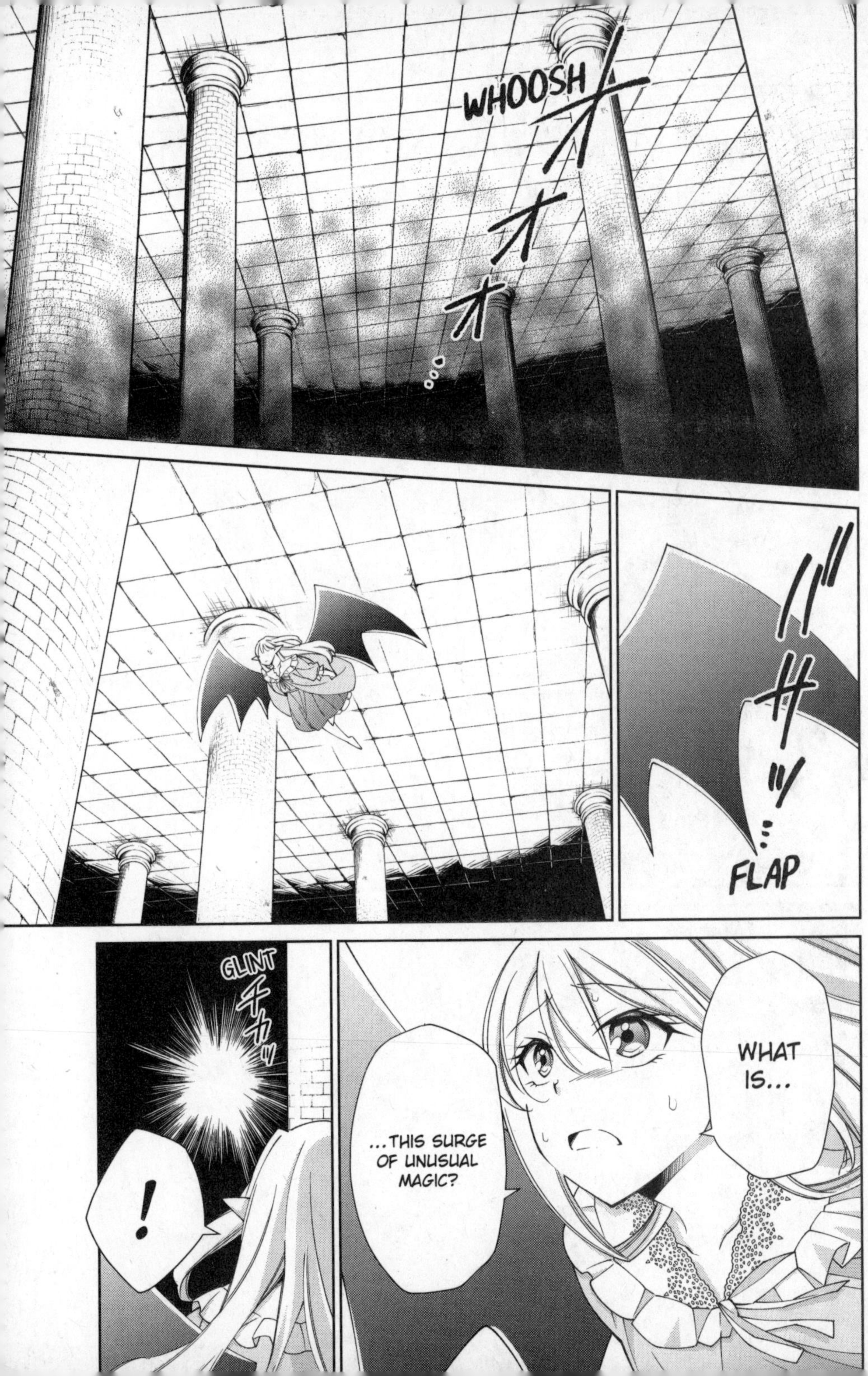
WHOOSH
バサッ
FLAP
WHAT IS...
...THIS SURGE OF UNUSUAL MAGIC?
GLINT
チカッ
!

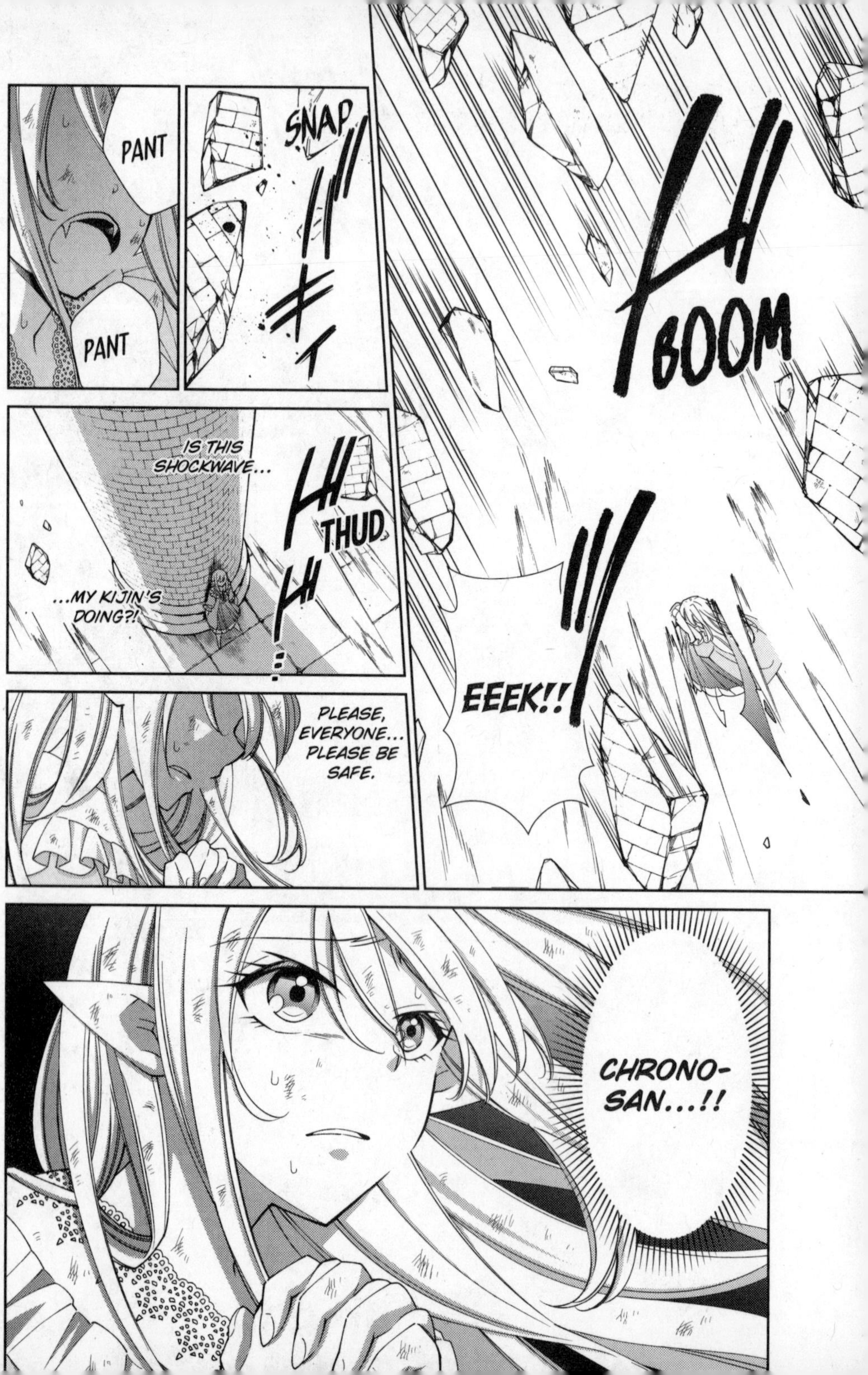
BOOM
EEEK!!
SNAP
PANT
PANT
THUD
IS THIS SHOCKWAVE...
...MY KIJIN'S DOING?!
PLEASE, EVERYONE... PLEASE BE SAFE.
CHRONO-SAN...!!

CHAPTER 12 CHRONO CELEBRATES A VICTORY

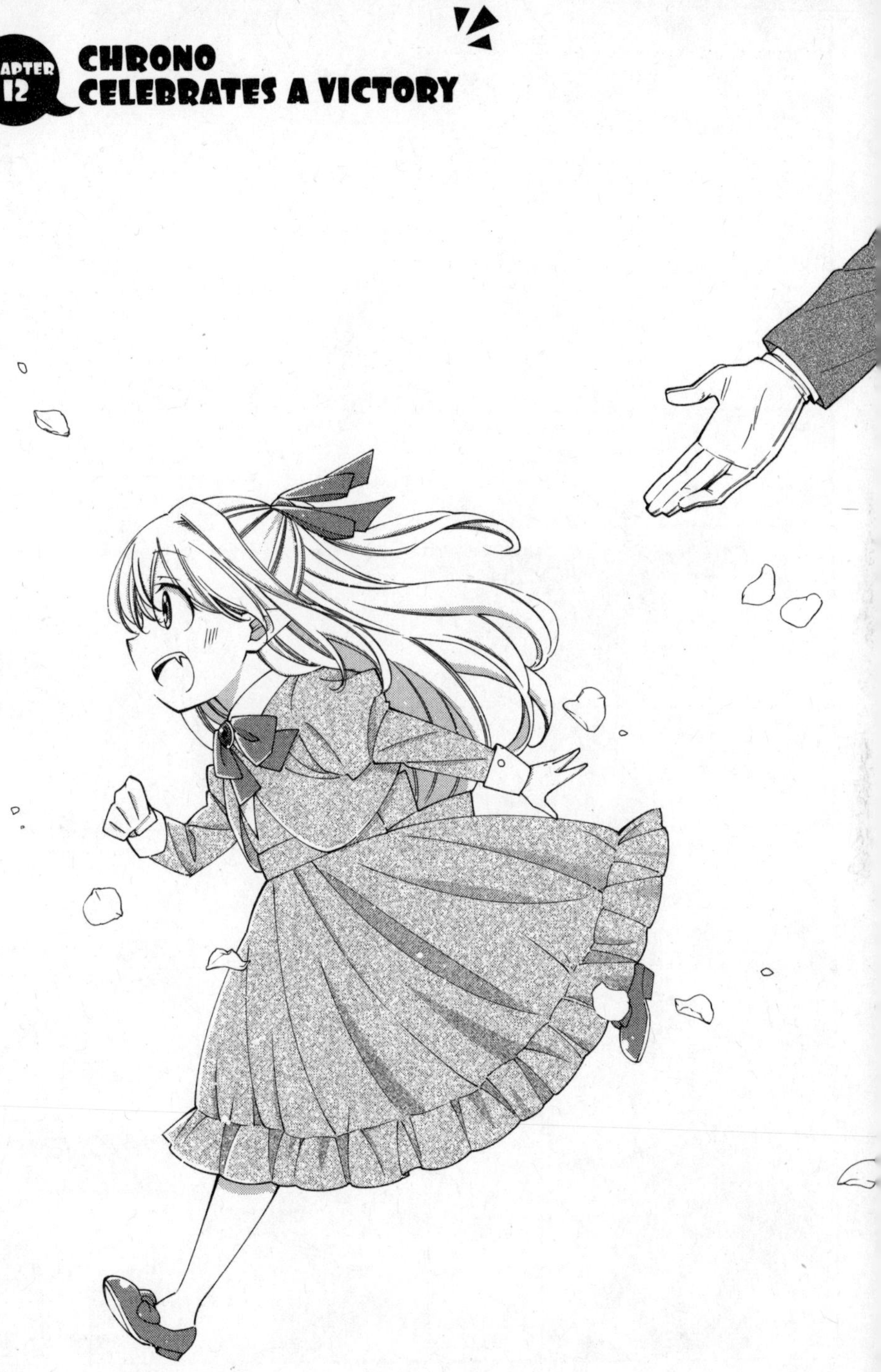

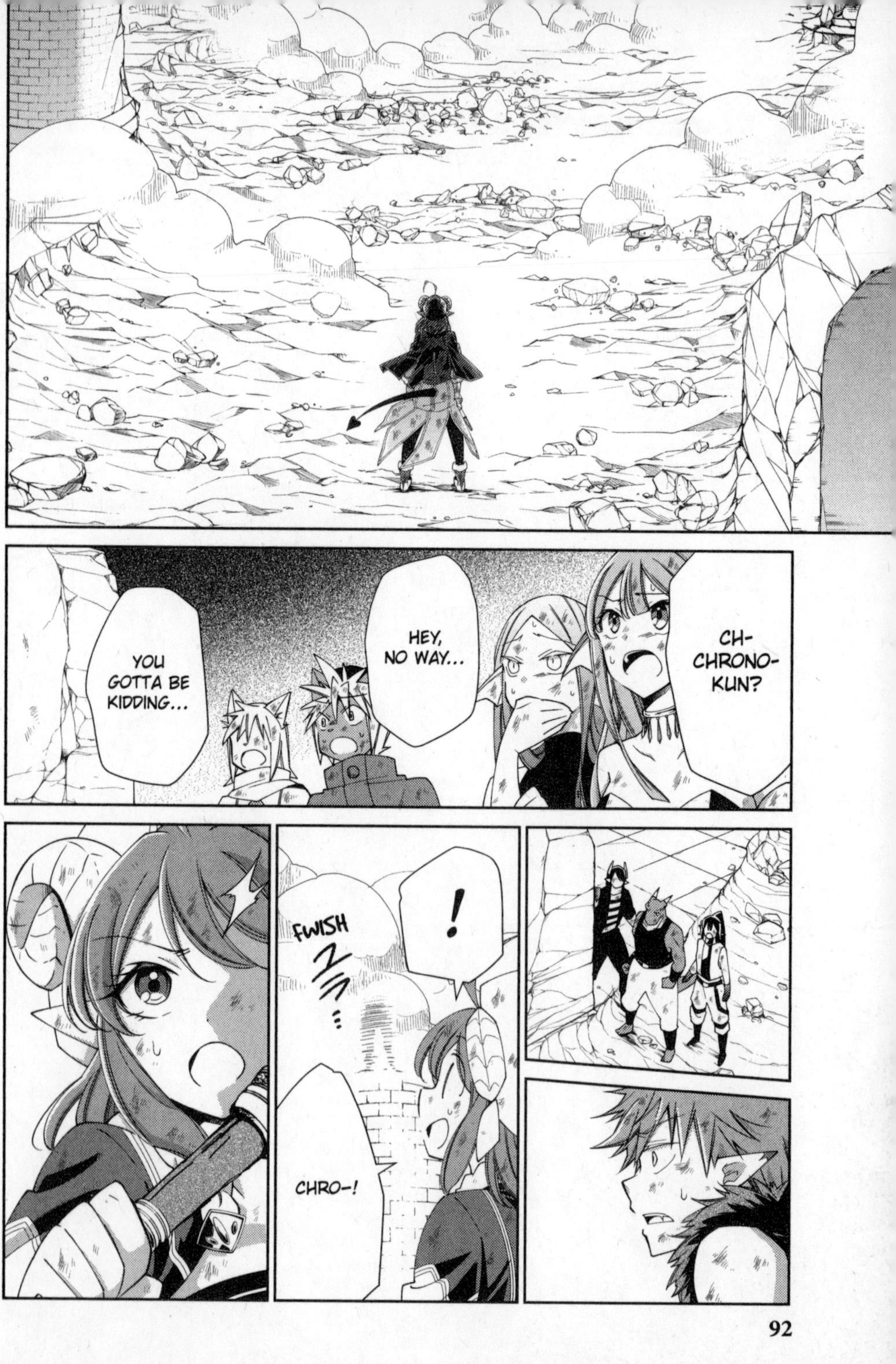
CH- CHRONO- KUN?
HEY, NO WAY...
YOU GOTTA BE KIDDING...
!
FWISH
CHRO-!

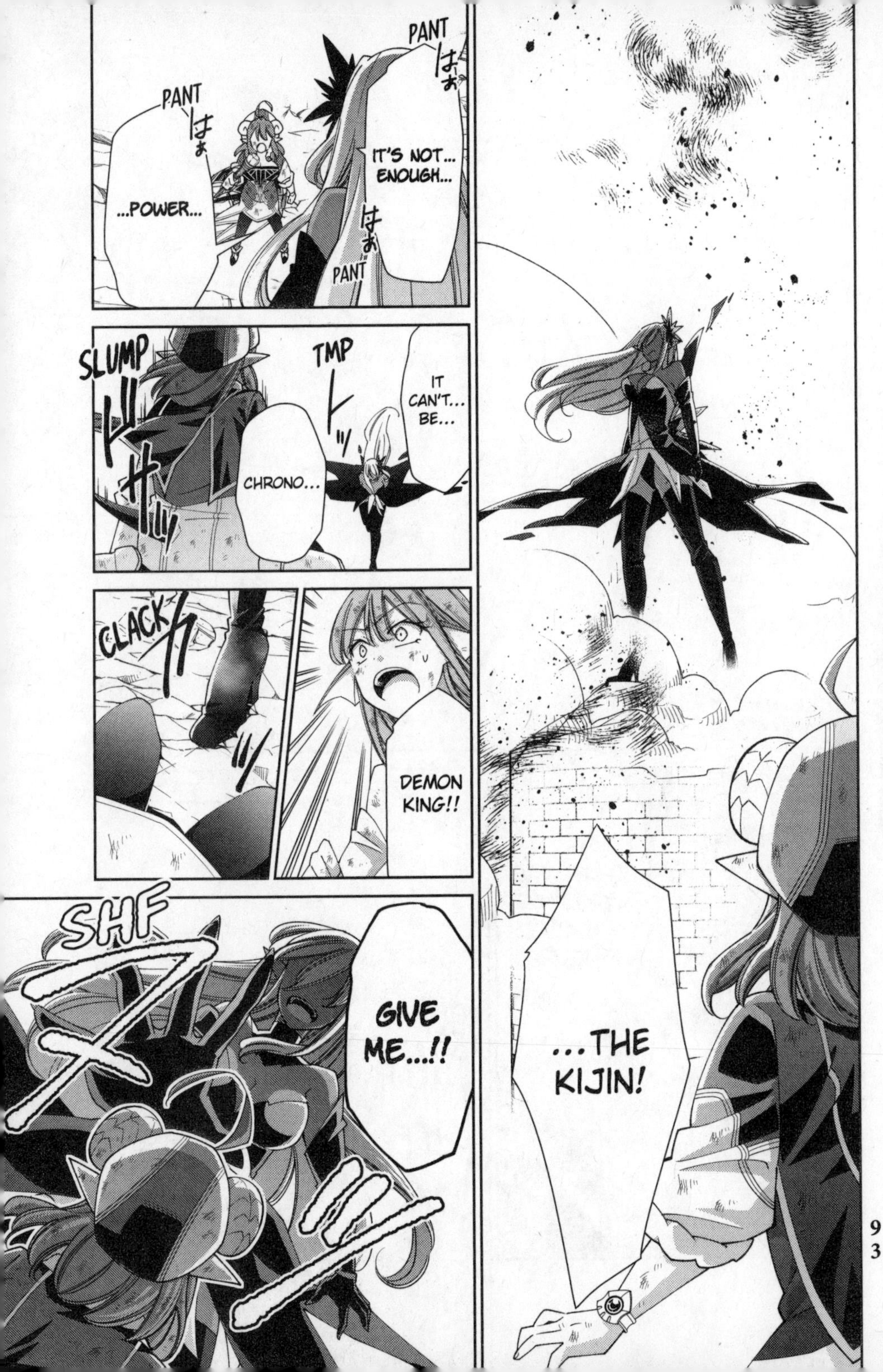
PANT はぉ
IT'S NOT... ENOUGH...
はぉ PANT
PANT はぉ
...POWER...
TMP
IT CAN'T... BE...
CHRONO...
SLUMP
CLACK
DEMON KING!!
SHF
GIVE ME...!!
...THE KIJIN!

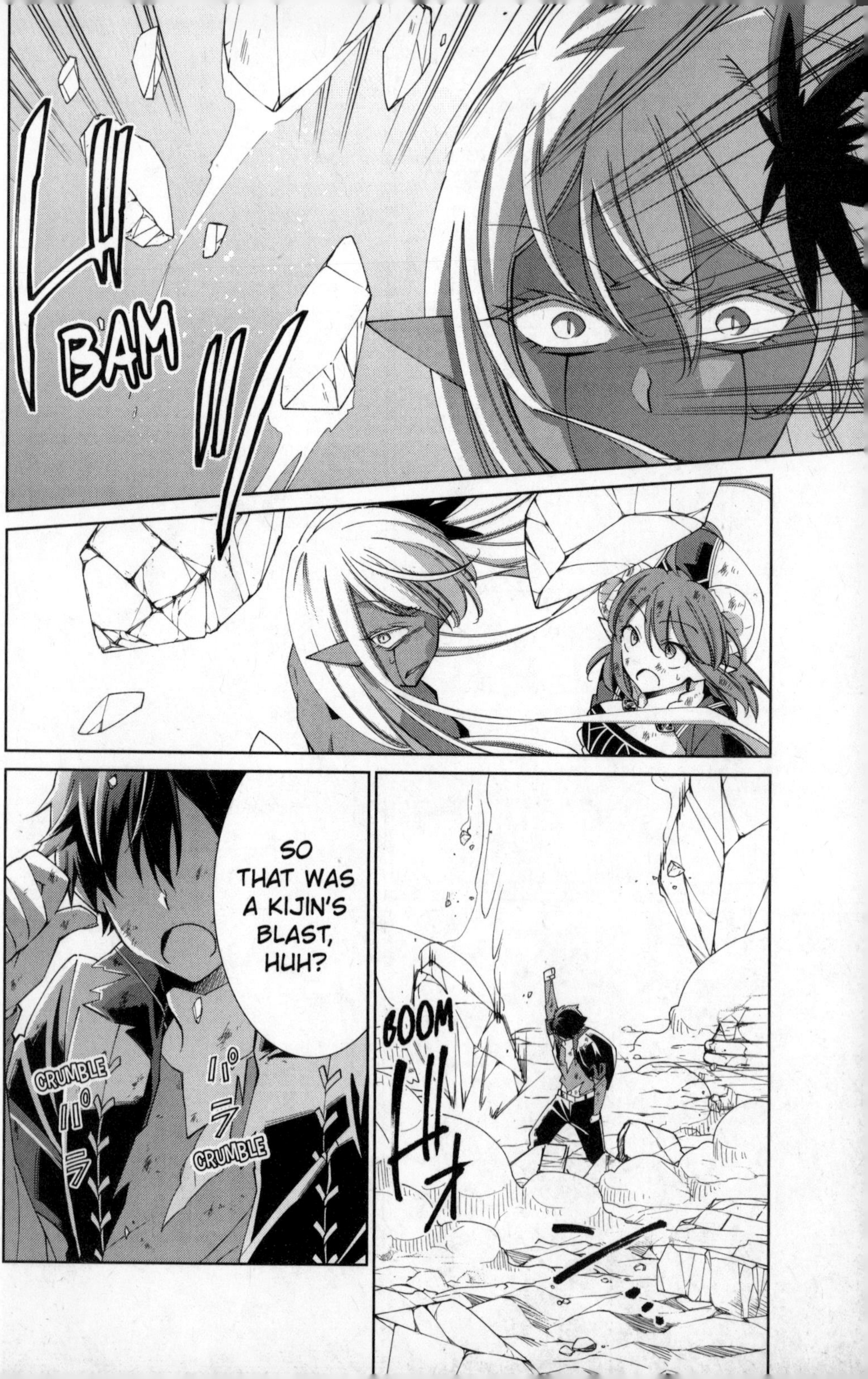
BAM
BOOM
SO THAT WAS A KIJIN'S BLAST, HUH?
パラ
CRUMBLE
パラ
CRUMBLE

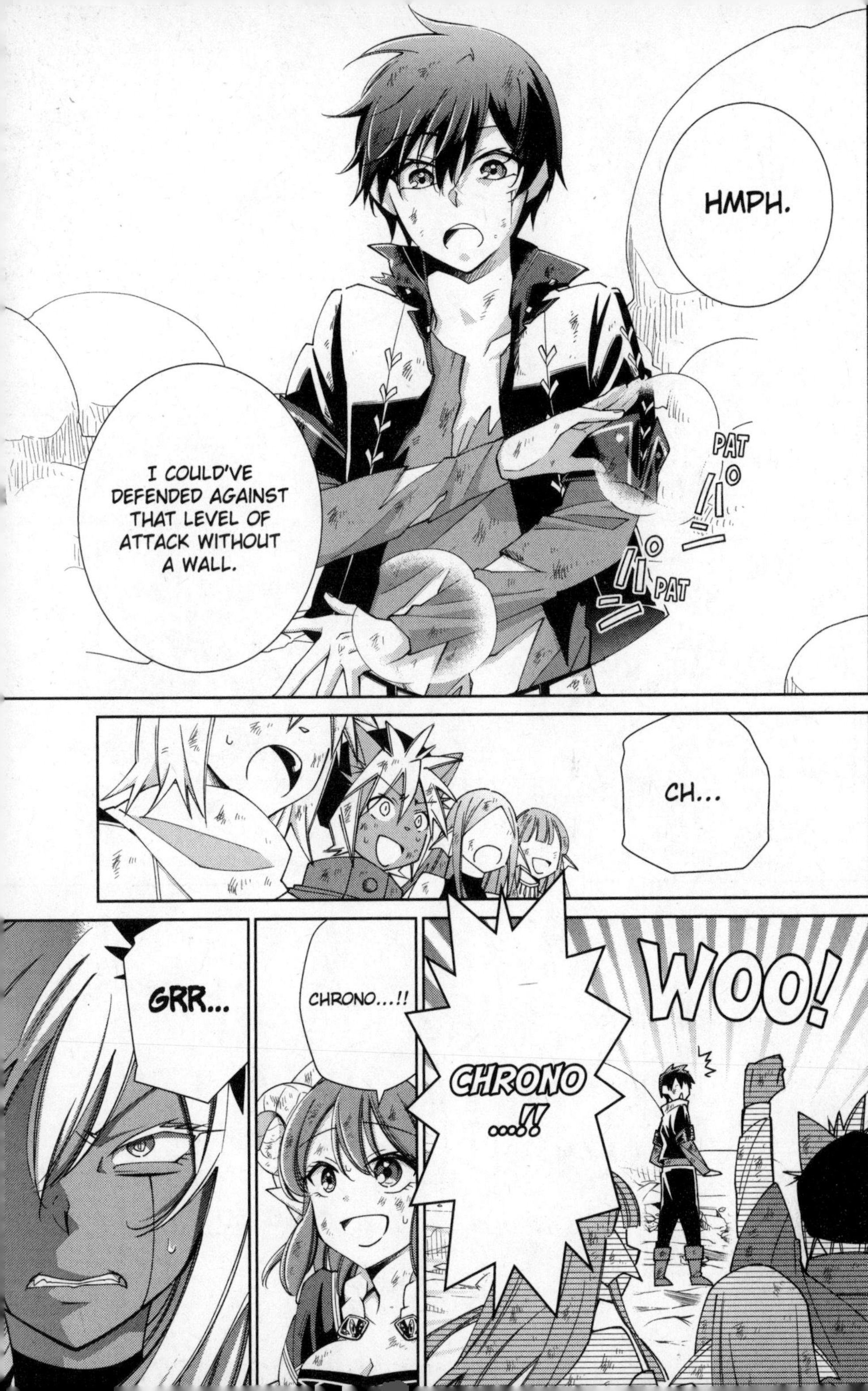
HMPH.
PAT
I COULD'VE DEFENDED AGAINST THAT LEVEL OF ATTACK WITHOUT A WALL.
PAT
CH...
WOO!
CHRONO ...!!
CHRONO...!!
GRR...

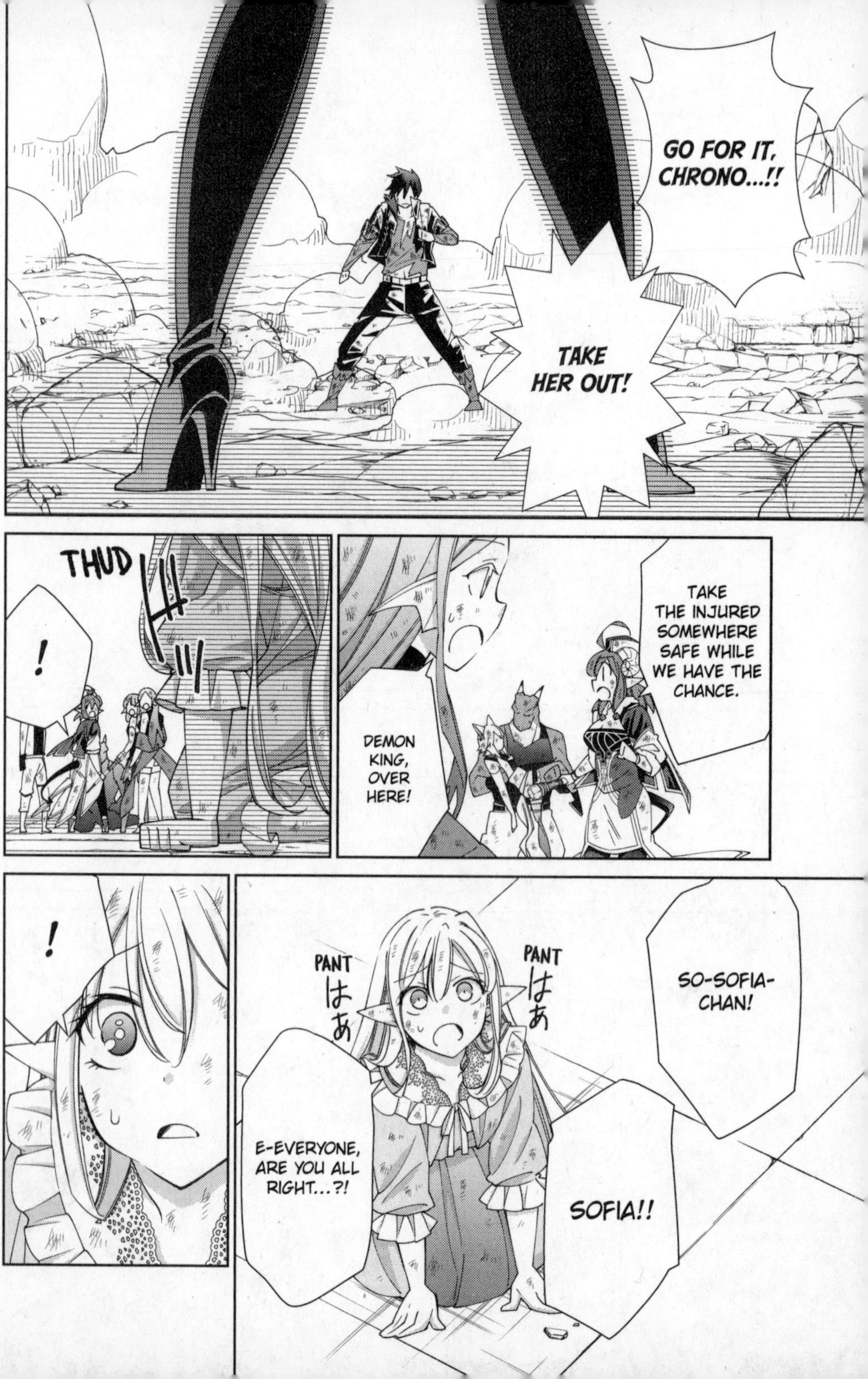
GO FOR IT, CHRONO...!!
TAKE HER OUT!
TAKE THE INJURED SOMEWHERE SAFE WHILE WE HAVE THE CHANCE.
DEMON KING, OVER HERE!
THUD
!
SO-SOFIA-CHAN!
PANT はあ
PANT はあ
SOFIA!!
E-EVERYONE, ARE YOU ALL RIGHT...?!
!

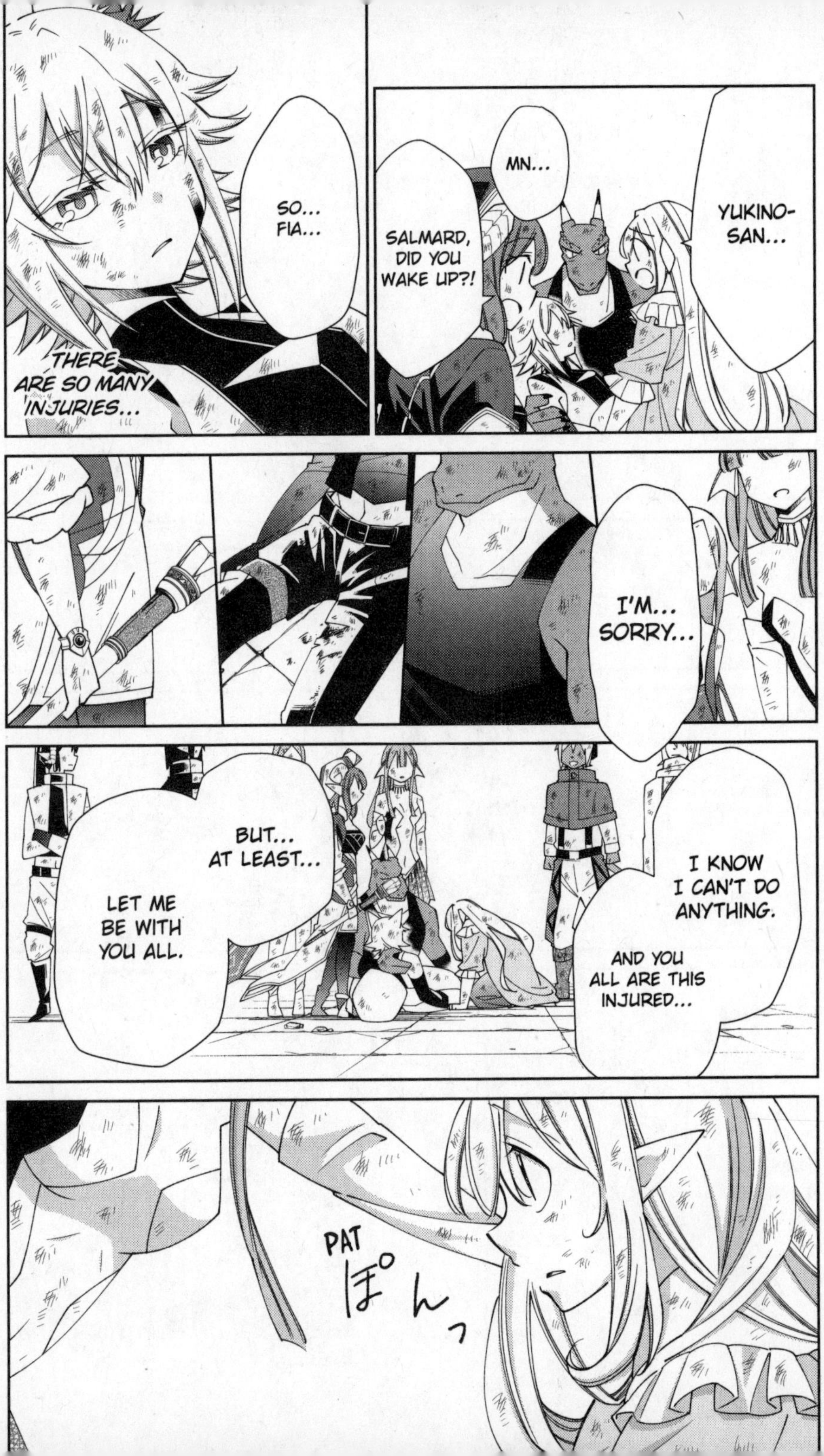
YUKINO-SAN...
MN...
SALMARD, DID YOU WAKE UP?!
SO... FIA...
THERE ARE SO MANY INJURIES...
I'M... SORRY...
I KNOW I CAN'T DO ANYTHING.
AND YOU ALL ARE THIS INJURED...
BUT... AT LEAST...
LET ME BE WITH YOU ALL.
PAT
ぽんっ

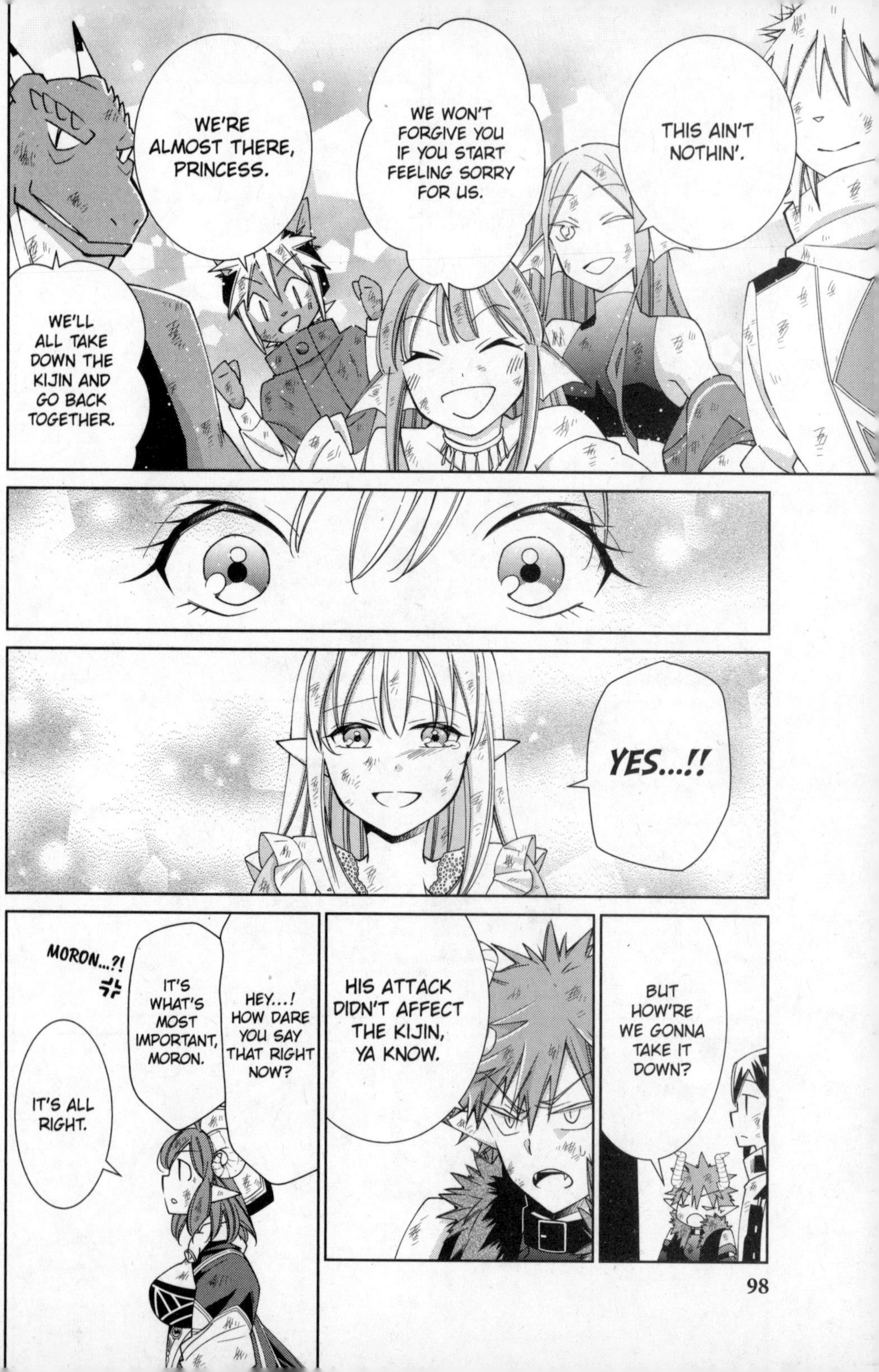
THIS AIN'T NOTHIN'.
WE WON'T FORGIVE YOU IF YOU START FEELING SORRY FOR US.
WE'RE ALMOST THERE, PRINCESS.
WE'LL ALL TAKE DOWN THE KIJIN AND GO BACK TOGETHER.
YES...!!
BUT HOW'RE WE GONNA TAKE IT DOWN?
HIS ATTACK DIDN'T AFFECT THE KIJIN, YA KNOW.
HEY...! HOW DARE YOU SAY THAT RIGHT NOW?
IT'S WHAT'S MOST IMPORTANT, MORON.
MORON...?!
IT'S ALL RIGHT.

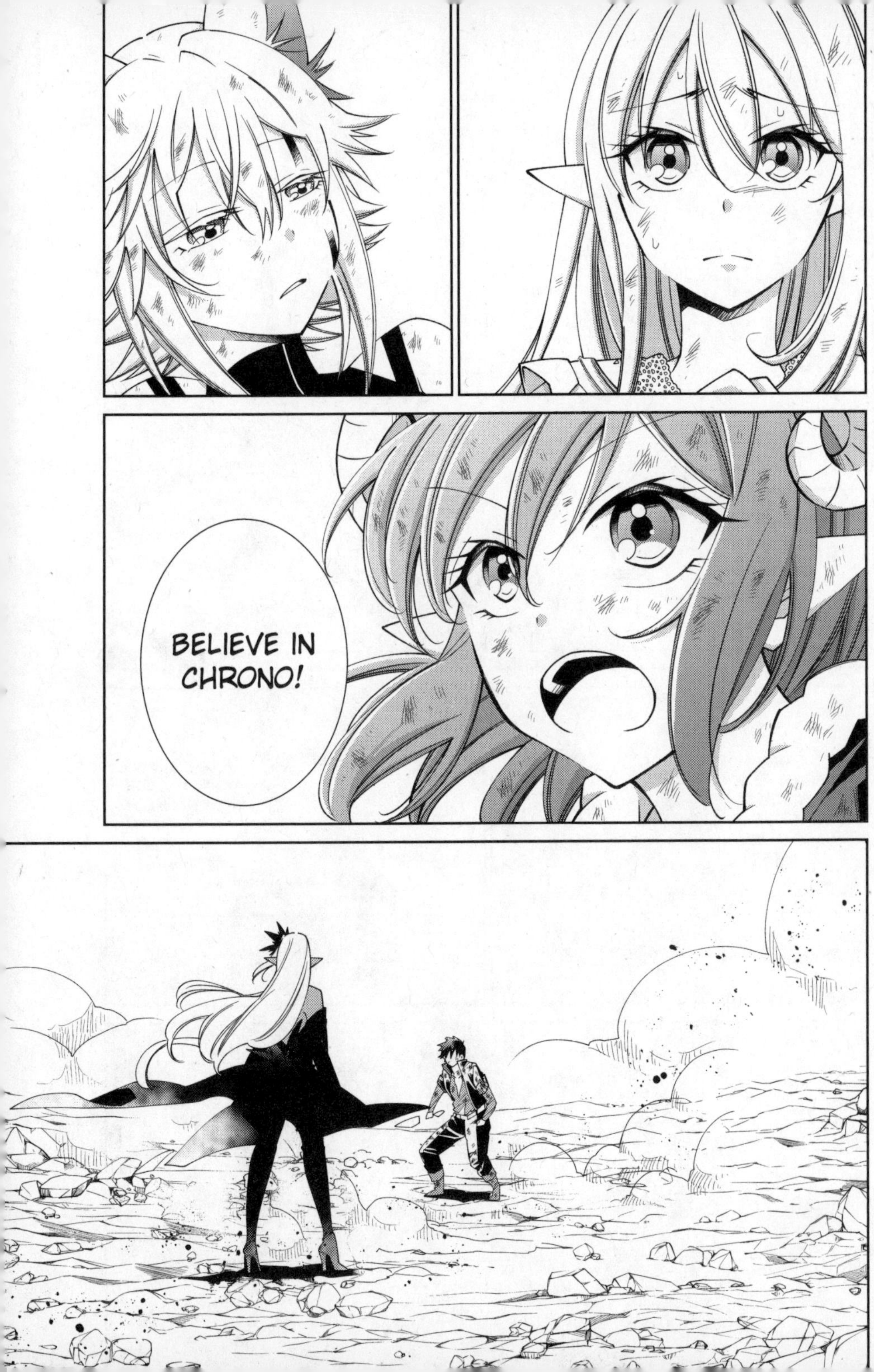
BELIEVE IN CHRONO!

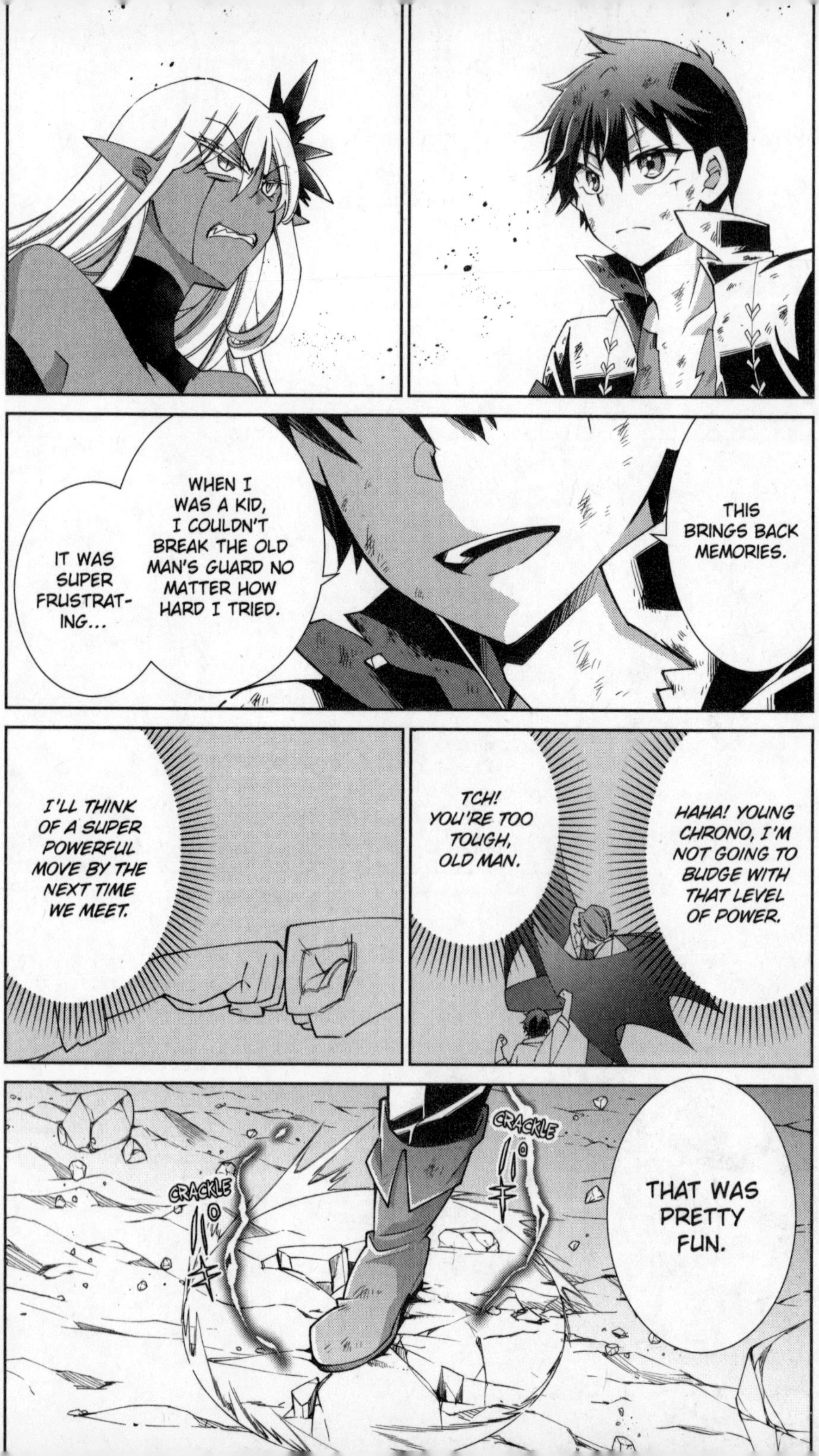
THIS BRINGS BACK MEMORIES.
WHEN I WAS A KID, I COULDN'T BREAK THE OLD MAN'S GUARD NO MATTER HOW HARD I TRIED.
IT WAS SUPER FRUSTRAT-ING...
HAHA! YOUNG CHRONO, I'M NOT GOING TO BUDGE WITH THAT LEVEL OF POWER.
TCH! YOU'RE TOO TOUGH, OLD MAN.
I'LL THINK OF A SUPER POWERFUL MOVE BY THE NEXT TIME WE MEET.
THAT WAS PRETTY FUN.
CRACKLE
CRACKLE

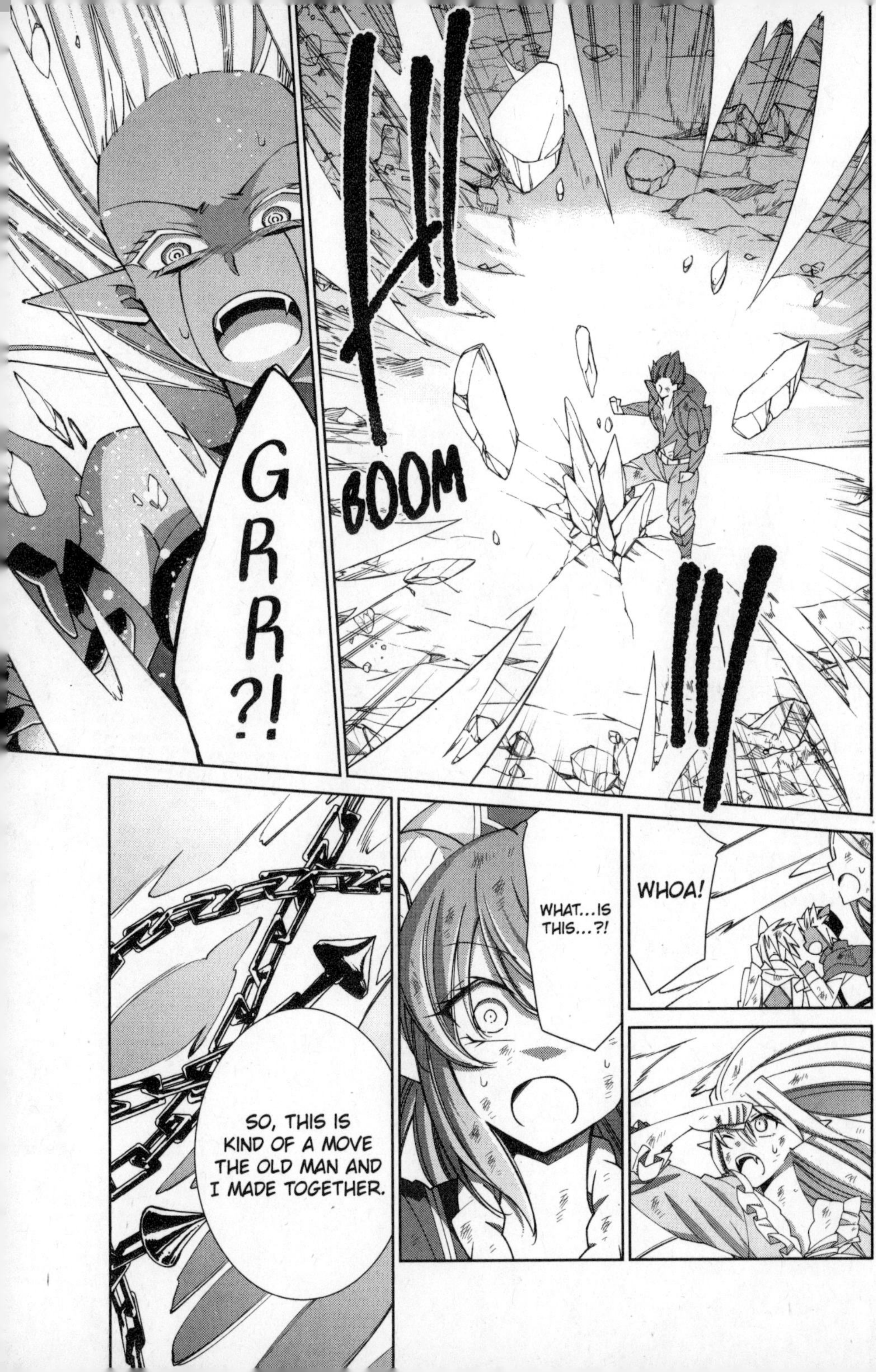
BOOM
GRR?!
WHOA!
WHAT…IS THIS…?!
SO, THIS IS KIND OF A MOVE THE OLD MAN AND I MADE TOGETHER.

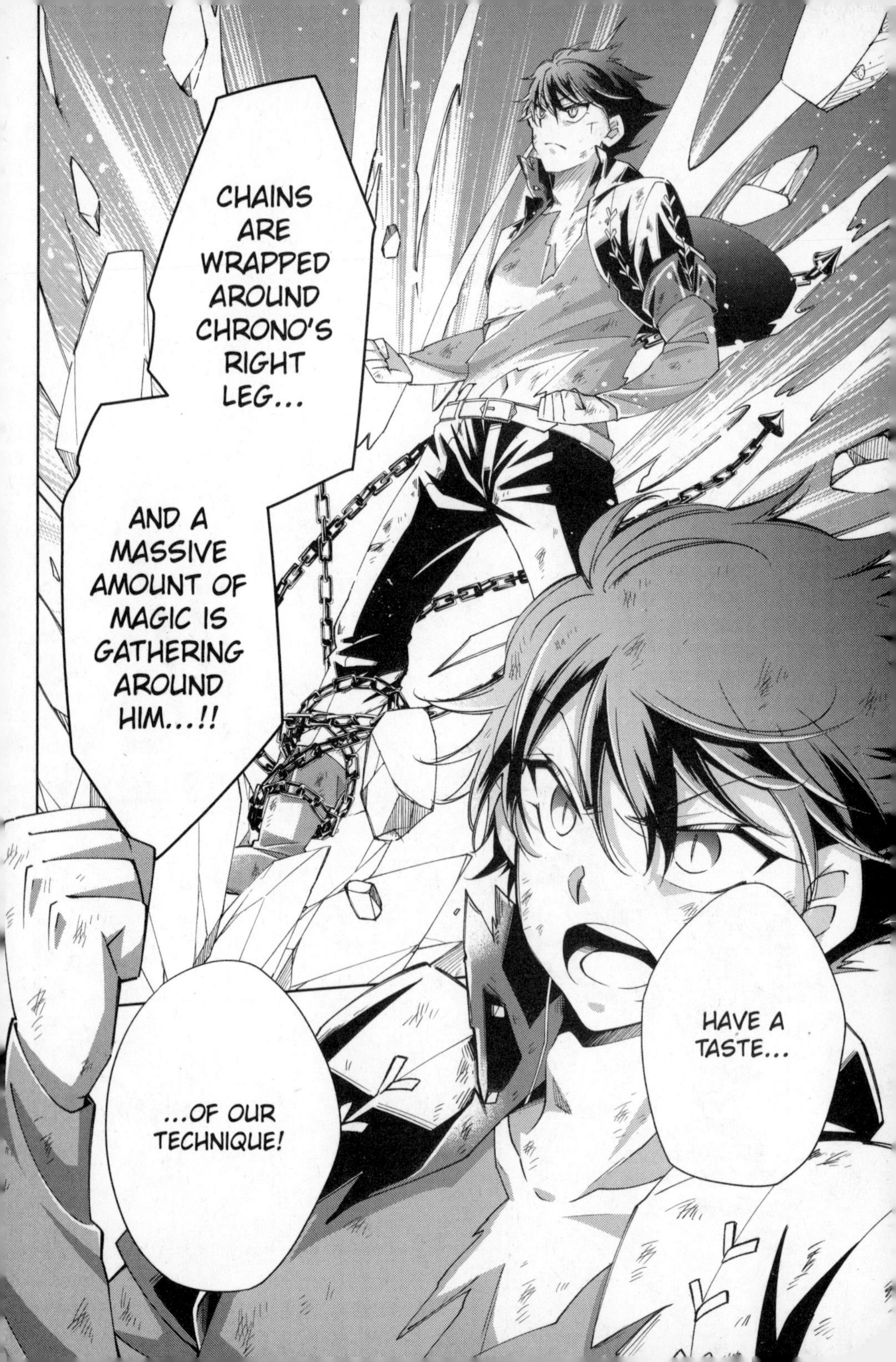
CHAINS ARE WRAPPED AROUND CHRONO'S RIGHT LEG...
AND A MASSIVE AMOUNT OF MAGIC IS GATHERING AROUND HIM...!!
HAVE A TASTE...
...OF OUR TECHNIQUE!

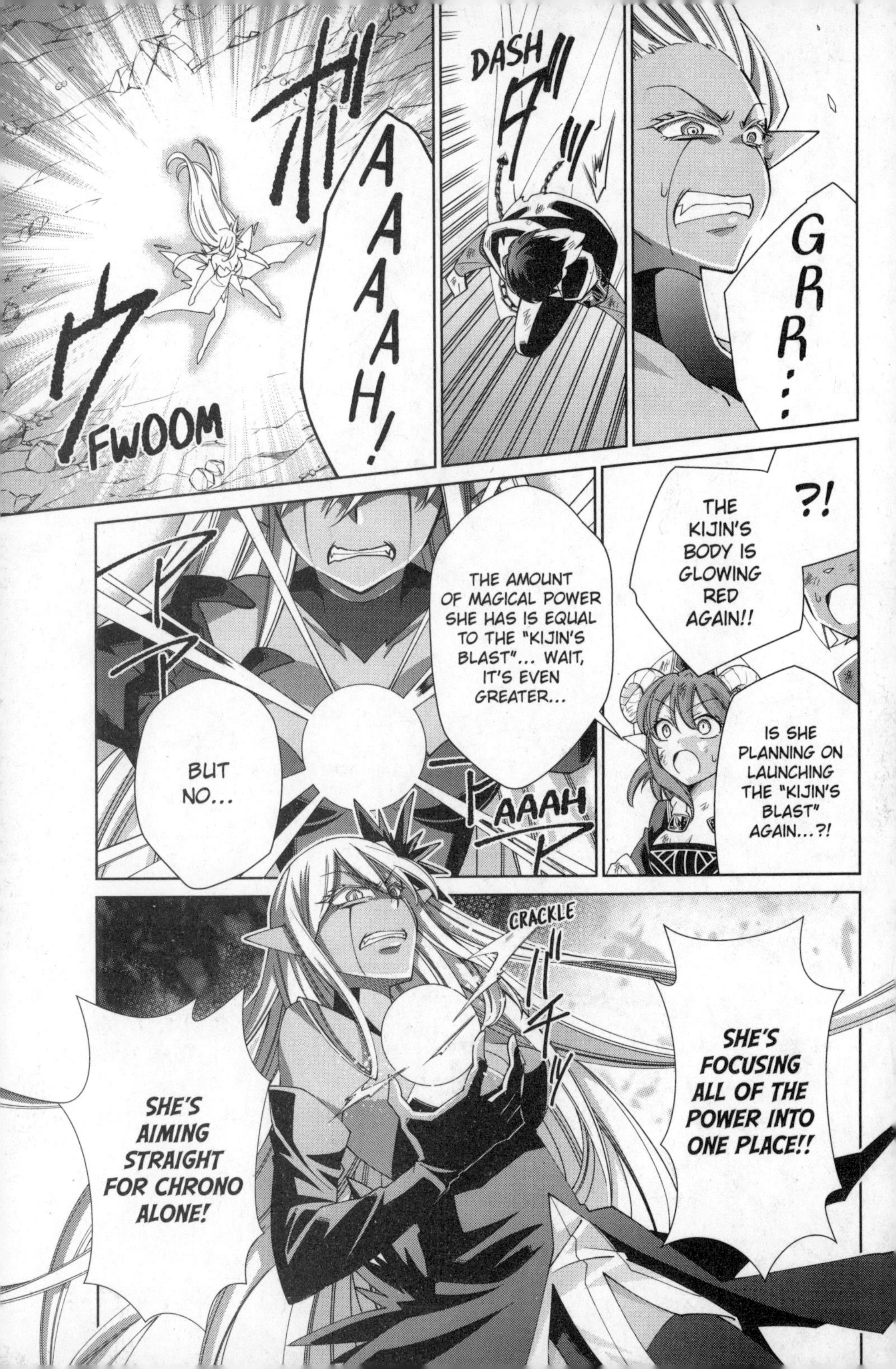
GRR...
DASH
AAAAAH!
FWOOM
?!
THE KIJIN'S BODY IS GLOWING RED AGAIN!!
IS SHE PLANNING ON LAUNCHING THE "KIJIN'S BLAST" AGAIN...?!
THE AMOUNT OF MAGICAL POWER SHE HAS IS EQUAL TO THE "KIJIN'S BLAST"... WAIT, IT'S EVEN GREATER...
AAAH
BUT NO...
SHE'S FOCUSING ALL OF THE POWER INTO ONE PLACE!!
CRACKLE
SHE'S AIMING STRAIGHT FOR CHRONO ALONE!

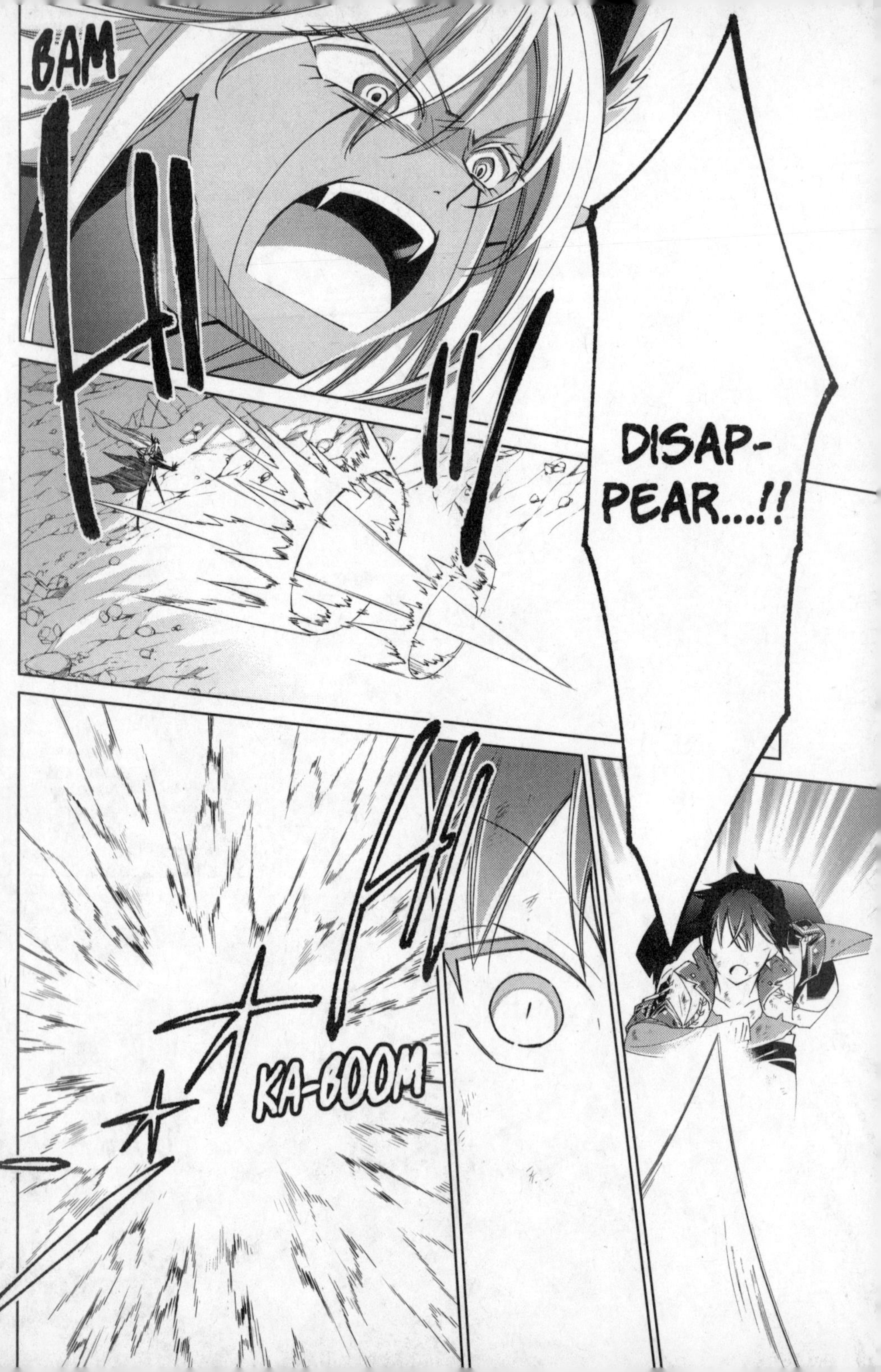
DISAP-
PEAR...!!
BAM
KA-BOOM

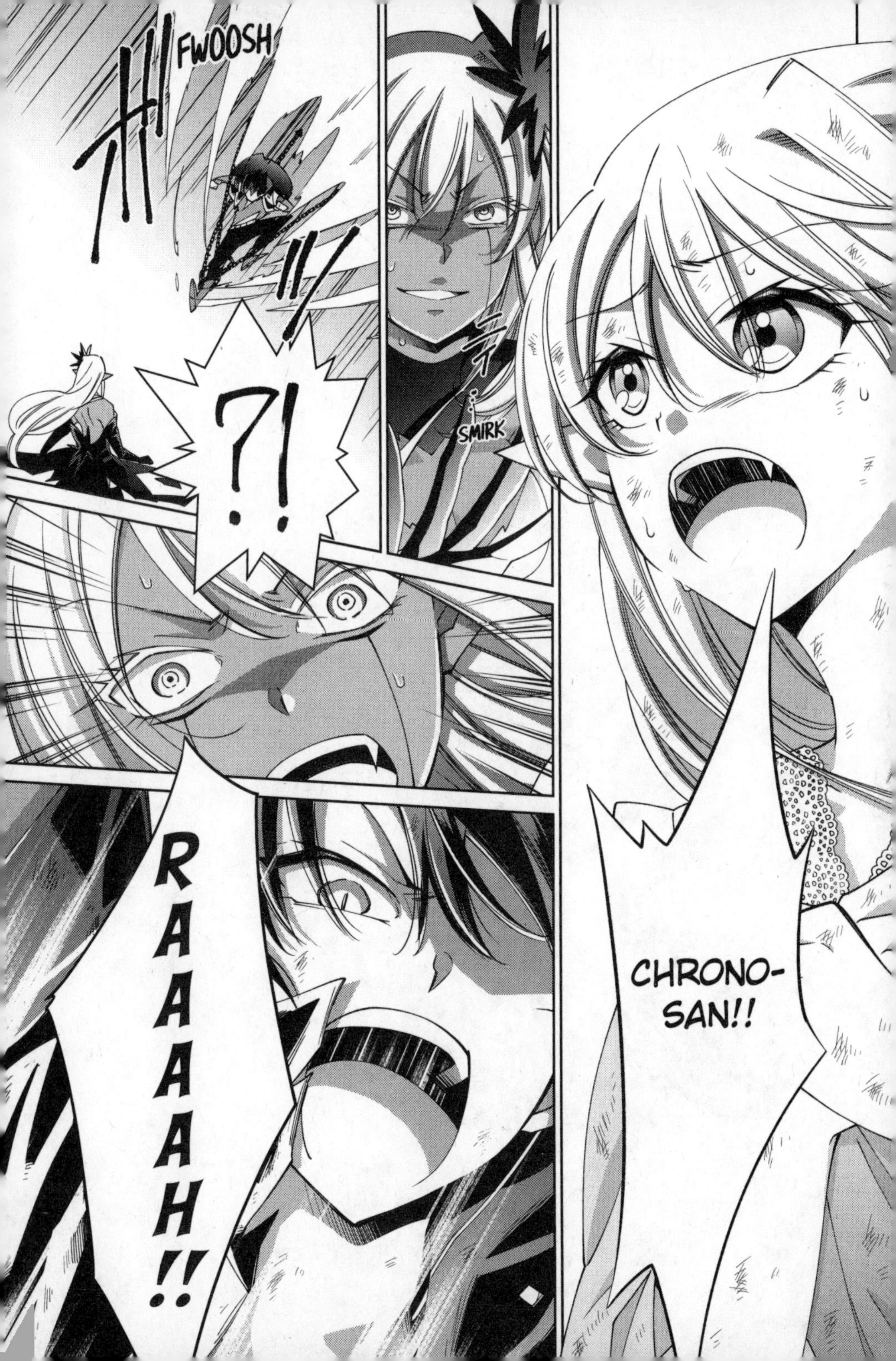
SMIRK
FWOOSH
?!
RAAAAH!!
CHRONO-SAN!!

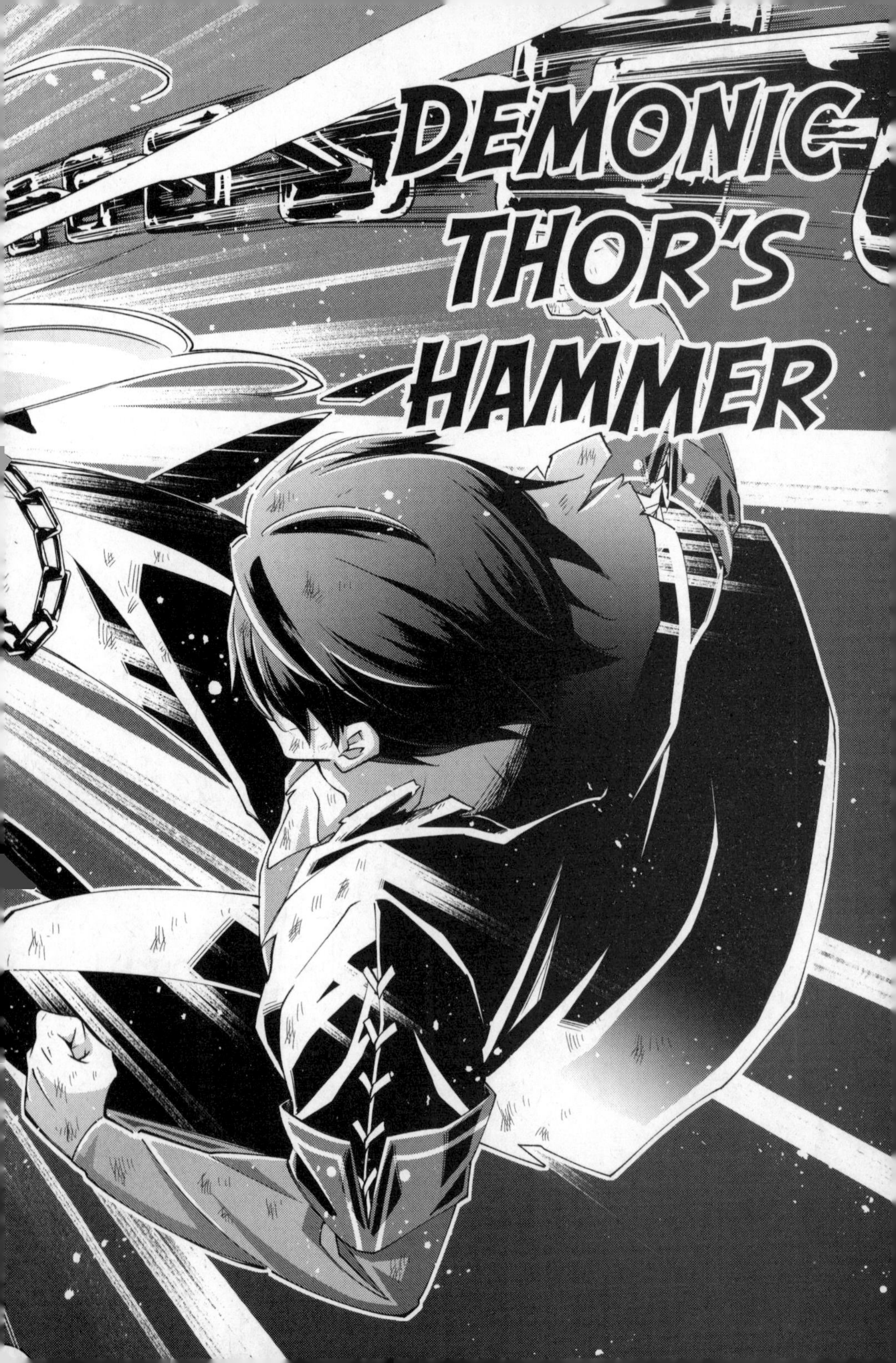
DEMONIC THOR'S HAMMER

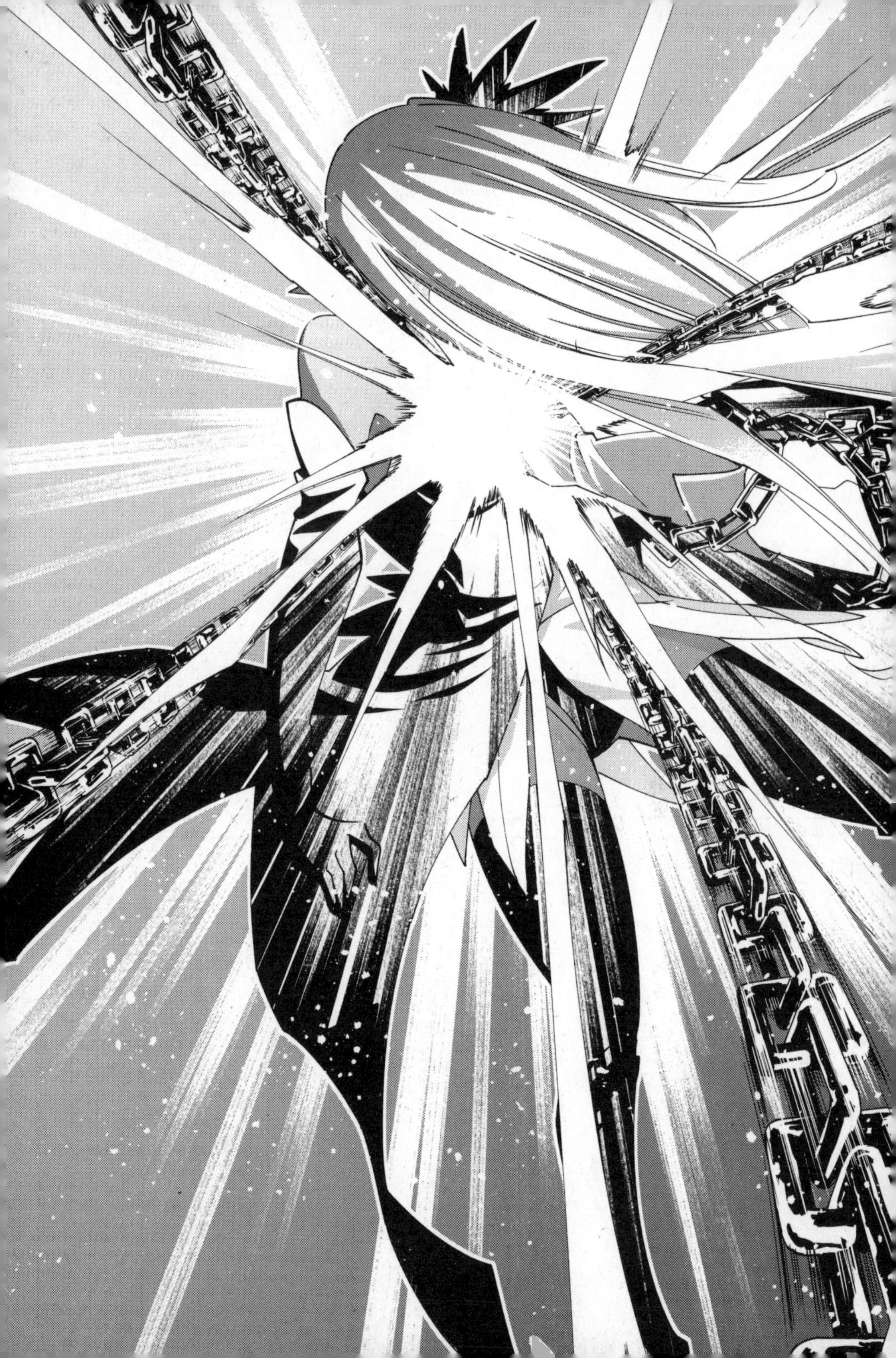

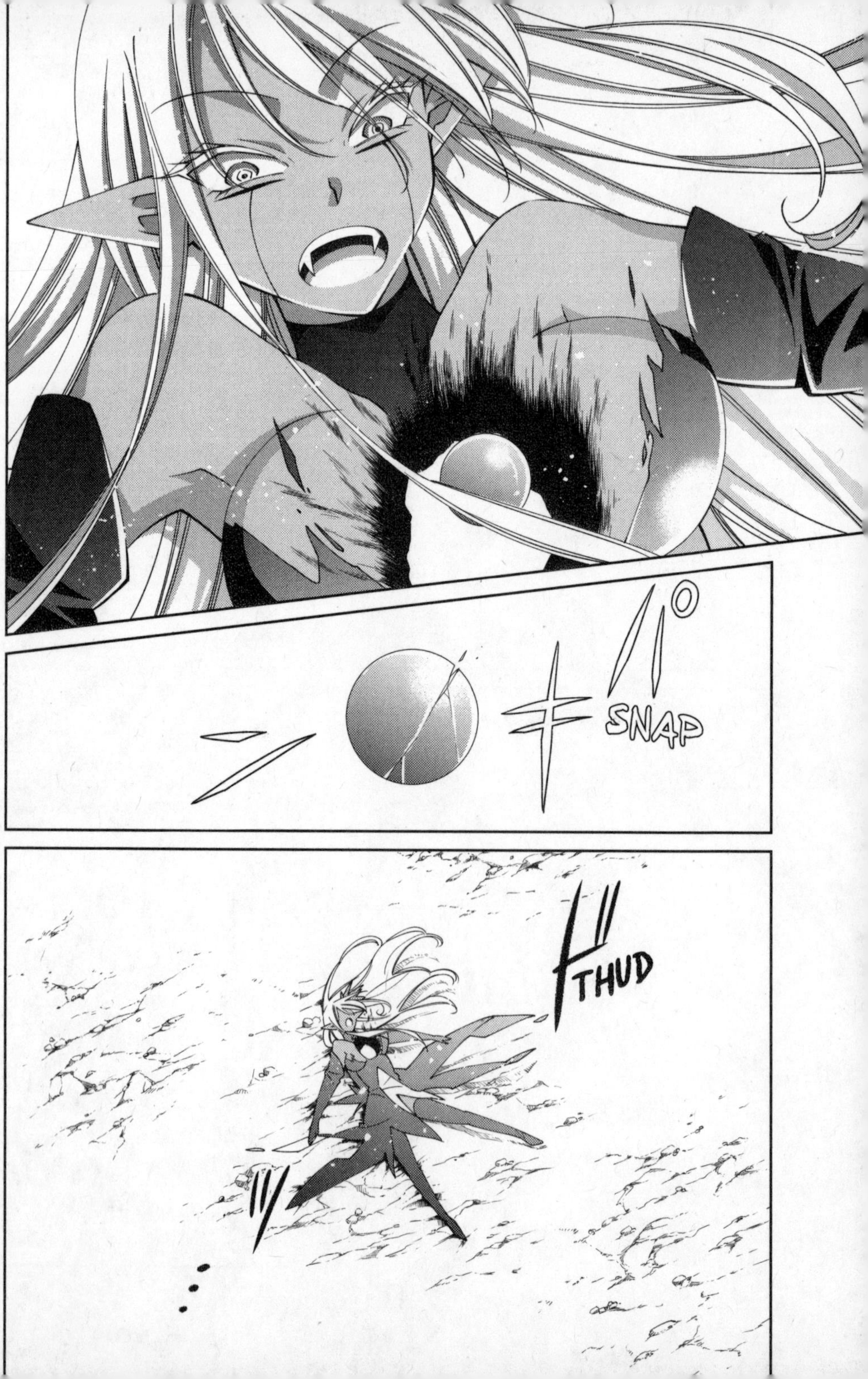
SNAP
THUD

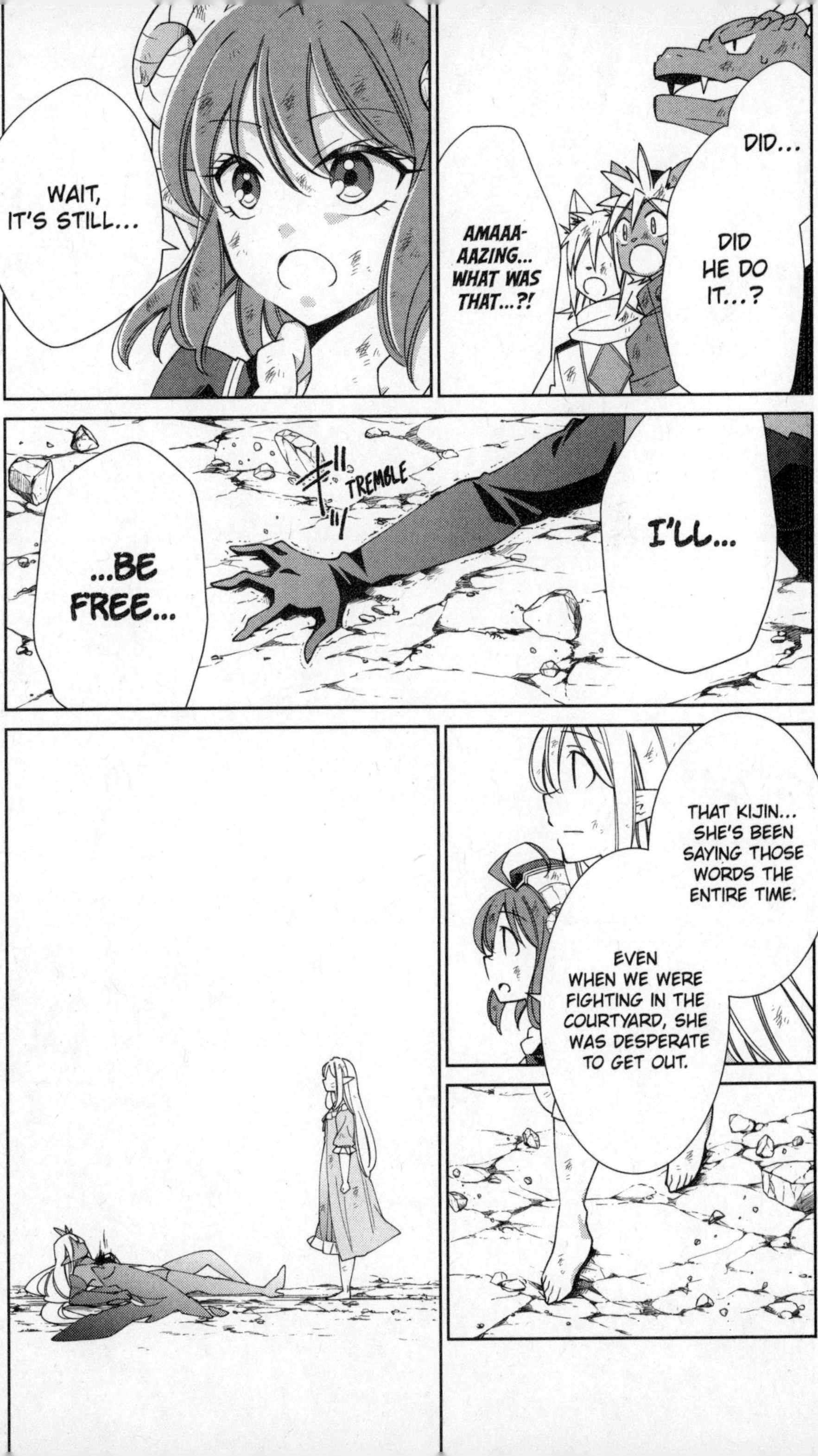
DID...
DID HE DO IT...?
AMAAAA-AAZING... WHAT WAS THAT...?!
WAIT, IT'S STILL...
I'LL...
TREMBLE
...BE FREE...
THAT KIJIN... SHE'S BEEN SAYING THOSE WORDS THE ENTIRE TIME.
EVEN WHEN WE WERE FIGHTING IN THE COURTYARD, SHE WAS DESPERATE TO GET OUT.

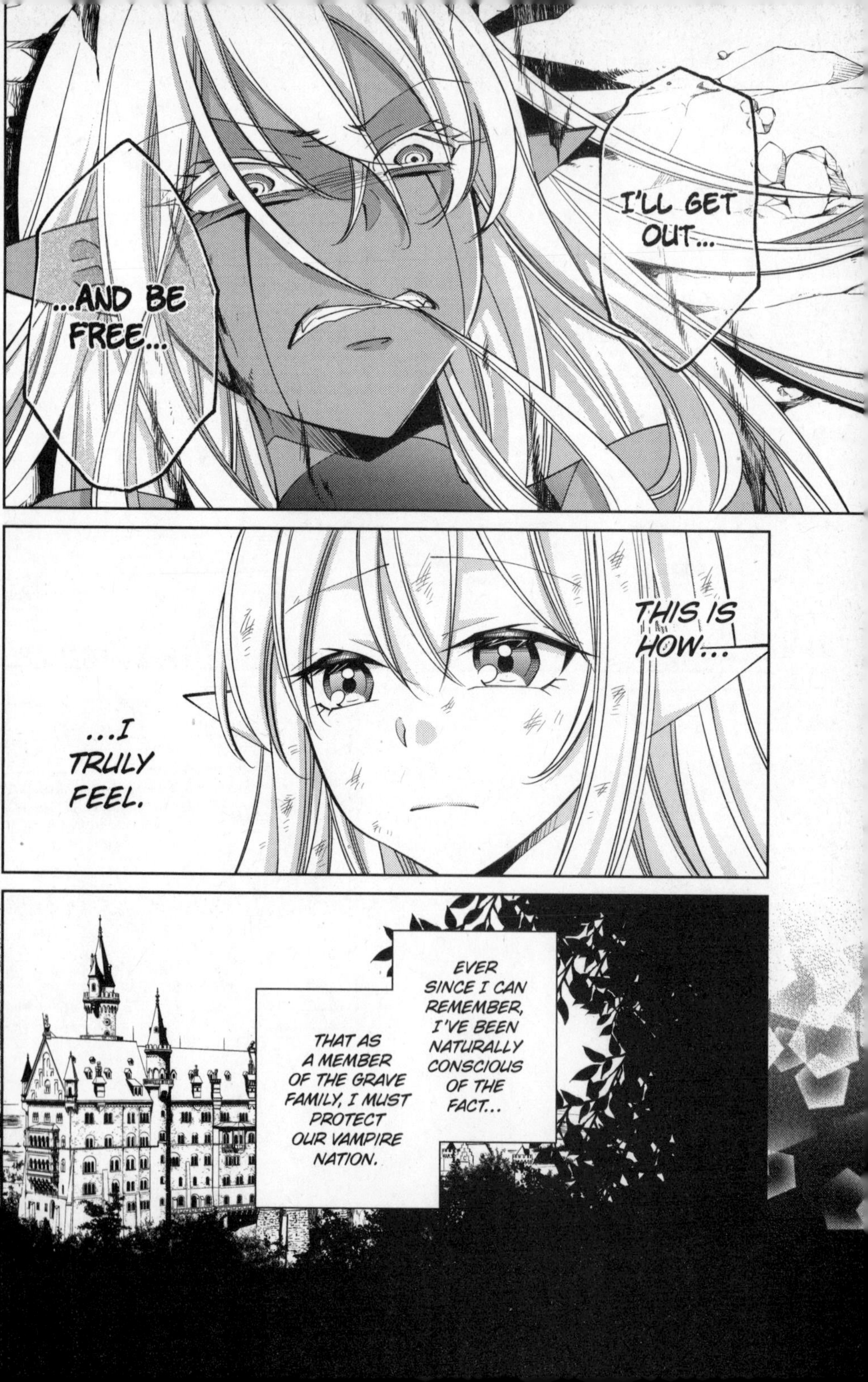
I'LL GET OUT...
...AND BE FREE...
THIS IS HOW...
...I TRULY FEEL.
EVER SINCE I CAN REMEMBER, I'VE BEEN NATURALLY CONSCIOUS OF THE FACT...
THAT AS A MEMBER OF THE GRAVE FAMILY, I MUST PROTECT OUR VAMPIRE NATION.

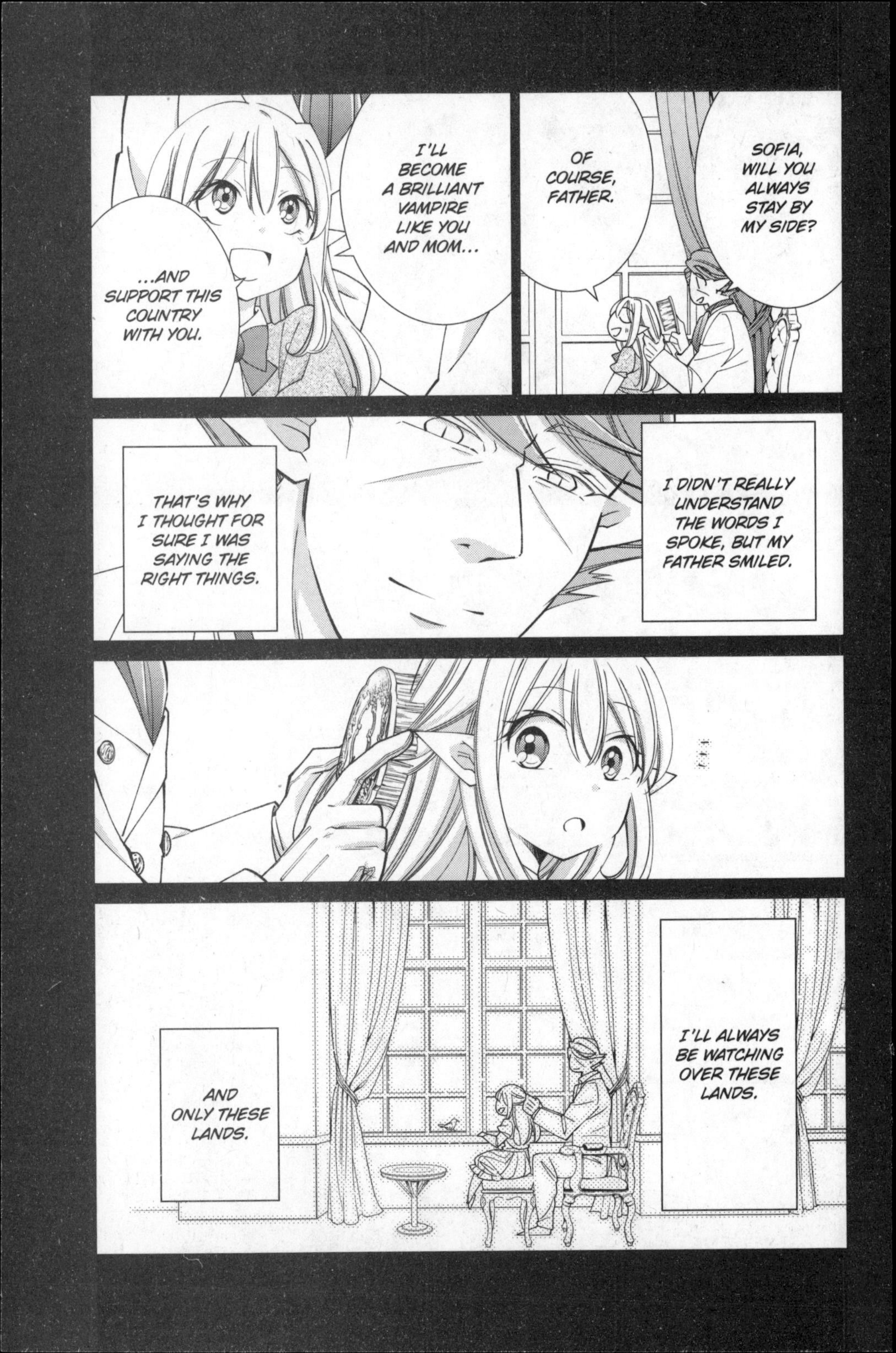
SOFIA, WILL YOU ALWAYS STAY BY MY SIDE?
OF COURSE, FATHER.
I'LL BECOME A BRILLIANT VAMPIRE LIKE YOU AND MOM...
...AND SUPPORT THIS COUNTRY WITH YOU.
I DIDN'T REALLY UNDERSTAND THE WORDS I SPOKE, BUT MY FATHER SMILED.
THAT'S WHY I THOUGHT FOR SURE I WAS SAYING THE RIGHT THINGS.
I'LL ALWAYS BE WATCHING OVER THESE LANDS.
AND ONLY THESE LANDS.

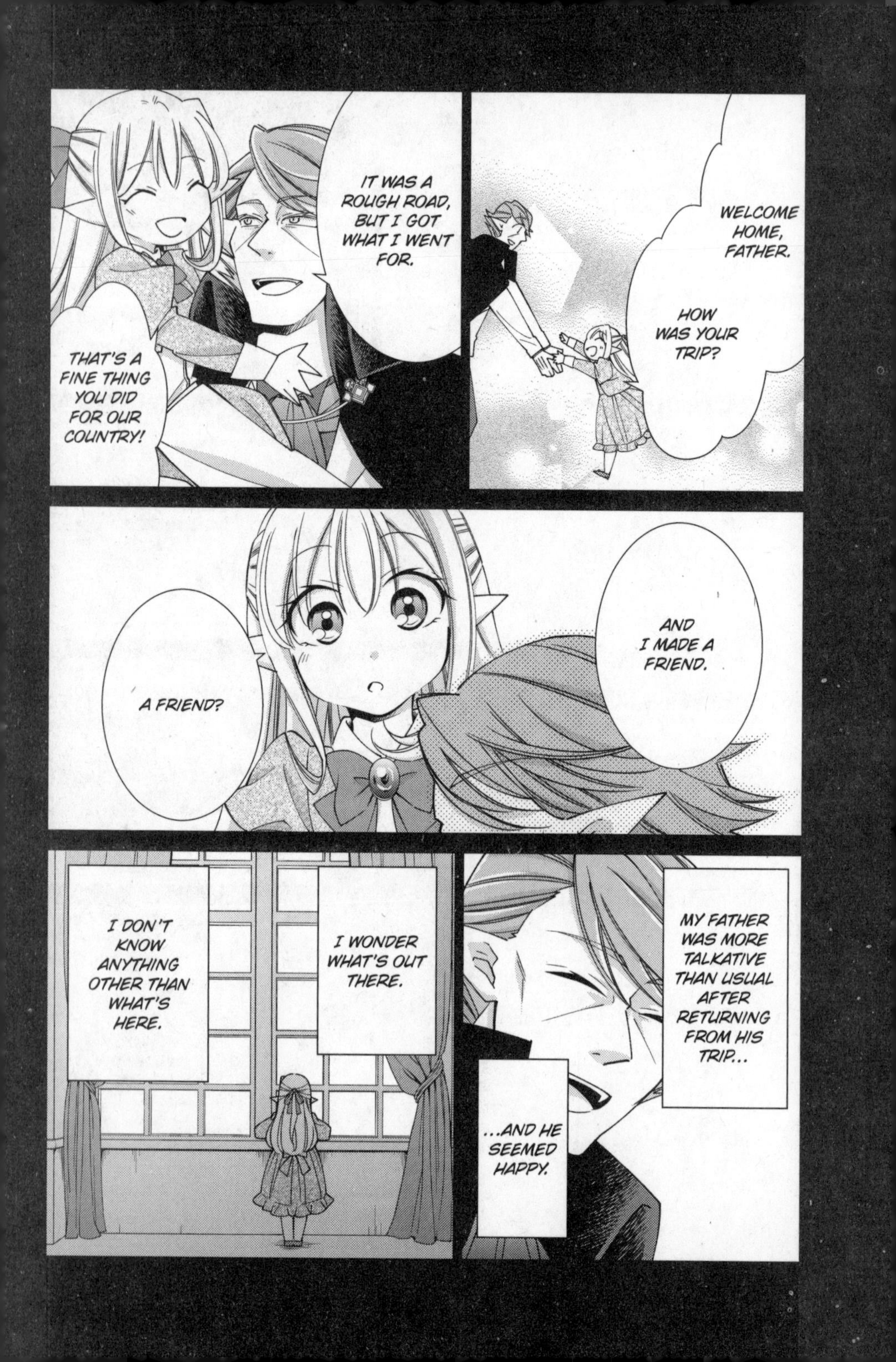
WELCOME HOME, FATHER.
HOW WAS YOUR TRIP?
IT WAS A ROUGH ROAD, BUT I GOT WHAT I WENT FOR.
THAT'S A FINE THING YOU DID FOR OUR COUNTRY!
AND I MADE A FRIEND.
A FRIEND?
MY FATHER WAS MORE TALKATIVE THAN USUAL AFTER RETURNING FROM HIS TRIP...
...AND HE SEEMED HAPPY.
I WONDER WHAT'S OUT THERE.
I DON'T KNOW ANYTHING OTHER THAN WHAT'S HERE.

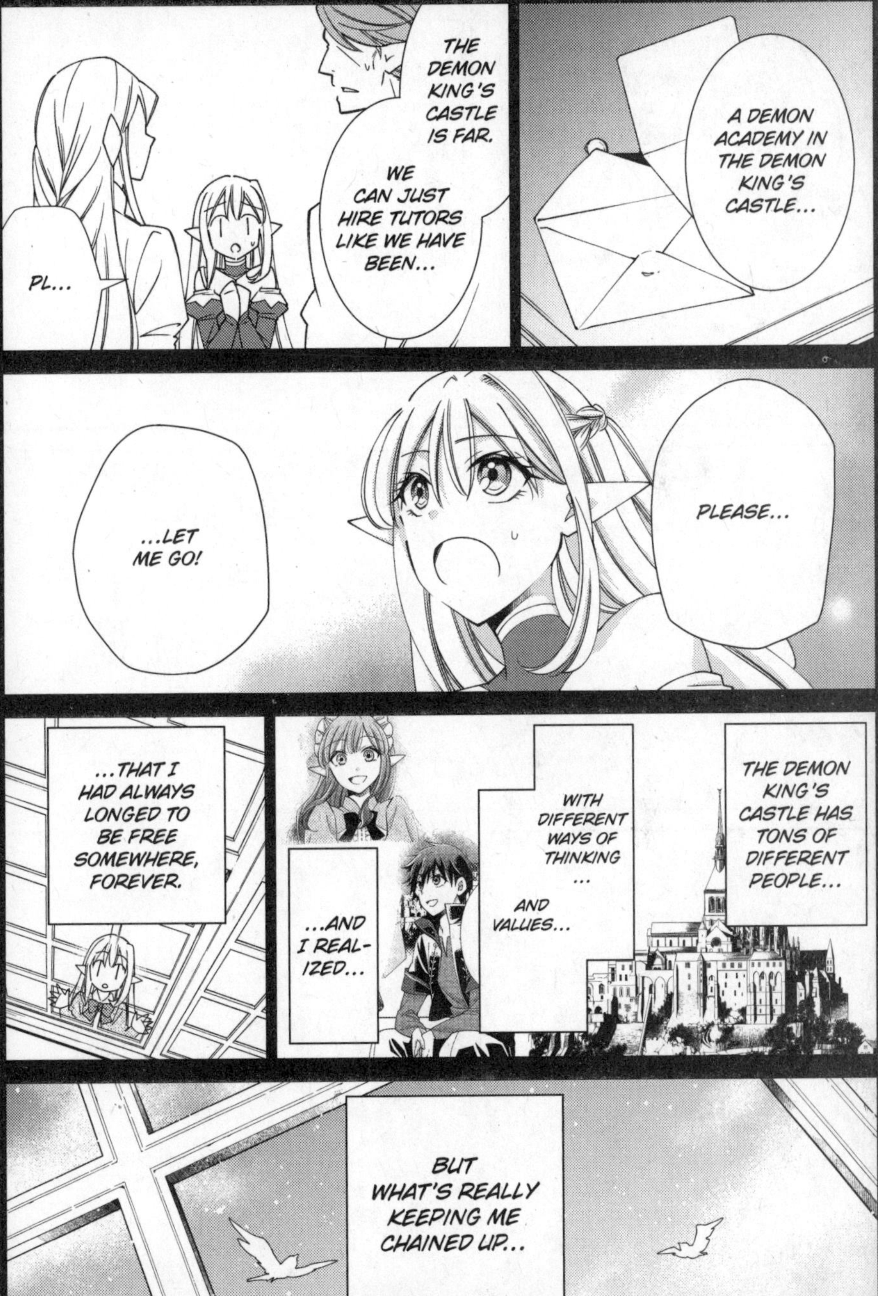
A DEMON ACADEMY IN THE DEMON KING'S CASTLE...
THE DEMON KING'S CASTLE IS FAR.
WE CAN JUST HIRE TUTORS LIKE WE HAVE BEEN...
PL...
PLEASE...
...LET ME GO!
THE DEMON KING'S CASTLE HAS TONS OF DIFFERENT PEOPLE...
WITH DIFFERENT WAYS OF THINKING...
AND VALUES...
...AND I REAL-IZED...
...THAT I HAD ALWAYS LONGED TO BE FREE SOMEWHERE, FOREVER.
BUT WHAT'S REALLY KEEPING ME CHAINED UP...

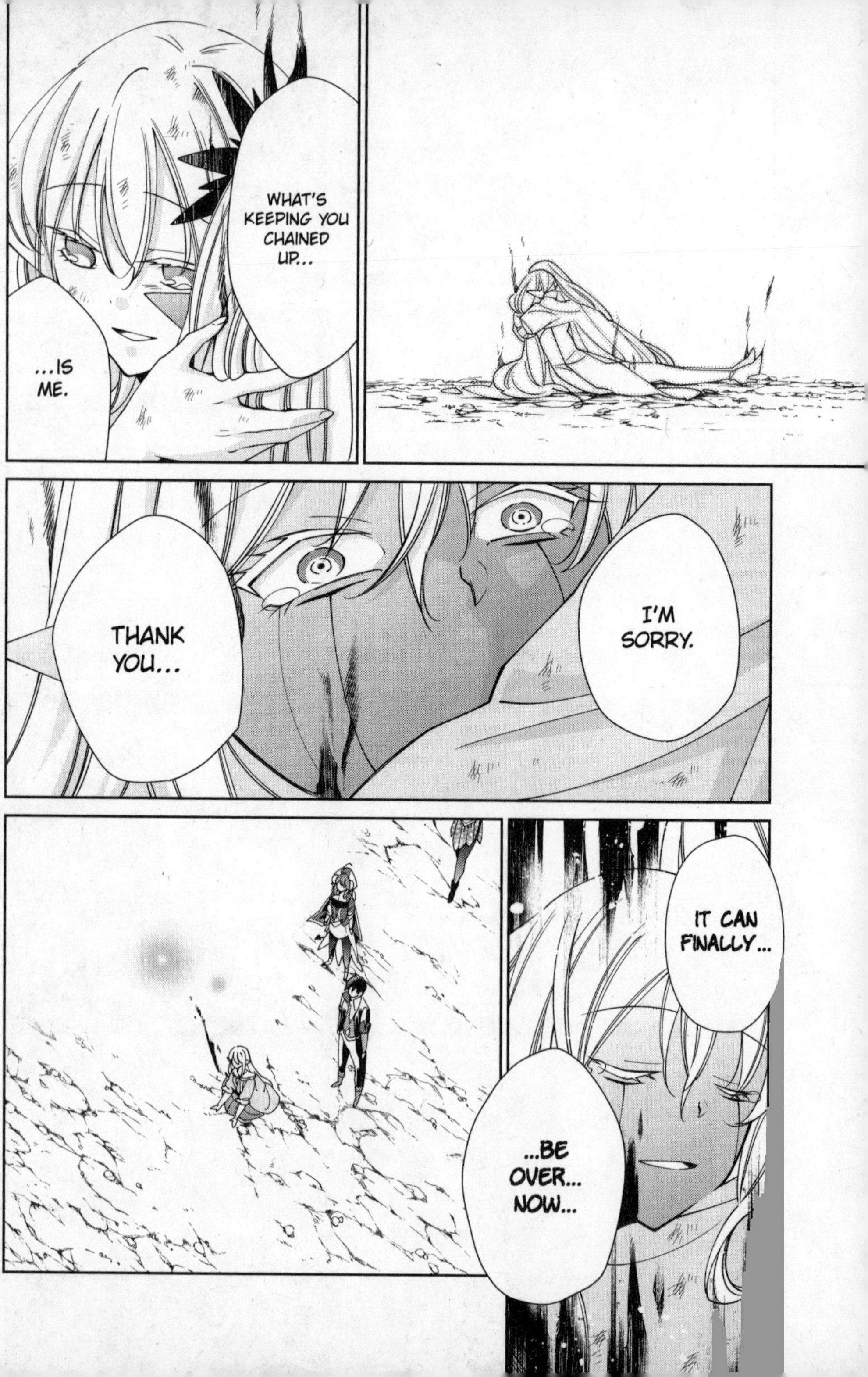
WHAT'S KEEPING YOU CHAINED UP...
...IS ME.
I'M SORRY.
THANK YOU...
IT CAN FINALLY...
...BE OVER... NOW...

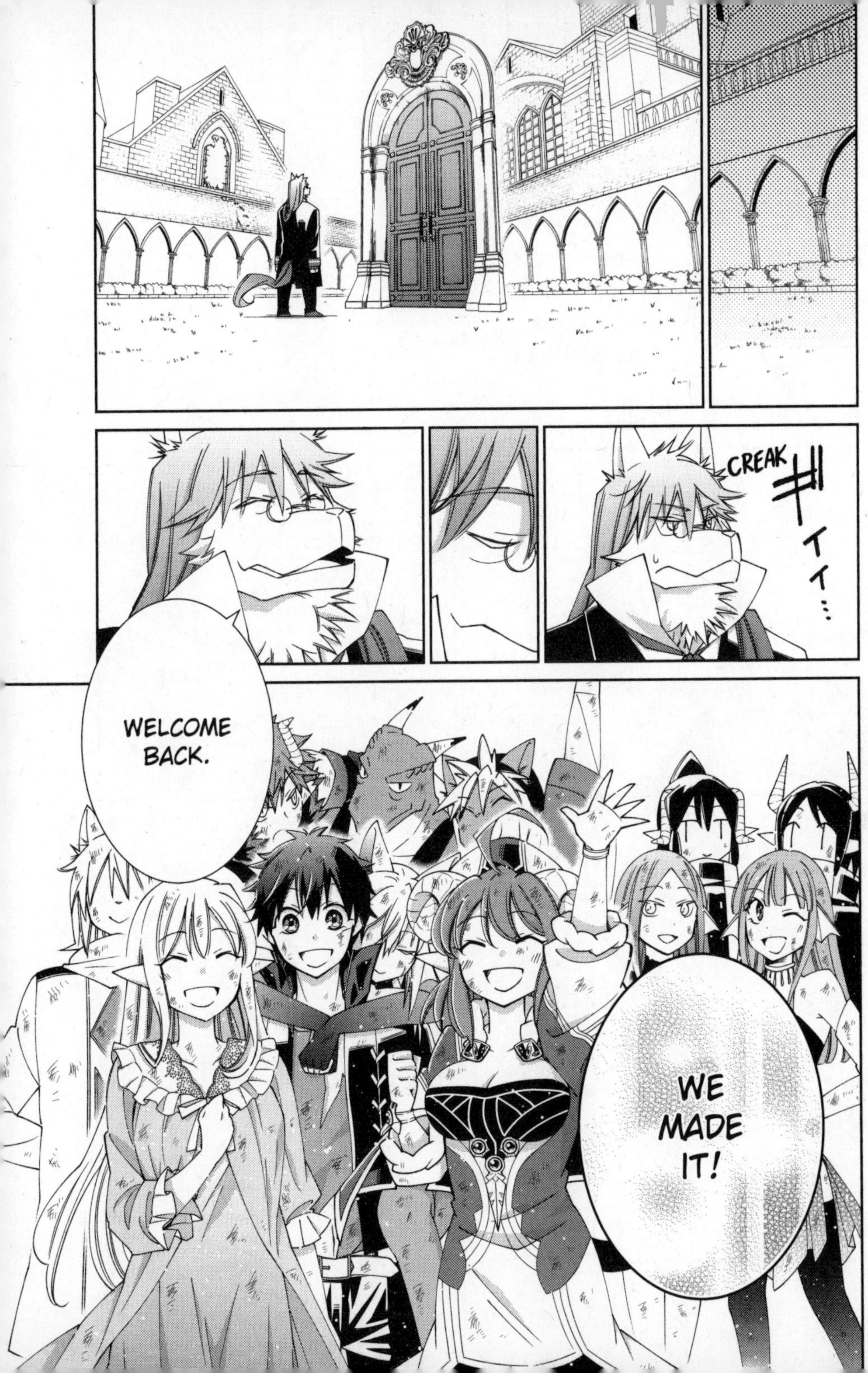
CREAK
WELCOME BACK.
WE MADE IT!

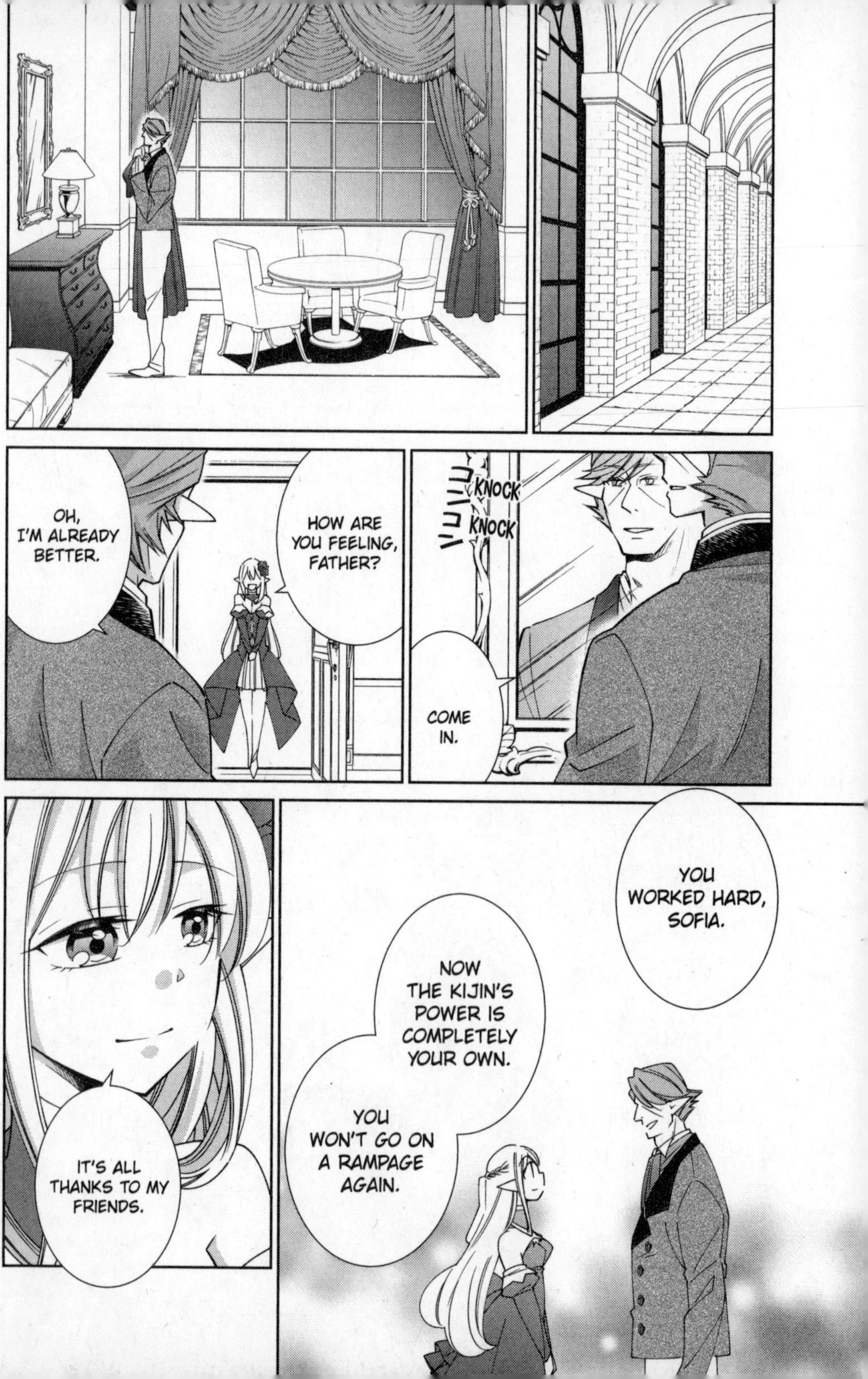
KNOCK
KNOCK
COME IN.
HOW ARE YOU FEELING, FATHER?
OH, I'M ALREADY BETTER.
YOU WORKED HARD, SOFIA.
NOW THE KIJIN'S POWER IS COMPLETELY YOUR OWN.
YOU WON'T GO ON A RAMPAGE AGAIN.
IT'S ALL THANKS TO MY FRIENDS.

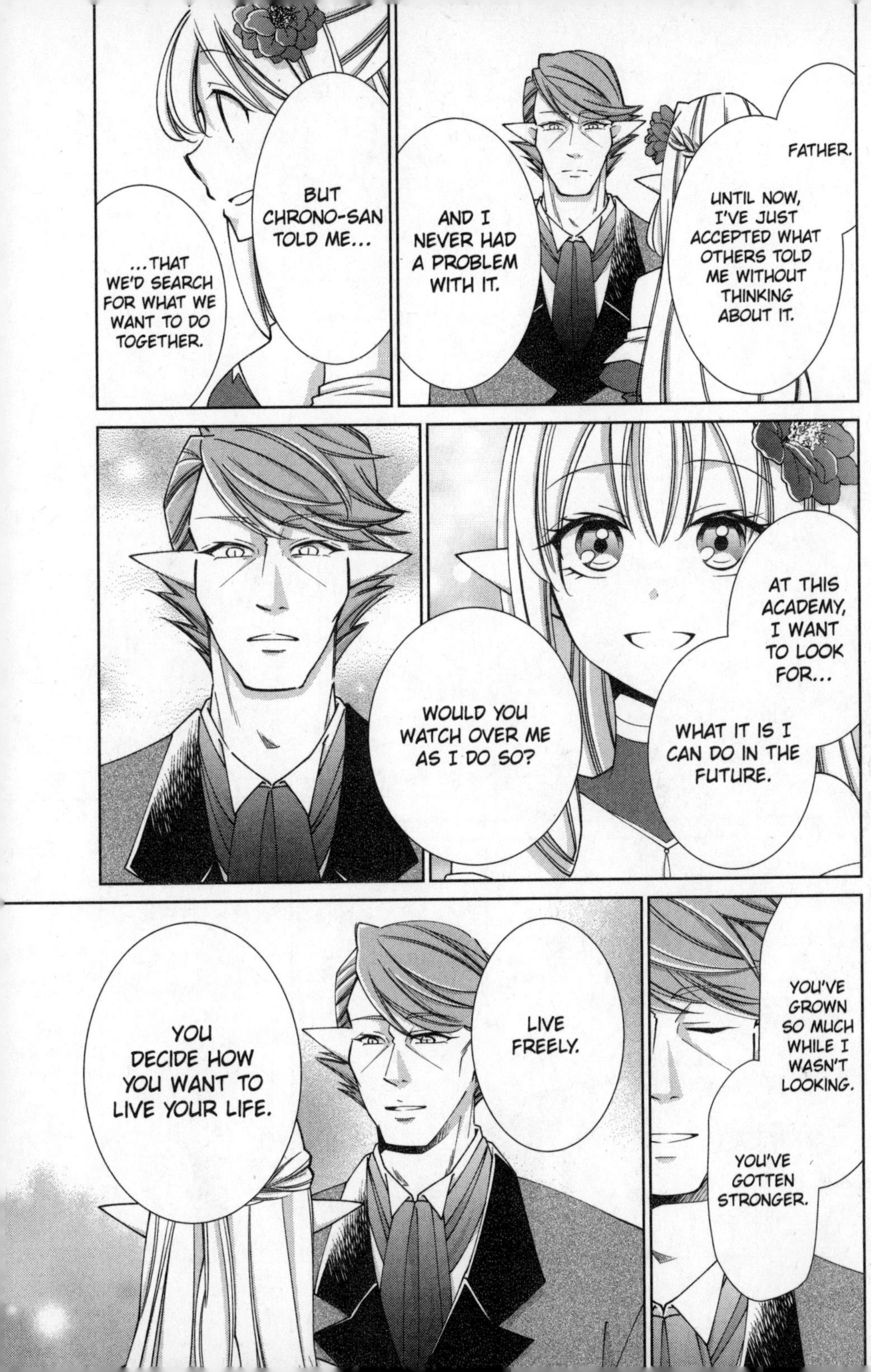
FATHER.
UNTIL NOW, I'VE JUST ACCEPTED WHAT OTHERS TOLD ME WITHOUT THINKING ABOUT IT.
AND I NEVER HAD A PROBLEM WITH IT.
BUT CHRONO-SAN TOLD ME...
...THAT WE'D SEARCH FOR WHAT WE WANT TO DO TOGETHER.
AT THIS ACADEMY, I WANT TO LOOK FOR...
WHAT IT IS I CAN DO IN THE FUTURE.
WOULD YOU WATCH OVER ME AS I DO SO?
YOU'VE GROWN SO MUCH WHILE I WASN'T LOOKING.
YOU'VE GOTTEN STRONGER.
LIVE FREELY.
YOU DECIDE HOW YOU WANT TO LIVE YOUR LIFE.

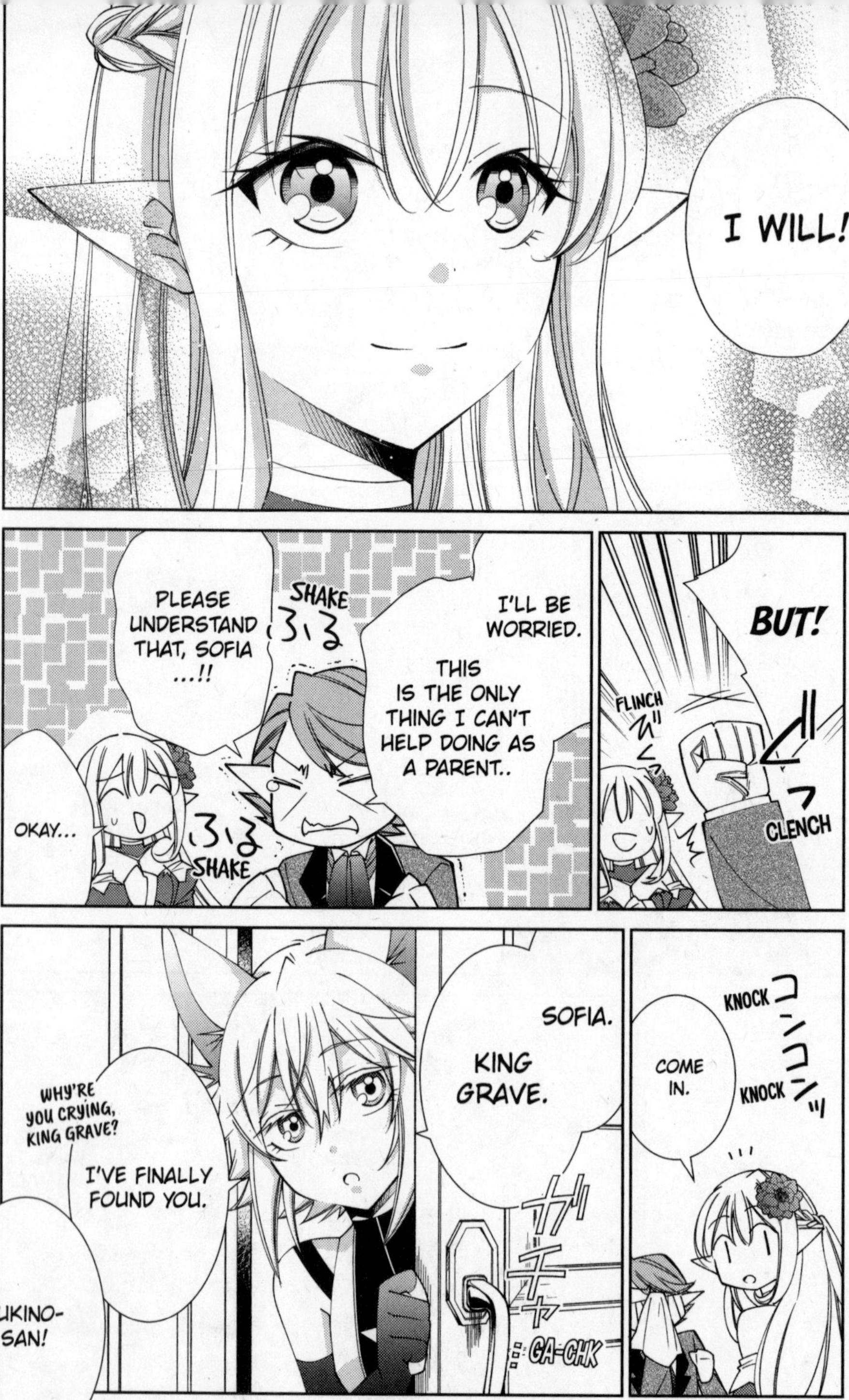
I WILL!
BUT!
FLINCH
CLENCH
I'LL BE WORRIED.
THIS IS THE ONLY THING I CAN'T HELP DOING AS A PARENT..
SHAKE ふる
PLEASE UNDERSTAND THAT, SOFIA ...!!
OKAY...
ふる SHAKE
KNOCK
KNOCK
COME IN.
GA-CHK
SOFIA.
KING GRAVE.
WHY'RE YOU CRYING, KING GRAVE?
I'VE FINALLY FOUND YOU.
YUKINO-SAN!

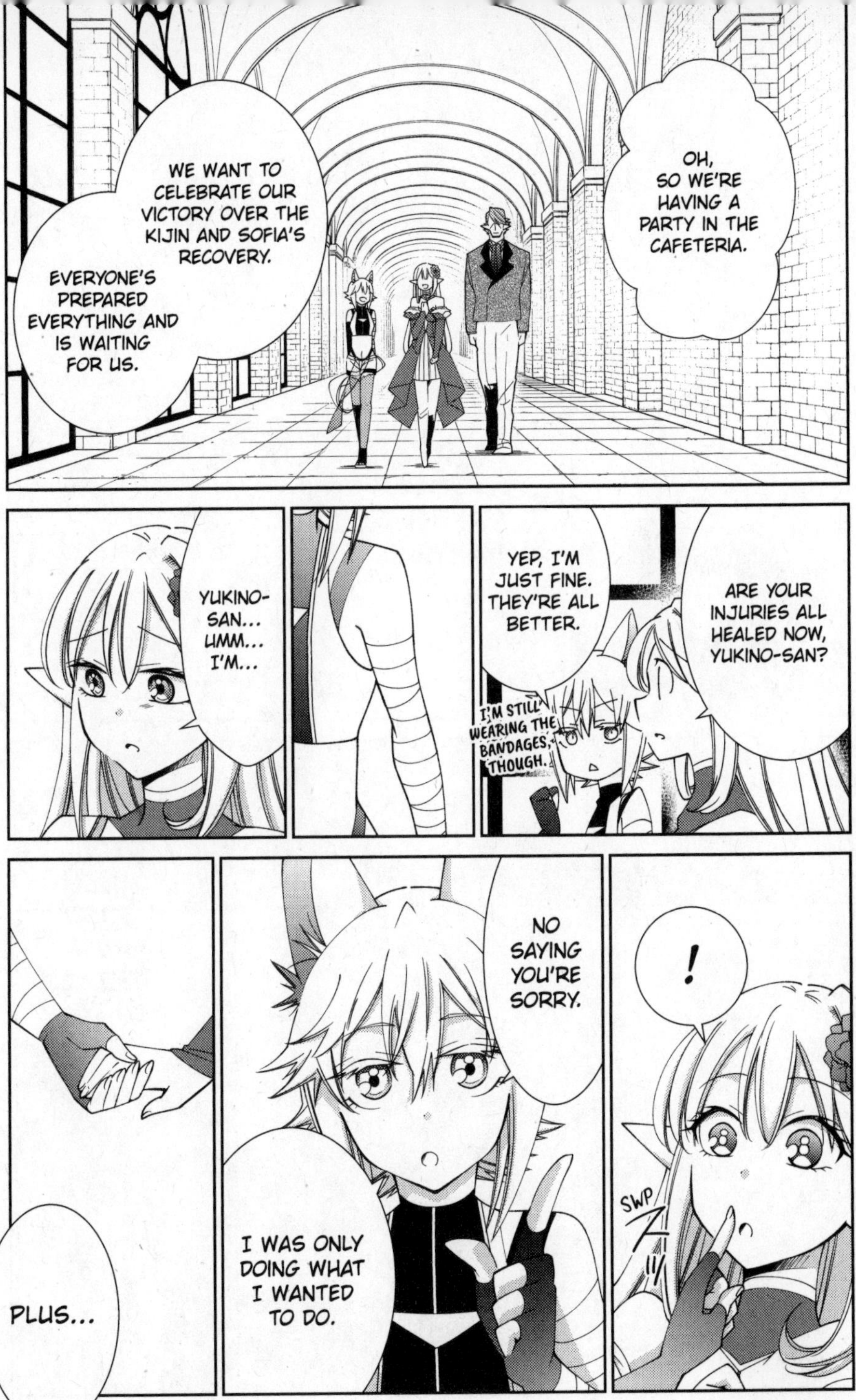
OH, SO WE'RE HAVING A PARTY IN THE CAFETERIA.
WE WANT TO CELEBRATE OUR VICTORY OVER THE KIJIN AND SOFIA'S RECOVERY.
EVERYONE'S PREPARED EVERYTHING AND IS WAITING FOR US.
ARE YOUR INJURIES ALL HEALED NOW, YUKINO-SAN?
YEP, I'M JUST FINE. THEY'RE ALL BETTER.
I'M STILL WEARING THE BANDAGES, THOUGH.
YUKINO-SAN... UMM... I'M...
!
SWP
NO SAYING YOU'RE SORRY.
I WAS ONLY DOING WHAT I WANTED TO DO.
PLUS...

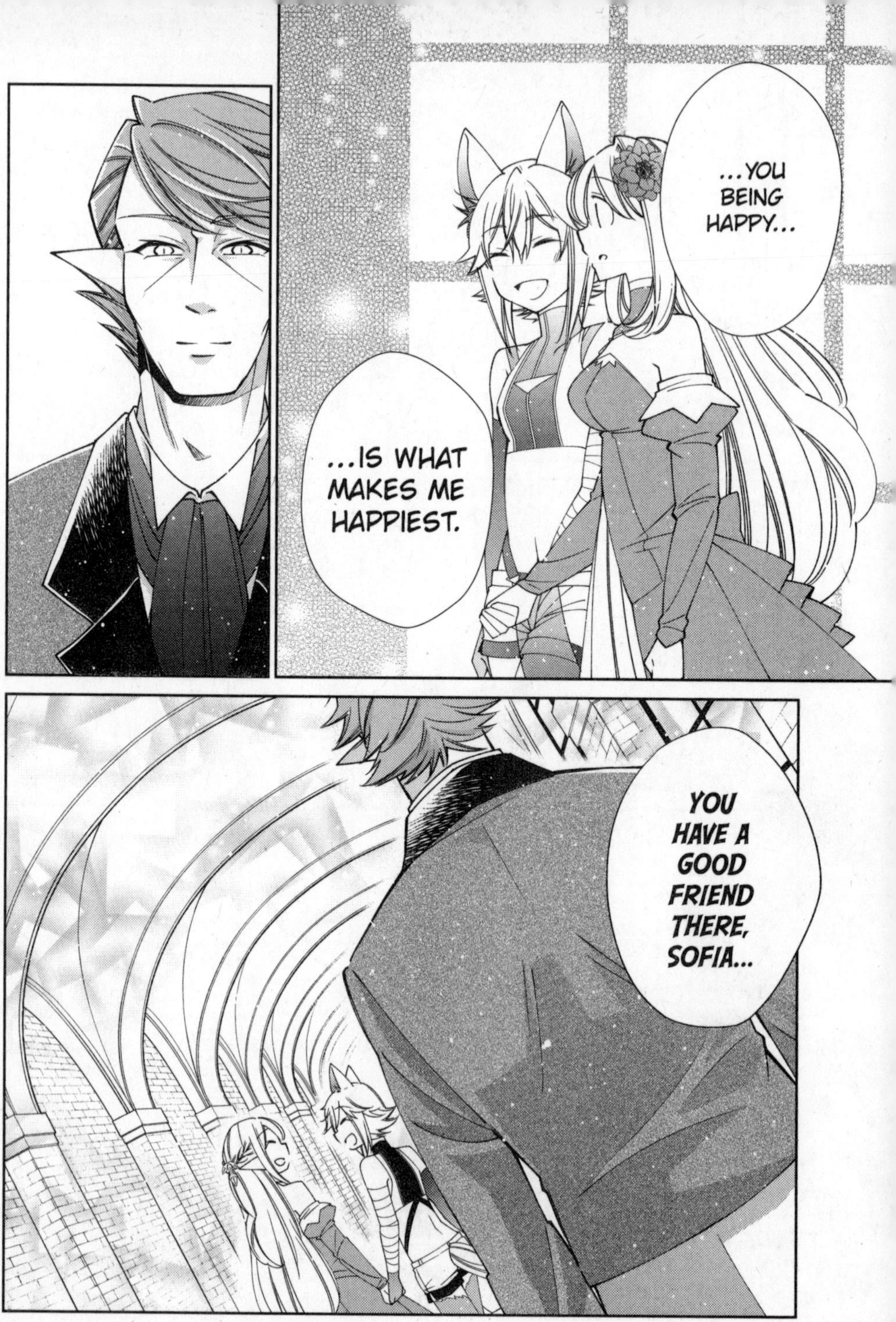
...YOU BEING HAPPY...
...IS WHAT MAKES ME HAPPIEST.
YOU HAVE A GOOD FRIEND THERE, SOFIA...

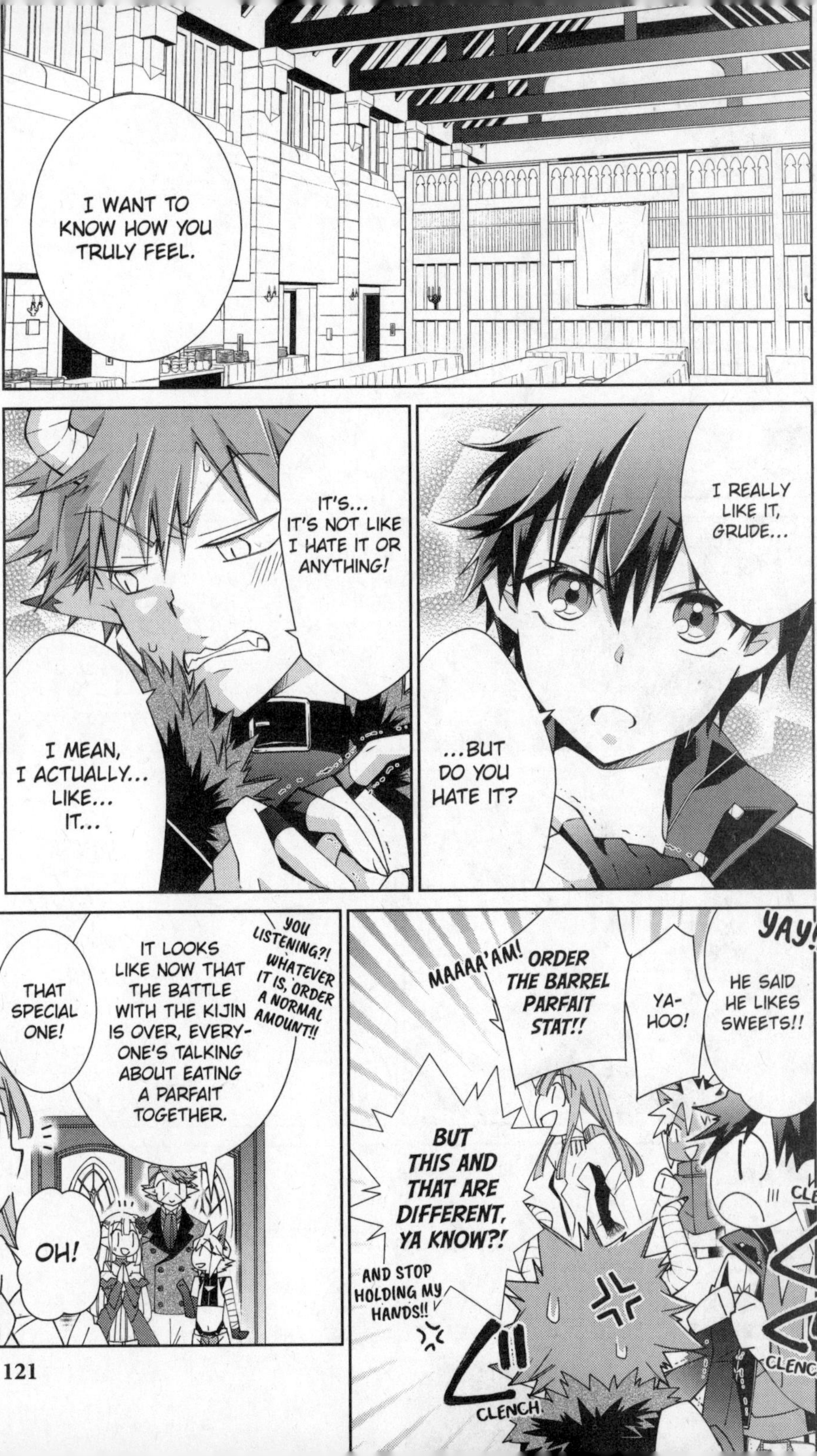

I WANT TO KNOW HOW YOU TRULY FEEL.
I REALLY LIKE IT, GRUDE...
...BUT DO YOU HATE IT?
IT'S... IT'S NOT LIKE I HATE IT OR ANYTHING!
I MEAN, I ACTUALLY... LIKE... IT...
YAY!!
HE SAID HE LIKES SWEETS!!
YA-HOO!
ORDER THE BARREL PARFAIT STAT!!
MAAAA'AM!
BUT THIS AND THAT ARE DIFFERENT, YA KNOW?!
AND STOP HOLDING MY HANDS!!
CLENCH
CLENCH
CLENCH
IT LOOKS LIKE NOW THAT THE BATTLE WITH THE KIJIN IS OVER, EVERY-ONE'S TALKING ABOUT EATING A PARFAIT TOGETHER.
THAT SPECIAL ONE!
YOU LISTENING?! WHATEVER IT IS, ORDER A NORMAL AMOUNT!!
OH!

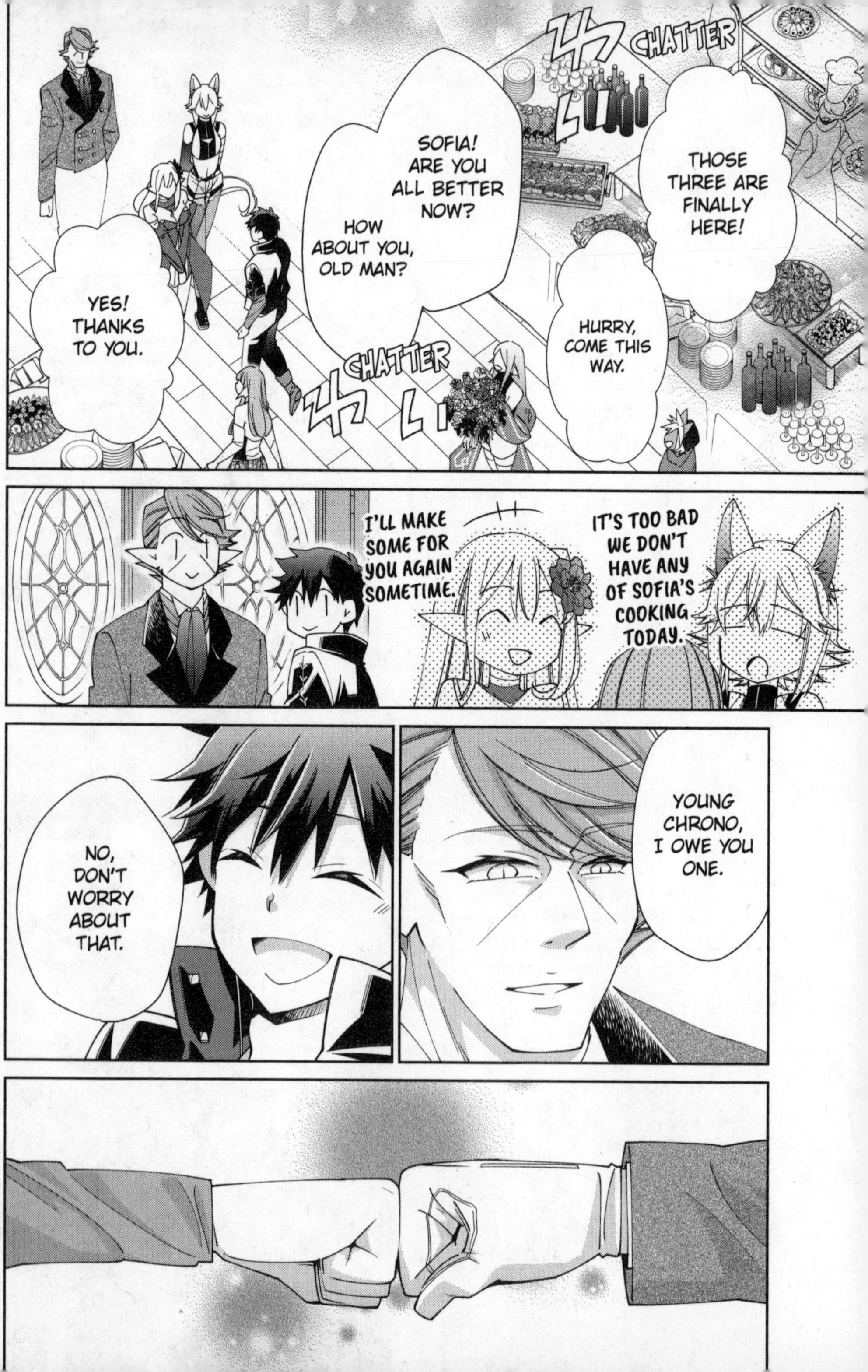
CHATTER
THOSE THREE ARE FINALLY HERE!
HURRY, COME THIS WAY.
SOFIA! ARE YOU ALL BETTER NOW?
HOW ABOUT YOU, OLD MAN?
CHATTER
YES! THANKS TO YOU.
IT'S TOO BAD WE DON'T HAVE ANY OF SOFIA'S COOKING TODAY.
I'LL MAKE SOME FOR YOU AGAIN SOMETIME.
YOUNG CHRONO, I OWE YOU ONE.
NO, DON'T WORRY ABOUT THAT.

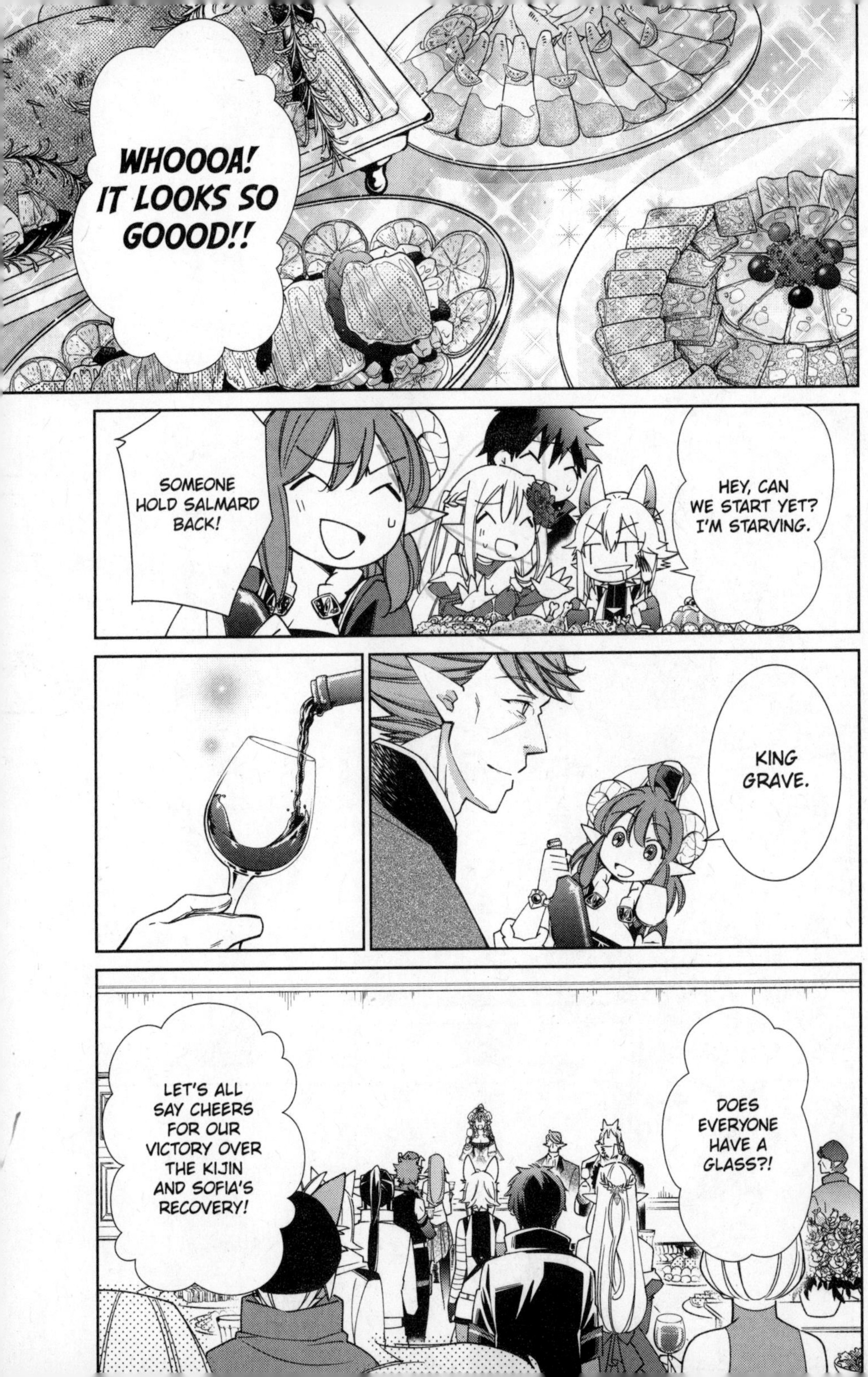
WHOOOA! IT LOOKS SO GOOOD!!
HEY, CAN WE START YET? I'M STARVING.
SOMEONE HOLD SALMARD BACK!
KING GRAVE.
DOES EVERYONE HAVE A GLASS?!
LET'S ALL SAY CHEERS FOR OUR VICTORY OVER THE KIJIN AND SOFIA'S RECOVERY!

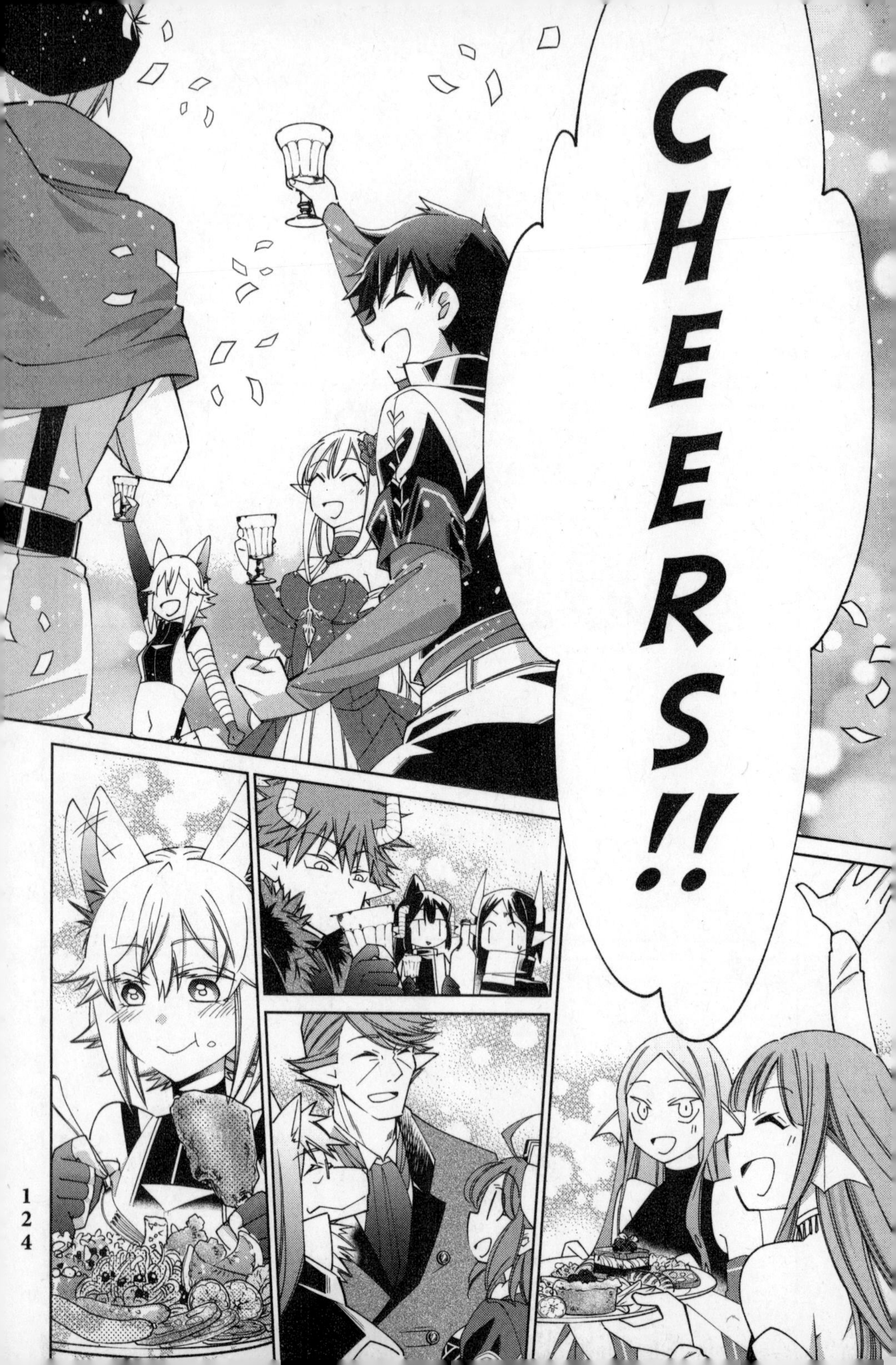
CHEERS!!

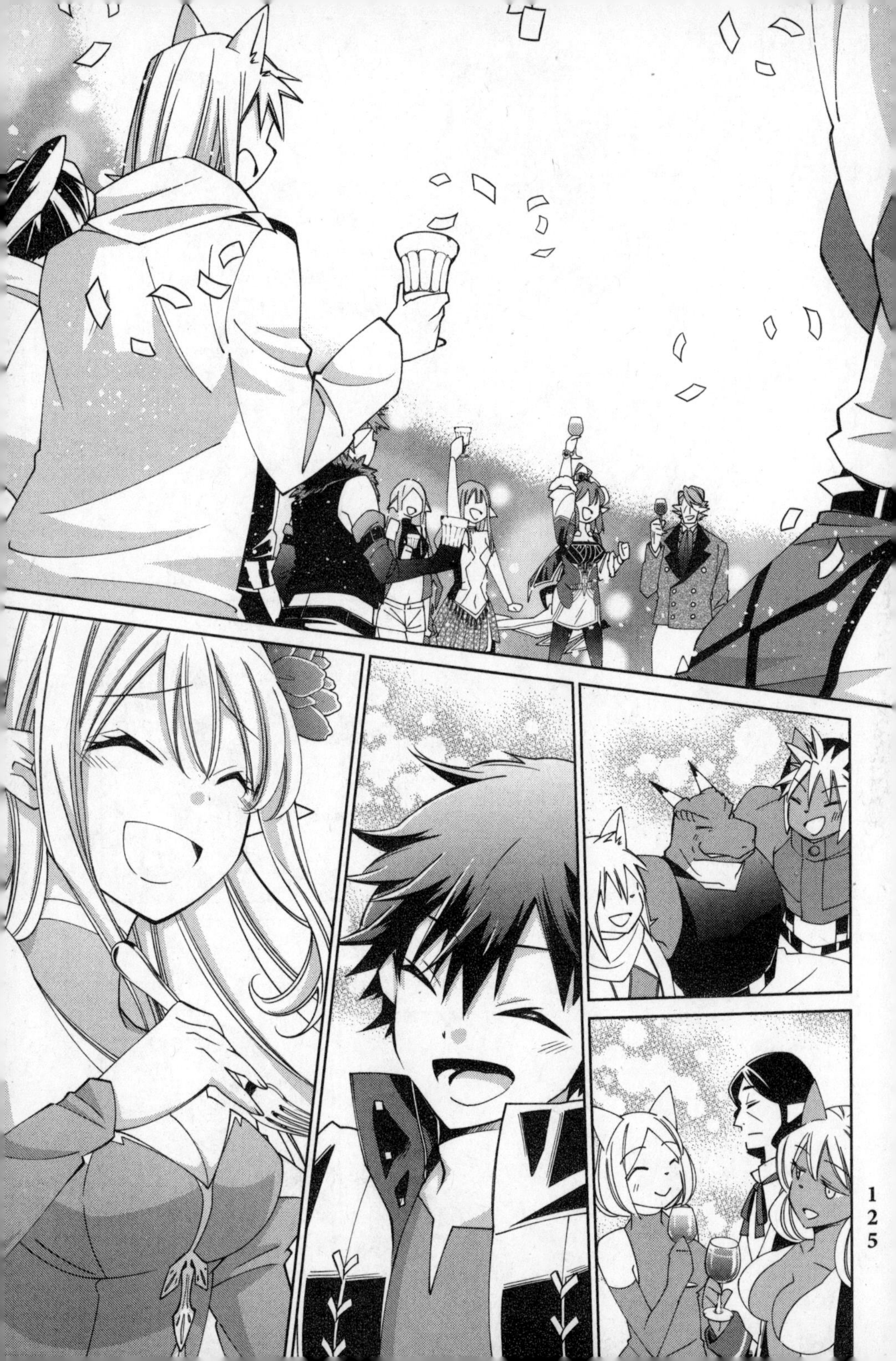

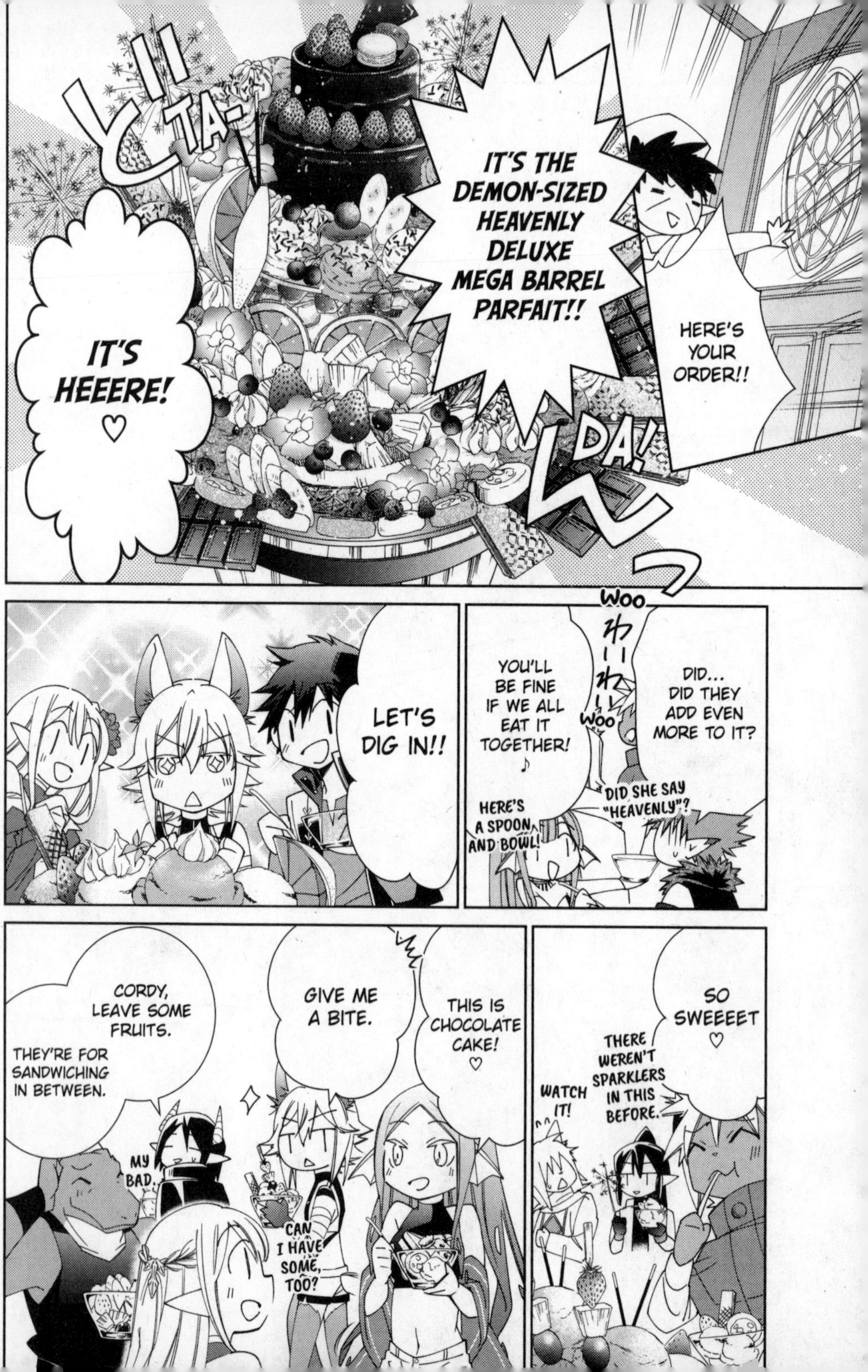
HERE'S YOUR ORDER!!
IT'S THE DEMON-SIZED HEAVENLY DELUXE MEGA BARREL PARFAIT!!
TA-
DA!
IT'S HEEERE! ♡
Woo
Woo
DID... DID THEY ADD EVEN MORE TO IT?
DID SHE SAY "HEAVENLY"?
YOU'LL BE FINE IF WE ALL EAT IT TOGETHER! ♪
HERE'S A SPOON AND BOWL!
LET'S DIG IN!!
SO SWEEEET ♡
THERE WEREN'T SPARKLERS IN THIS BEFORE.
WATCH IT!
THIS IS CHOCOLATE CAKE! ♡
GIVE ME A BITE.
CAN I HAVE SOME, TOO?
CORDY, LEAVE SOME FRUITS.
THEY'RE FOR SANDWICHING IN BETWEEN.
MY BAD.

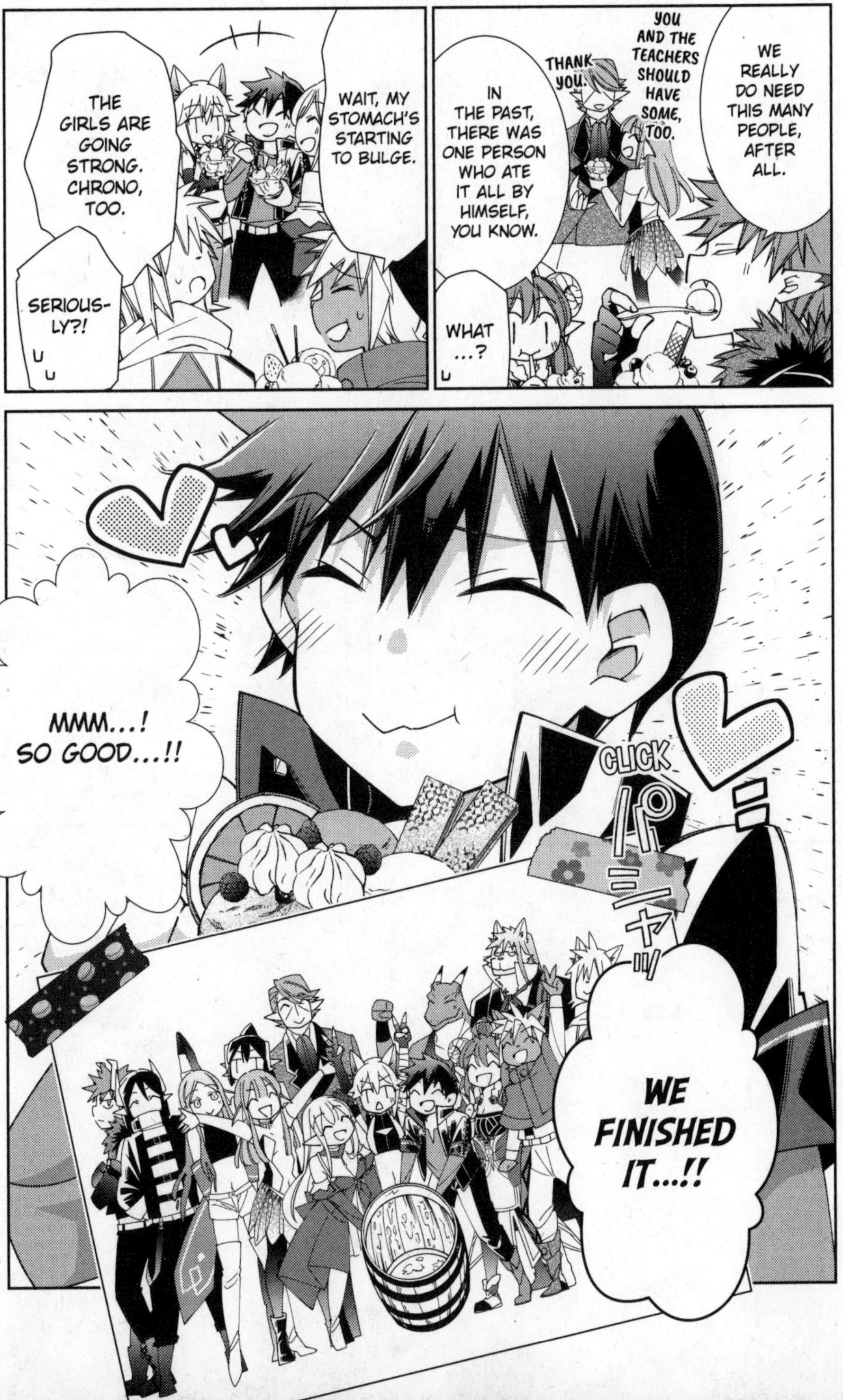
WE REALLY DO NEED THIS MANY PEOPLE, AFTER ALL.
YOU AND THE TEACHERS SHOULD HAVE SOME, TOO.
THANK YOU.
IN THE PAST, THERE WAS ONE PERSON WHO ATE IT ALL BY HIMSELF, YOU KNOW.
WHAT ...?
WAIT, MY STOMACH'S STARTING TO BULGE.
THE GIRLS ARE GOING STRONG. CHRONO, TOO.
SERIOUS-LY?!
MMM...! SO GOOD...!!
CLICK
WE FINISHED IT...!!

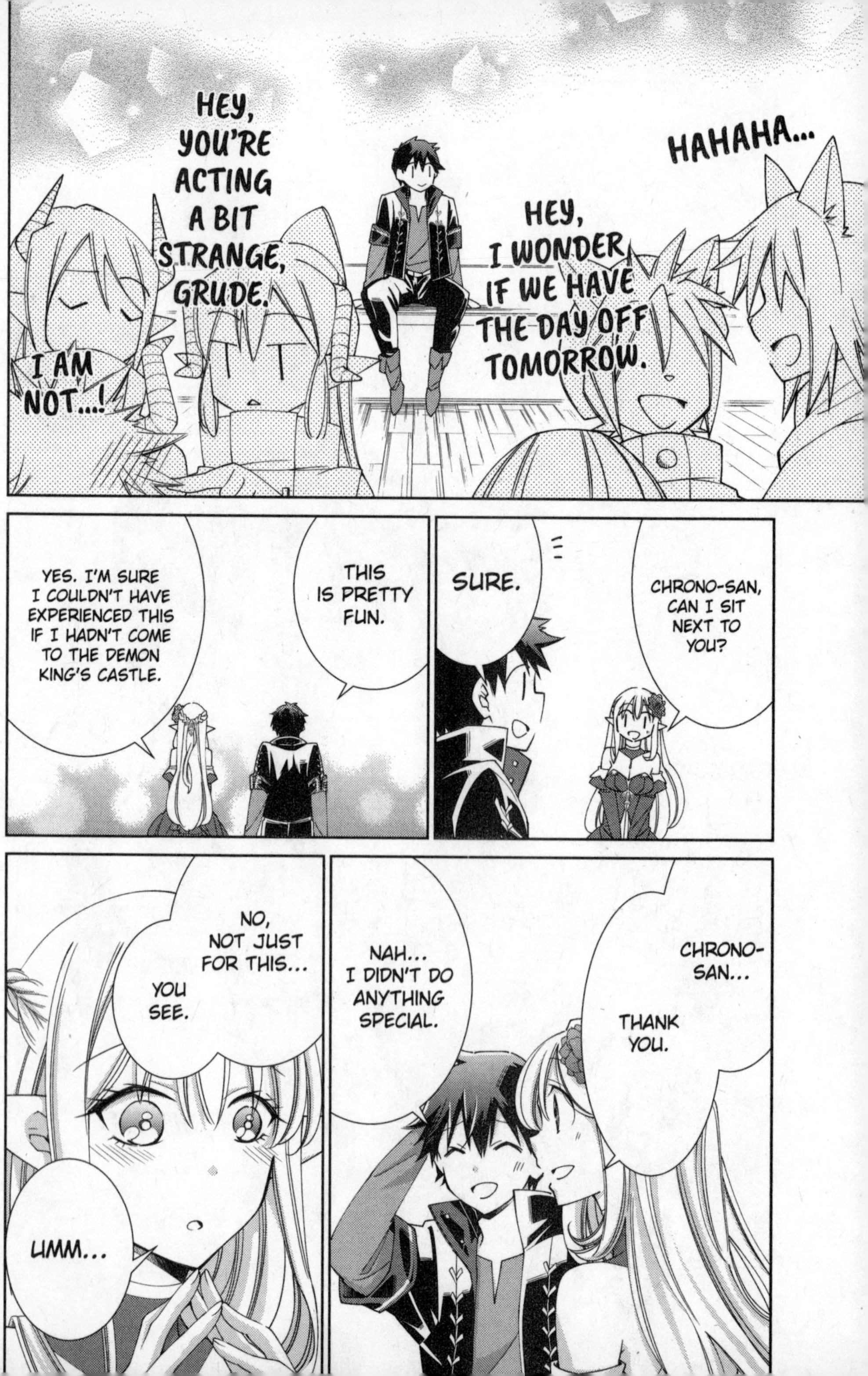
HAHAHA...
HEY, I WONDER IF WE HAVE THE DAY OFF TOMORROW.
HEY, YOU'RE ACTING A BIT STRANGE, GRUDE.
I AM NOT...!
CHRONO-SAN, CAN I SIT NEXT TO YOU?
SURE.
THIS IS PRETTY FUN.
YES. I'M SURE I COULDN'T HAVE EXPERIENCED THIS IF I HADN'T COME TO THE DEMON KING'S CASTLE.
CHRONO-SAN...
THANK YOU.
NAH... I DIDN'T DO ANYTHING SPECIAL.
NO, NOT JUST FOR THIS...
YOU SEE.
UMM...

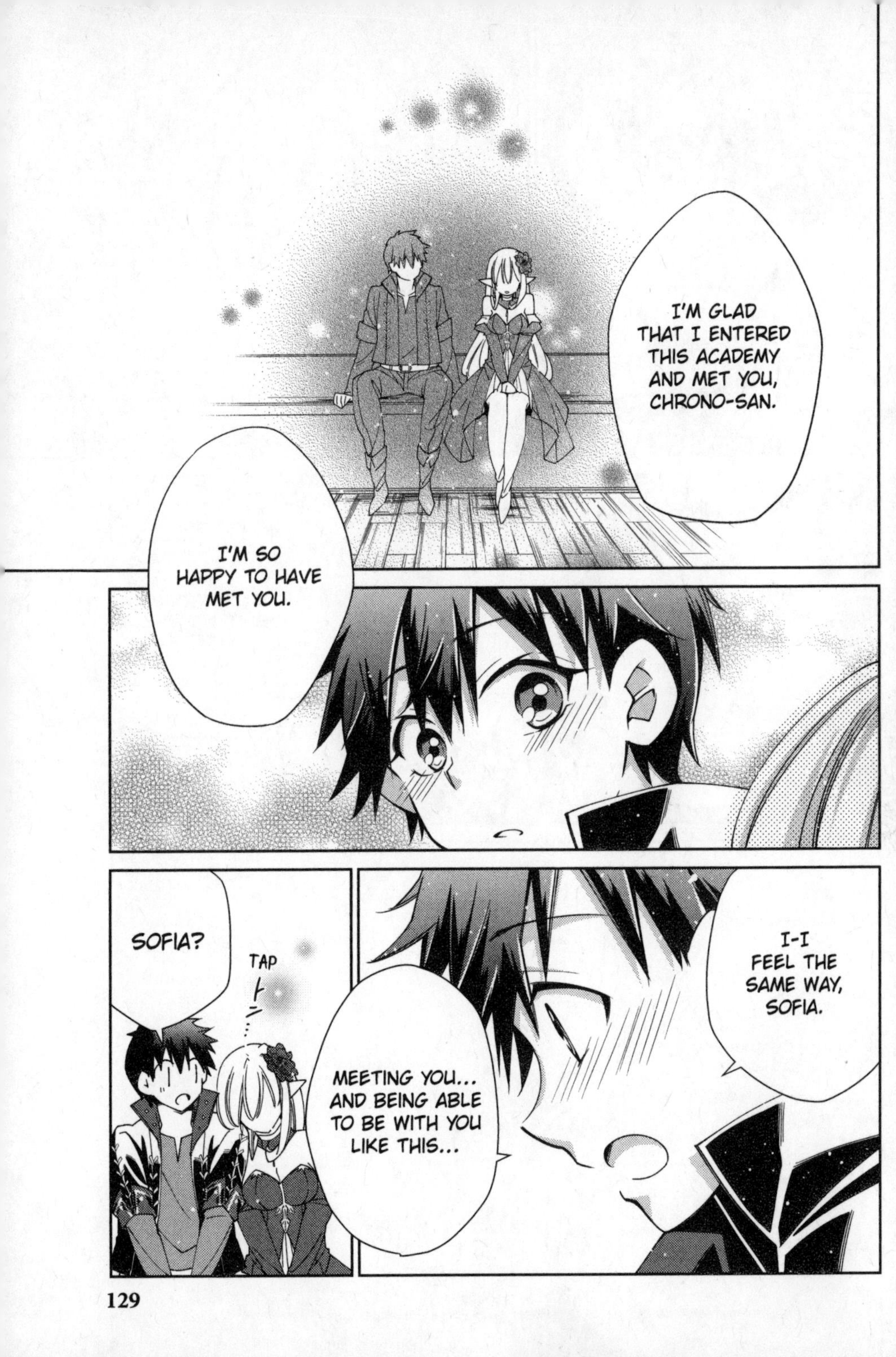
I'M GLAD THAT I ENTERED THIS ACADEMY AND MET YOU, CHRONO-SAN.
I'M SO HAPPY TO HAVE MET YOU.
I-I FEEL THE SAME WAY, SOFIA.
MEETING YOU... AND BEING ABLE TO BE WITH YOU LIKE THIS...
TAP
SOFIA?

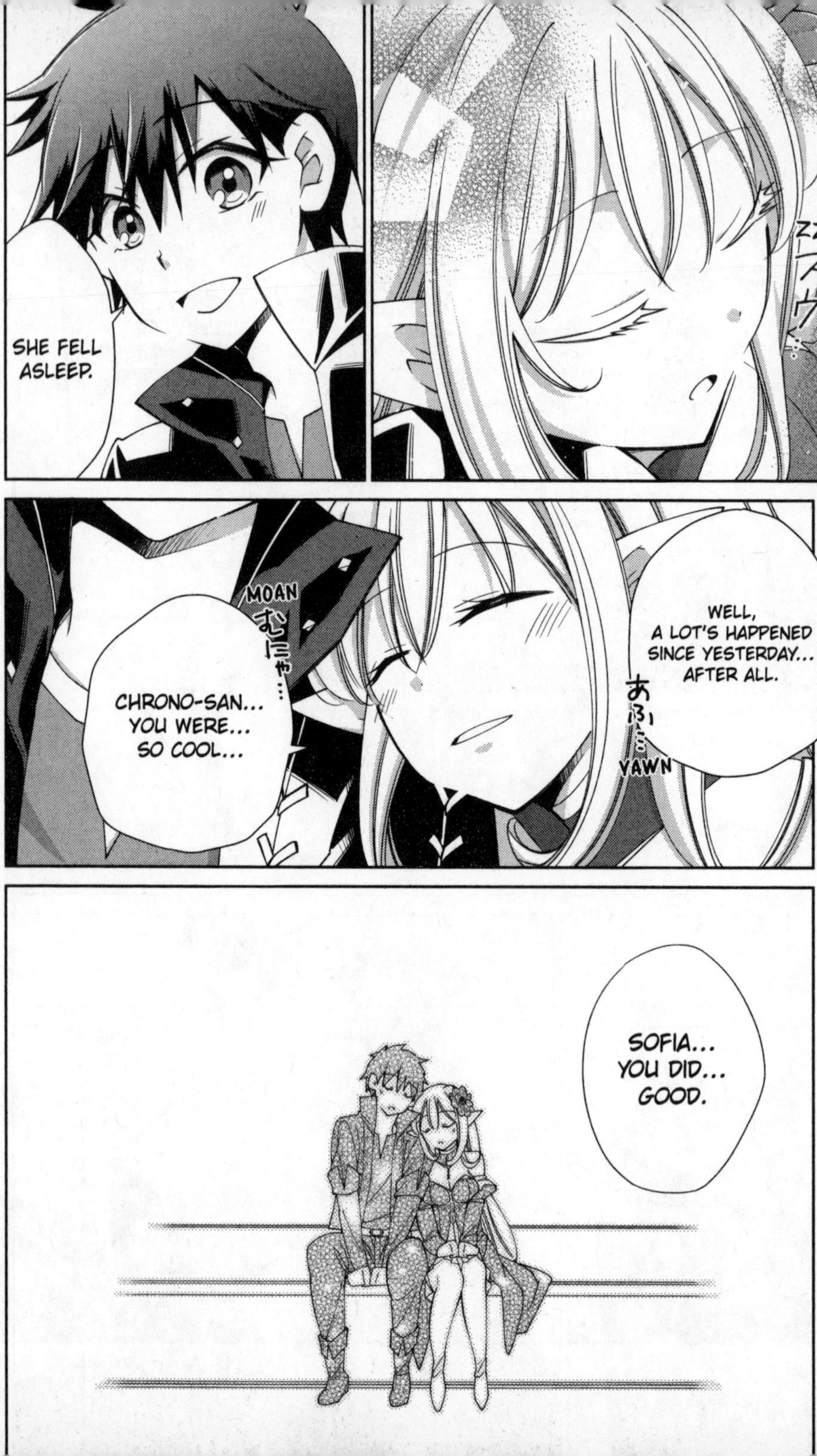
ZZZ...
SHE FELL ASLEEP.
WELL, A LOT'S HAPPENED SINCE YESTERDAY... AFTER ALL.
YAWN
MOAN
むにゃ…
CHRONO-SAN... YOU WERE... SO COOL...
SOFIA... YOU DID... GOOD.

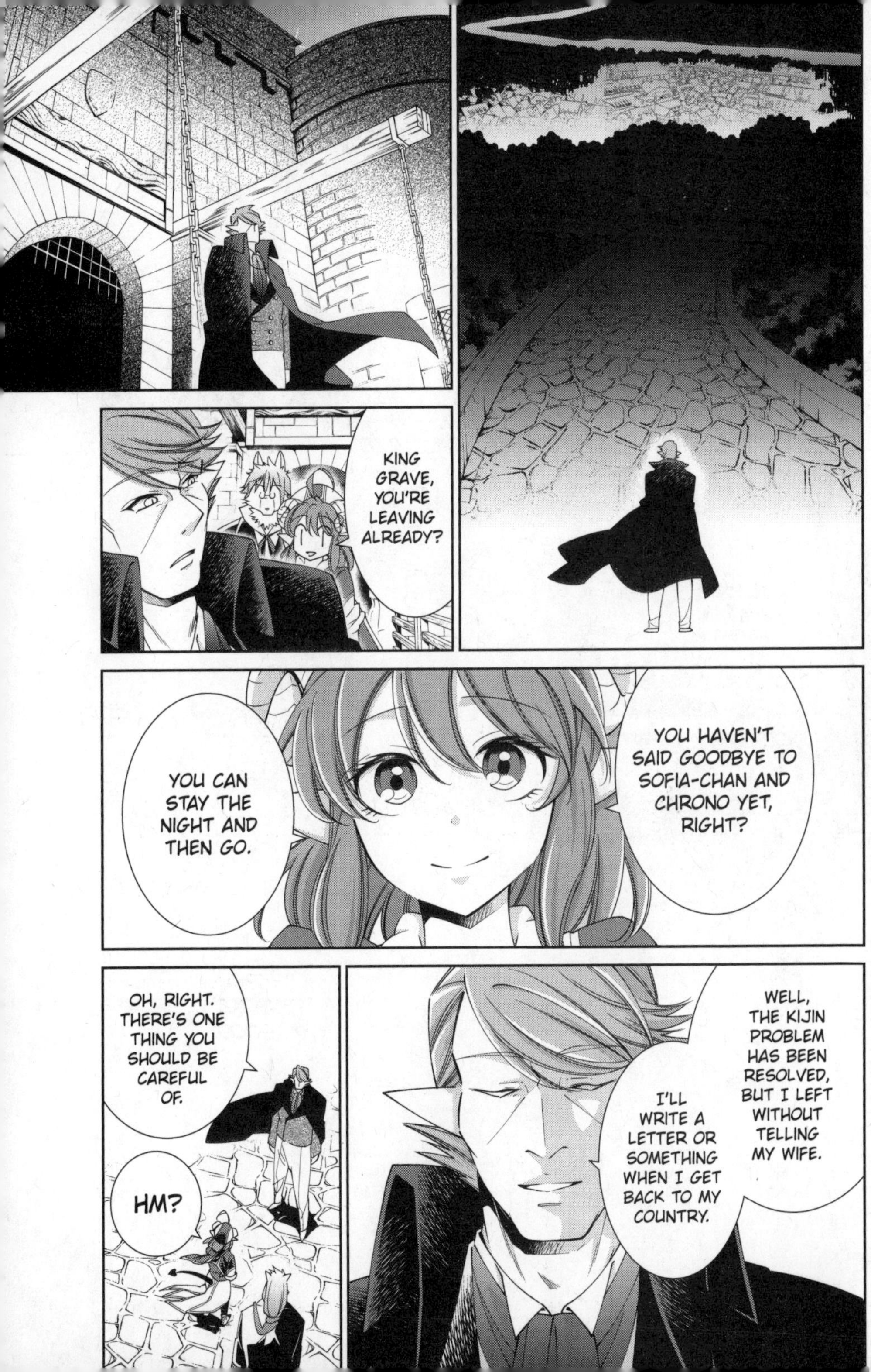
KING GRAVE, YOU'RE LEAVING ALREADY?
YOU HAVEN'T SAID GOODBYE TO SOFIA-CHAN AND CHRONO YET, RIGHT?
YOU CAN STAY THE NIGHT AND THEN GO.
WELL, THE KIJIN PROBLEM HAS BEEN RESOLVED, BUT I LEFT WITHOUT TELLING MY WIFE.
I'LL WRITE A LETTER OR SOMETHING WHEN I GET BACK TO MY COUNTRY.
OH, RIGHT. THERE'S ONE THING YOU SHOULD BE CAREFUL OF.
HM?

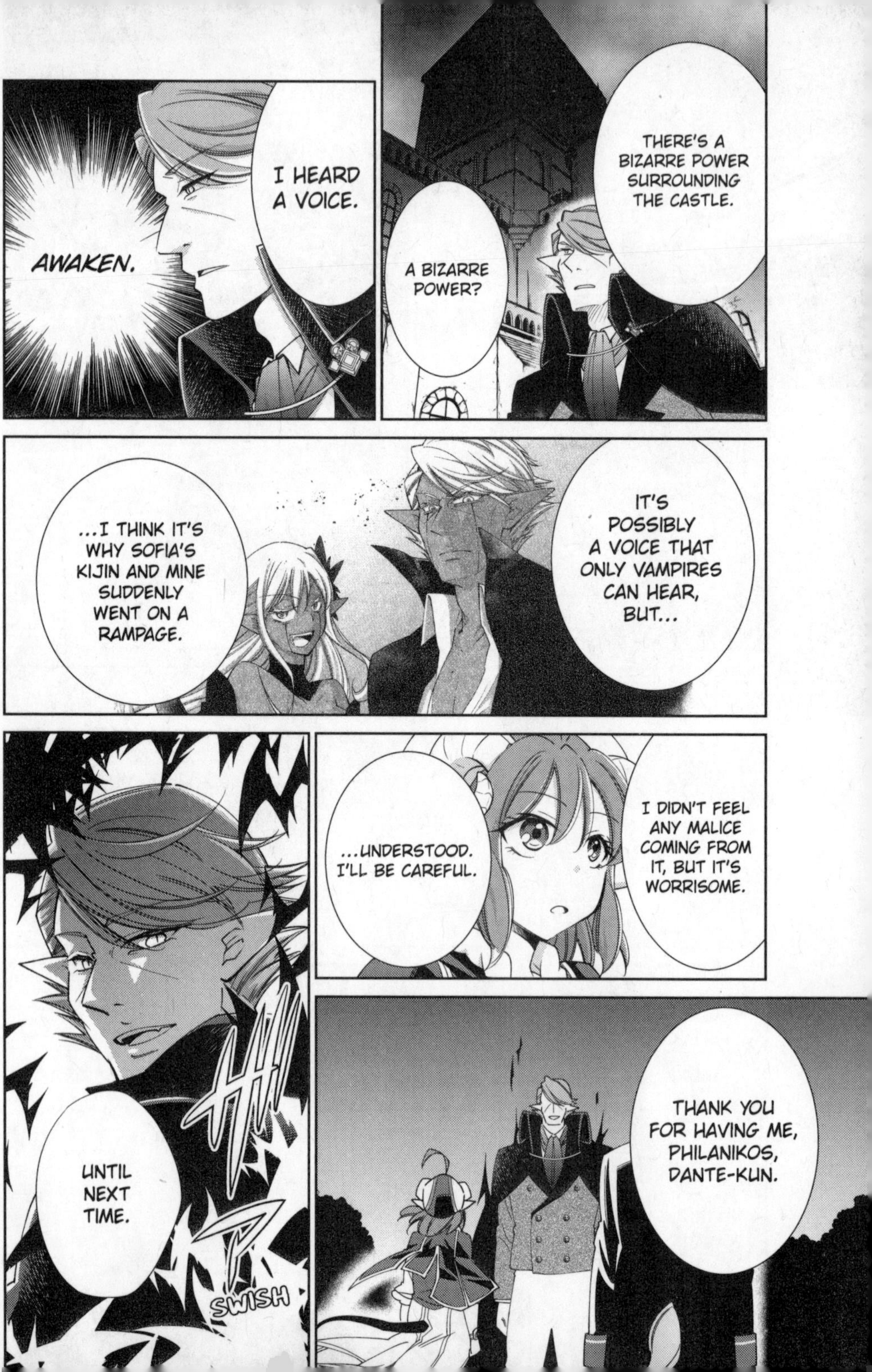
THERE'S A BIZARRE POWER SURROUNDING THE CASTLE.
A BIZARRE POWER?
I HEARD A VOICE.
AWAKEN.
IT'S POSSIBLY A VOICE THAT ONLY VAMPIRES CAN HEAR, BUT...
...I THINK IT'S WHY SOFIA'S KIJIN AND MINE SUDDENLY WENT ON A RAMPAGE.
I DIDN'T FEEL ANY MALICE COMING FROM IT, BUT IT'S WORRISOME.
...UNDERSTOOD. I'LL BE CAREFUL.
THANK YOU FOR HAVING ME, PHILANIKOS, DANTE-KUN.
UNTIL NEXT TIME.
SWISH

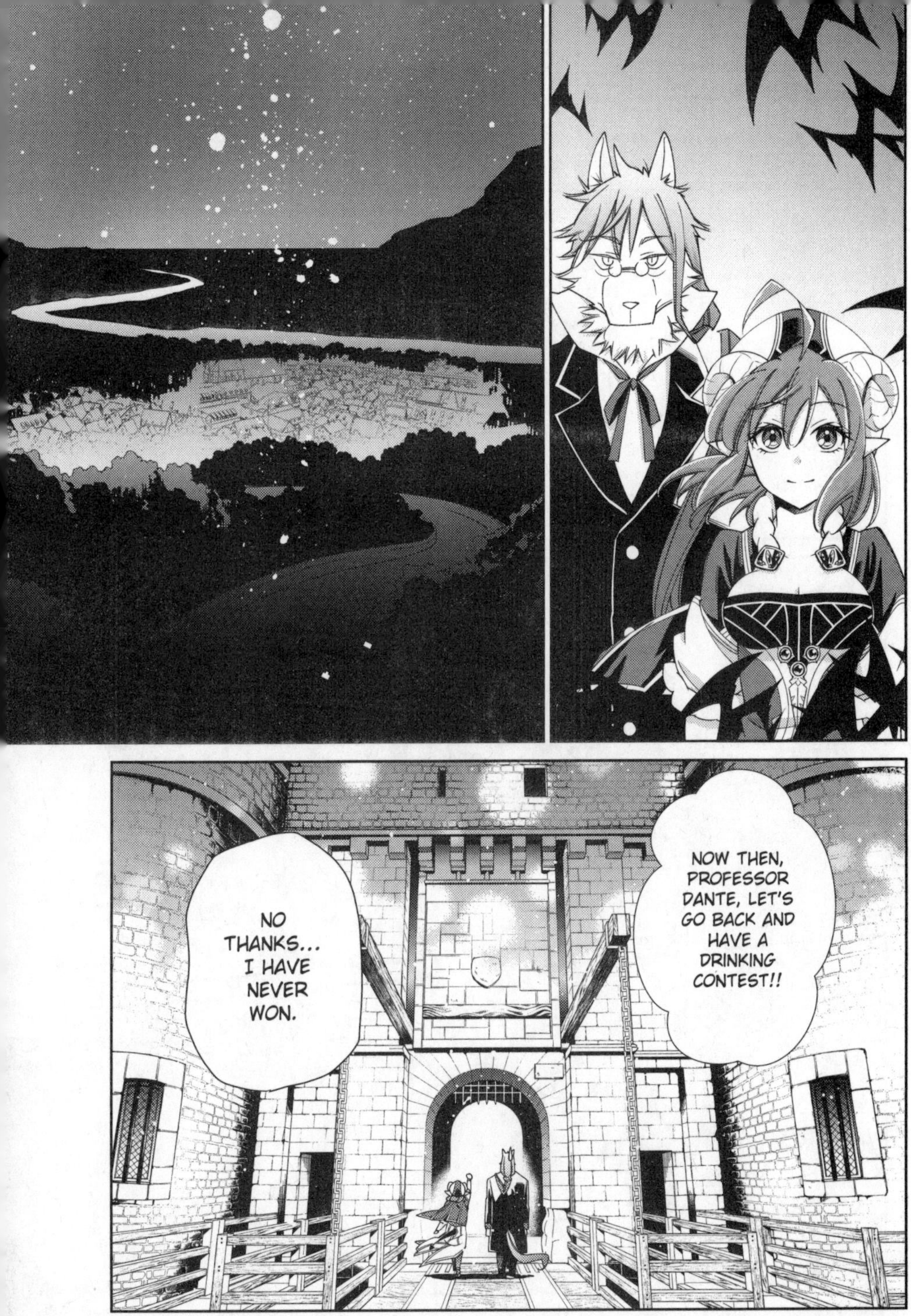
NOW THEN, PROFESSOR DANTE, LET'S GO BACK AND HAVE A DRINKING CONTEST!!
NO THANKS... I HAVE NEVER WON.

EXTRA MANGA - TO MYSELF ON THAT DAY

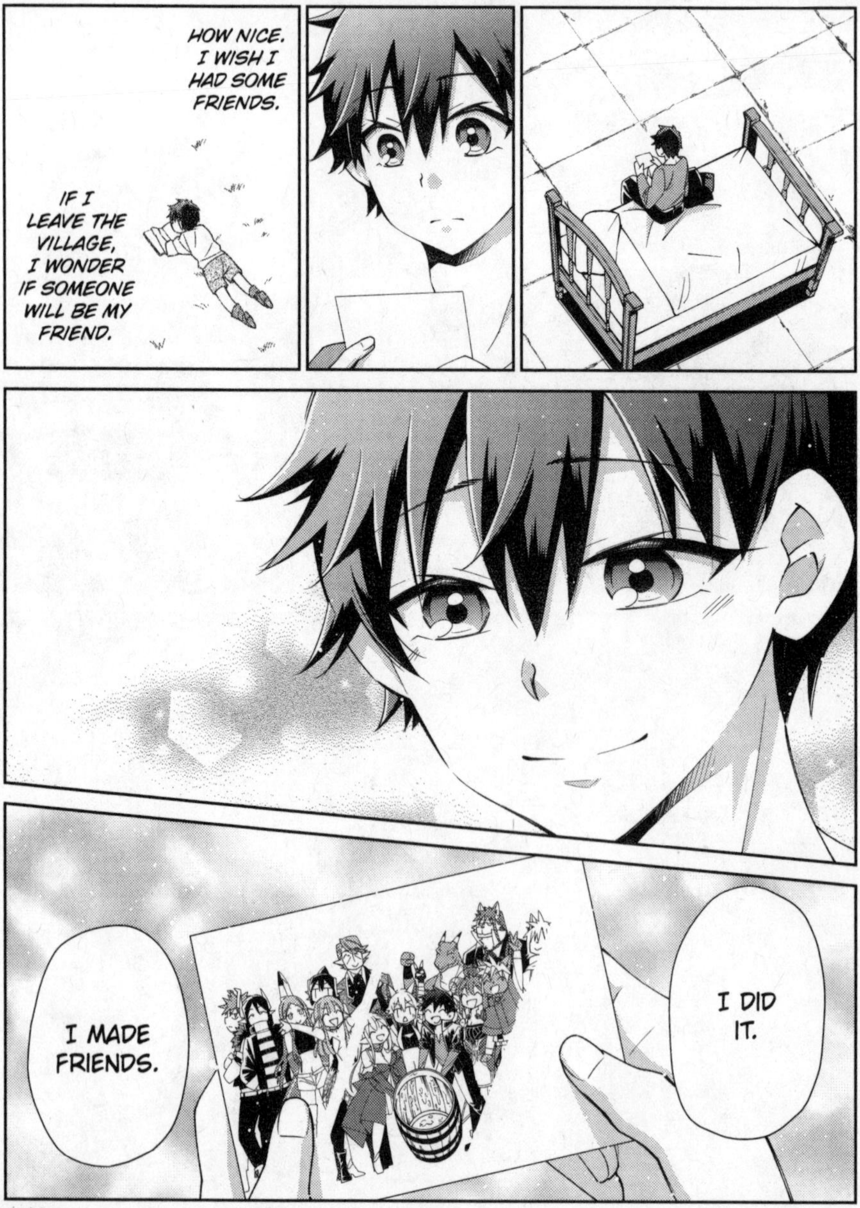
HOW NICE. I WISH I HAD SOME FRIENDS.
IF I LEAVE THE VILLAGE, I WONDER IF SOMEONE WILL BE MY FRIEND.
I DID IT.
I MADE FRIENDS.

END

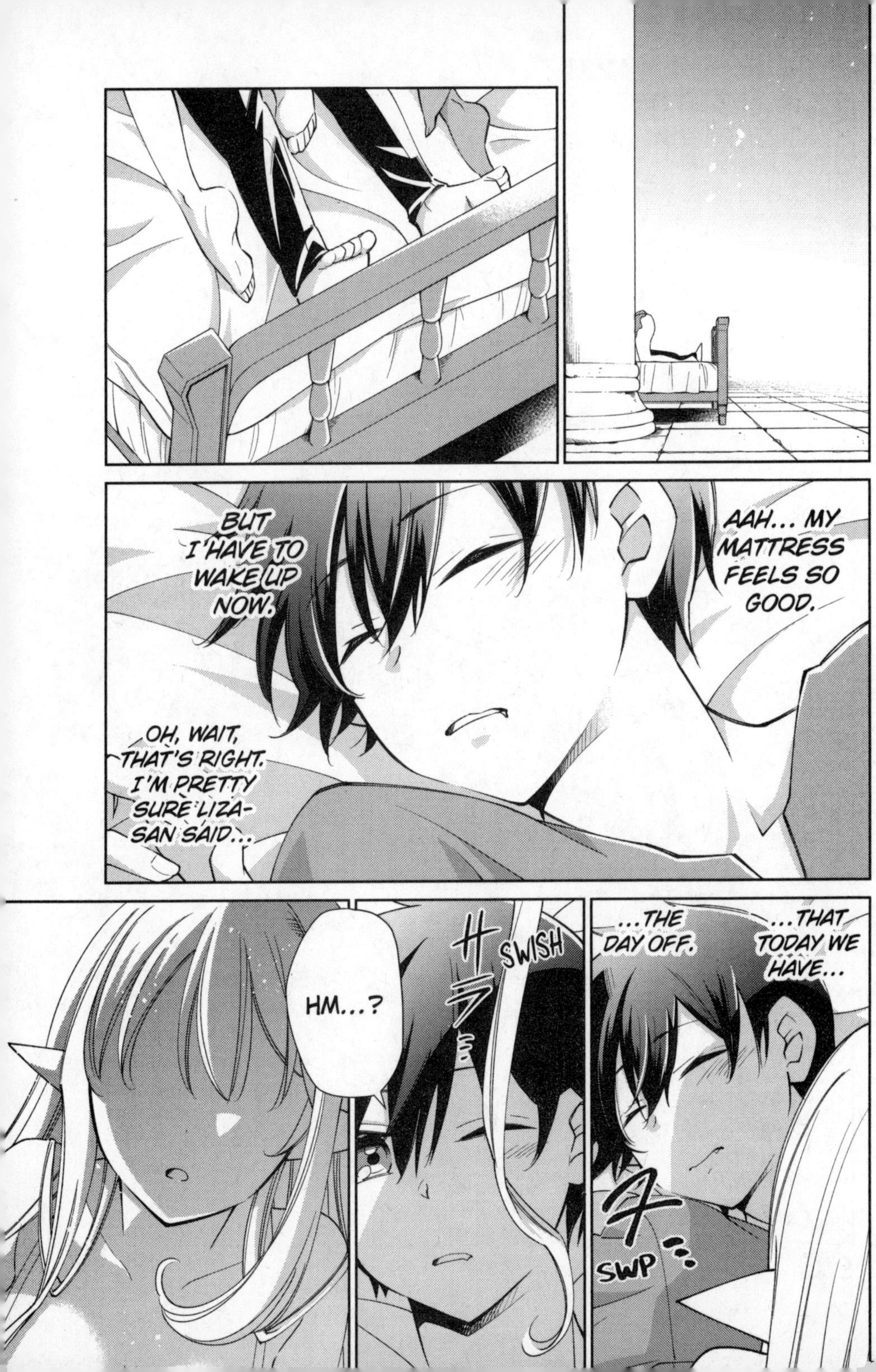
AAH... MY MATTRESS FEELS SO GOOD.
BUT I'HAVE TO WAKE UP NOW.
OH, WAIT, THAT'S RIGHT. I'M PRETTY SURE LIZA-SAN SAID...
...THAT TODAY WE HAVE...
...THE DAY OFF.
SWP
SWISH
HM...?

CHAPTER 13 CHRONO MAKES A DECISION

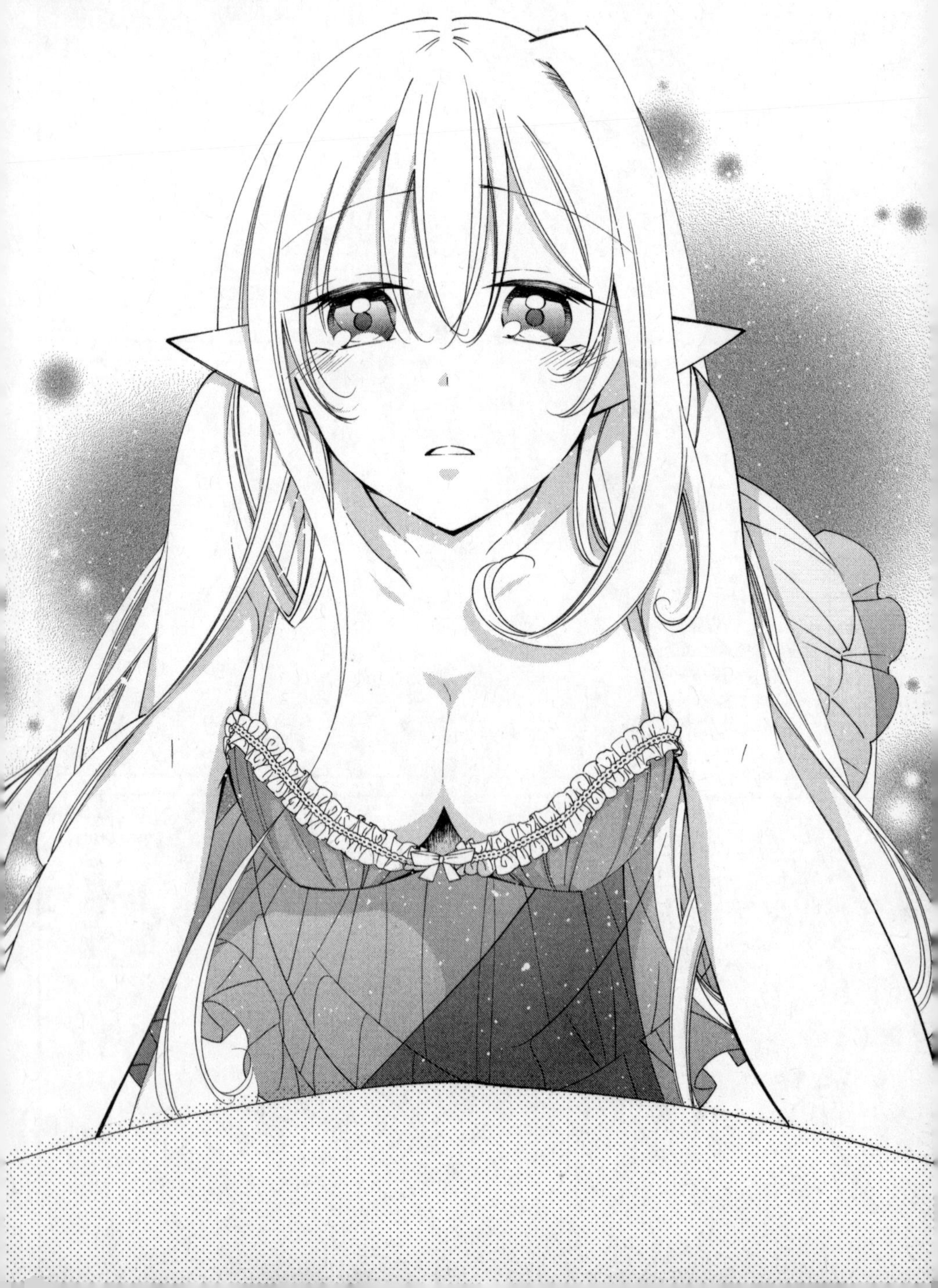

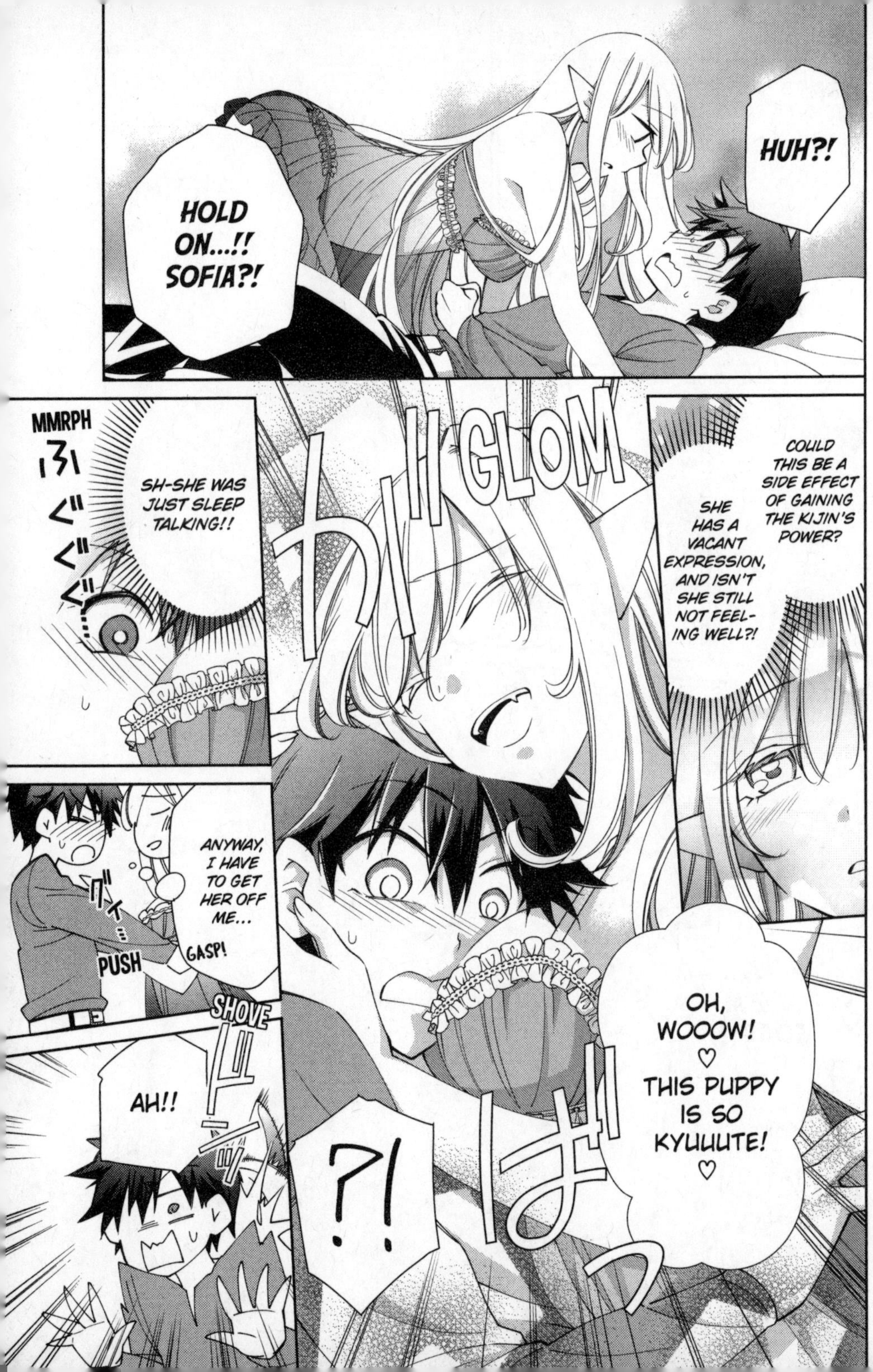
HUH?!
HOLD ON...!! SOFIA?!
COULD THIS BE A SIDE EFFECT OF GAINING THE KIJIN'S POWER?
SHE HAS A VACANT EXPRESSION, AND ISN'T SHE STILL NOT FEELING WELL?!
GLOM
OH, WOOOW! ♡ THIS PUPPY IS SO KYUUUTE! ♡
MMRPH
SH-SHE WAS JUST SLEEP TALKING!!
?!
ANYWAY, I HAVE TO GET HER OFF ME...
GASP!
PUSH
SHOVE
AH!!

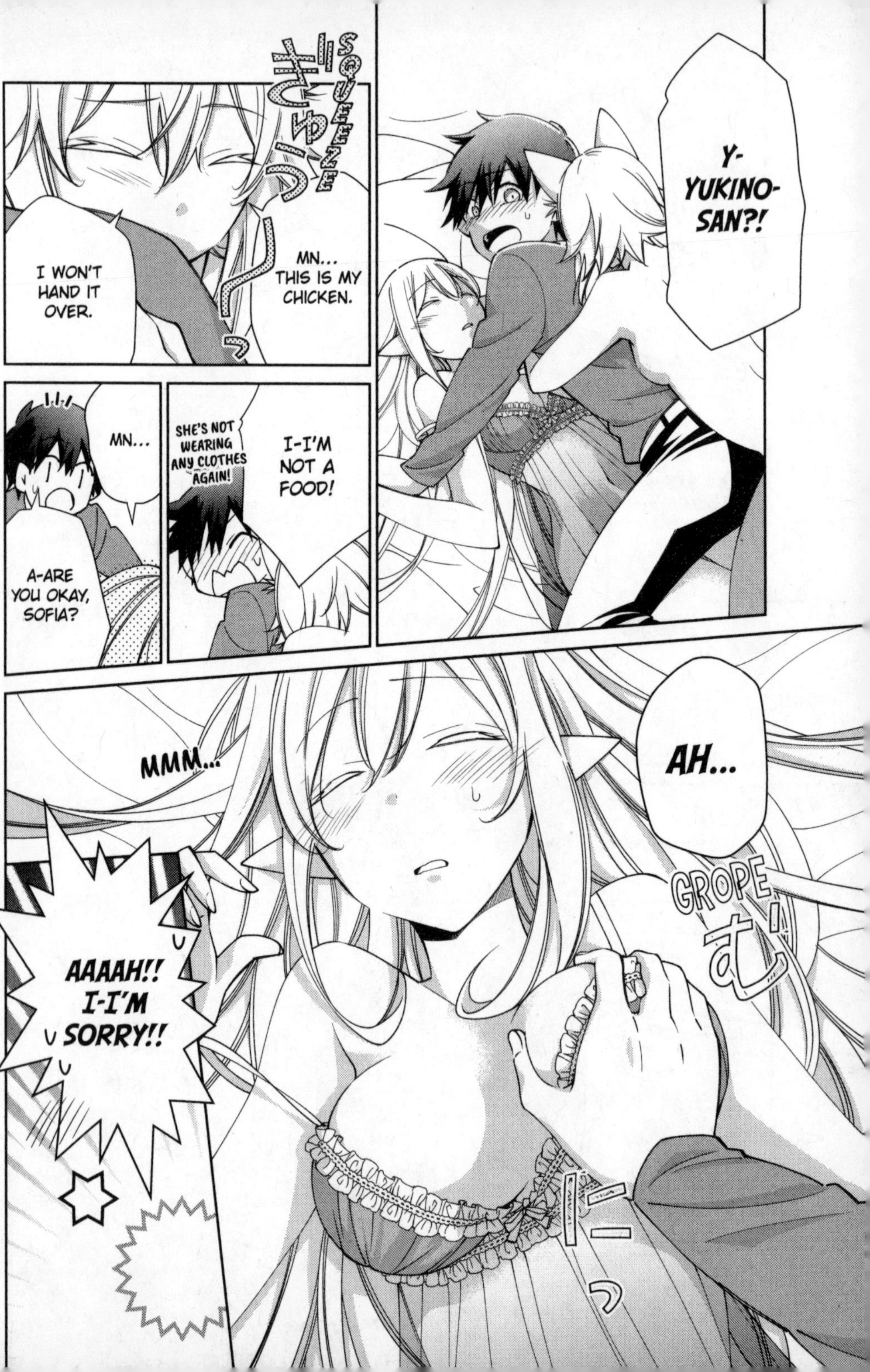
Y-YUKINO-SAN?!
SQUEEZE
MN... THIS IS MY CHICKEN.
I WON'T HAND IT OVER.
I-I'M NOT A FOOD!
SHE'S NOT WEARING ANY CLOTHES AGAIN!
MN...
A-ARE YOU OKAY, SOFIA?
AH...
GROPE
MMM...
AAAAH!! I-I'M SORRY!!

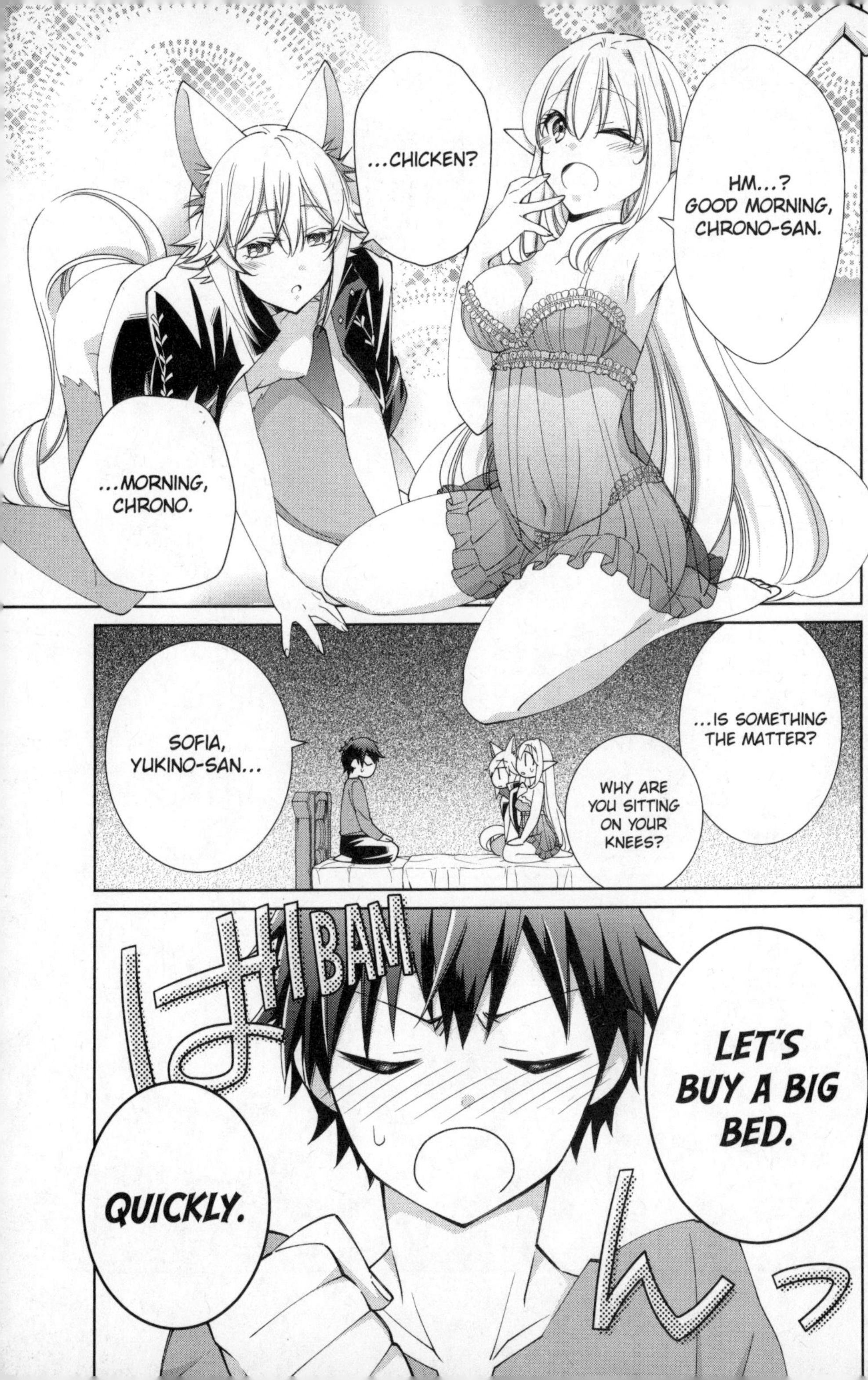
HM...? GOOD MORNING, CHRONO-SAN.
...CHICKEN?
...MORNING, CHRONO.
...IS SOMETHING THE MATTER?
WHY ARE YOU SITTING ON YOUR KNEES?
SOFIA, YUKINO-SAN...
BAM
LET'S BUY A BIG BED.
QUICKLY.

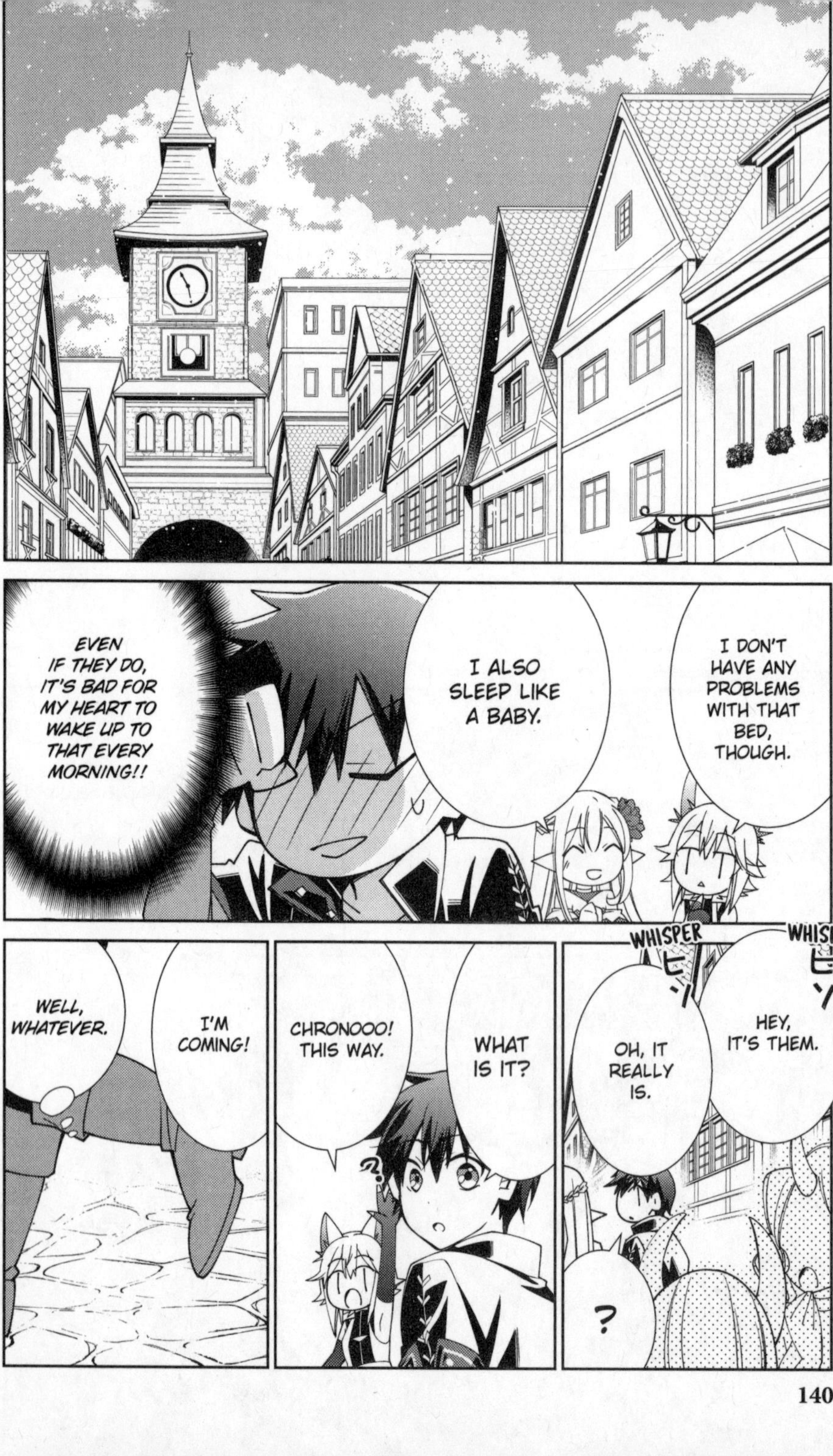
I DON'T HAVE ANY PROBLEMS WITH THAT BED, THOUGH.
I ALSO SLEEP LIKE A BABY.
EVEN IF THEY DO, IT'S BAD FOR MY HEART TO WAKE UP TO THAT EVERY MORNING!!
WHISPER
ヒソ
WHISPER
ヒソ
HEY, IT'S THEM.
OH, IT REALLY IS.
?
WHAT IS IT?
CHRONOOO! THIS WAY.
I'M COMING!
WELL, WHATEVER.

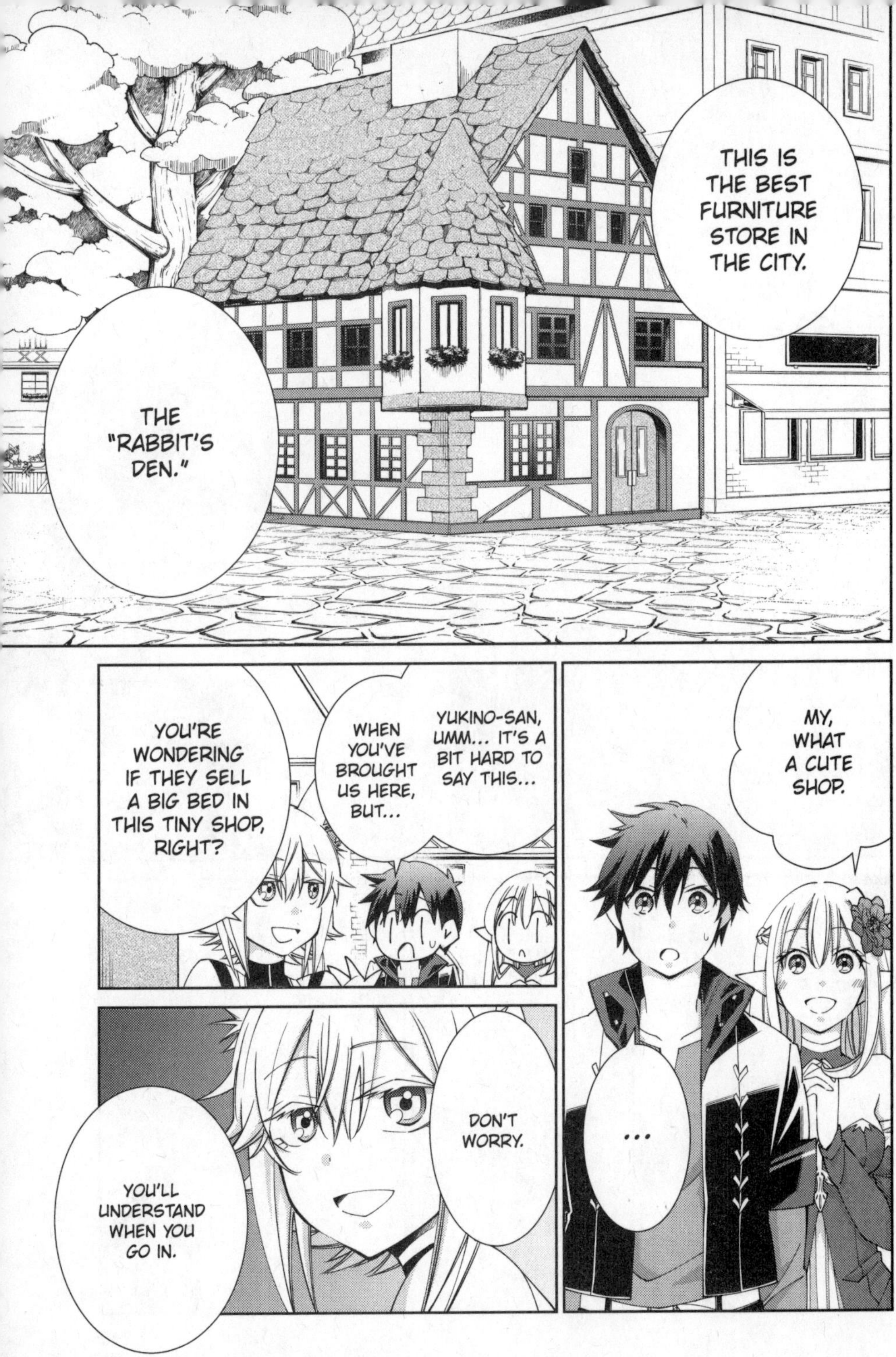
THIS IS THE BEST FURNITURE STORE IN THE CITY.
THE "RABBIT'S DEN."
MY, WHAT A CUTE SHOP.
...
YUKINO-SAN, UMM... IT'S A BIT HARD TO SAY THIS...
WHEN YOU'VE BROUGHT US HERE, BUT...
YOU'RE WONDERING IF THEY SELL A BIG BED IN THIS TINY SHOP, RIGHT?
DON'T WORRY.
YOU'LL UNDERSTAND WHEN YOU GO IN.

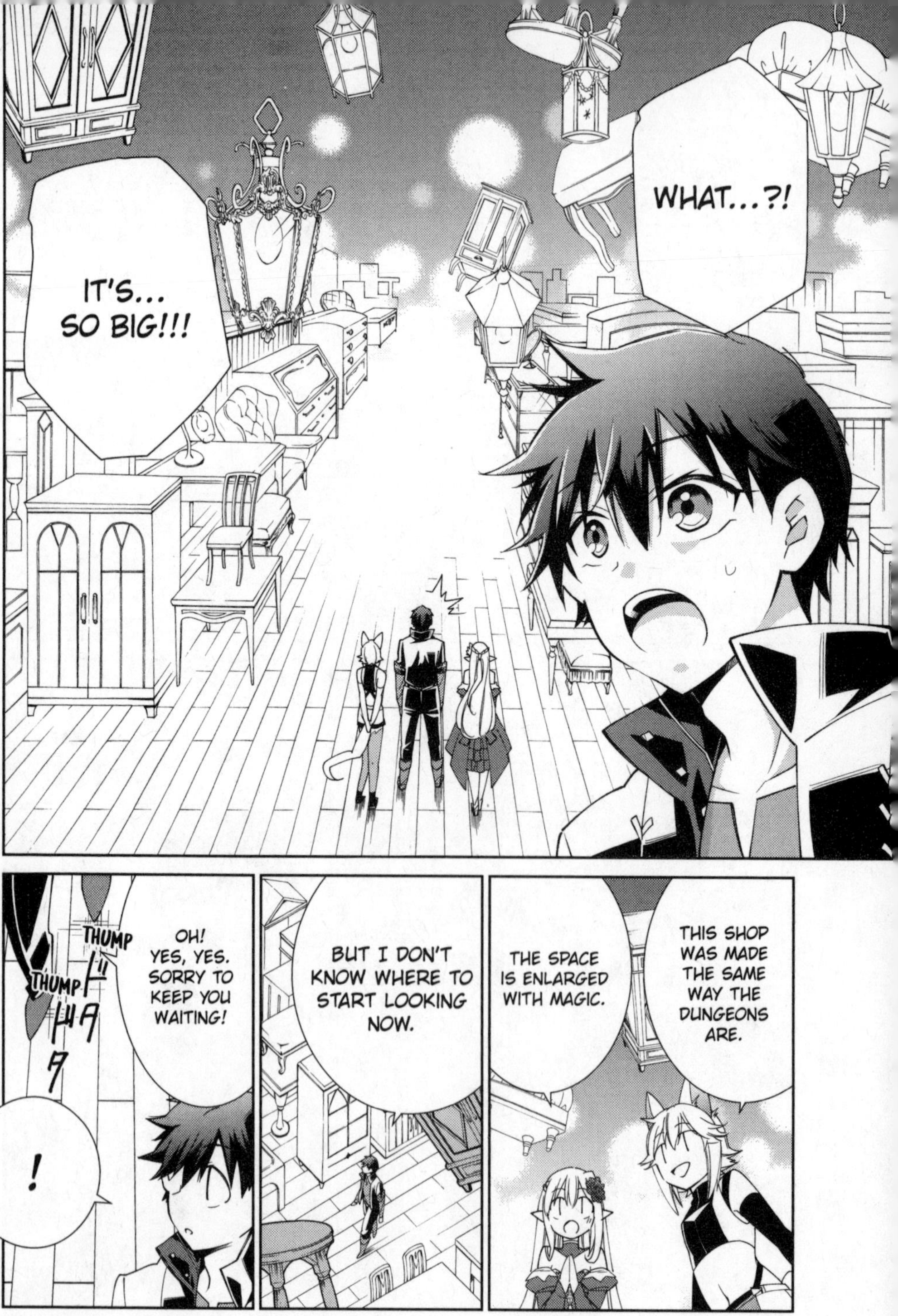
WHAT...?!
IT'S... SO BIG!!!
THIS SHOP WAS MADE THE SAME WAY THE DUNGEONS ARE.
THE SPACE IS ENLARGED WITH MAGIC.
BUT I DON'T KNOW WHERE TO START LOOKING NOW.
THUMP
THUMP
OH! YES, YES. SORRY TO KEEP YOU WAITING!
!

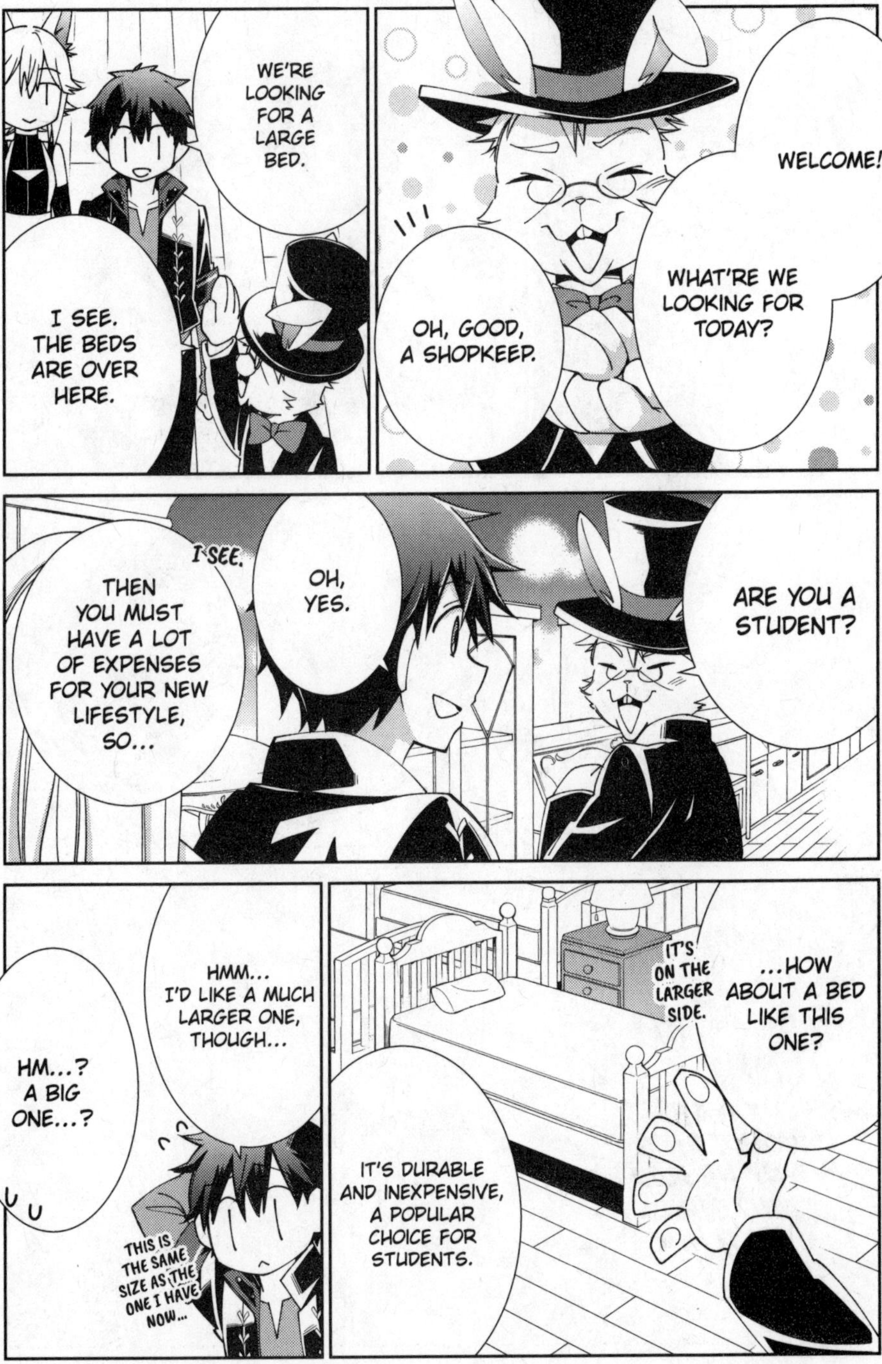
WELCOME!
WHAT'RE WE LOOKING FOR TODAY?
OH, GOOD, A SHOPKEEP.
WE'RE LOOKING FOR A LARGE BED.
I SEE. THE BEDS ARE OVER HERE.
ARE YOU A STUDENT?
OH, YES.
I SEE.
THEN YOU MUST HAVE A LOT OF EXPENSES FOR YOUR NEW LIFESTYLE, SO...
...HOW ABOUT A BED LIKE THIS ONE?
IT'S ON THE LARGER SIDE.
IT'S DURABLE AND INEXPENSIVE, A POPULAR CHOICE FOR STUDENTS.
HMM... I'D LIKE A MUCH LARGER ONE, THOUGH...
HM...? A BIG ONE...?
THIS IS THE SAME SIZE AS THE ONE I HAVE NOW...

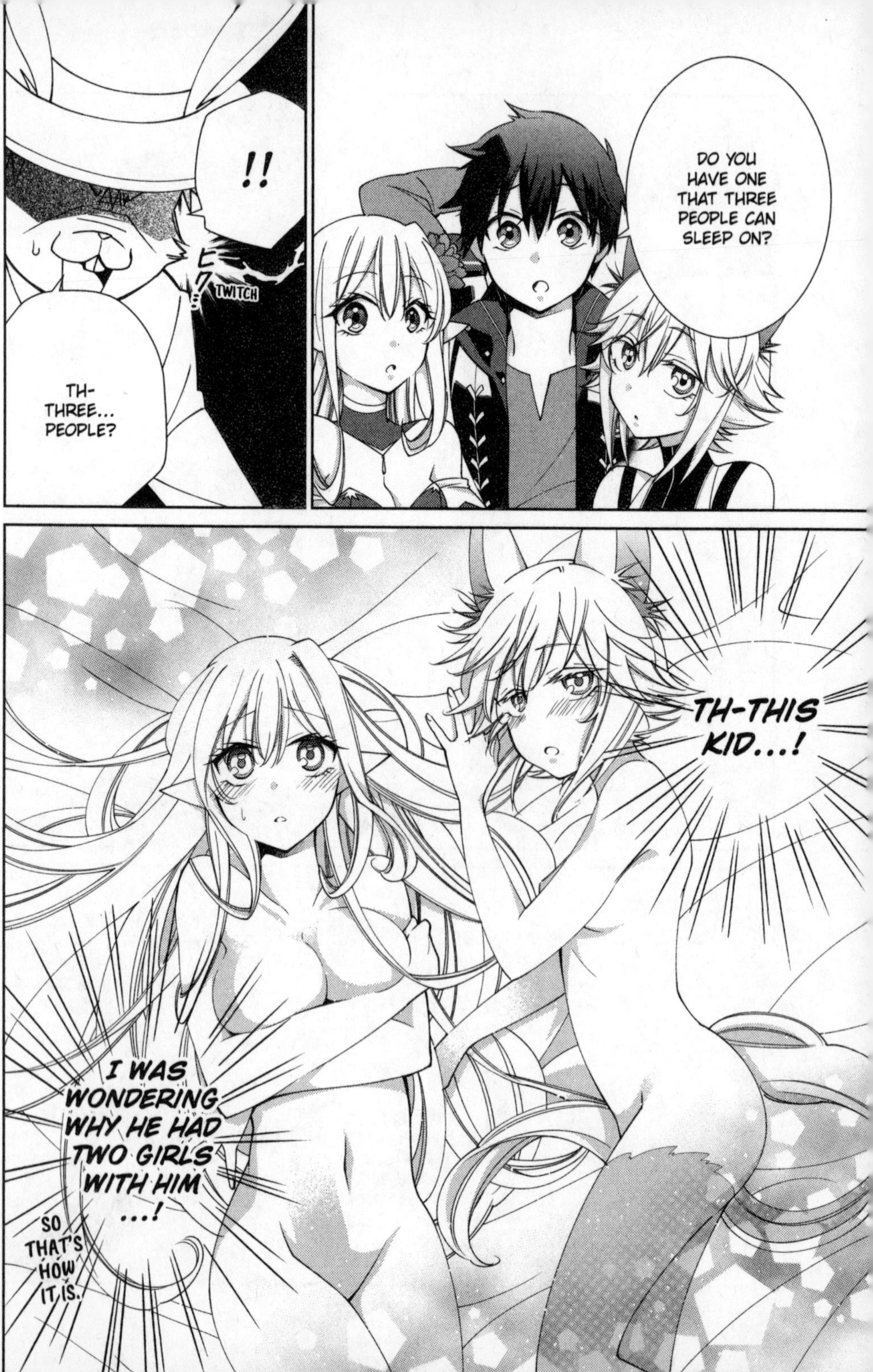
DO YOU HAVE ONE THAT THREE PEOPLE CAN SLEEP ON?
!!
TWITCH
TH-THREE... PEOPLE?
TH-THIS KID...!
I WAS WONDERING WHY HE HAD TWO GIRLS WITH HIM ...!
SO THAT'S HOW IT IS.

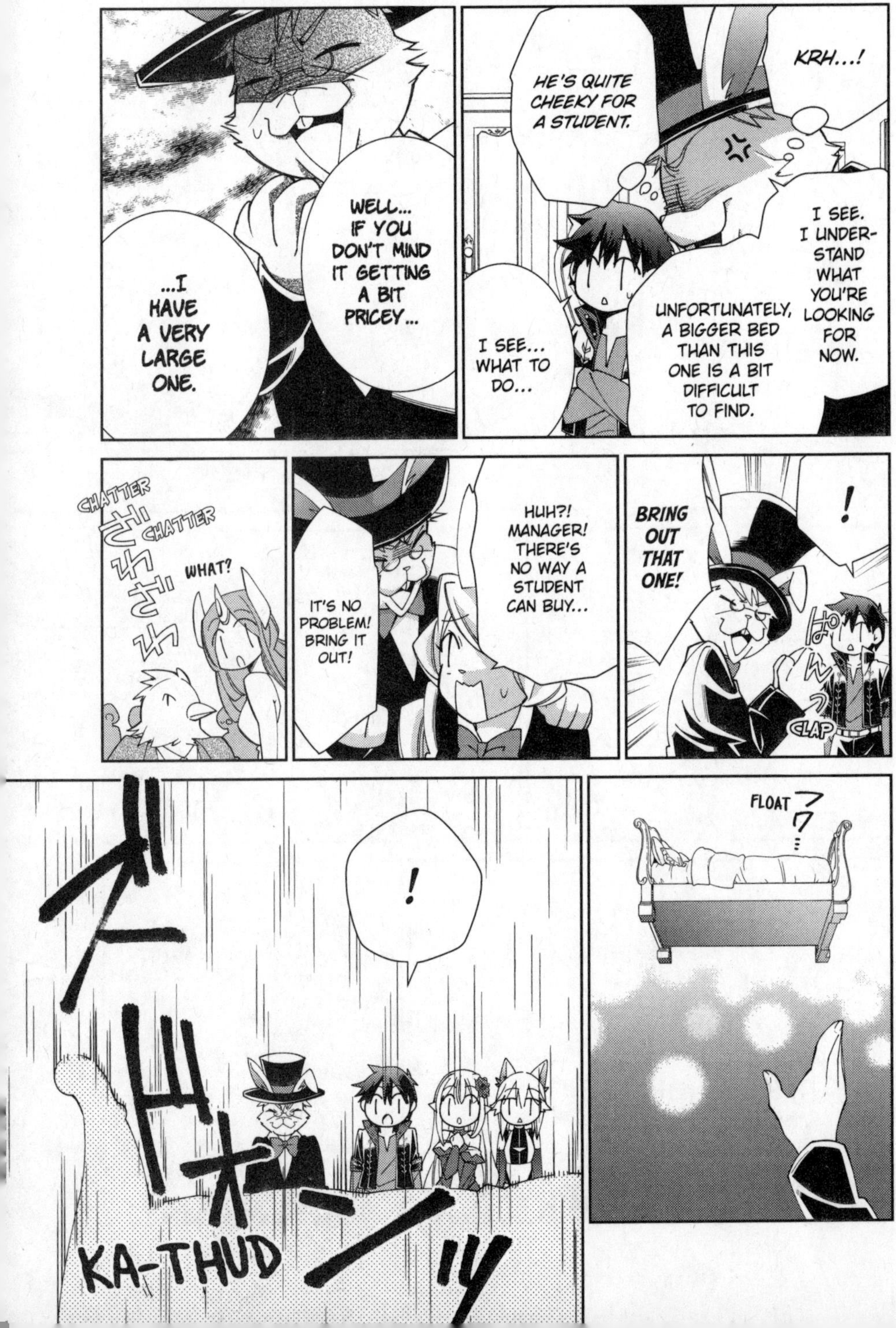
KRH...!
HE'S QUITE CHEEKY FOR A STUDENT.
I SEE. I UNDER-STAND WHAT YOU'RE LOOKING FOR NOW.
UNFORTUNATELY, A BIGGER BED THAN THIS ONE IS A BIT DIFFICULT TO FIND.
I SEE... WHAT TO DO...
WELL... IF YOU DON'T MIND IT GETTING A BIT PRICEY...
...I HAVE A VERY LARGE ONE.
!
BRING OUT THAT ONE!
CLAP
HUH?! MANAGER! THERE'S NO WAY A STUDENT CAN BUY...
IT'S NO PROBLEM! BRING IT OUT!
CHATTER
CHATTER
WHAT?
FLOAT
!
KA-THUD

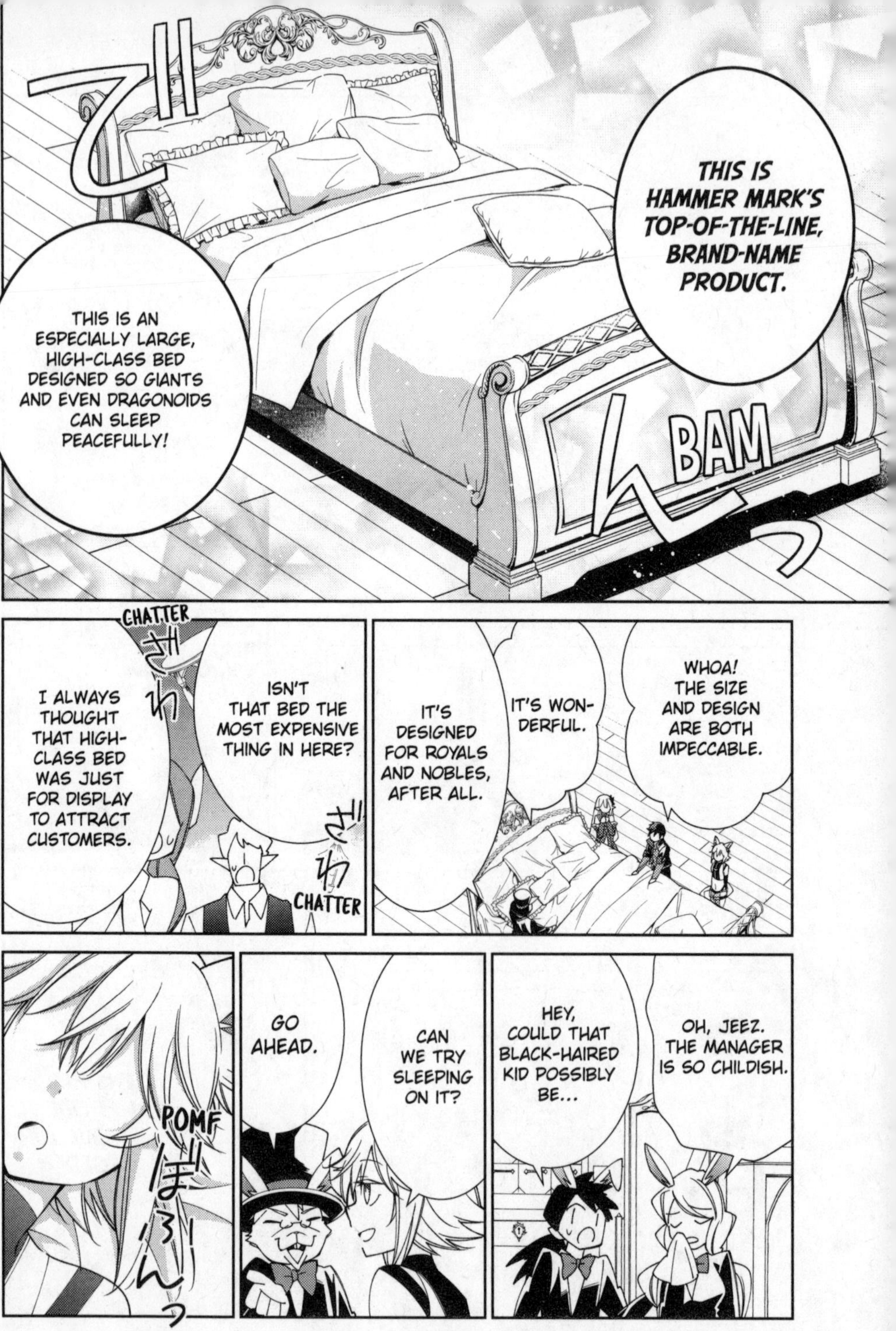

THIS IS HAMMER MARK'S TOP-OF-THE-LINE, BRAND-NAME PRODUCT.
THIS IS AN ESPECIALLY LARGE, HIGH-CLASS BED DESIGNED SO GIANTS AND EVEN DRAGONOIDS CAN SLEEP PEACEFULLY!
BAM
WHOA! THE SIZE AND DESIGN ARE BOTH IMPECCABLE.
IT'S WON-DERFUL.
IT'S DESIGNED FOR ROYALS AND NOBLES, AFTER ALL.
CHATTER
ISN'T THAT BED THE MOST EXPENSIVE THING IN HERE?
I ALWAYS THOUGHT THAT HIGH-CLASS BED WAS JUST FOR DISPLAY TO ATTRACT CUSTOMERS.
CHATTER
OH, JEEZ. THE MANAGER IS SO CHILDISH.
HEY, COULD THAT BLACK-HAIRED KID POSSIBLY BE...
CAN WE TRY SLEEPING ON IT?
GO AHEAD.
POMF

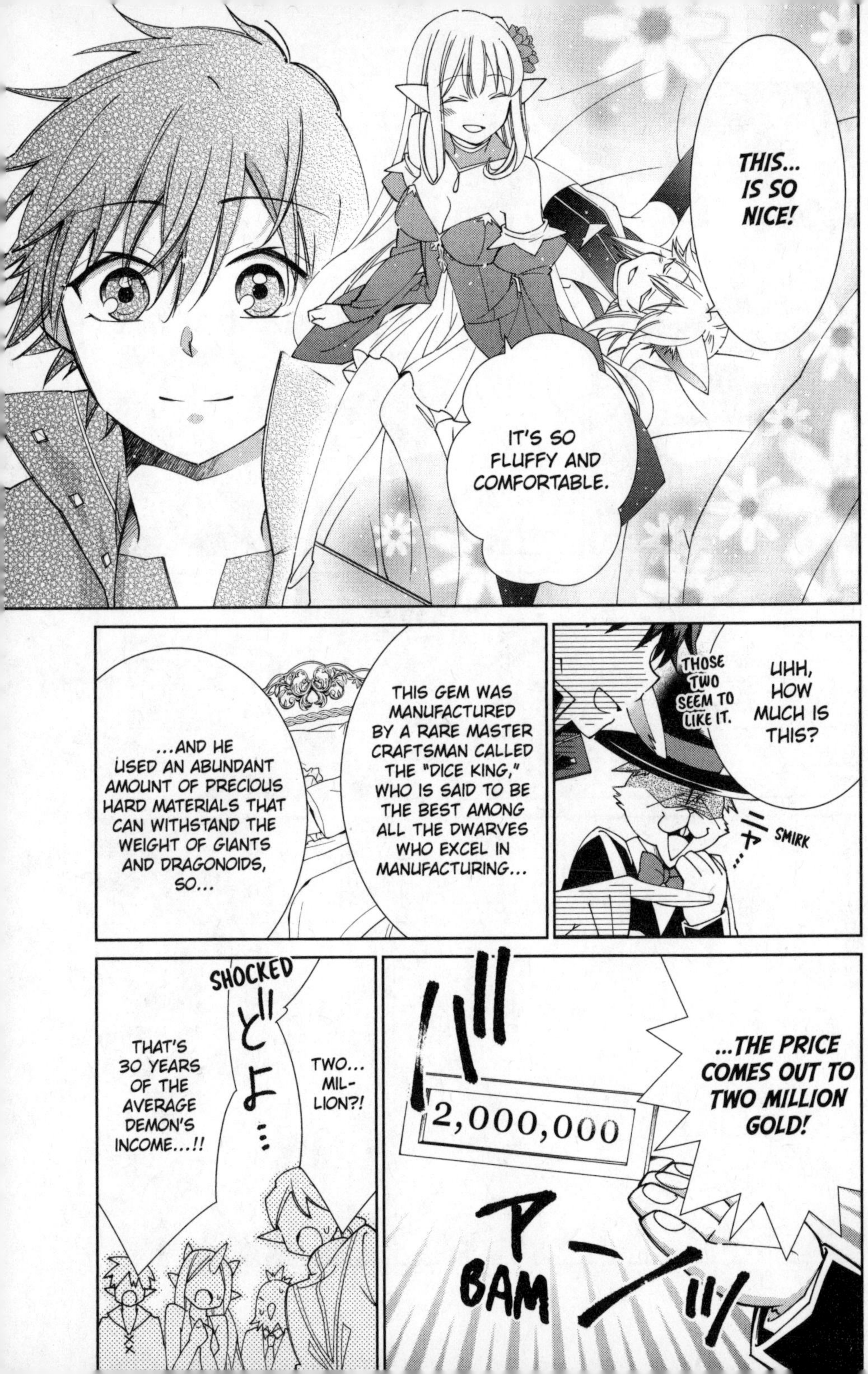
THIS... IS SO NICE!
IT'S SO FLUFFY AND COMFORTABLE.
UHH, HOW MUCH IS THIS?
THOSE TWO SEEM TO LIKE IT.
SMIRK
THIS GEM WAS MANUFACTURED BY A RARE MASTER CRAFTSMAN CALLED THE "DICE KING," WHO IS SAID TO BE THE BEST AMONG ALL THE DWARVES WHO EXCEL IN MANUFACTURING...
...AND HE USED AN ABUNDANT AMOUNT OF PRECIOUS HARD MATERIALS THAT CAN WITHSTAND THE WEIGHT OF GIANTS AND DRAGONOIDS, SO...
...THE PRICE COMES OUT TO TWO MILLION GOLD!
2,000,000
BAM
TWO... MIL-LION?!
SHOCKED
THAT'S 30 YEARS OF THE AVERAGE DEMON'S INCOME...!!

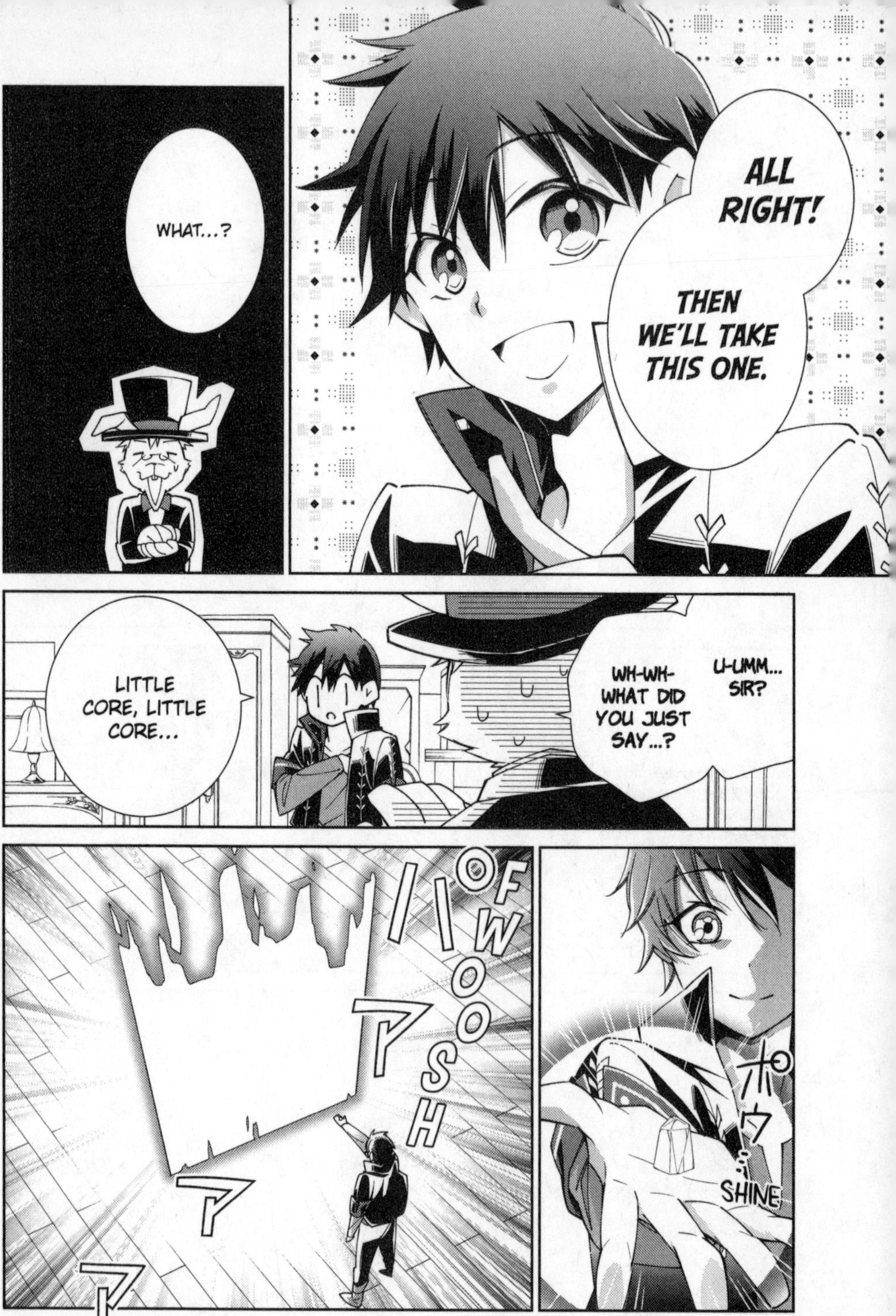
ALL RIGHT!
THEN WE'LL TAKE THIS ONE.
WHAT...?
U-UMM... SIR?
WH-WH-WHAT DID YOU JUST SAY...?
LITTLE CORE, LITTLE CORE...
SHINE
FWOOOSH

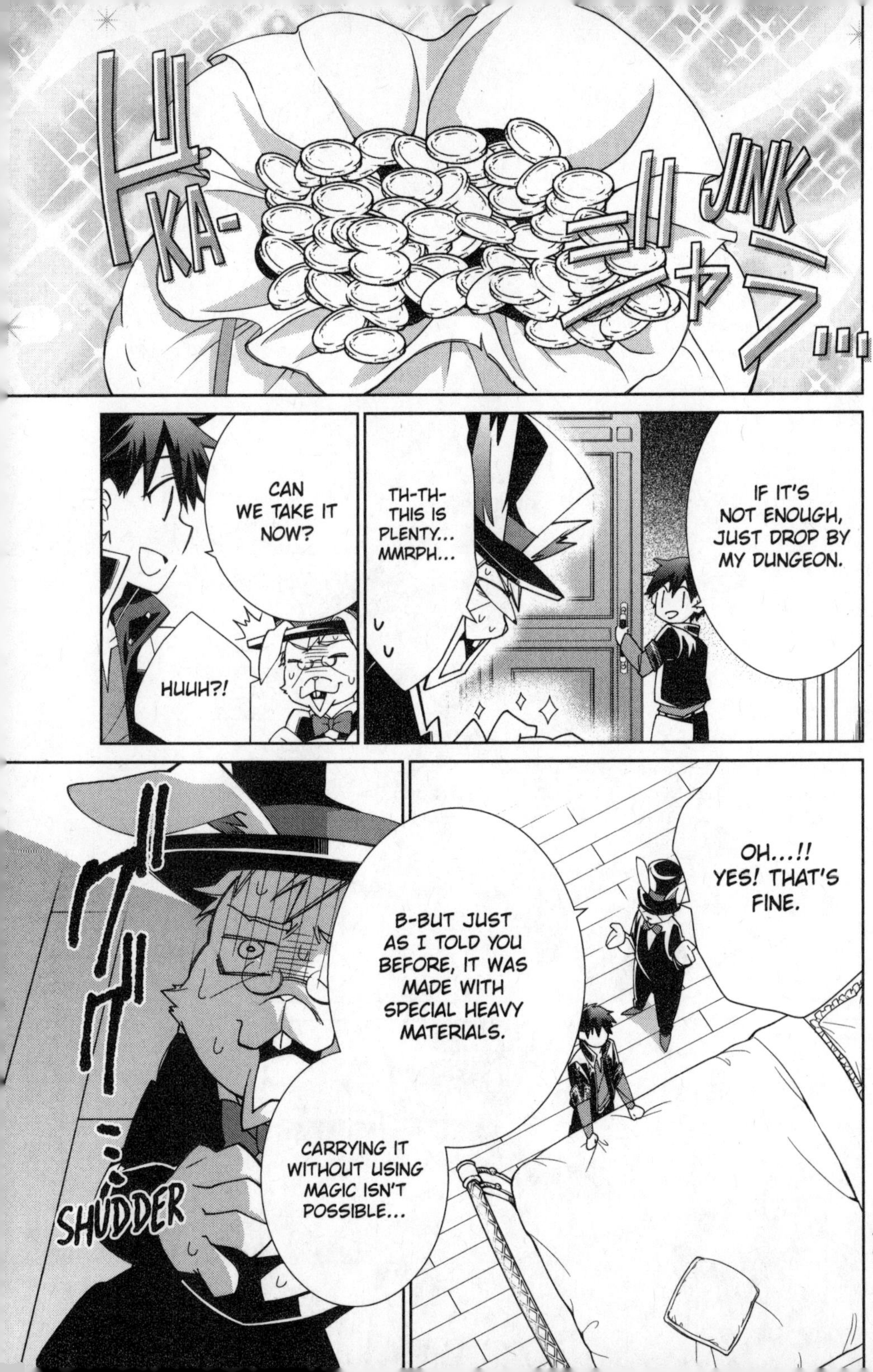
JINK...
KA-
IF IT'S NOT ENOUGH, JUST DROP BY MY DUNGEON.
TH-TH- THIS IS PLENTY... MMRPH...
CAN WE TAKE IT NOW?
HUUH?!
OH...!! YES! THAT'S FINE.
B-BUT JUST AS I TOLD YOU BEFORE, IT WAS MADE WITH SPECIAL HEAVY MATERIALS.
CARRYING IT WITHOUT USING MAGIC ISN'T POSSIBLE...
SHUDDER

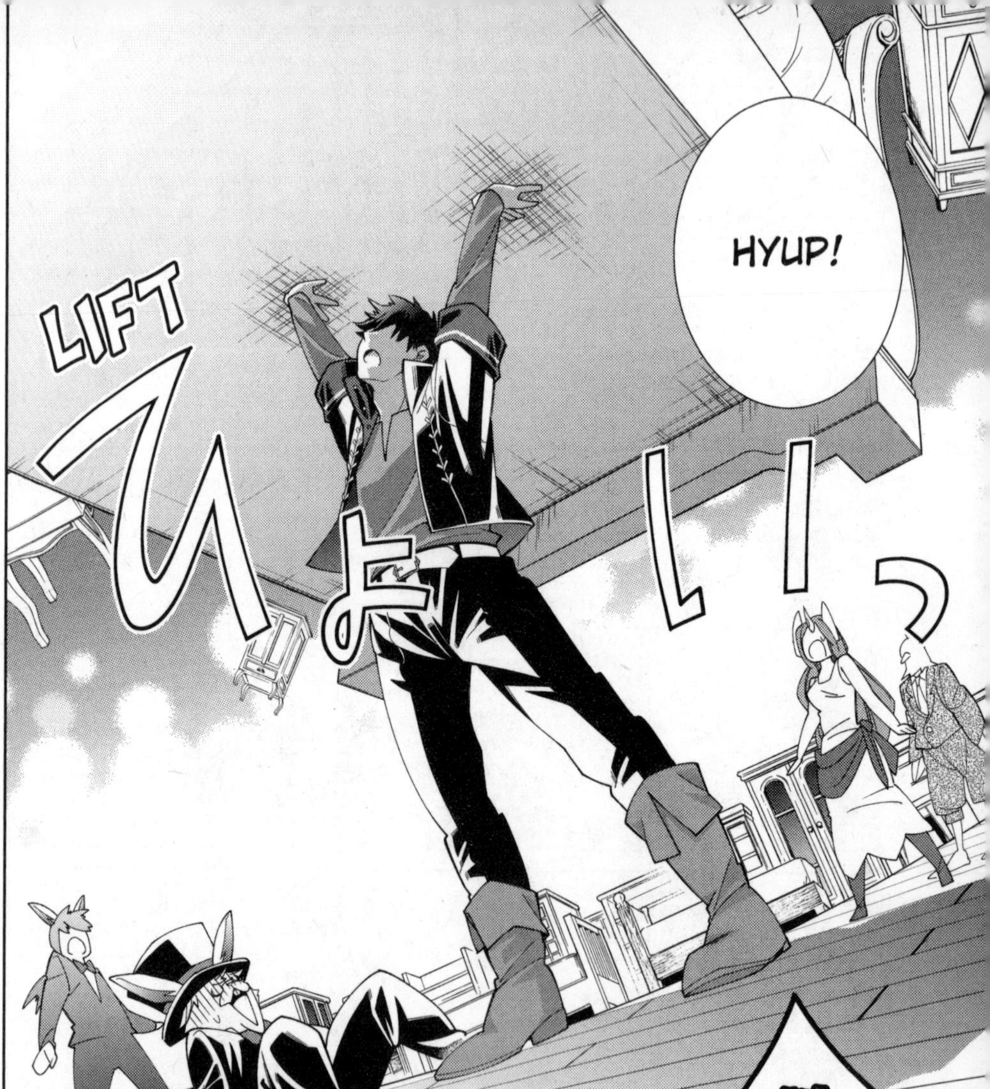
HYUP!
LIFT
ひょいっ
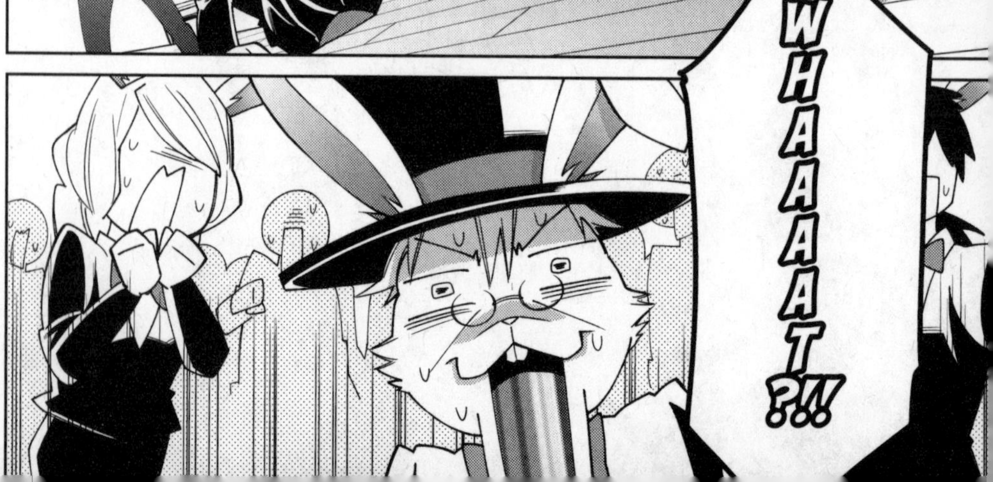
WHAAAAAT?!!

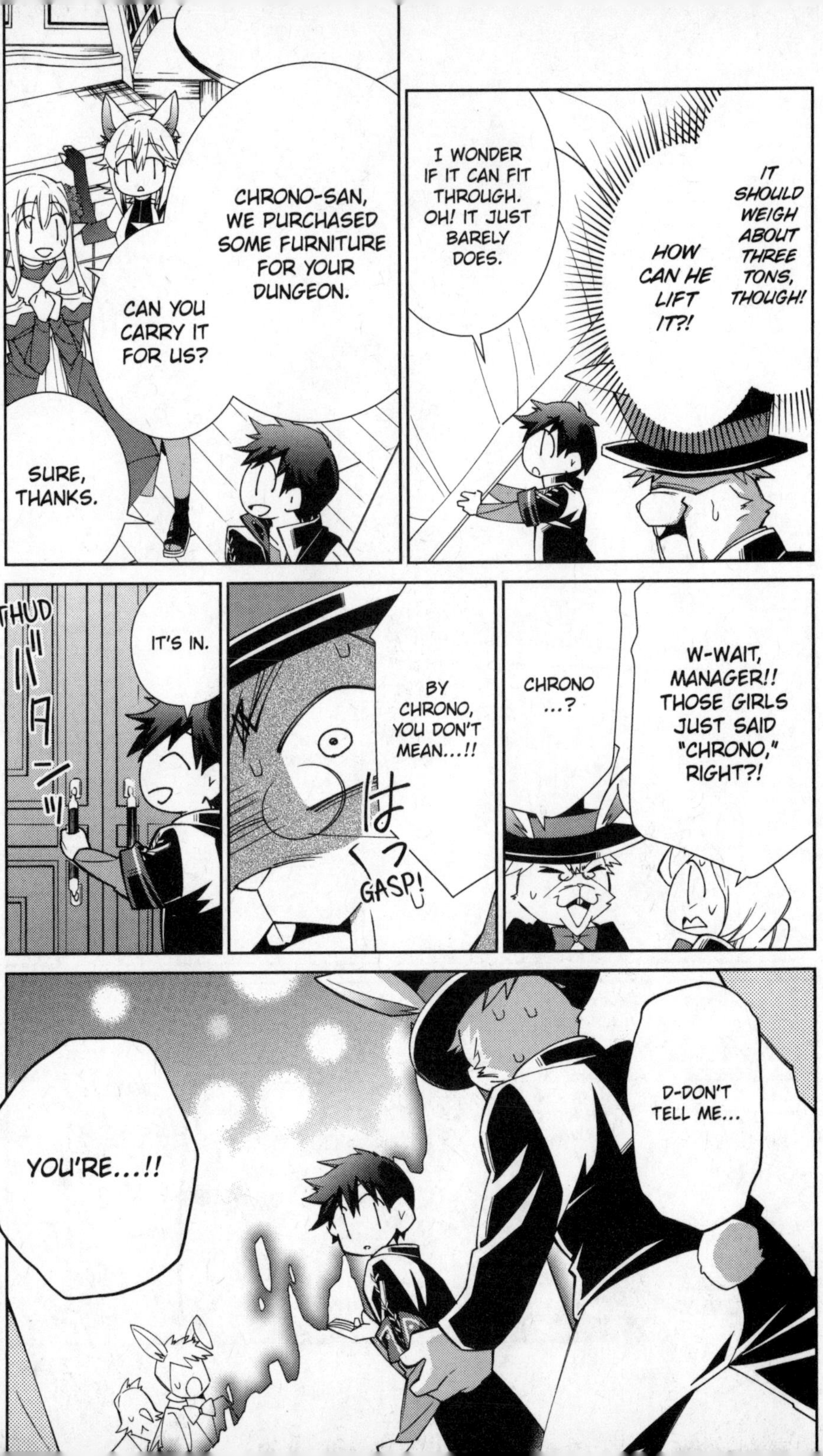

IT SHOULD WEIGH ABOUT THREE TONS, THOUGH!
HOW CAN HE LIFT IT?!
I WONDER IF IT CAN FIT THROUGH. OH! IT JUST BARELY DOES.
CHRONO-SAN, WE PURCHASED SOME FURNITURE FOR YOUR DUNGEON.
CAN YOU CARRY IT FOR US?
SURE, THANKS.
W-WAIT, MANAGER!! THOSE GIRLS JUST SAID "CHRONO," RIGHT?!
CHRONO ...?
BY CHRONO, YOU DON'T MEAN...!!
GASP!
IT'S IN.
THUD
D-DON'T TELL ME...
YOU'RE...!!

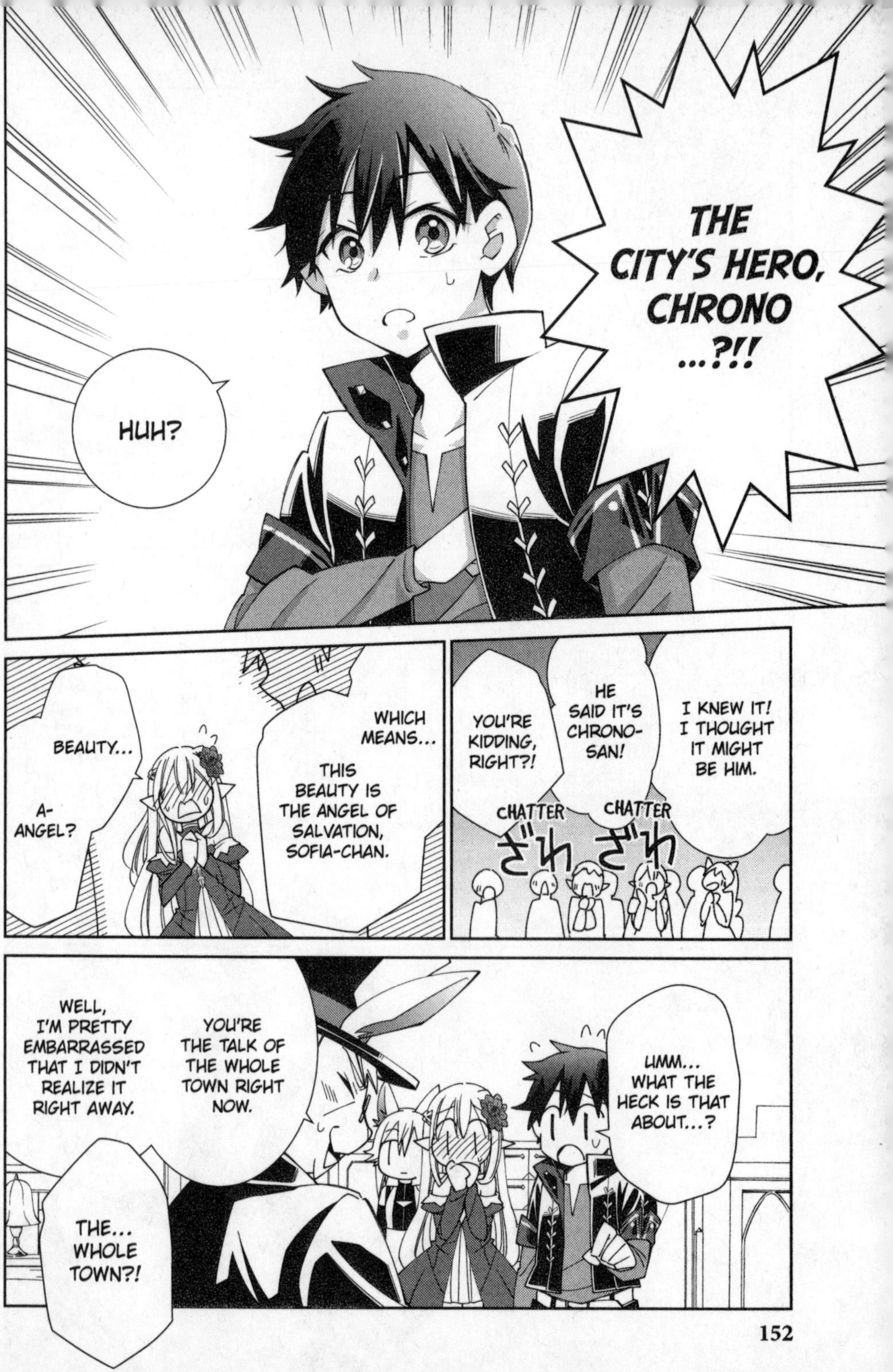
THE CITY'S HERO, CHRONO ...?!!
HUH?
I KNEW IT! I THOUGHT IT MIGHT BE HIM.
HE SAID IT'S CHRONO-SAN!
YOU'RE KIDDING, RIGHT?!
CHATTER
CHATTER
ざわざわ
WHICH MEANS...
THIS BEAUTY IS THE ANGEL OF SALVATION, SOFIA-CHAN.
BEAUTY...
A-ANGEL?
UMM... WHAT THE HECK IS THAT ABOUT...?
YOU'RE THE TALK OF THE WHOLE TOWN RIGHT NOW.
WELL, I'M PRETTY EMBARRASSED THAT I DIDN'T REALIZE IT RIGHT AWAY.
THE... WHOLE TOWN?!

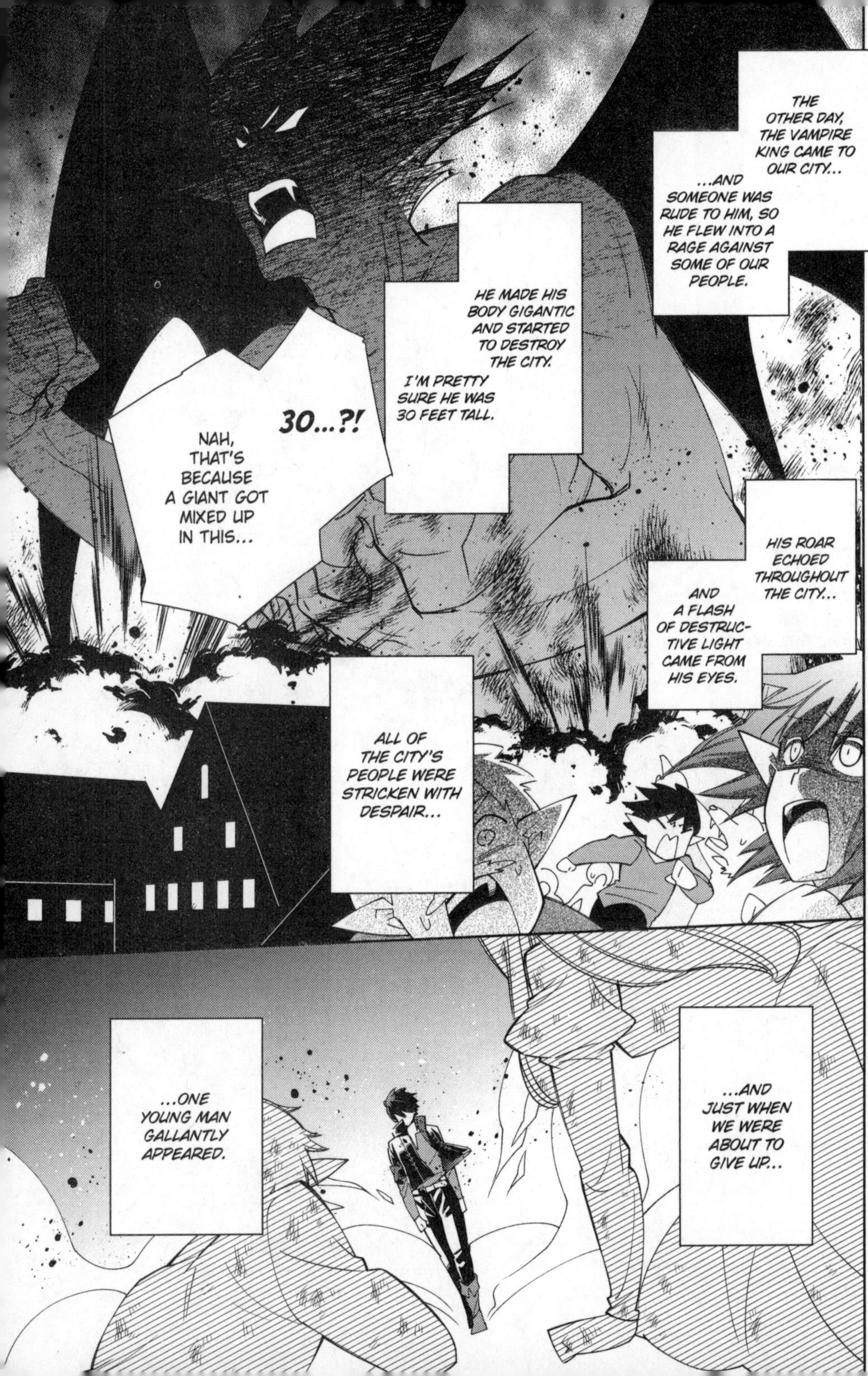
THE OTHER DAY, THE VAMPIRE KING CAME TO OUR CITY...
...AND SOMEONE WAS RUDE TO HIM, SO HE FLEW INTO A RAGE AGAINST SOME OF OUR PEOPLE.
HE MADE HIS BODY GIGANTIC AND STARTED TO DESTROY THE CITY.
I'M PRETTY SURE HE WAS 30 FEET TALL.
30...?!
NAH, THAT'S BECAUSE A GIANT GOT MIXED UP IN THIS...
HIS ROAR ECHOED THROUGHOUT THE CITY...
AND A FLASH OF DESTRUCTIVE LIGHT CAME FROM HIS EYES.
ALL OF THE CITY'S PEOPLE WERE STRICKEN WITH DESPAIR...
...AND JUST WHEN WE WERE ABOUT TO GIVE UP...
...ONE YOUNG MAN GALLANTLY APPEARED.

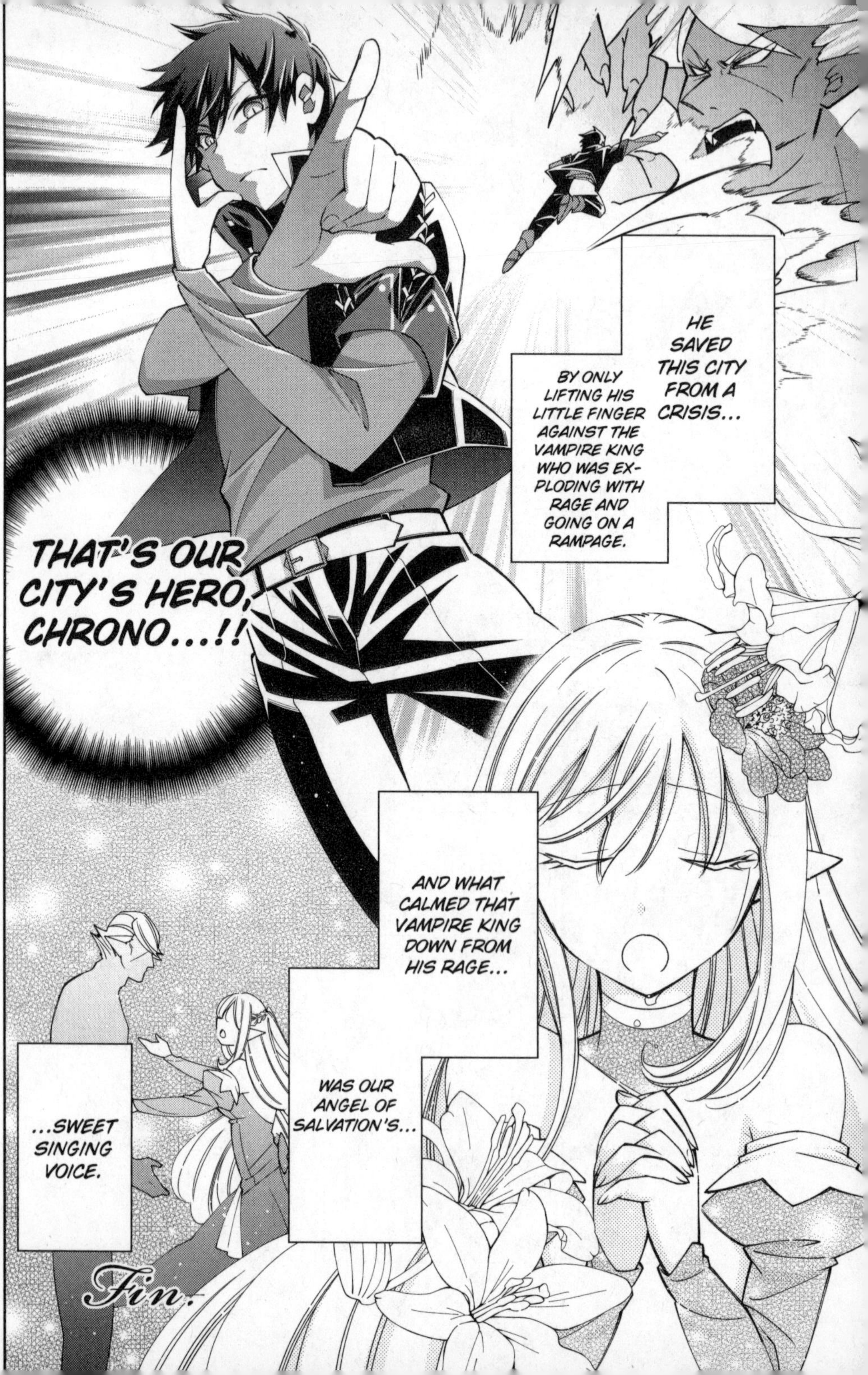
HE SAVED THIS CITY FROM A CRISIS...
BY ONLY LIFTING HIS LITTLE FINGER AGAINST THE VAMPIRE KING WHO WAS EX-PLODING WITH RAGE AND GOING ON A RAMPAGE.
THAT'S OUR CITY'S HERO, CHRONO...!!
AND WHAT CALMED THAT VAMPIRE KING DOWN FROM HIS RAGE...
WAS OUR ANGEL OF SALVATION'S...
...SWEET SINGING VOICE.
Fin.

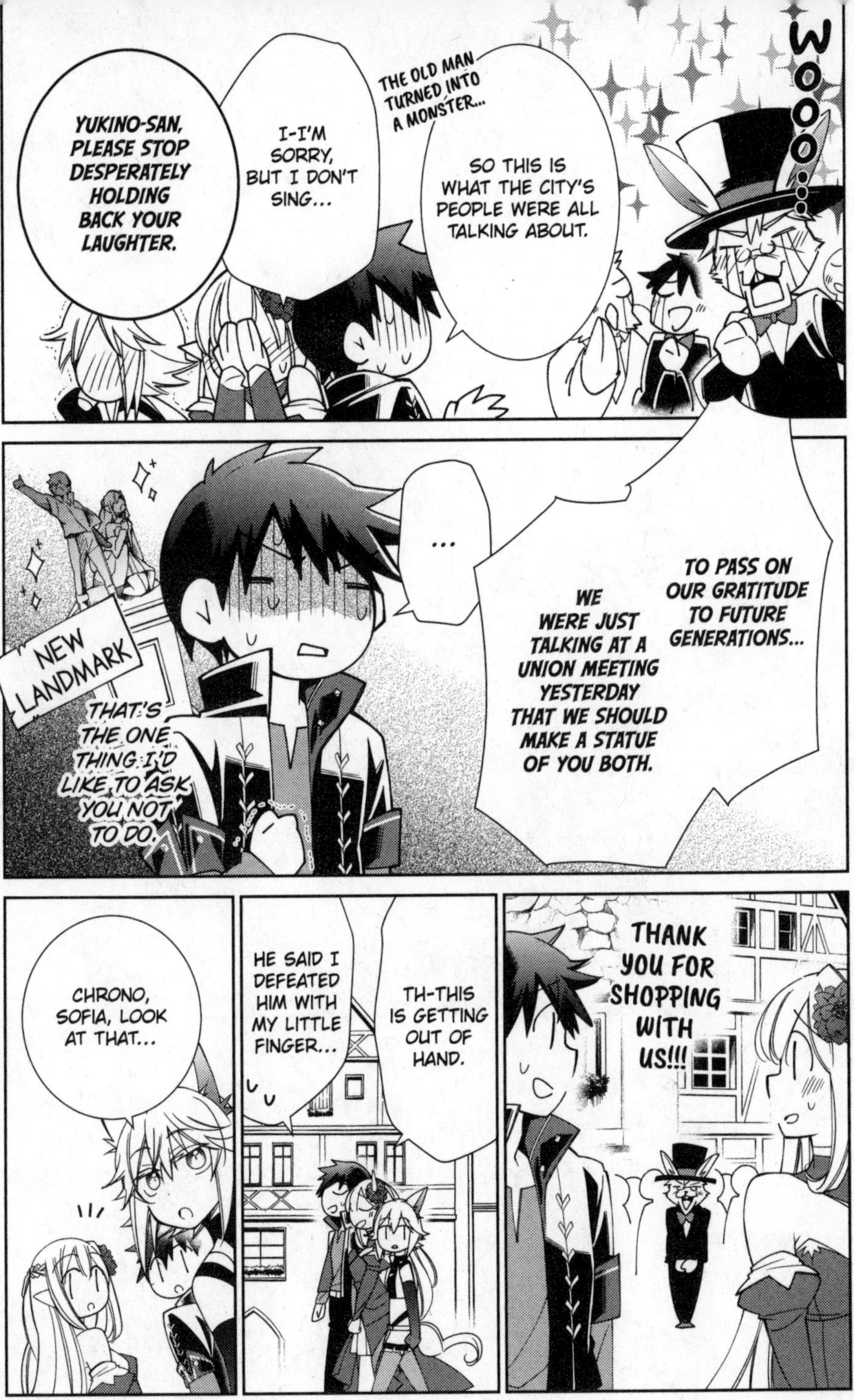
WOOO...
THE OLD MAN TURNED INTO A MONSTER...
SO THIS IS WHAT THE CITY'S PEOPLE WERE ALL TALKING ABOUT.
I-I'M SORRY, BUT I DON'T SING...
YUKINO-SAN, PLEASE STOP DESPERATELY HOLDING BACK YOUR LAUGHTER.
TO PASS ON OUR GRATITUDE TO FUTURE GENERATIONS...
WE WERE JUST TALKING AT A UNION MEETING YESTERDAY THAT WE SHOULD MAKE A STATUE OF YOU BOTH.
...
NEW LANDMARK
THAT'S THE ONE THING I'D LIKE TO ASK YOU NOT TO DO.
THANK YOU FOR SHOPPING WITH US!!!
TH-THIS IS GETTING OUT OF HAND.
HE SAID I DEFEATED HIM WITH MY LITTLE FINGER...
CHRONO, SOFIA, LOOK AT THAT...

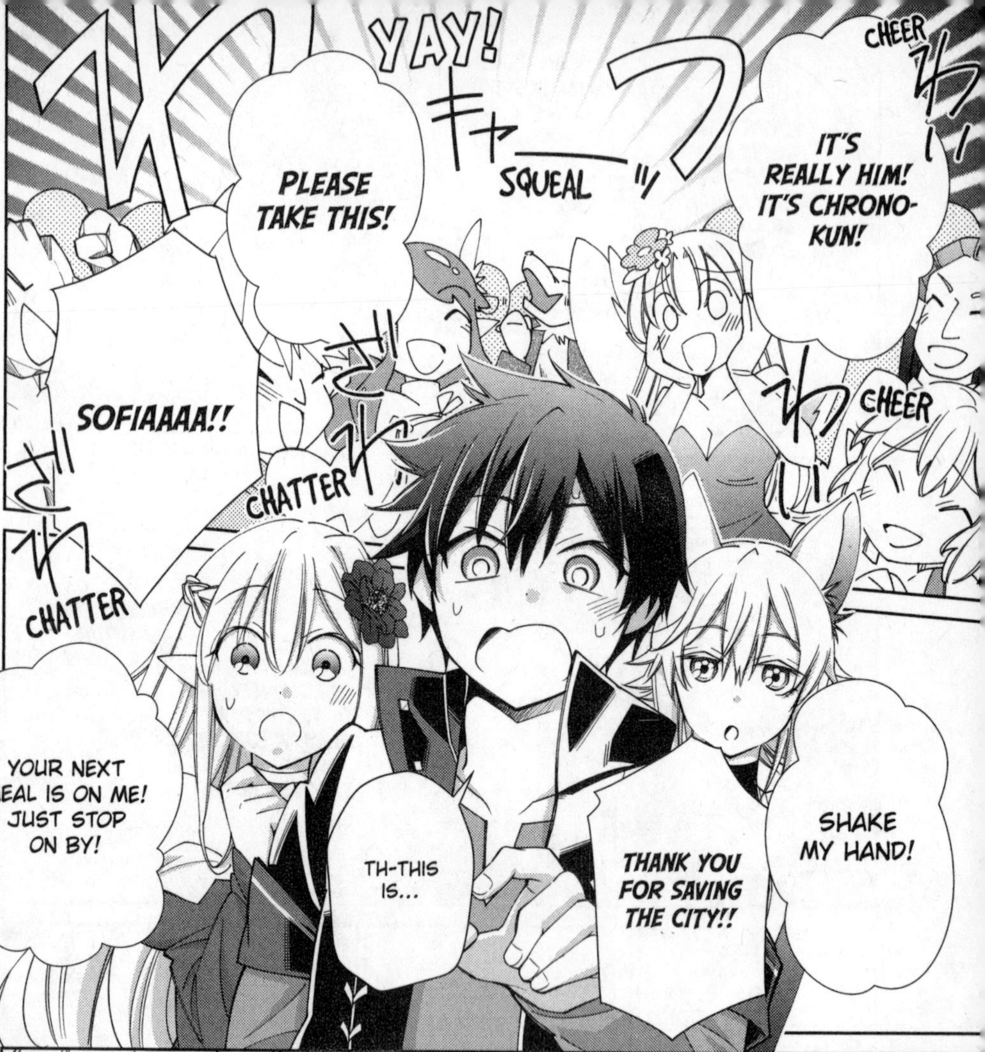
CHEER
IT'S REALLY HIM! IT'S CHRONO-KUN!
YAY!
SQUEAL
PLEASE TAKE THIS!
SOFIAAAA!!
CHEER
CHATTER
CHATTER
SHAKE MY HAND!
THANK YOU FOR SAVING THE CITY!!
TH-THIS IS...
YOUR NEXT MEAL IS ON ME! JUST STOP ON BY!
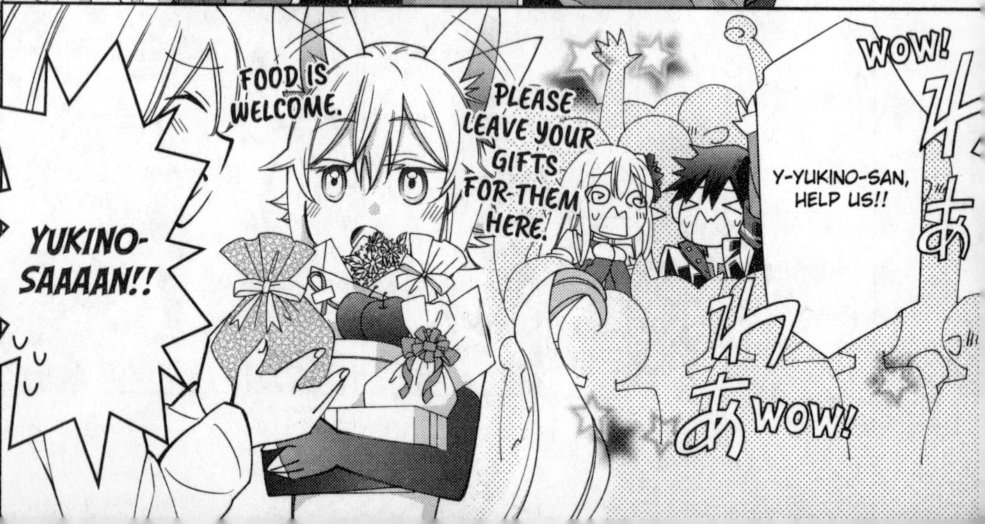
WOW!
Y-YUKINO-SAN, HELP US!!
PLEASE LEAVE YOUR GIFTS FOR THEM HERE.
FOOD IS WELCOME.
YUKINO-SAAAAN!!
WOW!

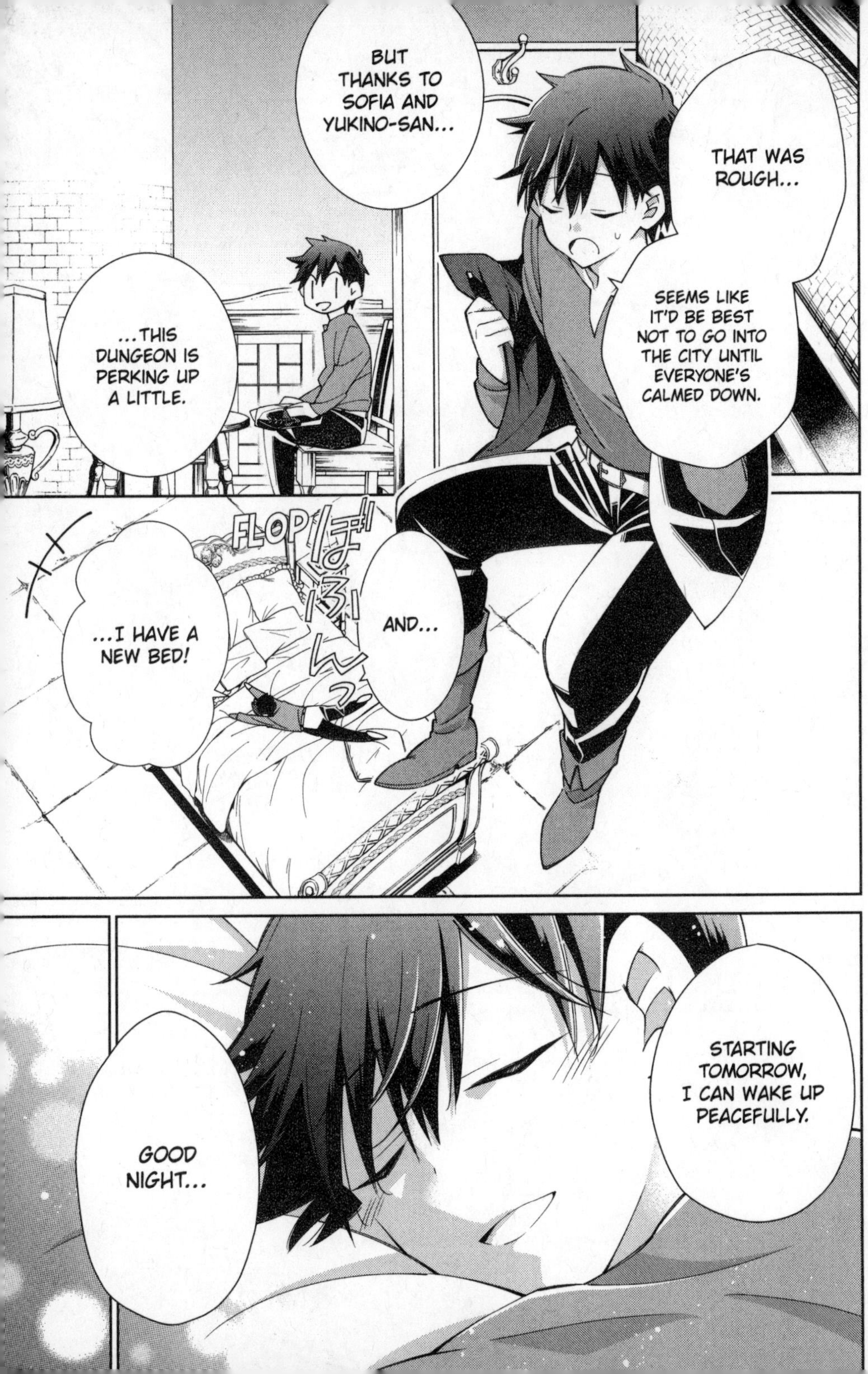
THAT WAS ROUGH...
SEEMS LIKE IT'D BE BEST NOT TO GO INTO THE CITY UNTIL EVERYONE'S CALMED DOWN.
BUT THANKS TO SOFIA AND YUKINO-SAN...
...THIS DUNGEON IS PERKING UP A LITTLE.
AND...
FLOP
...I HAVE A NEW BED!
STARTING TOMORROW, I CAN WAKE UP PEACEFULLY.
GOOD NIGHT...

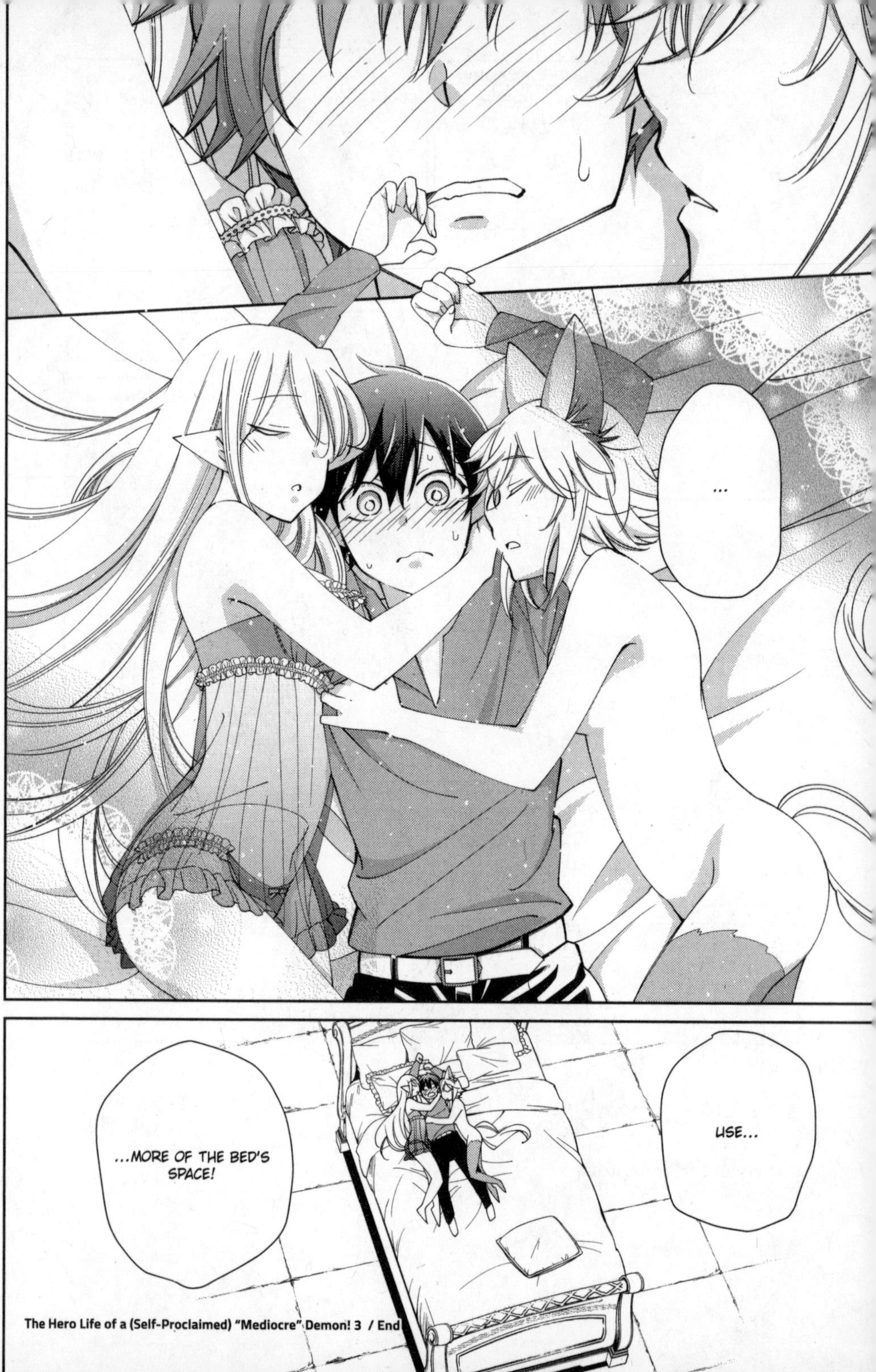
...
USE...
...MORE OF THE BED'S SPACE!

The Hero Life of a (Self-Proclaimed) "Mediocre" Demon! 3 / End

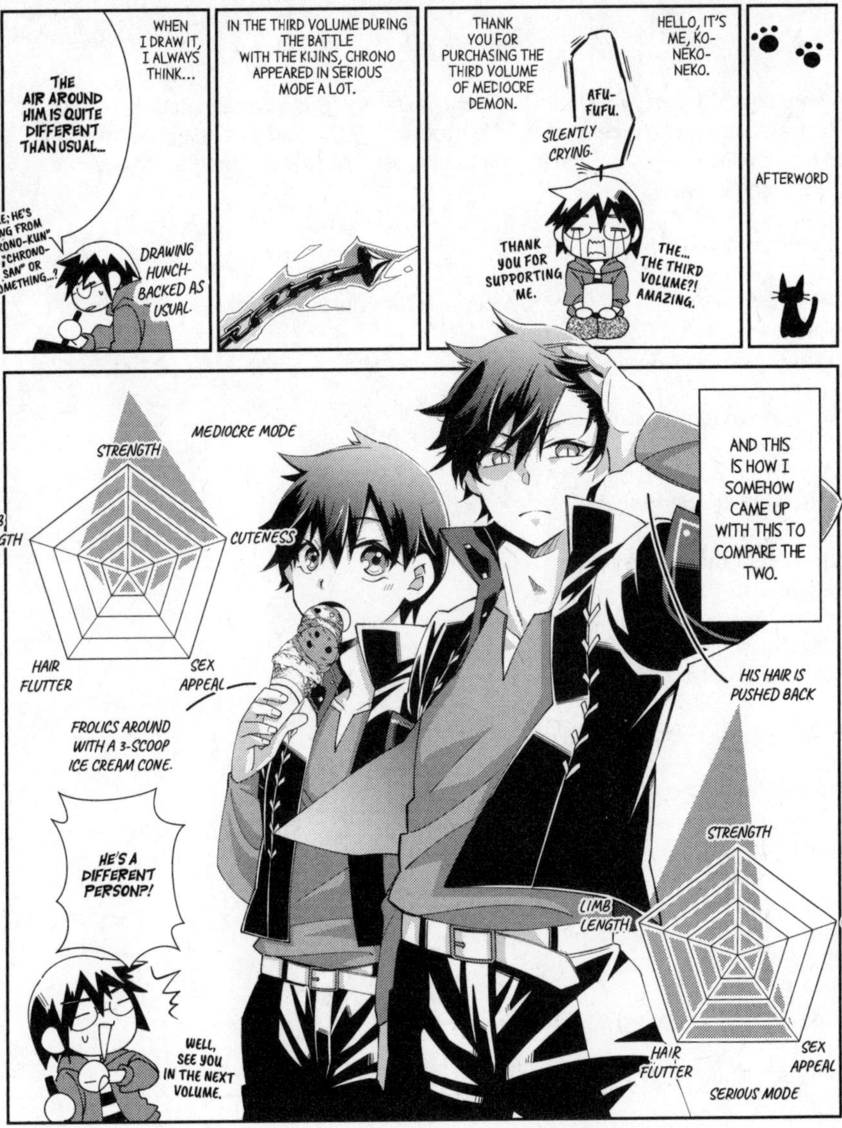
AFTERWORD
HELLO, IT'S ME, KO-NEKO-NEKO.
THANK YOU FOR PURCHASING THE THIRD VOLUME OF MEDIOCRE DEMON.
AFU-FUFU.
SILENTLY CRYING.
THE... THE THIRD VOLUME?! AMAZING.
THANK YOU FOR SUPPORTING ME.
IN THE THIRD VOLUME DURING THE BATTLE WITH THE KIJINS, CHRONO APPEARED IN SERIOUS MODE A LOT.
WHEN I DRAW IT, I ALWAYS THINK...
THE AIR AROUND HIM IS QUITE DIFFERENT THAN USUAL...
DRAWING HUNCH-BACKED AS USUAL.
LIKE; HE'S GOING FROM "CHRONO-KUN" TO "CHRONO-SAN" OR SOMETHING...?
AND THIS IS HOW I SOMEHOW CAME UP WITH THIS TO COMPARE THE TWO.
MEDIOCRE MODE
STRENGTH
CUTENESS
SEX APPEAL
HAIR FLUTTER
LIMB LENGTH
FROLICS AROUND WITH A 3-SCOOP ICE CREAM CONE.
HIS HAIR IS PUSHED BACK
HE'S A DIFFERENT PERSON?!
STRENGTH
CUTENESS
SEX APPEAL
HAIR FLUTTER
LIMB LENGTH
SERIOUS MODE
WELL, SEE YOU IN THE NEXT VOLUME.

Special Thanks

I'D LIKE TO THANK EVERYONE WHO BOUGHT THIS BOOK FROM THE BOTTOM OF MY HEART.

ASSISTANT
MAEDA-CHAN
TSUBAKI NAKAHARA-SAN
NAMINO-SAN
EIKICHI-SAN
MEIKO SHINODA-SAN

ORIGINAL STORY: SHIROICHI AMAUI-SAMA
CHARACTER DRAFT: TAMAGONOKIMI-SAMA
EDITOR IN CHARGE: NAKAMA-SAMA
COMICS EDITOR IN CHARGE:
TSUKAMOTO-SAMA
DAD, MOM, BIG SIS.

and you!!

A Kodansha Trade Paperback Original

The Hero Life of a (Self-Proclaimed) Mediocre Demon! 3 copyright © 2019 Shiroichi Amaui / Konekoneko / Tamagonokimi
English translation copyright © 2021 Shiroichi Amaui / Konekoneko / Tamagonokimi

Published in the United States by
Kodansha USA Publishing, LLC, New York.

Publication rights for this English edition arranged through
Kodansha Ltd., Tokyo.

First published in Japan in 2019 by Kodansha Ltd., Tokyo as
Jishō! Heibon mazoku no eiyū raifu 3.

ISBN 978-1-64651-336-9

Printed in the United States of America.

1st Printing

Translation: Jessica Latherow / amimaru
Lettering: Chris Burgener / amimaru
Additional Lettering: Phil Christie
Editing: David Yoo
Kodansha USA Publishing edition cover design by Matt Akuginow

Publisher: Kiichiro Sugawara

Director of Publishing Services: Ben Applegate
Associate Director, Publishing Operations: Stephen Pakula
Publishing Services Managing Editors: Madison Salters, Alanna Ruse
Production Managers: Emi Lotto, Angela Zurlo

KODANSHA.US

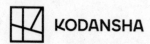